SELF-ESTEEM
ACROSS THE LIFESPAN

SELF-ESTEEM
ACROSS THE LIFESPAN

ISSUES AND INTERVENTIONS

EDITED BY MARY H. GUINDON

Routledge
Taylor & Francis Group
New York   London

Routledge
Taylor & Francis Group
270 Madison Avenue
New York, NY 10016

Routledge
Taylor & Francis Group
27 Church Road
Hove, East Sussex BN3 2FA

Printed in the United States of America on acid-free paper
10 9 8 7 6 5 4 3 2 1

International Standard Book Number: 978-0-415-99699-0 (Hardback)

Library of Congress Cataloging-in-Publication Data

Self-esteem across the lifespan : issues and interventions / [edited by] Mary H.
Guindon.
    p. cm.
Includes bibliographical references and index.
ISBN 978-0-415-99699-0 (hardcover : alk. paper)

1. Self-esteem. I. Guindon, Mary H.
BF697.5.S46S447 2009
155.2--dc22   2009012537

Visit the Taylor & Francis Web site at
http://www.taylorandfrancis.com

and the Routledge Web site at
http://www.routledgementalhealth.com

This book is dedicated to my three grandsons:
Payton Vellenga, Spencer Guindon, and Parker Guindon.

Their healthy self-esteem levels amaze and delight
their significant others, especially their Grammy.

Contents

SECTION III   ADOLESCENCE

SECTION IV   YOUNG ADULTHOOD

SECTION V   MIDLIFE

Preface

Back in the 1980s, I was asked to create a self-esteem group for a then newly opened women's in-patient unit at a private psychiatric hospital. Since I was interested in women's issues, I eagerly accepted. I asked the hospital staff for some guidance and was told something like, "Oh, you know, just make them feel better about themselves." I asked colleagues if they had materials I might draw on to develop the program and received the same approximate answer. In fact, most everyone looked at me as if I had asked an obvious, elemental question whose answer was known to all, it appeared, but me. The next week, I happened to be going to New York and took the opportunity to stop into the biggest bookstore in Manhattan. To my astonishment, I found rack after rack of books with the word *self-esteem* in the title. In fact, an entire section of the store was devoted to the subject. There was no question that the idea of self-esteem was popular. I felt slightly embarrassed that I had been totally unaware of this huge area, but as I looked through book after book, I realized that most of them didn't seem to know much more about how to help people with low self-esteem than I.

I settled on a few of the more promising books and headed home to read, study, and create a program that might work, combining what I could glean from these books with what I already knew about human development (a little), psychology of personality (not much), and the various approaches to individual and group therapy (enough to practice ethically). I ran the group two evenings a week for almost three years, and by trial and error (I hope not much of the latter), I slowly honed a program that seemed to have good results.

A few years later, when I needed to decide on a topic for my doctoral dissertation, self-esteem seemed a natural. This was still before the Internet made literature searches armchair work. I wandered through the University of Virginia library's stacks of journals, old theses and dissertations, and lane upon lane of academic books. It was then that I discovered there was, indeed, an academic body of inquiry on the self-esteem construct. Yet only a relatively few resources defined self-esteem well. I next discovered the monumental works of Morris Rosenberg and Stanley Coopersmith and had my "Aha!" moment. I finally found out what I had assumed everyone else knew: what self-esteem is. However, despite the fact that a substantial body of research on the self-esteem construct existed then (and exists today), I found most people, even those in the helping professions, didn't seem to be aware of any more of it than I was. I felt like I was somehow the keeper of a well-kept secret.

Over the last 25 years, I have facilitated many self-esteem groups for my clients or addressed their self-esteem needs in individual sessions. I have made presentations, facilitated professional workshops, and taught courses on the subject. I continue to be amazed by how, even today, so many practitioners are not particularly knowledgeable about self-esteem, although they tell me that low self-esteem plagues their clients. It seemed to me that what was needed was accountability in the use of the self-esteem construct that included understanding what it is and what has been shown to effectively enhance it.

Although I have had the luxury of offering self-esteem-specific strategies to clients and to teach students and other practitioners about self-esteem programs that work, I have found that many clinicians are not in a position, especially in a managed care climate, to provide interventions that exclusively address self-esteem issues. Although they recognize the importance of self-esteem enhancement and, more often than not, include it in treatment goals, few practitioners that I have met have the opportunity to specifically create and apply programs that only target self-esteem. That is what led me to consider that self-esteem might be successfully enhanced through the existing interventions that practitioners already use with their clients, if only they learned the same basic information that I had learned. For those that can offer self-esteem programs, I provide an overview of specific self-esteem strategies in this book. For those that may not be able to, I have asked experts on various clinical issues all across the life span to apply the self-esteem knowledge base to their areas of expertise. I am enthusiastic with the result and sincerely hope you will come to share my enthusiasm.

Each contributor has been willing to add to his or her own knowledge of the self-esteem literature. They incorporate principles of self-esteem to address an identified self-esteem issue at a specific developmental stage. They present at least one aspect of self-esteem that is most pertinent to their population and include suitable intervention strategies that support it. They discuss the self-esteem issues of their population, address diversity, include the crucial role of the mental health practitioner, and where relevant, present information on assessment. Each chapter contains a case study for your consideration. I thank these contributors for their hard work and their wholehearted willingness to join me in this project. I have learned much from them.

I continue to refine and add to my own knowledge, both professionally and personally. I am grateful to every one of the legitimate and responsible self-esteem writers for what they have taught me over the years, although I have known them only through their writings. I am perhaps most grateful for every client and every student who has tested me and challenged me as I have tried to assist them with their self-esteem needs. They have taught me about the nobleness of the human spirit even in the worst of personal circumstances.

About the Editor

Mary H. Guindon, PhD, is former chair of and associate professor in the Department of Counseling and Human Services at Johns Hopkins University, where she created programs in organizational counseling, counselor clinical supervision, and contemporary trauma response. She holds a PhD from the University of Virginia and was formerly associate professor at Rider University and collegiate professor at University of Maryland University College–Europe, where she continues to teach distance education courses. Her 25 years of clinical practice, consulting, and teaching experience includes counselor training and supervision, mental health and career development, adult transitions, grief and loss, and global counseling issues. She has published in the professional and popular press and has presented nationally and internationally on self-esteem accountability. She previously served on the Maryland State Board of Professional Counselors and Therapists, the Maryland Work/Life Alliance Advisory Board, the publications committee of the American Counseling Association, the professional development committee of the National Career Development Association, the editorial board of *Career Development Quarterly*, and is a member of the Maryland Professional Volunteer Corps for the Office of Preparedness and Response. Formerly, she was president of the New Jersey Mental Health Counselors Association, president of New Jersey Association of Counselor Education and Supervision, and Mid-Atlantic district consultant for the American Mental Health Counselors Association. A licensed psychologist and licensed clinical professional counselor, Dr. Guindon maintains a private practice in executive, personal, and career coaching; consulting; and counselor supervision. She currently serves as a consultant providing short-term, problem-solving counseling to the U.S. military bases in the United States and Europe.

About the Contributors

Deryl F. Bailey, PhD, is an associate professor at the University of Georgia. He earned BS and master's degrees from Campbell University, and his education specialist and PhD degrees from the University of Virginia. He believes strongly in the power of education and is committed to providing equitable opportunities to promote the betterment of societal existence for everyone. Dr. Bailey is an accomplished professional in the areas of school counseling, diversity, multicultural education, adolescent development, and African American adolescent male development, and is a published scholar.

Mary Bradbury-Bailey, EdS, holds a BS degree in science teaching from the University of North Carolina–Chapel Hill, a master's degree in science education from North Carolina State University, and an education specialist degree from Piedmont College in Athens, Georgia. She is a National Board Certified teacher. She is an experienced teacher of 29 years and has extended her educational and leadership expertise beyond the classroom through both professional and community activities. She has taught on the secondary and college level, served as science department chair, developed and implemented secondary science courses in three schools, served as a master teacher for a biotechnology initiative, served as a mentor teacher for three school systems, and facilitated the SACS accreditation process for one high school as its instructional lead teacher. She has been teacher of the year in three states, and in 2003 she was selected as a semifinalist for the state teacher of the year. Ms. Bradbury-Bailey also serves as the associate director for Empowered Youth Programs, an academic enrichment initiative for children and adolescents that she developed with her husband 20 years ago. She has also coauthored several journal articles and book chapters.

Rebecca L. Brickwedde, MSEd, is a licensed professional counselor, licensed marriage and family therapist, and certified medical psychotherapist. She holds a master's degree in counseling psychology and is a fellow and diplomate of the American Board of Medical Psychotherapists. She currently serves on the board of governors of the European branch of the American Counseling Association and is coordinating editor of the award-winning publication *Neues Perspectives for the European Counselor*. She has been researching the mind–body connection, and its effect on health and self-esteem, for 25 years. She was both founder and director of Self-Esteem Builders, Inc., and has worked as a psychotherapist in private practice, as well as in psychiatric and medical hospitals. Also a teacher, certified in the areas of emotional disturbance, learning disabilities, and art, she has worked as an educator in the public school system and in various hospital education programs. She has presented internationally on the topic of health psychology, the mind–body connection, and uses of imagery in counseling. She is also an artist and has participated in art exhibitions in the United States and Germany.

Mary C. Burke, PhD, is a faculty member in the psychology department at Carlow University, where she is the director of training for the doctoral program in counseling psychology. During the summer months, Dr. Burke serves as affiliate faculty in the Department of Counseling and Human Services at Johns Hopkins University in Baltimore, Maryland. Dr. Burke's commitment to social justice and equity is manifest in her research, teaching, and activism. Currently she represents the Association for Women in Psychology on the United Nations Conference of Non-Governmental Organizations Committee on Mental Health. In addition to her participation in various national and international professional associations, Dr. Burke collaboratively founded and directs the Project to End Human Trafficking (www.endhumantrafficking.org). This United States-based nonprofit group works regionally, nationally, and internationally to raise awareness about the enslavement and economic exploitation of human beings. In this role, Dr. Burke has given over 100 talks about human trafficking and has begun antitrafficking coalitions in Pennsylvania, Virginia, and Maryland.

David A. Crenshaw, PhD, is board certified in clinical psychology and a registered play therapist supervisor. For 30 years, he served as clinical director of two separate residential treatment centers for emotionally disturbed children. He is the author of *Evocative Strategies in Child and Adolescent Psychotherapy*; *Therapeutic Engagement of Children and Adolescents: Play, Symbol, Drawing and Storytelling Strategies*; and editor of *Child and Adolescent Psychotherapy: Wounded Spirits and Healing Paths*. He is also the coauthor of two books with John B. Mordock, *A Handbook of Play Therapy with Aggressive Children* and *Understanding and Treating the Aggression of Children: Fawns in Gorilla Suits*. All of these books were published by Jason Aronson/Rowman & Littlefield Publishers. Dr. Crenshaw is past president of the New York Association for Play Therapy. He now serves on the board of directors of Astor Child and Family Services, where he previously worked as clinical director for more than 23 years. The Rhinebeck Child and Family Center, www.childtherapytechniques.com, provides training and consultation to public and private agencies serving at-risk children and adolescents.

Francesca G. Giordano, PhD, is an associate professor of counseling at Northern Illinois University. For the past 10 years, she has been an administrator and counselor educator with a specialization in mental health, consultation, and ethics. She received her doctorate from the University of Virginia. A licensed clinical professional counselor, she is vice chair of the Illinois Professional Counselor Licensing and Disciplinary Board and is a board member for the Illinois Mental Health Counselors Association. She offers workshops for the Illinois Mental

Health Counselors Association, including an exam preparation workshop for the LCPC license and workshops on legal and ethical Issues. She is also the Illinois Counseling Association (ICA) Ethics Committee chair and the editor for ICA's newsletter. She consults with mental health centers in the areas of effective treatment planning, ethical issues, working with adolescents, and therapeutic change. Her research interests include transformational anger, counseling with at-risk, low-income urban populations, and sexuality counseling.

Samuel T. Gladding, PhD, is chair of and a professor in the Department of Counseling at Wake Forest University in Winston-Salem, North Carolina. He is a fellow in the American Counseling Association and its former president (2004–2005). He has also served as president of the Association for Counselor Education and Supervision (ACES), the Association for Specialists in Group Work (ASGW), and Chi Sigma Iota. He is the former editor of the *Journal for Specialists in Group Work* and a current member of the American Counseling Association Foundation and the North Carolina Board of Licensed Professional Counselors. Dr. Gladding has authored numerous professional publications, including 30 books. In 1999, he was cited as being in the top 1% of contributors to the *Journal of Counseling & Development*. A national certified counselor (NCC), a certified clinical mental health counselor (CCMHC), and a licensed professional counselor (North Carolina), his specialty in counseling is creativity.

Eric J. Green, PhD, is chair of the MA Clinical Psychology Department and an associate professor at the Chicago School of Professional Psychology. A licensed clinical professional counselor and a registered play therapist supervisor, he also maintains a part-time, private practice in child psychotherapy, focusing on clinical work with young children affected by diminished self-esteem, behavioral disorders, and trauma. He has published over 20 journal articles and book chapters on the mental health treatment of children. He was 2008–2009 president of Counselors for Social Justice and a past recipient of the Ohana award.

Barbara Herlihy, PhD, is presently university research professor and counseling graduate program coordinator at the University of New Orleans. She is the coauthor of 3 current books and 20 book chapters, and has authored or coauthored over 50 refereed journal articles. Her primary research interests are counselor ethics, multiculturalism and social justice, supervision, and feminist therapy. She has served as chair of the American Counseling Association Ethics Committee, and served on the ACA Ethics Code Revision Taskforce (2002–2005). Her professional experience includes serving as a counselor in schools, community agencies, and private practice. She is a licensed professional counselor and board-approved supervisor in Louisiana and Texas. She recently was the recipient of the Southern Association for Counselor Education & Supervision 2008 Courtland Lee Social Justice award.

Tana Hope, PhD, assistant director of the Child and Family Therapy Clinic in the Behavioral Psychology Department of the Kennedy Krieger Institute, obtained her doctorate from Louisiana State University and completed her predoctoral internship at the Kennedy Krieger Institute and the Johns Hopkins School of Medicine. She is also an instructor in the Department of Psychiatry at the Johns Hopkins School of Medicine and a faculty associate in the Department of Counseling and Human Services at Johns Hopkins University. Her research and clinical interests include the assessment and treatment of children with anxiety, depression, Asperger's disorder, and reactive attachment disorder.

Brandon Hunt, PhD, is a professor of counselor education at Penn State University, where she has been employed since she received her doctorate from the University of Virginia in 1992. She teaches undergraduate students in rehabilitation and human services as well as master's- and doctoral-level counselor education students. The majority of her counseling experience is focused on people with disabilities, particularly people with addictions or mental health concerns. Her research areas include assessing counselor knowledge and attitudes, grief counseling, and counseling gay, lesbian, bisexual, and transgendered clients. Dr. Hunt served on the Council for Accreditation of Counseling and Related Educational Programs Board of Directors for six years, and she currently serves on the board of directors for the National Board for Certified Counselors. She is also the associate editor for qualitative research for the *Journal of Counseling & Development*.

Charles Jason Jacobs, MEd, is currently a PhD student in counselor education at Penn State University. He is a clinical mental health counselor and graduate fellow at Penn State.

Bryan S. K. Kim, PhD, is a professor of psychology and director of the MA Program in Counseling Psychology at the University of Hawaii at Hilo. He received a PhD in counseling, clinical, and school psychology with an emphasis in counseling psychology from the University of California–Santa Barbara in 2000. Prior to UH–Hilo, Dr. Kim held faculty positions at the University of California at Santa Barbara and the University of Maryland at College Park. Dr. Kim currently has over 50 publications in the areas of multicultural counseling process and outcome, measurement of cultural constructs, counselor education and supervision, and immigrant experiences. Dr. Kim is currently associate editor of *The Counseling Psychologist* and *Cultural Diversity and Ethnic Minority Psychology*, and serves on the editorial boards of four other journals of the American Psychological Association. Dr. Kim is a recipient of early career awards from the Asian American Psychological Association, Society of Counseling Psychology, and Society of the Psychological Study of Ethnic Minority Issues. He also received research awards from the American Counseling Association and the Association for Assessment in Counseling and Development. Most recently, in 2008, Dr. Kim was awarded fellow status by the APA.

Amie C. Kolos, MS, is a licensed clinical professional counselor who conducts therapy with families affected by addiction and trauma. She earned a postmaster's certificate in play therapy from Johns Hopkins University in 2008, and she currently works at Johns Hopkins Bayview Medical Center.

Jennifer Lee, PhD, is a clinical psychologist practicing in Kingston, New York, where she specializes in the treatment of adolescents and their families. She graduated from Teachers College, Columbia University, where she began her research and development of mindfulness-based cognitive therapy for children (MBCT-C), an intervention for anxiety in school-aged children. She has authored several articles and book chapters on mindfulness-based treatments for children and adolescent identity development. As an adjunct instructor in the Mental Health Counseling Program at Marist College, she teaches a course on couples and family counseling to master's-level clinicians. Her interest in systems and organizations also drew her to Nonbox Consulting, where she serves as a business consultant, and to the A. K. Rice Institute, where she is training to become a certified group relations conference consultant.

Beth Martin, MA, received a master's degree in counseling from Wake Forest University and an undergraduate degree in human and organizational development from Vanderbilt University. Research interests include the use of creativity and the arts in counseling and the use of choice theory in counseling children in schools. She currently lives in Vienna, Austria, where she shares a variety of programming and general responsibilities for the Wake Forest University residential study center located there.

Elizabeth A. Mellin, PhD, is an assistant professor in the Department of Counselor Education, Counseling Psychology, and Rehabilitation Services at Penn State University. Prior to joining Penn State University as an assistant professor in 2006, Dr. Mellin was a child and adolescent counselor, clinical supervisor, and grant writer for a large, public community mental health program in Atlanta, Georgia, where she often worked with families affected by parental mental illness. She is a nationally published author on child and adolescent mental health topics. Her research is focused on building capacity in child and adolescent mental health, with a specific interest in community-based, ecologically relevant approaches. Dr. Mellin has also been an invited speaker to workshops, conferences, and certification programs to share her expertise in relational aggression, crisis intervention, and female adolescent development.

Stephanie Mihalas, PhD, is currently a postdoctoral fellow in the Behavior Management Clinic at Kennedy Krieger Institute and the Johns Hopkins University School of Medicine. She attended Northwestern University for her undergraduate studies in psychology and learning and organizational change. Her graduate work was completed at the University of South Florida. Dr. Mihalas's main research interests include relational aggression, depression in children, and minority psychopathology. Clinically, Dr. Mihalas's main focus is treating economically disadvantaged youth via a family systems and cognitive-behavioral framework.

Michelle C. Muratori, PhD, is a senior counselor/researcher at the Center for Talented Youth at Johns Hopkins University, where she works with highly gifted middle school and high school students who participate in the Study of Exceptional Talent (SET) and their families. She received her PhD in counselor education from the University of Iowa (UI), where she developed her research and clinical interests in gifted education. Her graduate research on the academic, social, and emotional adjustment of young college entrants earned her recognition from the Iowa Talented and Gifted Association, the National Association for Gifted Children, and the Mensa Education and Research Foundation and Mensa International, Ltd. At UI, Muratori also earned the Howard R. Jones Achievement Award, the Albert Hood Promising Scholar Award, and the First in the Nation in Education (FINE) Scholar Award. Since 2005, Muratori has been a faculty associate in the Counseling and Human Services Department at Johns Hopkins. Muratori developed a practical guide about early college entrance that steers all of the stakeholders through the difficult decision-making process (*Early College Entrance: A Guide to Success*, Prufrock Press, 2007) and is currently coauthoring a book on clinical supervision with Drs. Robert Haynes, Gerald Corey, and Patrice Moulton.

Lindsey Marie Nichols, MEd, is currently a PhD student in counselor education at Penn State University. She is a professional school counselor and special educator.

Spencer G. Niles, EdD, is professor and department head for Counselor Education, Counseling Psychology, and Rehabilitation Services at Penn State University and director of the Center for the Study of Career Development and Public Policy at Penn State. Former president of the National Career Development Association (NCDA), he is the recipient of the NCDA's Eminent Career Award, an NCDA fellow, an American Counseling Association (ACA) fellow, and has received the ACA's David Brooks Distinguished Mentor Award, the ACA Extended Research Award, and the University of British Columbia Noted Scholar Award. He is the editor of the *Journal of Counseling & Development* and past editor of *Career Development Quarterly*. Niles has authored or coauthored approximately 95 publications and delivered over 90 presentations on career development theory and practice. He is an honorary member of the Japanese Career Development Association, honorary member of the Italian Association for Educational and Vocational Guidance, and a lifetime honorary member of the Ohio Career Development Association.

Yong S. Park, MA, is a doctoral candidate in the Counseling/Clinical/School Psychology Program at University of California (UC)–Santa Barbara. He is currently completing his predoctoral internship at UC–San Diego's Counseling and Psychology Services. His clinical interests include Asian American mental health and family issues, career and vocational counseling, and cross-cultural communication. He is also actively involved in the student division of the Asian American Psychological Association.

Alexandria E. Pilecki, MS, received her master's degree in counseling from Carlow University. She is a therapist at the Persad Center in Pittsburgh,

Pennsylvania. The Persad Center is the nation's second oldest counseling center for the lesbian, gay, bisexual, and transgender (LGBT) community. In addition, Ms. Pilecki cofacilitates the Closing the Gap program, which specializes in outreach to at-risk youth.

Gina Richman, PhD, is currently the director of the Child and Family Therapy Clinic in the Behavioral Psychology Department of the Kennedy Krieger Institute. She graduated from Florida State University with a PhD in child clinical and school psychology. Dr. Richman completed her predoctoral internship at the University of Maryland School of Medicine and postdoctoral fellowship at Kennedy Krieger Institute and the Johns Hopkins School of Medicine. She is also an assistant professor of Psychiatry and Behavioral Sciences at the Johns Hopkins School of Medicine, and a faculty associate in the Department of Counseling and Human Services at Johns Hopkins University. Her clinical and research interests include working with culturally disadvantaged families and assessing and treating children experiencing anxiety, depression, and issues related to self-esteem, along with ADHD and anger management.

Lee J. Richmond, PhD, is a professor in the Department of Education Specialties, Loyola College in Maryland, where she teaches counseling and career development courses to both school and pastoral counseling students. Currently, Dr. Richmond is a member of the board of educational affairs of the Maryland Psychological Association, and the editorial board of the *Journal of Counseling & Development*. A past president of the National Career Development Association, the American Counseling Association, the Maryland Association for Counseling and Development, and the Baltimore Psychological Association, Dr. Richmond has coauthored four books and has written seven book chapters along with numerous journal articles. Her recent research relates to career development and the development of spirituality in women. Dr. Richmond is the mother of four adult children and grandmother of 11, who range in age from 6 to 22. She relates that her interest in self-esteem in aging is personal as well as professional.

Lee Covington Rush, PhD, is an assistant professor of counseling at Northern Illinois University. He teaches courses in the areas of multicultural counseling, life span career counseling and interventions, family counseling, and counseling theories. His current research interests include investigating the intersection of personal and career counseling and reflective approaches for enhanced multicultural counseling competency. Dr. Rush is a nationally certified counselor.

Ann Jacob Smith, PhD, received her doctorate in counseling from George Washington University and a master's degree in rehabilitation counseling from University of North Carolina–Chapel Hill before becoming part of the behavioral staff at Duke University Diet and Fitness Center. While at Duke, she helped to develop and implement a binge eating disorder treatment program. While pursuing her doctoral work, she worked for the George Washington University Women's Exercise Research Center, the George Washington University Weight

Management Program, and the Washington Center for Eating Disorders and Adolescent Obesity. She has taught courses in counseling and eating disorders at Johns Hopkins University and George Washington University, and has presented at national eating disorders association meetings. A licensed clinical professional counselor, Smith has a private practice in Chevy Chase, Maryland, working with adolescents and their families.

Zarus E. Watson, PhD, is associate professor of counselor education at the University of New Orleans. His current teaching and research interests include social systems theory, organizational counseling, and consultation/evaluation modeling. Dr. Watson is also the research director of the UNO Research Center for Multiculturalism and Counseling and has been principal or coprincipal investigator on numerous projects conducted with the New Orleans-area public school systems, National Finance Center's Department of Workforce Services of the United States Department of Agriculture, Institute of Mental Hygiene, Louisiana State University Health Sciences Center, Baptist Community Ministries, United States Department of Housing and Urban Development, and other nonprofit and faith-based institutions. He is a licensed professional counselor and is a member of Chi Sigma Iota and Phi Delta Kappa honor societies.

Joy S. Whitman, PhD, is associate professor and program director in the human services and counseling program at DePaul University in Chicago. She is past president of the Association for Lesbian, Gay, Bisexual, and Transgender Issues in Counseling and has served on the American Counseling Association's ethics committee. She has written and presented nationally on the topics of clinical issues for lesbian, gay, bisexual, and transgender clients, counselor education for working with LGBT clients, and positive aspects of lesbian and gay identities. She advocates for safe schools for LGBT students through workshops and training for school personnel and maintains a small private practice in Chicago that serves the lesbian community.

Section *I*

Introduction

S elf-esteem as an area of inquiry has a rich history. Subsumed under the category of self-concept (the totality of thoughts and feelings about the self [Rosenberg and Owens, 2001]), it has been researched for more than a century. Today, it is also highly popularized, as a Web search or a visit to any bookstore shows. For example, one branch of a well-known bookstore on just one day contained 42 books on the subject. A recent Google search on the word *self-esteem* brought up over 3 million sites, while a book search under Amazon.com yielded more than 135,000 results. Although mental health practitioners and educators have available to them a massive amount of information about esteem-enhancing programs from academic, field/clinical-based, and popular/commercial sources, the majority of them seem to recommend ways to enhance self-esteem without regard to any evidence of what actually works. A few available resources are based on sound research, some on anecdotal material, and far too many on opinion, personal experience, or insight alone.

A continued proliferation of self-esteem research and its popularity in the trade media attests to the widely held belief of its significance as a personality variable. Self-esteem appears to be a wonder trait, a solution for all one's problems. Yet, most people do not seem to have a clear understanding of the construct. As a result, many helping professionals from various disciplines who routinely include self-esteem in their strategies do so without having accurate knowledge about it.

The goal of this book is to help clinicians have a good conceptualization of what self-esteem is and how interventions for specific populations can address underlying self-esteem issues. This first part of the book addresses the definitional maze (Smelser, 1989) that is self-esteem, discusses its controversies, and presents information on intervention strategies that actually can make a difference.

REFERENCES

Rosenberg, M., & Owens, T. J. (2001). Low self-esteem people: A collective portrait. In T. J. Owens, S. Stryker, & N. Goodman (Eds.), *Extending self-esteem theory and research* (pp. 400–436). New York: Cambridge University Press.

Smelser, N. (1989). Self-esteem and social problems: An introduction. In A. M. Mecca, N. J. Smelser, & J. Vasconcellos (Eds.), *The social importance of self-esteem* (pp. 294–326). Berkeley: University of California Press.

1

What Is Self-Esteem?

MARY H. GUINDON

INTRODUCTION

Researchers and clinicians from many disciplines focus on self-esteem as an area of importance. Self-esteem affects motivation, functional behavior, and life satisfaction, and is significantly related to well-being throughout life. It is possible that behaviors meant to maintain and enhance a positive sense of self are universal, that self-esteem is a basic human need (Greenberg, 2008). What individuals choose to do and the way they do it in part may be dependent upon their self-esteem. Low self-esteem has been shown to be related to many negative phenomena, including higher rates of teen pregnancy, alcohol and drug abuse, and violence, depression, social anxiety, and suicide. Such factors as gender, race, economic level, sexual orientation, immigrant status, and more seem to influence its levels (Twenge & Campbell, 2002; Twenge & Crocker, 2002). In fact, the need for positive self-esteem may be a significant feature of mainly European/American cultures (Heine, Lehman, Markus, & Kitayama, 1999).

The *Diagnostic and Statistical Manual of Mental Disorders* (*DSM–IV–TR;* American Psychiatric Association, 2000) includes self-esteem among diagnostic criteria for several mental disorder categories, and it is correlated strongly with depression. In a recent study of 1,190 individuals attending psychiatric outpatient services, Silverstone and Salsali (2003) concluded that all psychiatric patients suffered some degree of lowered self-esteem, with the lowest levels in patients diagnosed with depressive disorders, eating disorders, and substance abuse. Those with comorbid diagnoses, especially when one of the diagnoses was a depressive disorder, tended toward lower self-esteem than those without dual or multiple diagnoses. They found "a vicious cycle between low self-esteem and onset of psychiatric disorders. Thus, low self-esteem increases the susceptibility for development of psychiatric disorders, and the presence of a psychiatric disorder, in turn, lowers self-esteem" (para. 4).

Yet self-esteem's conceptualization and operationalization have been inconsistent, and many writers have criticized its meaning and usage. For example, countless studies have been conducted on student self-esteem and academic performance. Factors influencing students' low academic performance point to low self-esteem as either an antecedent or consequent component. In general, high self-esteem appears to be a consequence of having experienced success. Other research, however, suggests that there is no positive correlation between self-esteem and academic achievement (Baumeister, Campbell, Krueger, & Vohs, 2003; Forsyth, Lawrence, Burnett, & Baumeister, 2007; Ginter & Dwinell, 1994). This lack of consistency and consensus means mental health practitioners and educators may be making their own assumptions about self-esteem's nature, relying on common sense. This is misleading and contributes to an impression of preciseness in treatment planning where none exists. Consequently, clients' concerns may not be addressed, and strategies meant to impact their levels of self-esteem may not fit them.

The dichotomy between self-esteem's popularity in the public consciousness and the professional body of knowledge leads to misconception and confusion. Try this example:

> Betsy, an attractive 16 year old, well dressed and stylish, walks into a crowded party. She is at the top of her junior class, takes two AP classes, is a cheerleader, and has lots of friends. Upon request and encouragement, she sings a contemporary song with perfection. Several other guests rush over to compliment her on her talent. Later, she whispers to her best friend, "So what if I can sing? What difference does it make? I still feel really bad about myself. I guess I have low self-esteem."

Is she talking about how she measures up to other singers? The fact she has a rip in her new silk blouse? That she thinks she is overweight? That she earned a 97 rather than 100 on her last exam? How she manages her part-time job? Her overall level of confidence? In short, what does she mean?

Despite myriad resources, most people do not know how to answer this basic question. Furthermore, it seems that few mental health practitioners actually use resources that are well grounded in the existing body of knowledge. How can this be? How can something so well known to the general public be so perplexing? It seems to be that "the popular definition of self-esteem may not match the psychological definition of self-esteem" (Koch, 2006, p. 262). Given the ubiquitous nature of self-esteem, the assumption that it needs to be attended to, the availability of both responsible and problematic resources, and the lack of consistency and consensus in the field, practitioners need an accurate understanding of self-esteem if they are to use interventions that impact positive self-esteem development and enhancement. As long as clinicians continue to write "increase self-esteem" on treatment plans without a good knowledge of what it is or what can help, there is a fundamental need for this information.

Self-esteem is first of all a construct, and constructs are by necessity grounded in theory and concomitant research. Self-esteem is not something we can see, but we believe it to exist through its artifacts. To know its artifacts, we must first examine self-esteem's definitional maze (Smelser, 1989) because any theory—and intervention—depends on how it is defined.

Over 30 years ago, Wells and Marwell (1976) classified ways of defining self-esteem. Their landmark work stands today. They exhaustively studied the existing self-esteem works up to that time and came to the conclusion that definitions fall into four distinct categories resulting in different perspectives. In the *object/attitudinal approach*, the self is an object of attention just like any other thing. We can have thoughts, feelings, and behaviors toward anything that is an object. Thus, we can also have these reactions toward ourselves, in this case toward that part of ourselves we call self-esteem. The *relational approach* is the relationship or difference between sets of attitudes. It is also reactional. For example, we can have varying and different thoughts, feelings, and behaviors when comparing our ideal self with our real self, or between our aspirations and our achievements. Wells and Marwell found this to be the most common type of definition. The *psychological responses approach*, as its name suggests, concerns psychological or emotional reactions toward the self. We can feel either positive or negative about some element of ourselves, such as our behavior or our appearance. Self-esteem defined this way is affective in nature. The fourth type is the *personality function/component approach*. Self-esteem is seen as being a part of personality (a construct itself), the self, or self-system, which is that part of personality concerned with motivation and self-regulation. For example, individuals evaluate themselves according to how they conform to socially sanctioned standards. Wells and Marwell thus categorized definitions as attitudinal toward the self as the object of attention; as relational between different sets of self-attitudes; as psychological responses toward the self; and as a function of personality, a part of the self-system. Despite these varying ways to defining self-esteem, Wells and Marwell concluded that nearly all definitions of self-esteem consist of two primary aspects: evaluation and its emotional experience or affect.

Smelser (1989) posited that cognitive, affective, and evaluative elements are the universally accepted components of self-esteem. These components indicate the possibility of different artifacts. The cognitive element expresses a part of the self in descriptive terms. It answers the question of what kind of person one is, such as secure, outgoing, or smart. The affective element is the positive or negative aspect of each of these attributes, or its valence. It determines whether self-esteem is high or low. The evaluative element is the level of worthiness assigned to each attribution. It is based on an ideal societal standard.

How these and other self-esteem researchers came to their conclusions is based on the history of previous conceptualizations about self-esteem. "Each usage is relative to the particular theoretical context in which it occurs, since it is from that theory that self-esteem gets its definition and, consequently, its meaning" (Wells & Marwell, 1976, p. 229). If we are to apply strategies meaningfully, we must come to a consensus on how we define self-esteem. To reach consensus, we should be well informed of past and current definitions. Mruk (2006) reminds us that definitions worth examining must pass the test of time, and that "every major definition is important because each one can show us some things about self-esteem that can only be seen from that particular point of view" (p. 9). We will now look at the main theories and key scholars that show the evolution of the construct across time.

HISTORY OF SELF-ESTEEM AS A CONSTRUCT

The study of self-esteem is not new. The concept of self-esteem has probably always been part of the human psyche. Campbell and Foster (2006) have argued for its evolution as an early human trait that "likely provided information about social standing and performance ..." (p. 345). Nevertheless, self-esteem as a distinct concept in all likelihood first appeared during the European Age of Enlightenment. John Milton (cited in Leonard, 2003) may have coined the word *self-esteem* when he wrote in *An Apology for Smectymnuus* in 1642: "Nothing profits more than self-esteem, grounded on what is just and right."

However, its beginnings as a modern psychological concept can be traced to William James (1890), who is generally credited as the earliest investigator of self psychology. He defined self-esteem as self-appreciation consisting of feelings and emotions toward the self. As a product of the scientific, positivistic period of time, he conceptualized self-esteem as an equation of self-evaluation—a ratio of our "pretensions" divided by our "successes" (p. 310). He believed there to be a connection among values, success, and competence. He proposed that one carries an average level of self-feeling at all times regardless of objective reality. That is, self-esteem is a trait. Individuals have a baseline feeling of worth, value, liking, and acceptance. Hence, James's definition is affective. One's trait level of self-esteem is relatively independent of objective circumstances, in contrast to state self-esteem, in which self-esteem changes in response to the successes and failures in one's life.

Cooley (1902) also viewed self-esteem as affective. Perhaps best known for his conceptualization of the looking-glass self, in which the understanding of the self is determined by perceptions of others' judgments, Cooley observed that who we believe ourselves to be is very much tied to our social environment. Significant others are the social mirror into which we look to discover their opinions toward us. We imagine our self to be what others think us to be, including all of our aspects, such as our character, looks, behaviors, and so forth.

Mead (1934) viewed the self as a product of interactions in which individuals experience themselves as reflected in the behavior of others. Although Mead did not address directly the concept of self-esteem, he discussed self-evaluation as an attitude toward self. In contrast to James and Cooley, his view is cognitive in nature. Mead believed that the self develops from the continual interaction of the *I* (the subjective, private, experiencing part of the self) with the *Me* (the objective, social aspect of the self). The I consists only of the awareness of experiences of thinking and feeling and is present from infancy. The Me grows gradually in children as they develop the ability to perceive objects distinct from themselves. For Mead, individuals experience themselves through their perceptions of the outside environment and community. The self is a product of the social world. The Me distinguishes attributes of the self from the perspective of this "generalized other" of society. "Mead's formulation implies a process through which the judgments of numerous significant others are somehow psychologically weighted in order to produce an overall sense of self-worth as a person" (Harter, 1999, p. 19). James, Cooley, and Mead believed the self-image to be influenced by the social environment, particularly through the individual's perceived appraisal by others.

Several early personality theorists contributed to our understanding of self-esteem. Neo-Freudian Karen Horney (1950) stated that each person is born with a unique potential, and that self-esteem derives from achieving it. Harry Stack Sullivan (1953) posited that self-esteem is the social need to be accepted and liked and to belong that is derived from social interaction mediated by reflected self-appraisal. Self-esteem is maintained by conforming to social expectations. Alfred Adler (1956) theorized that people construct their own views of self. They strive for meaning; they work toward the goal of wholeness and for superiority. Although he did not define self-esteem directly, he used the term *self-acceptance*, which entails perceptions of competence and achievement. He said that false superiority is an inefficient way of gaining self-esteem. He believed in coping rather than avoiding life's problems. Gordon Allport (1961) saw the development of self-esteem as a central issue for early childhood. He equated self-esteem to the sense of pride that comes from recognition that one can do things on one's own. White (1963) stated that self-esteem has two sources: an internal source of a sense of accomplishment and an external source of affirmation from others. He described self-esteem as a developmental process and recognized competence as a key factor.

Humanists also described self-esteem. Rogers (1951) defined self-esteem as the extent to which people like, value, and accept themselves. He believed that the self develops from a combination of what is experienced and what is interjected, derived from values and affective preferences. The individual conceptualizes an ideal self, or the "person you would like to be"; the actual self-image, or the "person you think you are"; and the true self, or the "person you actually are." The more congruent are these three aspects of the self, the healthier the self-esteem. In his hierarchy of human needs, Maslow (1968) included self-esteem as a basic need, second only to self-actualization. He defined it as "the desire for strength, for achievement, for adequacy, for mastery and competence, ... and for independence and freedom" (p. 45).

Morris Rosenberg (1965, 1979) and Stanley Coopersmith (1967) were the first researchers to develop theories of self-esteem as a significant personality construct grounded in empirical methods. Although they researched different populations, they reached similar conclusions.

Rosenberg (1965) researched the development of the self-image during adolescence and its consequences for adolescents and adults. He emphasized the self-image as a global aspect of the personality. He concluded that self-esteem is an attitude toward a specific object, the self. Each characteristic of the self is evaluated and results in an estimate of that characteristic. Every element of the self is evaluated according to a value that has developed during childhood and adolescence. Feedback from others, particularly significant others, is a key element of self-esteem (Rosenberg, 1979). This feedback can be actual or perceived.

Rosenberg recognized a dual nature in self-esteem. It is at once a situational evaluation and a general one. Self-esteem is a combination of specific estimates of the individual's numerous and varied characteristics. Although this process can be out of awareness, people assign varying negative or positive values to each characteristic—or domain—and add them together. This results in a general evaluation of the self. Furthermore, people place importance on, or weigh, some domains more than others. The weight of each value will vary depending upon how important that particular characteristic is to the individual. In other words, how much each constituent characteristic matters to the individual determines the weight given, or its salience. Perceived reactions from others, particularly significant others, is an important element of self-esteem. People socially rank and evaluate many elements, including their personal attributes, life roles, and present circumstances. Consequently, the individual's sense of personal worth can be contingent upon the perceived prestige of the element. Therefore, a person's global self-esteem is based "not solely on an assessment of his constituent qualities but on an assessment of the qualities that *count*" (Rosenberg, 1979, p. 18). For example, an individual may place a weak negative evaluation on looks, a medium negative evaluation on physical prowess, a weak positive evaluation on mathematical ability, and an extremely high evaluation on social sense and belongingness. Together these would add up to an overall positive sense of self-esteem, assuming these qualities were particularly salient. Conversely, if belongingness and mathematical ability were not important and physical prowess was most important, overall self-esteem would be negative. Nevertheless, although Rosenberg discussed specific estimates of various parts of the self, he argued for a unidimensional concept of self-esteem that he termed global self-esteem, or "the feeling that one is 'good enough'" (1965, p. 31).

Coopersmith (1967) researched the development of self-esteem in presecondary school children and believed self-esteem to be a complex phenomenon consisting of self-evaluation and manifestations of defensive reactions to that evaluation. Comprised of two parts—subjective expression and behavioral manifestation—self-esteem is a self-evaluation of personal worthiness. It is a judgmental process in which "performance, capacities, and attributes" (Coopersmith, 1981, p. 5) are examined according to personal standards and values that developed during childhood. As an acquired trait, individuals learn their worth initially from their parents, which is then reinforced by others. Coopersmith addressed true self-esteem (seen in those who actually feel worthy and valuable) and defensive self-esteem (seen in those who feel unworthy but who cannot admit this threatening information). This definition focuses on the "relatively enduring estimate of general self-esteem rather than on specific and transitory changes in evaluation" (Coopersmith, 1981, p. 5).

Following their original works and not particularly related to them, self-esteem as a popular phenomenon exploded during the human potential movement of the 1960s and 1970s. Self-esteem now entered the national consciousness. The centrality of self-esteem to success and well-being has since become part of American culture. Helping professionals, teachers, and parents have made efforts to increase self-esteem in the belief that high self-esteem will result in a plethora of positive outcomes, but with little substantive evidence (Baumeister et al., 2003; Swann,

Chang-Schneider, & Larsen McClarty, 2007). As an example, the California Task Force to Promote Self-Esteem and Personal and Social Responsibility (1990) embarked on an ambitious program to promote enhancing self-esteem as a method of bolstering its state's economy and cure social problems. It published a committee-generated definition based on task force recommendations. Stated as its official definition was, "Appreciating my own worth and importance and having the character to be accountable for myself and to act responsibly toward others" (California Task Force, p. 1). This was a notable exception to academic definitions. Later on, Dr. Sidney B. Simon spawned a self-esteem industry with the development of the IALAC (I am loveable and capable) curriculum.

The search for the meaning of self-esteem and the refining of its definition continues to this day. Nathaniel Branden (1969) defined self-esteem as a standard by which one judges oneself, an estimate, an emotion, and as "the experience that we are appropriate to life and to the requirements of life" (1992, p. 8). His early work was the first to clearly include both competence and worthiness. He added the dimension of the relationship between personal self-efficacy and self-respect.

Epstein's (1973) cognitive-experiential self theory (CEST) views self-esteem as a basic human need. Self-enhancement is a basic motive. Self-esteem is conceptualized as a consequence of one's understanding of the world and others, and who one is in relation to them. The self strives to maintain equilibrium through compromises among various motives. This accounts for how low- or high-self-esteem people respond to positive and negative feedback differently. Two experiences most directly affecting self-esteem are success/failure and acceptance/rejection (Epstein, 1979). Epstein noted that there are different levels of self-esteem: global, intermediate, and situational. Global is the general evaluation of the self. Intermediate involves specific domains, such as competence, lovability, self-control, and body appearance. Situational is the day-to-day manifestation of self-esteem that varies with circumstances. Global and intermediate self-esteem affect situational self-esteem.

Gecas (1982) differentiated between self-esteem based on a sense of competence, power, or efficacy and self-esteem based on a sense of virtue or moral worth. Self-esteem based on competence involves effective performance and is associated with self-attribution and social comparison processes. Self-esteem based on self-worth is associated with values and norms of personal and interpersonal conduct. These two aspects are interrelated; sense of worth may be affected by sense of competence, and vice versa.

Harter (1999) discussed both global and domain-specific evaluations of the self. In reviewing the literature she came to the conclusion that it is necessary "to distinguish between self-evaluations that represent global characteristics of the individual (e.g., 'I am a worthwhile person') and those that reflect the individual's sense of adequacy across particular domains such as one's cognitive competence (e.g., 'I am smart'), social competence (e.g., 'I am well liked by my peers'), athletic competence (e.g., 'I am good at sports'), and so forth" (p. 5). Harter reiterated Mead's and Cooley's contentions that evaluations of the self are a social construction that develops in childhood from the perceived opinions of significant others. Children internalize the standards and values of important significant others, "including the values of the larger society" (p. 13). She pointed out that general self-esteem is not a summary of self-evaluations of different domains.

Brown (1993) supported conceptualizing self-esteem in terms of global feelings separate from specific self-evaluation. He made a case for global self-esteem affecting specific self-evaluations, not the reverse. Rather than seeing a qualitative difference between specific and global self-esteem, Wylie (1974) and Gurney (1986) proposed a hierarchic relationship. Evidently, generalizations cannot be made from the global to the specific or from the specific to the global (Harter, 1999).

Mruk (1995, 2006), in presenting his phenomenological theory of self-esteem, reviewed previous definitions and presented self-esteem in a two-factor theory in which an interaction between worthiness and competence occurs. He has conceptualized a self-esteem matrix showing a continuum of low to high competence-based self-esteem and low to high worthiness-based self-esteem. His work has substantiated worth and competence as the major elements in defining self-esteem. A similar line of inquiry presents self-esteem as self-competence and self-liking. Self-competence corresponds "to one's history of success and failure in meeting goals" (Tafarodi & Milne, 2002, p. 467), and self-liking derives from "appraisals of worth conveyed by others or reflexively generated by the 'generalized other' of self-judgment" (p. 468).

In recent years the emphasis in definitions has shifted to various aspects of self-esteem. Contributors to the self-esteem body of knowledge continue to further refine the construct. *Collective self-esteem* refers to the positivity of the self-concept derived from identifying oneself as a member in one or more social groups. Level of self-worth is mainly based on the emotional significance attached to a specific social group and one's role in it (Luhtanen & Crocker, 1992). Collective self-esteem is an especially important factor to understand when working with those who are not ethnic members of the traditional White Euro-American culture, or who are marginalized by it.

Contingent self-esteem refers to feelings about the self that are dependent upon measuring up to external sources of perceived standards and expectations (Crocker, 2006; Crocker & Wolfe, 2001; Deci & Ryan, 1995). "Contingent self-esteem is experienced by people who are preoccupied with questions of worth and esteem, and who see their worth as dependent upon reaching certain standards, appearing certain ways, or accomplishing certain goals. It is not just that they are motivated, but also that they are strongly motivated by the desire to appear worthy to self and others," whereas noncontingent self-esteem "characterizes persons for whom the issue of self-esteem is not salient, largely because they experience themselves on a fundamental level as worthy of esteem and love" (Ryan & Brown, 2003, p. 72). Those with contingent self-esteem issues "are preoccupied with their standings on specific evaluative dimensions (e.g., How attractive am I?) and how they are viewed by others (Do people think I am smart?) ..." (Kernis & Goldman, 2006, p.79).

Implicit self-esteem refers to unconscious self-evaluations (Kernis, 2003; Koole, Dijksterhuis, & van Knippenberg, 2001). It is "the introspectively unidentified (or inaccurately identified) effect of the self-attitude on evaluation of self-associated and self-dissociated objects" (Greenwald & Banaji, 1995, p. 11). *Explicit self-esteem* is conscious and may be influenced by the need for positive self-presentation. Yamaguchi et al. (2007) have suggested that while explicit self-esteem may not be universal, implicit self-esteem may very well be universal, based on their studies of students in Japan, China, and the United States.

An emphasis on the difference between state and trait self-esteem has also emerged. *Self-esteem lability* is a trait: one's excessive reactions to everyday stressors and positive and negative occurrences. Self-esteem can be stable or unstable (Trzesniewski, Donnellan, & Robins, 2003), and secure or fragile (Kernis, Lakey, & Heppner, 2008). These and other newer developments in conceptualizing self-esteem keep the discipline vibrant and open to debate and controversy.

SELF-ESTEEM DEFINED

With such variation in definitions in the literature, we must clarify self-esteem as defined in this book. In reviewing the history of the self-esteem construct we can come to some conclusions. First and foremost, self-esteem is an attitude, namely, the individual's evaluation of the self-concept. Competence and achievement appear to be integral elements of self-esteem, and these two elements appear to be intertwined with a judgment of self-worth. Worth is dependent on societal values and in part is shaped and maintained through the perceived judgment of opinions and feedback from significant others. Moreover, self-esteem appears to be dual in nature. It is at once a general evaluation (global) and a specific evaluation of elements of the self (selective). This means, as many theorists have suggested, that individuals attach evaluations to all the different qualities and aspects of the self that vary in importance to them. They also sum these qualities, presumably unconsciously, to generate an overall evaluation of the self. Furthermore, self-esteem appears to vary across different areas of experience and according to role-defining characteristics. Self-esteem, then, seems to fluctuate, influenced by "changing roles, expectations, performances, responses from others, and other situational characteristics" (Demo, 1985, p. 1491). It appears to be situational—high at one moment or low at another—depending upon to which specific identity element, or domain, such as academic ability or achievement, physical prowess, body image, or family and peer relationships, the individual attends. People may have positive attitudes about the self in general, but, in certain circumstances, feel better or worse about themselves. Furthermore, it is possible to have a good overall self-esteem level, but have low self-esteem about a specific trait or quality, especially when that trait has a high meaning or significance. When a trait or group of traits is especially salient, global self-esteem can be affected.

It is this very dual nature that leads to imprecise strategies intended to enhance or remediate self-esteem issues, resulting in the possibility that a practitioner may be addressing one quality or attribute in the client when another quality or attribute altogether may be of concern to the client. "Jane, for example, may have a strong sense of general, or global, self-esteem, but may manifest feelings of low self-esteem about the size of her nose, or her inability to do math; may exhibit feelings of high self-esteem about her popularity among her peers; and may temporarily show characteristics of low self-esteem when she is in a situation where she feels incompetent or demeaned by someone important to her" (Guindon, 2002, p. 206). Or, " John may play the piano exceptionally well but if it doesn't matter to him, if this accomplishment carries a low weight, his counselor's well-intentioned validation of his piano-playing skill as a way to bolster his self-esteem is ineffective" (Guindon, 2002, p. 207).

Consequently, mental health clinicians and others who are concerned about self-esteem in those who receive their services need ways to address self-esteem by conceptualizing a consistent definition that has utility. To that end and for the purposes put forth in this book, the following is a general definition grounded in the professional literature:

> *Self-esteem* is "the attitudinal, evaluative component of the self; the affective judgments placed on the self-concept consisting of feelings of worth and acceptance which are developed and maintained as a consequence of awareness of competence and feedback from the external world." (Guindon, 2002, p. 207)

Furthermore, we must recognize that self-esteem is not one entity. We can assume self-esteem exists as a *self-esteem system* made up of a global component and a selective component. It consists of interrelated concepts that can be addressed separately:

> *Global self-esteem:* An overall estimate of general self-worth; a level of self-acceptance or respect for oneself; a trait or tendency relatively stable and enduring, composed of all subordinate traits and characteristics within the self.
>
> *Selective self-esteem:* An evaluation of specific and constituent traits or qualities within the self, at times situationally variable and transitory, that are weighted and combined into an overall evaluation of self, or global self-esteem. (Guindon, 2002, p. 207)

These definitions allow us to assess and attend to different domains of the self—those traits and circumstances within individuals that most matter to them. To operationalize self-esteem, we need to recognize that accomplishment and achievement are manifestations of competence that can be addressed in counseling and psychotherapy. We also need to recognize that societal, family, and personal values play major roles in the sense of worthiness and self-acceptance and can likewise be addressed. Both areas emphasize the need to understand the extent that salience (i.e., weight) plays in each individual's level of selective self-esteem. The contributors to this book present information that explicitly speaks to the issues of their expertise. They connect what they know to be effective in treating their populations to one or more specific elements that make up the self-esteem system. They show us how and in what ways their interventions and strategies can address self-esteem issues. Practitioners who include self-esteem in their treatment plans thus have a framework from which to work responsibly.

SELF-ESTEEM APPRAISAL

Accurate appraisals about self-esteem level and stability help us plan interventions that have the best chance of working. The practitioner's decision needs to match the client's experience (Figure 1.1).

If a client's experience of her self-esteem is low, and the practitioner correctly decides the client has low self-esteem, he can then develop effective and appropriate treatment goals to attempt to raise it. If he is incorrect, he will falsely attribute manifest behaviors and feelings to low self-esteem and his attempts at increasing self-esteem are unwarranted. On the other hand, if the client's experience of her self-esteem is adequate or high, and the practitioner correctly decides the client has no self-esteem issues, self-esteem is not a treatment goal. If he is incorrect, he might then develop unwarranted and ineffective treatment goals and inappropriate interventions. Clearly, informed choices through appraisal are necessary.

Unfortunately, evidence points to the fact that few clinicians actually use methods to assess self-esteem. As an example, I investigated perceptions and practices pertaining to self-esteem among 418 participants, mainly school counselors, in New Jersey. A majority of the total survey participants (73.4%) indicated that they had specialized knowledge or training about self-esteem. Nevertheless, when asked if they used assessment methods to determine students' self-esteem levels, only 57 (13.6%) of the 418 survey participants answered yes. A majority of 81.8% answered no, and 19 respondents did not answer the question (Guindon, 1996).

What can we make of the fact that despite the overwhelming majority of these counselors' belief that schools are responsible for addressing the issue of self-esteem in their students, so few of them assess levels of self-esteem? Is its manifestation assumed? Without some basis to objectively assess self-esteem levels, upon what

Client's Experience	Counselor Decision (based on perception/assumption of client's experience)	
	Self-esteem Adequate/High	Self-esteem Low/False
Self-esteem Adequate/High	Correct Decision ↑ SE ≠ treatment goal	Incorrect Decision ↑ SE = ineffective treatment goal/ inappropriate interventions
Self-esteem Low/False	Incorrect Decision ↑ SE = ineffective treatment goal/ False attribution of behavior/feelings/thoughts	Correct Decision ↑ SE = appropriate/effective treatment goal. Assess global and selective SE

Figure 1.1   Client experience and counselor decision.

are counselors relying to develop self-esteem interventions? Surely, if addressing self-esteem is to be considered at all, assessing it is essential.

Although no shortage of instruments claiming to measure self-esteem exists, the current state of assessment is just as confusing as self-esteem's definitional maze. Just as we found with an Internet search of the word *self-esteem* by itself, pairing it with *test* garnered over 4 million sites, and with *assessment* resulted in over 2½ million. We can safely assume that most of these sites are problematic at best.

Standardized Assessment Instruments

Of course, there are many well-constructed, professionally accountable assessment instruments that include a self-esteem measurement. There are well over 2,000 self-esteem-related assessment instruments in existence. Most are self-report questionnaires. They contain inherent difficulties common to all self-report measures, such as question format and social desirability and self-presentation biases, and can be misleading. Some instruments purporting to measure self-esteem in actuality are a sum of various self-descriptions that may measure concepts other than self-esteem. In a review of self-esteem assessments almost 20 years ago, Blascovich and Tomaka (1991) stated: "Neither a firm body of evidence nor a convincing definitional rationale to justify many of the 'self-esteem' measures exists" (p. 119). Achieving a sound degree of scientific validity is difficult. Nevertheless, the use of standardized pencil-and-paper self-report instruments is the primary and most reliable means of ascertaining self-esteem levels. Although there are limits to what clinicians can realistically expect in self-esteem instruments, the most commonly used instruments suitable for self-esteem measurements include the Self-Esteem Inventory (SEI; Coopersmith, 1981), Tennessee Self-Concept Scale (TSCS; Roid & Fitts, 1988), Piers-Harris Children's Self-Concept Scale (P-HCSCS; Piers, 1984), Body-Esteem Scale (BES; Franzoi & Shields, 1984), and Culture-Free Self-Esteem Inventories (CFSEI-3; Battle, 2002). Arguably, the most widely used instrument is the Rosenberg Self-Esteem Scale (Rosenberg, 1965). A measure of global self-esteem, it is not published by a testing company. Used mainly for research with high face validity, it may not be suitable as an appraisal of any one individual's self-esteem (see Wylie, 1974; Table 1.1).

Other useful assessments include the Self-Perception Profile for Children (Harter, 1985) and Self-Perception Profile for Adolescents (Harter, 1988), Self-Liking and Self-Competence Scale (Tafarodi & Swann, 2001), Implicit Association Test (IAT; Greenwald, McGhee, & Schwartz, 1998), and Kernis and Paradise Contingent Self-Esteem Scale (Kernis & Goldman, 2006).

Other Methods of Assessing Self-Esteem

Relying on a single form of measurement is not enough. Clinicians have several other options: interviews, behavioral observation, and ratings by others (e.g., teachers, counselors, medical professionals, parents). A responsible way to approximate self-esteem levels is through triangulation, the use of multiple methods.

TABLE 1.1   Assessment Instruments Appropriate for Self-Esteem Measurement

Instrument with Citation	Purpose G/S[a]	Format	Age Range	Number of Items	Concerns
Self-Esteem Scale (SES; Rosenberg, 1965) (Also available is a 6-item SES targeted toward children below high school age, see Rosenberg & Simmons, 1972)	G only. Unidimensional measure of global feelings of self-worth and acceptance; estimates positive or negative feelings about the self	4-point reponses to self-descriptive statements	High school through adult	10	Susceptible to social desirability response. Tends to be negatively skewed for college age
Self-Esteem Inventory (SEI; Coopersmith, 1981)[b]	Form A: G and S with caution. Form B: G only. Measure "self-regard." Form A has three subscales: Social Self-Peers, Home-Parents, School-Academic, plus a lie scale	Forced choice ("like me," not like me") reponses to self-descriptive statements	Ages 8 through 15	Form A: 50 Form B: 25 (first half of Form A)	Susceptible to social desirability response. Tends to be negatively skewed
Tennessee Self-Concept Scale (TSCS; Roid & Fitts, 1988)	G (total score). S (social, family, physical, moral-ethical, personal categories. Multidimensional view of the self-concept; popular as a general measure of self-esteem	5-point responses to self-descriptive statements	Ages 12 and above	100	Support only for family, physical, and social subscales (Marsh & Richards, 1988)
Piers-Harris Children's Self-Concept Scale (P-HCSCS; Piers, 1984)	G only. Measures self-concept; synonymous with self-esteem regard. Subscales demonstrate substantial overlap (Blascovich & Tomaka, 1991)	Forced choice (yes/no) responses to predominantly self-descriptive statements	Ages 8 through 18	80	Susceptible to social desirability response; most suitable to younger groups

—continued

TABLE 1.1   Assessment Instruments Appropriate for Self-Esteem Measurement (*continued*)

Instrument with Citation	Purpose G/S[a]	Format	Age Range	Number of Items	Concerns
The Body-Esteem Scale (BES; Franzoi & Shields, 1984)	S only. Meaures degree of feelings with various body parts or processes	5-point responses rating feelings about body parts and functions including gender-specific subscales	College age	40	Social desirability response bias not determined but considered moderate (Blascovich & Tomaka, 1991)
Culture-Free Self-Esteem Inventories, 2nd edition (CFSEI-2; Battle, 1992)	Measures perception of self, self-esteem independent of cultural context. Form A: (general items subscale), S with caution. Subscales are Social/Peers Related; Academic/School Related; Parents/Home Related; and lie items. Form B: G only. Form AD: G (general items subscale). S with caution. Subscales are social, personal, and lie items.	Forced choice (yes/no) self-report checklists	Forms A&B: Grades 3–12. Form AD: Adults	Form A: 60 Form B: 30 Form AD: 40	True "culture free" status in question. Tends to be negatively skewed.

Source: Guindon (2002, p. 211).

[a] G= suitable as a measure of global self-esteem.   S = suitable as a measure of selective self-esteem.

[b] Adult form adapted from Form B is also available.

In fact, just as with other issues, appraisal does not begin with administering an assessment instrument alone, but by observing and monitoring the client. Ratings by others, behavioral observations, and interview methods are subjective means of assessment. They can clarify distinctions between experienced and presented self-esteem (Demo, 1985). Experienced self-esteem is that which is evaluated by the individual, whereas presented self-esteem is that which is evident to others through observing verbal and nonverbal behaviors. Self-ratings, however good at capturing personal information unavailable to others, are inherently fallible because minor changes in questions' wording, format, or context can result in major differences in results (Schwarz, 1999). Then again, observer ratings provide information observed by others, such as parents or teachers, but these ratings must infer information. This makes them susceptible to obscuring and distorting an individual's self-esteem, especially given the likelihood of observers not having a sound grounding in what self-esteem actually is. Clearly, all these alternatives to standardized measurements can contribute corroborative evidence but are also susceptible to distortion.

Although necessary, regrettably, assessing self-esteem is an imprecise activity. No one alternative method can accurately pinpoint self-esteem levels or consistently make accurate judgments on any one client. Practitioners should therefore take advantage of one or more standardized assessment instruments and supplement the information with one or more of the alternative methods whenever possible.

SELF-ESTEEM CHARACTERISTICS

Self-esteem exists on a continuum and can be high, medium, low, or defensive. When considering optimal self-esteem, the curvilinear model seems to be most apt, with too low and too high self-esteem being less adaptive than medium self-esteem. Too strong a belief in one's competence, for example, may actually make one more vulnerable to life's pitfalls because the individual does not recognize realistic limitations. Extreme high self-esteem can be indicative of narcissism and destructiveness (Baumeister, Smart, & Boden, 1996). On the other hand, some people who exhibit signs of high self-esteem may actually be experiencing feelings of low self-esteem through the mechanism of defensive, pseudo-high, or false self-esteem. The person with false high self-esteem is characterized by an overinflated sense of self (Hoyle, Kernis, Leary, & Baldwin, 1999), which in actuality covers up a sense of low self-worth. This person lacks self-awareness and may be defensive, destructive, and aggressive, all the while professing a strong evaluative sense of self. The combination of self-esteem level and instability may result in hostility; self-esteem reactivity may be one characteristic of childhood aggression. Those with unstable high self-esteem may be more likely to act angry and hostile than those with high stable self-esteem (Esposito, Kobak, & Little, 2005). Baumeister et al. (1996) have proposed that the combination of high self-esteem (associated with narcissism), low empathy, excessive need for approval, and unstable self-esteem results in a tendency toward violence. Others disagree, saying that those with low self-esteem are more likely to report violent thoughts (Harter, Low, & Whitesell,

2003, cited in Harter, 2006). The person with healthy and genuine high or medium self-esteem will be assertive rather than aggressive. Those with genuinely low self-esteem tend to be avoidant, rather than aggressive.

Low self-esteem is highly correlated with depression (Beck, Brown, Steer, & Kuyken, 2001; Silverstone & Salsali, 2003), and a significant relationship exists between suicidal ideation and self-esteem. Self-esteem is also correlated with locus of control (Brockner, 1979; Judge, Erez, Bono, & Thoresen, 2002). Many studies support the fact that high-self-esteem individuals seem to be more self-directed and independent than low-self-esteem individuals. High-self-esteem people are more open to feedback and can perceive situations more realistically. Lower-self-esteem individuals tend to be more cautious, self-protective, and conservative than higher-self-esteem people. Self-esteem stability seems to play a role. Stability is "the magnitude of short-term fluctuations that people experience in their current, contextually based feelings of self-worth" (Kernis, 2005, p. 1). Instability may be associated with greater sensitivity to feedback. When highly unstable-self-esteem people receive negative feedback, their self-esteem declines in reaction to this feedback more than that of stable-self-esteem people (Kernis, Cornell, Sun, Berry, & Harlow, 1993).

Rosenberg and Owens (2001) have provided us with a portrait of low-self-esteem people drawn from surveys and experimental studies. Those with low self-esteem are more sensitive than others to experiences that threaten to damage their self-esteem. They are more troubled by criticism and have more severe emotional reactions to failure. Additionally, they are more likely to magnify events as negative or perceive noncritical remarks as critical. Those with low self-esteem are more likely than others to experience social anxiety, exhibiting high levels of public self-consciousness. Low-self-esteem people have low interpersonal confidence. They feel "awkward, shy, conspicuous, and unable to adequately express themselves when interacting with others" (p. 409). This lack of interpersonal confidence lowers interpersonal success, which then results in damaged global self-esteem. Although not necessarily obvious to an observer, high- and low-self-esteem individuals vary greatly in their motives for personal growth and improvement. High-self-esteem people seek growth, whereas low-self-esteem people seek to protect the self and focus on not making mistakes. Moreover, those with low self-esteem experience substantially less happiness and more emotional distress, including depression and anxiety. Low-self-esteem individuals tend to be pessimistic, cynical, and have negative attitudes toward institutions as well as toward people and groups. Low-self-esteem people exhibit unconstructive thinking such as rigidity and inflexibility. They are more likely to be indecisive and slower to respond when they need to make decisions. They experience greater depersonalization, experiencing themselves as detached onlookers. However, Rosenberg and Owens (2001) point out that this type of depersonalization is distinct from the DSM disorder.

People with low self-esteem also tend to have lower self-efficacy and confidence in their own judgments and opinions. Self-efficacy and self-confidence are related parts of the self-concept. Self-efficacy refers to people's assessments of their effectiveness and competency and causal agency (Bandura, 1977; Gecas, 1989). However, high self-esteem does not necessarily reflect strong feelings of efficacy, nor does a good sense of self-efficacy ensure high self-esteem. Self-confidence is defined as the "anticipation of successfully mastering challenges or overcoming obstacles ..." (Rosenberg, 1979, p. 31). High-self-esteem individuals are confident in the accuracy of their perceptions and judgments and believe that they can favorably resolve their efforts (Coopersmith, 1967). Yet global self-esteem seems to be distinct from social confidence.

Baumeister et al. (2003) found that self-esteem and happiness are strongly interrelated: Enhanced initiative, pleasant feelings, and better physical health and longevity are positive outcomes of high self-esteem. Those with high self-esteem are less likely to be depressed in response to stressful, traumatic events. They seem to perform better in the workplace and experience more occupational success, persist following failure, sometimes perform better in groups, and perceive themselves as well liked and popular. Low self-esteem is linked to depression, may be a risk factor for it, and is associated with victimization.

Perhaps the most overriding and important difference between low- and high-self-esteem people identified by Rosenberg and Owens (2001) is in their approach to life. Low-self-esteem people engage in self-protective behaviors, whereas high-self-esteem people engage in self-enhancing behaviors. Low-self-esteem people avoid risk taking, especially in their interpersonal encounters. They tend to restrict their interactions with others, are less likely to express their opinions and views, keep their emotions private, and conceal their thoughts, which are often hostile and suspicious of others. Consequently, those with low self-esteem are less spontaneous, more passive, lonelier, more interpersonally inept, and more alienated than those with high self-esteem. Overall, low-self-esteem people are most concerned with safety and protection of the self. Rosenberg and Owens (2001) sound one cautionary note: "The features of the LSE [low-self-esteem] personality are generally not qualitatively different from those of most other people; they are largely an *accentuation* of characteristics that appear among many people.... Many people with self-esteem problems are able to function reasonably well in life, even while their self-esteem problems cause pain, difficulty, failure, and worry.... It would be no exaggeration to say that it *damages* their lives in many ways" (p. 431).

Crocker and Park (2004) have suggested that when perceiving threats to the self-concept, both high- and low-self-esteem people act to enhance self-esteem, but do so differently. Those with high self-esteem are concerned with presenting their abilities; they discount negative feedback and seek feedback on competence. Low-self-esteem people pursue self-esteem by seeking acceptance. Kaplan (2001) states, "People characteristically behave so as to minimize the experience of self-rejecting attitudes and maximize the experience of positive self-attitudes."

How aware are helping professionals of these self-esteem characteristics? In the survey of school counselors discussed earlier in this chapter, participants were asked to list five characteristics each that best describe students with high self-esteem and students with low self-esteem (Table 1.2).

A majority of the participants in this study (63.9%) saw students with high self-esteem, first and foremost, as confident. The second most frequent characteristic was friendly/outgoing (43.8%), with the third most frequent being happy (36.6%). Other characteristics included positive/optimistic and motivated. The most frequent characteristics of low-self-esteem students were withdrawn/shy/quiet and

TABLE 1.2   Top 15 Characteristics of High- and Low-Self-Esteem Students

High Self-Esteem	n	Low Self-Esteem	n
1. Confident	267	1. Withdrawn/shy/quiet	140
2. Friendly/outgoing	189	2. Insecure	138
3. Happy	153	3. Underachieving	131
4. Positive/optimistic	118	4. Negative (attitude)	120
5. Motivated	98	5. Unhappy	110
6. Achieving	89	6. Socially inept	101
7. Competitive/risk taker	88	7. Angry/hostile	91
8. Accepting/tolerant	85	8. Unmotivated	84
9. Involved/active	78	9. Depressed	83
10. Secure/well adjusted	75	10. Dependent/follower	82
11. Comfortable w/ self	74	11. Poor self-image	75
12. Assertive	59	12. Non-risk taker	66
13. Caring	53	13. Lacks self-confidence	62
14. Independent	52	14. Poor communicator	47
15. Responsible	50	15. Acts out	39
Other[a]	432	Other[b]	578

Note: 412 of 418 respondents answered this question.
n = number of responses.
[a] 27 additional terms.
[b] 34 additional terms.

insecure, each of which was listed by approximately one-third of the respondents. Other top characteristics included underachieving (31.8%), negative attitude (26.7%), and unhappy (26.3%; Guindon, 1996).

The most noteworthy finding points to the disparity with which respondents described characteristics. Well over 1,000 words, phrases, and terms were used to describe either high- or low-self-esteem students. In some cases, the same terms, such as assertive and competitive, appeared on both lists. Depending on how self-esteem is conceptualized, aggressive children may appear to have both a low and a high self-esteem. This possibility was confirmed by Diamantopoulou, Rydell, and Henricsson (2008) in their study of 652 twelve-year-olds. Low levels of global self-esteem and overinflated self-esteem (which was disputed by their peers) were related to aggression, and aggressive children seem to have both a low and a high self-esteem, which may depend upon how self-esteem is conceptualized. On the other hand, shyness may not be indicative of implicit low self-esteem. Kemple (1995) has suggested that while teachers viewed the shy students as having lower self-esteem, the students themselves did not share a similar view.

Is it potentially damaging to consider shyness or quietness, for example, a trait of low self-esteem? Or to being motivated only a characteristic of high self-esteem? Most experts today teach us to be wary of our interpretations of behavior without attending to context, including culture and values. Yet when it comes to self-esteem, no such caveat is evident.

REFERENCES

Adler, A. (1956). *The individual psychology of Alfred Adler* (H. L. Ansbacher & R. R. Ansbacher, Eds.). New York: Harper & Row.

Allport, G. (1961). *Pattern and growth in personality.* New York: Holt.

American Psychiatric Association. (2000). *Diagnostic and statistical manual of mental disorders* (4th ed., text rev.). Washington, DC: Author.

Bandura, A. (1977). Self-efficacy: Toward a unifying theory of behavioral change. *Psychological Review, 84,* 191–215.

Battle, J. (2002). *Culture-free self-esteem inventories* (3rd ed.). Austin, TX: Psychological Assessment Resources.

Baumeister, R., Campbell, J., Krueger, J., & Vohs, K. (2003). Does high self-esteem cause better performance, interpersonal success, happiness, or healthier lifestyles? *Psychological Science in the Public Interest, 4,* 1–44.

Baumeister, R. F., Smart, L., & Boden, J. M. (1996). Relation of threatened egotism to violence and aggression: The dark side of self-esteem. *Psychological Review, 103,* 5–33.

Beck, A. T., Brown, G. K., Steer, R. A., & Kuyken, W. (2001). Psychometric properties of the Beck Self-Esteem Scales. *Behaviour Research & Therapy, 39,* 115–124.

Blascovich, J., & Tomaka, J. (1991). Measures of self-esteem. In J. P. Robinson, P. R. Shaver, & S. Wrightsman (Eds.), *Measures of personality and social psychological attitudes* (pp. 115–160). San Diego: Academic Press.

Branden, N. (1969). *The psychology of self-esteem.* New York: Bantam.

Branden, N. (1992). *The power of self-esteem.* Deerfield Beach, FL: Health Communications.

Brockner, J. (1979). The effects of self-esteem: Success-failure, and self-consciousness on task performance. *Journal of Personality and Social Psychology, 37,* 1732–1741.

Brown, J. D. (1993). Self-esteem and self-evaluation: Feeling is believing. In J. Suls (Ed.), *Psychological perspectives on the self* (pp. 27–58). Hillsdale, NJ: Lawrence Erlbaum Associates.

California Task Force to Promote Self-Esteem and Personal and Social Responsibility. (1990). *Toward a state of self-esteem: The final report of the California Task Force to Promote Self-Esteem and Personal and Social Responsibility.* Sacramento: California Department of Education.

Campbell, W. K., & Foster, J. D. (2006). Self-esteem: Evolutionary roots and the historical cultivation. In M. H. Kernis (Ed.), *Self-esteem issues and answers: A sourcebook of current perspectives* (pp. 340–346). New York: Psychology Press.

Cooley, C. H. (1902). *Human nature and the social order.* New York: Scribner.

Coopersmith, S. (1967). *The antecedents of self-esteem.* San Francisco: W. H. Freeman & Co.

Coopersmith, S. (1981). *SEI: Self-esteem inventories.* Palo Alto, CA: Consulting Psychologists Press.

Crocker, J. (2006). What is optimal self-esteem? In M. H. Kernis (Ed.), *Self-esteem issues and answers: A sourcebook of current perspectives* (pp. 119–123). New York: Psychology Press.

Crocker, J., & Park, L. E. (2004). The costly pursuit of self-esteem. *Psychological Bulletin, 130,* 392–414.

Crocker, J., & Wolfe, C. T. (2001). Contingencies of self-worth. *Psychological Review, 108,* 593–623.

Deci, E. L., & Ryan, R. M. (1995). Human agency: The basis for true self-esteem. In M. H. Kernis (Ed.), *Efficacy, agency, and self-esteem* (pp. 31–50). New York: Springer.

Demo, D. H. (1985). The measurement of self-esteem: Refining our methods. *Journal of Personality and Social Psychology, 48,* 1490–1500.

Diamantopoulou, S., Rydell, A., & Henricsson, L. (2008). Can both low and high self-esteem be related to aggression in children? *Social Development, 17,* 682–698.

Epstein, S. (1973). The self-concept revisited or a theory of a theory. *American Psychologist, 28,* 405–416.

Epstein, S. (1979). The ecological study of emotions in humans. In K. Blenstein (Ed.), *Advances in the study of communications and affect* (pp. 47–83). New York: Plenum.

Esposito, A. J., Kobak, R., & Little, M. (2005). Aggression and self-esteem: A diary study of children's reactivity to negative interpersonal events. *Journal of Personality, 73,* 887–905.

Forsyth, D. R., Lawrence, N. K., Burnette, J. L., & Baumeister, R. R. (2007). Attempting to improve the academic performance of struggling college students by bolstering their self-esteem. *Journal of Social & Clinical Psychology, 26,* 447–459.

Franzoi, S. L., & Shields, S. A. (1984). The Body-Esteem Scale: Multidimensional structure and sex differences in a college population. *Journal of Personality Assessment, 48,* 173–178.

Gecas, V. (1982). The self concept. In R. H. Turner & J. F. Short, Jr. (Eds.), *Annual review of sociology* (Vol. 8, pp. 1–33). Palo Alto, CA: Annual Reviews, Inc.

Gecas, V. (1989). The social psychology of self-efficacy. *Annual Review of Sociology, 15,* 291–316.

Ginter, E. J., & Dwinell, P. L. (1994). The importance of perceived duration: Loneliness and its relationship to self-esteem and academic performance. *Journal of College Student Development, 35,* 456–460.

Greenberg, J. (2008). Understanding the vital human quest for self-esteem. *Perspectives on Psychological Science, 3,* 48–55.

Greenwald, A. G., & Banaji, M. R. (1995). Implicit social cognition: Attitudes, self-esteem, and stereotypes. *Psychological Review, 102,* 4–27.

Greenwald, A. G., McGhee, D. E., & Schwartz, J. L. K. (1998). Measuring individual differences in implicit cognition: The Implicit Association Test. *Journal of Personality and Social Psychology, 74,* 1464–1480.

Guindon, M. H. (1996, July). Definitions, perceptions, and interventions for self-esteem in New Jersey school. In M. H. Guindon & N. Westburg, *Hope and self-esteem: Applications for practice, research, and education.* Paper presented at the annual conference of the American Psychological Association, Toronto, Canada.

Guindon, M. H. (2002). Toward accountability in the use of the self-esteem construct. *Journal of Counseling & Development, 80,* 204–214.

Gurney, P. W. (1986). Self-esteem in the classroom. *School Psychology International, 7,* 199–209.

Harter, S. (1985). *Manual for the self-perception for children.* Denver, CO: University of Denver.

Harter, S. (1988). *Manual for the self-perception for adolescents.* Denver, CO: University of Denver.

Harter, S. (1999). *The construction of the self.* New York: Guilford Press.

Harter, S. (2006). Where do we go from here? In M. H. Kernis (Ed.), *Self-esteem issues and answers: A sourcebook of current perspectives* (pp. 430–438). New York: Psychology Press.

Heine, S. J., Lehman, D. R., Markus, H. R., & Kitayama, S. (1999). Is there a universal need for positive self-regard? *Psychological Review, 106,* 766–794.

Horney, K. (1950). *Neurosis and human growth.* New York: W.W. Norton & Company.

Hoyle, R. H., Kernis, M. H., Leary, M. R., & Baldwin, M. W. (1999). *Selfhood: Identity, esteem, regulation*. Boulder, CO: Westview Press.

James, W. (1890). *Principles of psychology*. New York: Henry Holt.

Judge, T., Erez, A., Bono, J. E., & Thoresen, C. J. (2002). Are measures of self-esteem, neuroticism, locus of control, and generalized self-efficacy indicators of a common core construct? *Journal of Personality and Social Psychology, 83*, 693–710.

Kaplan, H. B. (2001). Self-esteem and deviant behavior: A critical review and theoretical integration. In T. J. Owens, S. Stryker, & N. Goodman (Eds.), *Extending self-esteem theory and research* (pp. 375–399). New York: Cambridge University Press.

Kemple, K. (1995). Shyness and self-esteem in early childhood. *Journal of Humanistic Education and Development, 33*, 173–182.

Kernis, M. H. (2003). Toward a conceptualization of optimal self-esteem. *Psychological Inquiry, 14*, 1–26.

Kernis, M. H. (2005). Measuring self-esteem in context: The importance of stability of self-esteem in psychological functioning. *Journal of Personality, 73*, 1–37.

Kernis, M. H., Cornell, D. P., Sun, C., Berry, A., & Harlow, T. (1993). There's more to self-esteem than whether it is high or low: The importance of stability of self-esteem. *Journal of Personality and Social Psychology, 65*, 1190–1204.

Kernis, M. H., & Goldman, B. M. (2006). Assessing stability of self-esteem and contingent self-esteem. In M. H. Kernis (Ed.), *Self-esteem issues and answers: A sourcebook of current perspectives* (pp. 77–85). New York: Psychology Press.

Kernis, M. H., Lakey, C. E., & Heppner, W. L. (2008). Secure versus fragile high self-esteem as a predictor of verbal defensiveness: Converging findings across three different markers. *Journal of Personality, 76*, 477–512.

Koch, E. J. (2006). Examining the role of self-esteem in psychological functioning and well-being. In M. H. Kernis (Ed.), *Self-esteem issues and answers: A sourcebook of current perspectives* (pp. 260–266). New York: Psychology Press.

Koole, S. L., Dijksterhuis, A., & van Knippenberg, A. (2001). What's in a name: Implicit self-esteem and the automatic self. *Journal of Personality and Social Psychology, 80*, 669–685.

Leonard, J. (2003). Introduction. In J. Milton, *Paradise lost: Edited with an introduction and notes by John Leonard* (pp. vii–xli). New York: Penguin Classics.

Luhtanen, R., & Crocker, J. (1992). A collective self-esteem scale: Self-evaluation of one's social identity. *Personality and Social Psychology Bulletin, 18*, 302–318.

Marsh, H.W., & Richards, G.E. (1988). Tennessee Self-Concept Scale: Reliability, internal structure, and construct validity. *Journal of Personality and Social Psychology, 55*, 612–624.

Maslow, A. (1968). *Toward a psychology of being* (2nd ed.). New York: Van Nostrand.

Mead, G. H. (1934). *Mind, self, and society*. Chicago: University of Chicago Press.

Mruk, C. (1995). *Self-esteem: Research, theory, and practice*. New York: Springer.

Mruk, C. (2006). *Self-esteem: Research, theory, and practice: Toward a positive psychology of self-esteem* (3rd ed.). New York: Springer.

Piers, E. V. (1984). *Piers-Harris Children's Self-Concept Scale* (rev.). Los Angeles: Western Psychological Services.

Rogers, C. (1951). *Client-centered therapy*. New York: Houghton-Mifflin.

Roid, G. H., & Fitts, W. H. (1988). *Tennessee Self-Concept Scale* (rev.). Los Angeles: Western Psychological Services.

Rosenberg, M. (1965). *Society and the adolescent self-image*. Princeton, NJ: Princeton University Press.

Rosenberg, M. (1979). *Conceiving the self*. New York: Basic Books.

Rosenberg, M., & Owens, T. J. (2001). Low self-esteem people: A collective portrait. In T. J. Owens, S. Stryker, & N. Goodman (Eds.), *Extending self-esteem theory and research* (pp. 400–436). New York: Cambridge University Press.

Rosenberg, M., & Simmons, R. G. (1972). *Black and white self-esteem: The urban school child.* Washington, DC: American Sociological Association.

Ryan, R. M., & Brown, K. W. (2003). Why we don't need self-esteem: On fundamental needs, contingent love, and mindfulness. *Psychological Inquiry, 14,* 27–82.

Schwarz, N. (1999). Self-reports: How the questions shape the answers. *American Psychologist, 54,* 93–105.

Silverstone, P. H., & Salsali, M. (2003). Low self-esteem and psychiatric patients. Part I. The relationship between low self-esteem and psychiatric diagnosis. *Annals of General Hospital Psychiatry.* Retrieved February 15, 2009, from http://www.general-hospital-psychiatry.com/content/

Smelser, N. (1989). Self-esteem and social problems: An introduction. In A. M. Mecca, N. J. Smelser, & J. Vasconcellos (Eds.), *The social importance of self-esteem* (pp. 294–326). Berkeley: University of California Press.

Sullivan, H. S. (1953). *The interpersonal theory of psychiatry.* Chicago: University of Chicago Press.

Swann, W. B., Jr., Chang-Scheider, C., & Larson McClarty, K. (2007). Do people's selfview matter? Self-concept and self-esteem in everyday life. *American Psychologist, 62,* 84–94.

Tafarodi, R. W., & Milne, A. B. (2002). Decomposing global self-esteem. *Journal of Personality, 70,* 443–483.

Tafarodi, R. W., & Swann, W. B., Jr. (2001). Two-dimensional self-esteem: Theory and measurement. *Personality and Individual Differences, 31,* 653–673.

Trzesniewski, K. H., Donnellan, M. B., & Robins, R. W. (2003). Stability of self-esteem across the life span. *Journal of Personality and Social Psychology, 84,* 205–220.

Twenge, J. M., & Campbell, W. K. (2002). Self-esteem and socioeconomic status: A meta-analytic review. *Personality and Social Psychology Review, 6,* 59–71.

Twenge, J. M., & Crocker, J. (2002). Race and self-esteem: Meta-analyses comparing Whites, Blacks, Latinos, Asians, and American Indians and comment on Gray-Little and Hafdahl (2000). *Psychological Bulletin, 128,* 371–408.

Wells, L. E., & Marwell, G. (1976). *Self-esteem: Its conceptualization and measurement.* Beverly Hills, CA: Sage.

White, R. (1963). Ego and reality in psychoanalytic theory: A proposal regarding independent ego energies. *Psychological Issues, 3,* 125–150.

Wylie, R. C. (1974). *The self-concept. A review of methodological considerations and measuring instruments* (rev. ed., Vol. 1). Lincoln: University of Nebraska Press.

Yamaguchi, S., Greenwald, A. G., Banaji, M. R., Murakami, F., Chen, D., Shiomura, K., et al. (2007). Apparent universality of positive implicit self-esteem. *Psychological Science, 18,* 498–500.

2

What Do We Know About Self-Esteem Interventions?

MARY H. GUINDON

L ittle question exists that the issue of self-esteem is present in many of the concerns brought to mental health practitioners. Sometimes it is addressed as a part of a broader issue; less often it is seen as a viable area for possible intervention in and of itself.

What evidence is there for the success of self-esteem interventions? Dissertations and theses are one indication of continued research interest. Altogether, over 14,000 dissertations and theses from 1900 to 2008 have studied self-esteem as the main topic of interest. Amazingly, 24.9%—nearly one-quarter—were published between 2000 and 2008. However, of these, only 23.1% actually address interventions or strategies. Put another way, of 3,490 dissertations in this century, only 807 have been concerned with what practitioners can do about it. Regrettably, in these and in the research of established scholars, evidence that interventions actually affect levels of self-esteem is not particularly encouraging. Efforts to increase self-esteem are inconsistent, mixed, or inconsequential. Therefore, much controversy swirls around the construct.

CONTROVERSIES

Many research findings on the results of self-esteem enhancement programs, even where significant, have shown weak effects. Evidence points to the fact that many claims—particularly in popular culture—are extravagant and unfounded, engendering doubts about the viability of the construct itself. Thus, not all scholars support the salubrious effects of self-esteem enhancement. Smelser (1989) concluded that "one of the disappointing aspects [of research] ... is how low the associations between self-esteem and its [presumed] consequences are ..." (p. 15).

Baumeister, Campbell, Krueger, and Vohs (2003) have found no evidence of positive effects for increasing self-esteem through therapeutic interventions or school programs. High self-esteem did not improve academic performance. Self-esteem had only a weak relationship to delinquency and was not related to aggression, although the authors contend that high self-esteem, particularly in the form of defensiveness or narcissism, may increase aggression and antisocial tendencies. Low self-esteem was not connected to drinking or taking drugs, smoking, or becoming sexually active at an early age. Krueger, Vohs, and Baumeister (2008) concluded, "Looking for the behavioral implications of self-esteem, we find a yawning gap. People with high self-esteem are happier, less depressed, and more self-satisfied than others, but what are they motivated to do other than try to prolong this pleasant state?" (p. 64). Baumeister and his colleagues do not support continued efforts to boost self-esteem in the belief that it will by itself result in positive outcomes. They have made a strong case that indiscriminate praise may promote narcissism and its less desirable consequences.

The self-esteem movement that began in the last part of the 21st century spawned programs throughout school systems across the nation. Self-esteem is now assumed to be a social cure and an inherent right throughout American society. Yet childhood narcissism is more common today than in past generations (Twenge, 2006). Many believe this to be an unintended result of the proliferation of programs whose primary goal was and is to increase self-esteem as part of educating children. "Childrearing and educational practices aimed at bolstering children's self-views may actually cultivate an excessive focus on the self and an inflated sense of entitlement" (Thomas, Stegge, Bushman, Olthof, & Denissen, 2008, p. 389).

On the other hand, other scholars call for a broader conceptualization and more refined strategies that do justify efforts to improve self-esteem. Debate continues about whether self-esteem is a unidimensional or multidimensional construct. While most studies assume that self-esteem is a stable trait, many theorists emphasize its state-like attributes and processes. In this case, self-esteem as an indicator of momentary beliefs about one's worthiness means that self-esteem levels react strongly to outside evaluation. They can change with external feedback. In other words, we must examine and address the current state level of self-esteem (i.e., the selective part of self-esteem) more closely than the general trait itself (i.e., global self-esteem) if we are to assist people in reaching their optimal level of functioning.

It may be that the pursuit of self-esteem rather than its level is the more important aspect of its state-like attribute (Crocker & Park 2004). It is likely that most people attempt to raise their self-esteem or avoid those circumstances that will lower it. "Because increases in self-esteem feel good, and decreases in self-esteem feel bad, state self-esteem has important motivational consequences [and] ... failure at the pursuit of self-esteem can lead to feelings of worthlessness, shame, sadness, and anger, leaving people feeling vulnerable to mortality or social rejection or feeling unable to cope with life events" (Crocker & Park, 2004, pp. 393, 396). Although secure self-esteem is desirable and healthy, striving for it in those with fragile self-esteem is problematic because self-evaluations are based on factors about which the individual is insecure or uncertain (Rhodewalt, 2006), making it not likely to change.

Opportunities to experience success affect those with low self-esteem differently than those with high self-esteem. Those with preexisting low-state self-esteem may avoid circumstances that will increase it because it results in anxiety and "triggers negative self-relevant thoughts" (Wood, Anthony, & Foddis, 2006, p. 289). Although people with low self-esteem may want others' favorable feedback, such positive evaluation may actually be threatening to them because it violates their personal view of the self (Harter, 1999).

Debates continue in various other areas. Many contributors to the self-esteem outcomes literature have argued that much of the previous research has methodological limitations. For example, cross-sectional designs, in which participants are measured only once, are overrepresented in research designs, whereas less frequently used longitudinal studies hold more promise because participants are measured over a period of time. Each design can yield different results. Self-esteem stability and instability take into consideration fluctuations across time and situations that only longitudinal studies are equipped to capture. In a longitudinal study of 1,037 members of a 1972–1973 cohort in New Zealand, Trzesniewski et al. (2006) found self-esteem to be a useful construct and a causal factor in determining future outcomes. Their research of the remaining 978 participants at age 26 suggests that low self-esteem in adolescence is likely to lead to poor health, criminal behavior, and limited economic prospects into adulthood.

Another area of controversy concerns whether assessment instruments measure implicit or explicit self-esteem. Some argue that self-reports are explicit measures that do not yield accurate information because they are susceptible to a host of conscious biases. Implicit measures are necessary to assess factors that are not accessible to consciousness (Kernis, 2003). Implicit measures, developed to get at unconscious material, have yielded different levels of high and low self-esteem than the more commonly used explicit measures. Others argue that qualities of self-esteem are defined entirely by their subjective form, and are a conscious experience, and that implicit tests do not tap into an unconscious form of self-esteem (Tafarodi & Ho, 2006). Thus, discrepancies between implicit and explicit measures of self-esteem are the result of conscious self-presentation tendencies rather than unconscious material (Olson, Fazio, & Hermann, 2007).

It could be that some of the controversy may have been generated because self-esteem as a weak predictor of outcomes is "rooted in misunderstanding of the concept that leads to the naïve application of self-esteem theory and methods" (Owens & Stryker, 2001, p. 2). Furthermore, it could be that an overlap among closely related parts of the self clouds the results of many studies. Watson and Clark (1984) believed that diverse research literatures "have developed around a number of personality traits, that despite dissimilar names, nevertheless intercorrelate so highly that they must be considered measures of the same construct" (p. 465). For example, assessment of self-esteem, locus of control, neuroticism, and self-efficacy could be indicators of a common construct (Judge, Erez, Bono, & Thoresen, 2002). Whether this is the case, substantial evidence points to self-esteem as an important factor in adaptation and well-being.

DuBois and Tevendale (2007) have argued that there is adaptive significance to the many facets of self-esteem for children and adolescents: Presented (i.e., observable) behaviors are evidence of feelings of self-worth and stability of self-esteem. These authors differentiate areas of assessment that target domain-specific (i.e., selective) positive and negative evaluations as separate dimensions of self-evaluation. Domain-specific evaluations include academic skills and achievement, body image, and school and family relations. They conclude that "domain-specific aspects of self-evaluation are important to consider during development both separately and in combination with one another" (p. 105).

Although Boden, Fergusson, and Horwood (2008) have indicated that adolescent self-esteem is only weakly related to later development, many other scholars do, in fact, present compelling evidence for the importance of self-esteem in development. High self-esteem seems to make an important contribution to positive adaptation in children and adolescents (Harter, 1999) and is the strongest factor in overall life satisfaction in college students (Diener & Diener, 1995). Moreover, depressive symptoms and expressed anger decreased as self-esteem increased in young adults (Galambos, Barker, & Krahn, 2006), and long-term, enduring psychosocial stressors decreased self-esteem in psychiatric patients (Salsali & Siverstone, 2003).

Last, there is the crucial issue of whether self-esteem can change. Change for anyone is difficult, especially for the client with low self-esteem. Both client and clinician find it one of the most challenging tasks in treatment. The difficulty in changing self-esteem levels may be due to nature playing a more significant role than nurture, that self-esteem, indeed, may be inherited (McGuire et al., 1999). Yet, although evidence suggests that genetics play a substantial role in self-esteem level and stability, shared environmental influences are also substantial (Niess, Sedikides, & Stevenson, 2002; Neiss et al., 2005). In a study of twins, Niess, Sedikides, and Stevenson (2006) concluded, "It is the unique environmental effects that individuals experience, not those shared with their siblings, which have the greatest impact on both level and perceived stability" (p. 261).

If environment plays a substantial role in the formation of self-esteem, does it also play a role in the possibility of change? The issue is as complex as the construct itself. The answer is, it depends. If we consider self-esteem as a general trait, it is less open to change than if we consider it to be a state. It seems that for some people self-esteem is stable across time, and for others it varies by different circumstances and over time (Harter, 2006).

EXAMPLES OF SELF-ESTEEM OUTCOMES RESEARCH

Despite the many controversies surrounding the self-esteem construct, self-esteem interventions "do at least as well as other types of interventions in changing other domains of functioning such as behaviors, self-reported personality functioning, and academic performance" (Haney & Durlak, 1998, p. 429, as cited in Trzesniewski et al., 2006). Treatment plans can and do include self-esteem as a factor to be ameliorated, and outcomes can make a difference in addressing self-esteem issues (O'Brien, Bartoletti, & Leitzel, 2006). Quite a few research studies indicate outcomes that have implications for self-esteem interventions for varying issues. Although overlap exists, these can be broadly categorized into (1) social support (including parenting), (2) cognitive-behavioral strategies, (3) individual and group strategies, (4) physical fitness strategies, and (5) other. Just a few of the many studies are cited below.

Social Support

Self-esteem appears to respond to experiences of social support (Kinnunen, Feldt, Kinnunen, & Pulkkinen, 2008). Those with low self-esteem, who typically askew risk taking, will seek self-enhancement opportunities if they perceive little risk of humiliation (Wood, Giordano-Beech, Taylor, Michela, & Gaus, 1994). Baumeister and his colleagues have suggested that high-self-esteem individuals perceive that they have more social support. People with strong social ties seem to have higher self-esteem; a sense of belongingness influences self-esteem (Denissen, Penke, Schmitt, & van Aken, 2008; Gailliot & Baumeister, 2007). In a study of depressed patients, Kuehner and Buerger (2005) found that self-esteem and social support are among the attributes that substantially contribute to the psychological and social domains of subjective quality of life. They concluded that therapy should help patients to establish and maintain supportive relationships as well as enhance self-appreciation skills.

Client-centered approaches offer such support and have been shown to be effective in changing self-esteem levels because they attempt to help the client bring the actual self in alignment with the ideal self. The Rogerian concept of unconditional positive regard and empathy can assist the client ultimately to develop internal sources of authentic self-esteem.

In studying attachment and achievement in college students, Fass and Tubman (2002) found that students manifested higher levels of self-esteem when they perceived high levels of parental and peer support, and showed higher perceived and actual overall academic competence. They concluded that their study reinforced the importance of significant relationships on self-esteem.

As in other areas of human development, parenting is a critical type of social support. Grolnick and Beiswenger (2006) recommend three ways in which parents, teachers, and other significant caregivers can facilitate self-esteem in children. First, they need to provide an environment in which they are positively involved with their children. They can help them succeed by offering resources, including their time and support. Second, they can provide opportunities for autonomy by giving children ways to initiate and solve their own problems and by offering them choices for their actions. Third, they need to provide structure by offering information and guidelines that articulate reasonable expectations. Each of these strategies helps to build competence and a sense of worth through achievement.

Achievement and self-worth are gained through incremental challenges. Children need to experience success and modify achievement goals as they handle failures. "Disappointments [should] serve to renew the child's resolve to continue, not demoralize them" (Covington, 2006, p. 247). Reasons for learning should be intrinsically satisfying, rather than based in competition in itself. Parents and other caregivers can teach children resilience in the face of failure by focusing on encouraging their self-worth. On the other hand, "attempts to encourage self-worth … simply by reinforcing their status as being 'special' will fail if feelings of 'well-being' are not justified by 'well-doing'" (Covington, 2006, p. 247). Thus, indiscriminant use of praise is problematic. Parents should not overemphasize the importance of the self or individualism and independence. Positive feedback in the form of praise should be earned. Baumeister et al. (2003) recommend using praise as a reward for socially desirable behavior.

Cognitive-Behavioral Strategies

Cognitive-behavioral strategies are perhaps the most common treatment approaches for most self-esteem issues and have been effective in treating people across the life span. Only a few examples are listed here. Taylor and Montgomery (2007) conducted a systematic review of cognitive-behavioral therapy for improving self-esteem among depressed adolescents aged 13–18 years. They found it to be an effective treatment for increasing global and academic self-esteem. Cognitive-behavioral therapy increased levels of self-esteem and decreased depressive systems in schizophrenic patients (Oestrich, Austin, Lykke, & Tarrier, 2007). The cognitive-behavioral techniques of relaxation, guided imagery, study skills, and self-instructional skills training reduced test anxiety and increased academic self-esteem in learning disabled college students (Wachelka & Katz, 1999). In a longitudinal study on the impact of cognitive-behavioral group therapy on depression and self-esteem, clinically depressed patients experienced a greater increase in self-esteem and depression relief than the control group (Chen, Lu, Chang, Chu, & Chou, 2006). The use of diaries and journals has an effect on self-esteem. In a study of self-esteem memories, college students and middle-aged adults were asked to describe past events in which they felt particularly good or bad about themselves. Positive self-esteem memories included achievement more often than interpersonal experiences (Pillemer, Ivcevic, Gooze, & Collins, 2007). These are a very few of many examples.

Individual, Family, or Group Strategies

Individual, family, and group approaches are not mutually exclusive. Many individuals profit from a combination of two or all three. Individual one-on-one counseling has been shown to be effective for raising self-esteem. It can center on identifying and working with specific needs of an individual in depth and detail and allow for practice over a longer course of time than group work (Mruk, 2006). Although one-on-one counseling can be the treatment of choice for any self-esteem issue, it may be most useful for those with severe self-esteem problems and when the group setting is not appropriate.

Issues of poor family functioning and ineffective parenting styles can be addressed through family therapy. It can be the treatment of choice for self-esteem issues that manifest in eating disorders, attention-deficit hyperactivity disorder, and many more issues in which family dynamics play a significant role.

Group counseling allows clients to interact with others outside the home in an appropriate, healthy way, a critical element for self-esteem enhancement. Yalom (1995) hypothesized that the cohesiveness that develops in group therapy is a precursor to collective self-esteem as well as hope for the self, personal self-esteem, and psychological well-being. Recent empirical research findings targeting different populations have supported Yalom's hypothesis. Examples of group work for self-esteem issues proven to be effective include severely mentally disordered individuals living in high-security settings (Laithwaite et al., 2007), women with disabilities (Hughes, Robinson-Whelen, Taylor, Swedlund, & Nosek, 2004), behaviorally disruptive elementary children (Larkin & Thyer, 1999), and gifted adolescents (Barnette, 1989).

Physical Fitness Strategies

Exercise and other forms of physical fitness strategies have shown promise in increasing self-esteem, especially when physical activity requires specific skill development. Successful sports involvement increases physical self-esteem. In early adolescence, sports participation had a strong impact on physical self-esteem of both boys and girls, although boys showed higher levels of global self-esteem. For boys, physical competence was a more significant predictor of global self-esteem than for girls (Bowker, 2006). In a study of 122 adolescents ranging in age from 12 to 18, Saunders-Ferguson, Barnett, Culen, and TenBroeck (2008) found that those who took part in a Florida 4-H horsemanship school moderately increased their levels of self-esteem. Middle-aged adults who participated in an exercise program improved their sense of physical self-efficacy, and it played a significant positive role in situational and global self-esteem (McAuley, Mihalko, & Bane, 1997). In elderly Chinese adults, tai chi positively impacted state self-esteem as well as health-related quality of life (Lee & Woo, 2007).

Other Strategies

Quite a few other strategies have been shown to be effective in enhancing self-esteem, depending upon the population. These include reality therapy, solution-focused therapy, narrative therapy, creative arts, and play therapy. Research has shown promise for use of eye-movement desensitization and reprocessing (EMDR) with self-esteem issues in children with behavioral problems (Wanders, Serra, & de Jongh, 2008), sand-tray group therapy for adolescent girls (Shen & Armstrong, 2008), and process-based forgiveness with diverse populations (Lundahl, Stevenson, & Roberts, 2008). In short, a wide range of intervention strategies can be effective if the practitioner is well versed in the self-esteem knowledge base, and matches treatment to the particular self-esteem need, keeping in mind the many factors associated with the construct.

SELF-ESTEEM AND DEPRESSION

Counseling interventions commonly used for depressive disorders can also affect self-esteem levels and stability. Substantial evidence suggests that unstable or fragile self-esteem is associated with vulnerability to depressive disorders and may play a major role in the onset and recurrence of depression (Franck & De Raedt, 2007; Kernis, Grannemann, & Mathis, 1991). Beck's cognitive theory of depression states that dysfunctional attitudes about the self lead to specific negative self-evaluations and lowered self-esteem (Beck, Brown, & Brown, 2001). Depression has been shown to be present in all inpatient psychiatric patients (Silverstone & Salsali, 2003) and is prevalent throughout society. We can assume that it is also present in many of the issues presented in this book, although it is not addressed as an issue in a separate chapter because of its pervasiveness.

Harter's (1999) research studies point to self-esteem as either an antecedent or consequent phenomenon in depression. Gender differences in adolescents tend to account for low self-esteem as an antecedent of depression. Girls are more likely to focus on appearance and social behavior, whereas boys focus on athletic or scholastic incompetence and conduct. Negative self-evaluations in either case can lead to depression. Low self-esteem as consequent to depression occurs in both genders generally as a result of rejection, conflict, and experiences of loss. Interventions should take into account whether antecedent or consequent factors are affecting the level and stability of self-esteem, and practitioners should adjust the initial focus of treatment plans accordingly.

SELF-ESTEEM STRATEGIES AND INTERVENTIONS

Self-esteem interventions can address self-esteem in two ways. They can be embedded in existing strategies for specific issues, or they can specifically target self-esteem issues.

Embedded Strategies

In this case, practitioners conceptualize and treat their clients using already existing interventions they know to be effective for specific disorders, and also understand how these interventions can positively affect self-esteem. They are informed about the self-esteem system and its many elements, such as competence, achievement, feedback from significant others, and worthiness or feelings of acceptance; the differences in global and selective self-esteem and its salience, in which specific attributes are weighted differently; and the importance of stability and contingency. They understand how what they do in the course of treating their clients can impact self-esteem levels. Many of the chapters that follow connect existing interventions for specific issues or populations to the self-esteem body of knowledge. In this way, the contributors show us how clinicians can be accountable for outcomes when they include self-esteem in their case conceptualizations and treatment plans.

Self-Esteem-Specific Strategies

The second way to address self-esteem is through interventions that specifically and directly target self-esteem enhancement. Several authors have discussed elements that should be included in planning self-esteem programs and strategies for children and adults.

Harter's Intervention Strategies

In her seminal work, Harter (1999) presented important issues in planning a self-esteem intervention for children. First, the clinician should consider whether global or selective self-esteem domains are the target of intervention. In recent years, improving skills in selective areas has been the more common focus. Next, the clinician should distinguish between the goal of a self-esteem program and the target of the intervention. Harter writes, "... while self-esteem enhancement may be a goal, intervention strategies should be directed at its determinants" (p. 311). Thus, strategies need to take into consideration the client's perceptions of early self-esteem experiences. The intervention should also use a guide or model grounded in a theoretical base. For Harter, self-worth and personal esteem are the central focus. Harter suggests the following strategies targeted toward the cognitive and social determinants of self-esteem development for children and adolescents (see Table 2.1). The principles described can easily be adapted to adults at all life stages as well.

Cognitive Determinants Harter recommends assisting clients in reducing the discrepancies between their aspirations and perceived adequacy by identifying selective self-esteem domains in which discrepancies exist, and using strategies to improve skills in those domains. Interventions should serve to enhance feelings of worthiness, target areas in which the client feels successful, and downplay those in which the client feels unsuccessful or inadequate. Harter notes that this cluster of strategies is not appropriate for young children who do not yet have the cognitive skills to identify discrepancies or self-evaluations accurately.

Second, clients should be encouraged to accurately self-evaluate. Harter differentiates between self-evaluation enhancement and accurate self-evaluation. The goal should be promoting realistic evaluations rather than unrealistically high self-evaluations that can be inappropriate or dangerous. She notes that some overestimation, if not excessive, can be beneficial, especially in those who have good levels of self-esteem, as it can preserve feelings of self-worth and improve task performance.

Next, clients should be assisted in realizing their potential for change. Clients can be taught to change the salience of—or how they weigh—their constituent selective characteristics. However, self-evaluations are difficult to change unless the various antecedents of negative self-views can be pinpointed. The possibility for change is dependent upon successful progression through developmental stages, and there are optimal points at which interventions can be effective. Children are more vulnerable to decreases in global self-esteem in developmental periods of transition. Practitioners should concentrate on both prevention and intervention for those in whom self-esteem is at risk of being adversely affected. Some

TABLE 2.1   Harter's Summary of Intervention Strategies
_____

Intervention Strategies Directed at Cognitive Determinants:

1. Reduction of discrepancies between aspirations and perceived adequacy
2. Encouragement of relatively accurate self-evaluations
3. The potential for change in the valence of self-representations
4. Attention to individuals' own theories about the causes of their self-representations

Intervention Strategies Directed at Social Factors Influencing Self-Evaluations:

1. Provisions to increase approval support
2. Internalization of the positive opinions of others
_____

Source: Harter (1999, p. 316). With permission.

self-evaluations may be resistant to change if negative views are strongly formed in early childhood. Using reframing techniques to revise clients' perceptions that their inadequacies cannot be changed may allow for a shift in self-conception and self-esteem level.

Finally, Harter suggests attending to clients' conceptualizations of the causes of their own self-representations. Understanding the client's cognitive constructions will lead to effective reframing strategies about attributions. Cognitive restructuring emphasizes successes rather than failures, and stresses selective self-esteem domains in which success has been experienced.

Social Determinants   Harter believes that opportunities for approval and support should be provided, especially for children and adolescents who lack support or are the recipients of disapproval and rejection from their significant others. She suggests beginning by determining if the perceptions are realistic and accurate. If so, and the source is parents, family therapy and parenting training are treatment goals. In the case of lack of peer support or rejection, children may be misreading cues about actual support. If so, children can be encouraged to develop more realistic evaluations. If the perceptions are realistic, finding the specific causes, such as deficits in interpersonal likeability, physical ability, or attractiveness should be undertaken. Social skills and athletic ability skills training or removal from nonsupportive to more supportive circumstances where feasible may be treatment goals. In both cases, providing alternate and supportive significant others may be helpful.

Next, teaching individuals to internalize positive feedback from others is a critical area for intervention. "There is considerable consensus that the healthiest developmental course is one in which realistic standards and positive opinions are *internalized,* such that they become truly *self*-evaluations that the child comes to personally own" (Harter, 1999, p. 337). Note that the goal is internalizing realistic standards, not fostering dependence on the opinions of others. The latter can lead to preoccupation with feedback and the risk for false-self behavior, impression management, and contingent self-esteem. Healthy internalization can be accomplished by providing opportunities for success that focus on the child's role in creating positive outcomes, encouraging pride in accomplishment, and helping the child set personal goals based on their own ideals. Children can also be encouraged to evaluate present performance against past performance rather than on comparisons to others. Parents and others who work with children should offer unconditional support rather than expecting them to meet unrealistically high standards in order to gain approval.

Mruk's Self-Esteem Enhancement Techniques

Mruk (2006), noting that there are no easy or quick-fix interventions, has delineated eight areas common to self-esteem programs that lead to effective self-esteem enhancement:

1. *Acceptance and caring.* Practitioners employ the humanistic approach of "unconditional positive regard" introduced by Rogers (1951). They develop rapport and build a working alliance.
2. *Consistent, positive (affirming) feedback.* The practitioner can become a significant other to the client. Feedback must be authentic. "Small, positive doses of positive feedback are likely to be more effective than larger ones because they are non-threatening ..." (p. 99) and likely to help self-esteem change over time.
3. *Cognitive restructuring.* Mruk discusses three steps on how to use positive self-feedback: identifying problematic habits, labeling them, and substituting more rational or realistic responses. This is similar to rational-emotive behavioral therapy and is expected to result in new habits in thinking, feeling, and acting.
4. *Natural self-esteem moments.* Because self-esteem is lived phenomenologically, clients can be taught to increase their awareness of the role of self-esteem in their lived experiences and make changes in the moment. Consciousness-raising techniques, challenge, and support foster change.
5. *Assertiveness training.* Programs that teach assertiveness skills are grounded in the belief of human worth and rights. "A deep sense of worth and actual behavioral competence at preserving it appears to be helpful in enhancing self-esteem" (p. 100).
6. *Modeling.* Exposure to those with appropriate levels of self-esteem, including the therapist, can assist the client in learning to model competence and worthiness.
7. *Problem-solving skills.* Since coping with life's challenges effectively is related to self-esteem, teaching clients how to solve their own problems can increase chances of success and increase competence, and hence self-esteem.
8. *Opportunities for practice.* Mruk emphasizes that practice is the most important factor. Enhancing self-esteem takes time and practice. Old thoughts and actions must be unlearned and new, more facilitative ones learned over time.

Other Strategies of Note

Other programs offer intervention strategies that inform us. Wood et al. (2006) have suggested three self-evaluations strategies that can increase self-esteem:

teaching clients to use less destructive self-evaluations, encouraging them to focus on positive attributes, and reminding them of the qualities that they value.

Concerning interventions for youth, DuBois and Tevendale (2007) remind us that intervention designs should address the multiple facets and components of self-esteem, not simply its global dimension. Programs should center on normative sources of self-esteem and on an adequate fit with child or adolescent environment. Programs should target specific populations and include components on positive racial and ethnic identity. Programs should also expand to directly address adaptive functioning that fosters and mutually reinforces connections between self-esteem and adjustment. Tutoring for increased competence is an example.

Cognitive restructuring is the main focus for McKay and Fanning (2000). They have recommended helping clients recognize cognitive distortions, bringing into awareness the internal operation of what they term the "pathological critic" (critical self-talk) and then refuting the critic through rebuttal and thought stopping. Clients then learn to identify their strengths and move on to work on self-acceptance. The McKay and Fanning program includes ways to reinforce healthy self-talk through teaching coping statements, hypnosis, visualization, and anchoring by the process of bringing into awareness past feelings of confidence and self-liking.

In discussing treatment, Roberts (2006) has identified three types of programs designed to boost self-esteem. Therapists address client cognitions to modify deeply held beliefs about the self through teaching clients to consider their thoughts a hypotheses rather than indicators of absolute facts, then to test evidence to confirm or deny their beliefs and develop alternative beliefs consistent with facts. Therapists can work with clients to feel good about themselves and competent enough to make behavioral changes. Facilitating adaptive behavior presumably raises self-esteem. Therapists can also work to help clients reduce their preoccupation with self-worth. This can be especially effective with depressed clients who tend to ruminate on their deficits.

DEVELOPMENT OF HIGH AND LOW SELF-ESTEEM AND THE TIMING OF INTERVENTIONS

Substantial research indicates consensus on a general trajectory of self-esteem level and stability across the life span. "Self-esteem is relatively high in childhood, drops during adolescence (particularly for girls), rises gradually throughout adulthood, and then declines sharply in old age.... These fluctuations in self-esteem reflect changes in our social environment as well as maturational changes such as puberty and cognitive declines in old age" (Robins & Trzesniewski, 2005, p. 158). Baldwin and Hoffman (2002) analyzed intraindividual changes in self-esteem for children ages 11 to 16 over seven years using sequential data from a family health study. For females, mean self-esteem increased until age 12, dropped until age 17, and began to rise after age 17. For males, mean self-esteem increased two years longer, until age 14, decreased until about age 16, then increased, although it dipped slightly at age 19. By the time adolescents reach young adulthood, gender differences decreased and self-esteem stabilized, although females continue to lag males in level. Although there can be individual differences, of course, domain-specific self-evaluations appear consistent, with very small changes over a four-year time period in young adulthood (Donnellan, Trzesniewski, Conger, & Conger, 2007). Additionally, children and adolescents who were higher (or lower) in self-esteem than their peers also tended to be higher (or lower) in self-esteem than their peers at a future point in time (Trzesniewski, Donnellan, & Robins, 2003).

These and other similar findings have strong implications for the timing of interventions. As important as addressing issues of self-esteem across the life span can be, the need for strategies in childhood and adolescence is critical.

Level and stability of self-esteem can have lifelong consequences. Those with low self-esteem may be depressed, feel hopeless about who they are and the circumstances they are in, and helpless about what to do about it. They may believe that very little of what matters in life is in their control. They unrealistically assign low estimates to most, or even all, of their individual characteristics. They compare themselves to an imaginary, ideal self and come up with a negative overall evaluation of themselves. People with appropriate high self-esteem, on the other hand, recognize that they have many good parts and some not so good parts to themselves. They realistically assign varying estimates to their individual characteristics. They know that there is no imaginary ideal self, that perfection is a fantasy. While some selective domains may be negative and others positive, and they may experience occasional feelings of lowered selective self-esteem, they recognize that this is determined by the immediate circumstance. They do not allow a particular situation to dictate the level of their global self-esteem. Adults with healthy levels of self-esteem may take other people's judgments of their behaviors and actions into account, but they do not allow themselves to be defined by anyone else.

People develop self-esteem early in life. In other words, they learn during the normal developmental processes of childhood and adolescence about their competence through their achievements and about their worth as human beings from the validation of others. Initially, children's ability to make social comparisons is inaccurate—and usually overestimated. Their determinations about their abilities are not realistic. As they mature, their estimates become more realistic and healthy. Unfortunately, for some people, problematic and inaccurate judgments persist through life, sometimes overestimated, but more often underestimated.

Consider the middle or secondary school student who is a class leader. She is not physically attractive as most of her peers, and her family is not well off financially. She isn't the most gifted or talented student. She seems to have nothing particularly special going for her. Yet everybody likes her and she likes herself. She is upbeat, confident, and admired by students and teachers alike. She is happy and successful, and most likely, she will continue to be so into adulthood.

How can she have so few of those qualities we assume make for healthy self-esteem and still exhibit attributes of high self-esteem? The answer is in how self-esteem is formed. One's sense of self, and hence the mechanism by which one evaluates oneself, results from three important components:

1. The kinds of reactions and responses we experience from persons who are important to us, or feedback from significant others
2. The knowledge of who we are, our sense of our own identity grounded in the values of our particular culture, or the belief in our worth
3. An understanding of those things we do well and an appreciation of our achievements, or the awareness of our levels of competence

We can see, then, that the student with high self-esteem learned from those persons significant in her life that she is a competent and fully functioning, capable person. Most likely she learned, beginning at an early age, that she can investigate, without undue criticism, the many facets of herself and her personality so that she is able to determine for herself a clear and accurate sense of her own identity, what she is good at, and what she isn't. She is learning to make realistic evaluations of worth. Since she is at the adolescent developmental stage, she has already learned about her sense of identity within her family unit, and she is learning who she is in the broader community and world context. She is learning what matters to her and what doesn't, and she is in the process of making decisions, possibly unconsciously, that her good points outweigh her bad points, so that her global self-esteem will be positive. This will allow her to get on with the business of living effectively without constantly worrying about how others evaluate her because what matters most will be how she evaluates herself.

However, when feedback from significant others is absent, damaging, or inaccurate, when the sense of identity and belief in worth is undermined or based on inauthenticity, and when competence is not evaluated realistically, large discrepancies between the authentic and the ideal self develop. Both global and selective self-esteem will be adversely impacted, resulting in low, defensive, compensatory, false high, or narcissistic high self-esteem.

Contrast the above student with the boy in the class who appears to have a lot going for him. He is good looking. He is bright, has many talents, and is well behaved. Yet he seems to have few close friends. Or, he has too many friends who make constant demands on him. He tries to please them all, all the time, regardless of the cost to himself in time or effort or emotional turmoil. He is unduly vulnerable to the pressures of his peers. He rarely speaks up for himself. And most people, students and teachers alike, may not give him much thought, and if they do, they probably feel a little sorry for him, somehow.

How could he have so many positive traits and still have such low self-esteem? He learned, too, beginning at a very young age, from those people around him who were important to his well-being. But his lessons were different. He may have learned, for example, that his opinions do not count nearly as much as other people's do. He may have learned that being good is more important than being inquisitive. He may have learned that being quiet is easier than being wrong, or he may have learned that it is better to be unseen than to be competent. Whatever his particular upbringing, he learned that the evaluations that matter the most were outside of himself. The result is that he is growing up not knowing his human worth or the extent of what he can do and, consequently, who he is, and he may very well have already given up trying.

Mental health practitioners who work with children and adolescents are in a unique and critical position to impact on their future by developing interventions that influence the development and enhancement of their levels of self-esteem. Periods of transitions across the life span can especially affect levels of self-esteem. Because individuals at all ages are in the process of learning about themselves, practitioners can influence their self-esteem by offering them acceptance and non-contingent regard, reinforcing their worth as human beings, giving them positive but realistic feedback on those qualities and characteristics that matter to them, assisting them in investigating all facets of their authentic selves, and facilitating opportunities for achieving competence.

25 STRATEGIES TO ENHANCE SELF-ESTEEM

When we consider the many ways in which self-esteem can be enhanced, clearly no one method works best. Before formulating any treatment plans, effective practitioners will discover the determinants of self-esteem problems, find out in what domains their clients are most invested both positively and negatively, then develop programs than best suit their unique self-esteem needs. These 25 strategies are grounded in the self-esteem system literature from theoretical and practical perspectives:

1. Begin with humanistic, client-centered techniques and return to them often.
2. Help clients understand that change can occur at any age or stage of life; instill hope.
3. Help clients recognize self-esteem as culture bound, based on societal and subsocietal values.
4. Work on authentic values clarification.
5. Teach clients how self-concept beliefs form in humans and help them discover how their own self-concept developed in their unique circumstances.
6. Help clients uncover and discuss childhood messages and concepts.
7. Develop and discuss a family self-esteem genogram; consider family counseling.
8. Use cognitive restructuring techniques.
   a. Bring into awareness negative self-talk by recognizing irrational beliefs.
   b. Teach clients to dispute their internal self-critic in a safe, nonthreatening way.
   c. Teach clients to substitute positive self-talk.
   d. Reframe negative attributions into more realistic attributions.
   e. Recognize low-self-esteem triggers.
9. Work with clients to let go of perceived shortcomings and failures and learn to forgive themselves for their humanness.
10. Assist clients in making a realistic assessment of self-elements and domains that are important and salient for them by:
    a. Reviewing and owning past accomplishments
    b. Recognizing authentic strengths and talents

11. Provide opportunities for taking small risks in interpersonal relationships by teaching clients to:
    a. Ask for positive feedback from significant others
    b. Accept positive feedback without alibi or discounting
12. Teach basic communication skills.
13. Teach decision-making skills.
14. Help clients set obtainable goals and follow through.
15. Provide positive feedback that is realistic and authentic.
16. Suggest an assertiveness training group or train in individual assertiveness techniques.
17. Train clients in stress management and relaxation techniques.
18. Provide opportunities to practice genuine/authentic self-affirmations.
19. Offer positive visualization, guided imagery, and meditation.
20. Introduce journal writing for processing awareness, forgiveness, and recording new thoughts and behaviors.
21. Reinforce and support small steps that help move clients toward internal locus of control that does not undermine collective self-esteem or cultural norms.
22. Provide parenting workshops in how to build self-esteem in children and adolescents.
23. Help clients refocus energies away from self-evaluations and social comparisons.
24. Encourage physical activity that is enjoyable and within individual ability level.
25. Model good self-esteem processes by attending to your own self-esteem needs.

Appendix A lists some responsible Web site resources and self-esteem books that you might find helpful in applying these strategies and also learning more about the self-esteem construct. Appendix B is an example of a group self-esteem intervention program originally developed for adult high-functioning women. It can be applied to other populations except children.

We will now turn to specific issues that can impact self-esteem levels at five life stages: childhood, adolescence, early adulthood, midlife, and late life.

REFERENCES

Baldwin, S. A., & Hoffman, J. P. (2002). Dynamics of self-esteem: A growth-curve analysis. *Journal of Youth and Adolescence, 31*, 101–113.

Barnette, E. L. (1989). A program to meet the emotional and social needs of gifted and talented adolescents. *Journal of Counseling & Development, 67*, 525–528.

Baumeister, R., Campbell, J., Krueger, J., & Vohs, K. (2003). Does high self-esteem cause better performance, interpersonal success, happiness, or healthier lifestyles? *Psychological Science in the Public Interest, 4*, 1–44.

Beck, A., Brown, G., & Brown, G. (2001). Psychometric properties of the Beck Self-Esteem Scales. *Behaviour Research & Therapy, 39*, 115–124.

Boden, J. M., Fergusson, D. M., & Horwood, D. M. (2008). Does adolescent self-esteem predict later life outcomes? A test of the causal role of self-esteem. *Development and Psychopathology, 20,* 319–339.

Bowker, A. (2006). The relationship between sports participation and self-esteem during early adolescence. *Canadian Journal of Behavioral Science, 38,* 214–229.

Chen, T., Lu, R., Chang, A., Chu, D., & Chou, K. (2006). The evaluation of cognitive-behavioral group therapy on patient depression and self-esteem. *Archives of Psychiatric Nursing, 20,* 3–11.

Covington, M. V. (2006). How can optimal self-esteem be facilitated in children and adolescents by parents and teachers? In M. H. Kernis (Ed.), *Self-esteem issues and answers: A sourcebook of current perspectives* (pp. 244–249). New York: Psychology Press.

Crocker, J., & Park, L. E. (2004). The costly pursuit of self-esteem. *Psychological Bulletin, 130,* 392–414.

Denissen, J. J. A., Penke, L., Schmitt, D. P., & van Aken, M. A. (2008). Self-esteem reactions to social interactions: Evidence for sociometer mechanisms across days, people, and nations. *Journal of Personality and Social Psychology, 95,* 181–196.

Diener, E., & Diener, M. (1995). Cross-cultural correlates of life satisfaction and self-esteem. *Journal of Personality and Social Psychology, 68,* 653–663.

Donnellan, M. B., Trzesniewski, K. H., Conger, K. J., & Conger, R. D. (2007). A three-wave longitudinal study of self-evaluations during young adulthood. *Journal of Research in Personality, 41,* 453–472.

DuBois, D. L., & Tevendale, H. D. (2007). Self-esteem in childhood and adolescence: Vaccine or epiphenomenon? In J. A. Nier (Ed.), *Taking sides: Clashing views in social psychology* (2nd ed., pp. 101–114). Dubuque, IA: McGraw-Hill.

Fass, M., & Tubman, J. (2002). The influence of parental and peer attachment on college students' academic achievement. *Psychology in the Schools, 39,* 561–573.

Franck, E., & De Raedt, R. (2007). Self-esteem reconsidered: Unstable self-esteem outperforms level of self-esteem as vulnerability marker for depression. *Behaviour Research & Therapy, 45,* 1531–1541.

Gailliot, M. T., & Baumeister, R. F. (2007). Self-esteem, belongingness, and worldview validation: Does belongingness exert a unique influence upon self-esteem? *Journal of Research in Personality, 41,* 327–345.

Galambos, N. L., Barker, E. T., & Krahn, H. J. (2006). Depression, self-esteem, and anger in emerging adulthood: Seven-year trajectories. *Developmental Psychology, 42,* 350–365.

Grolnick, W. S., & Beiswenger, K. L. (2006). Facilitating children's self-esteem: The role of parents and teachers. In M. H. Kernis (Ed.), *Self-esteem issues and answers: A sourcebook of current perspectives* (pp. 230–237). New York: Psychology Press.

Harter, S. (1999). *The construction of the self.* New York: Guilford Press.

Harter, S. (2006). The development of self-esteem. In M. H. Kernis (Ed.), *Self-esteem issues and answers: A sourcebook of current perspectives* (pp. 144–150). New York: Psychology Press.

Hughes, R. B., Robinson-Whelen, S., Taylor, H. B., Swedlund, N., & Nosek, M. A. (2004). Enhancing self-esteem in women with physical disabilities. *Rehabilitation Psychology, 49,* 295–302.

Judge, T., Erez, A., Bono, J. E., & Thoresen, C. J. (2002). Are measures of self-esteem, neuroticism, locus of control, and generalized self-efficacy indicators of a common core construct? *Journal of Personality and Social Psychology, 83,* 693–710.

Kernis, M. H. (2003). Toward a conceptualization of optimal self-esteem. *Psychological Inquiry, 14,* 1–26.

Kernis, M. H., Grannemann, B. D., &. Mathis, L. C. (1991). Stability of self-esteem as a moderator of the relation between level of self-esteem and depression. *Journal of Personality and Social Psychology*, 61, 80–84.

Kinnunen, M., Feldt, T., Kinnunen, U., & Pulkkinen, L. (2008). Self-esteem: An antecedent or a consequence of social support and psychosomatic symptoms? Cross-lagged associations in adulthood. *Journal on Research on Personality*, 42, 333–347.

Krueger, J. I., Vohs, K. D., & Baumeister, R. F. (2008). Is the allure of self-esteem a mirage after all? *American Psychologist*, 63, 64–65.

Kuehner, C., & Buerger, C. (2005). Determinants of subjective quality of life in depressed patients: The role of self-esteem, response, styles, and social support. *Journal of Affective Disorders*, 86, 205–213.

Laithwaite, H. M., Gumley, A., Benn, A., Scott, E., Downey, K., Black, K., et al. (2007). Self-esteem and psychosis: A pilot study investigating the effectiveness of a self-esteem programme on the self-esteem and positive symptomatology of mentally disordered offenders. *Behavioural and Cognitive Psychotherapy*, 35, 569–577.

Larkin, R., & Thyer, B. (1999). Evaluating cognitive-behavioral group counseling to improve elementary school students' self-esteem, self-control, and classroom behavior. *Behavioral Interventions*, 14, 147–161.

Lee, D., & Woo, J. (2007). Effect of Tai Chi on state self-esteem and health-related quality of life in older Chinese residential care home residents. *Journal of Clinical Nursing*, 16, 1580–1582.

Lundahl, B., Stevenson, R., & Roberts, K. (2008). Process-based forgiveness interventions: A meta-analytic review. *Research on Social Work Practice*, 18(5), 465–478.

McAuley, E., Mihalko, S., & Bane, S. (1997). Exercise and self-esteem in middle-aged adults: Multidimensional relationships and physical fitness and self-efficacy influences. *Journal of Behavioral Medicine*, 20, 67–83.

McGuire, S., Manke, B., Saudino, K. J., Reiss, D., Heatherington, E. M., & Plomin, R. (1999). Perceived competence and self-worth during adolescence: A longitudinal behavioral genetic study. *Child Development*, 70, 1283–1296.

McKay, M., & Fanning, P. (2000). *Self-esteem* (3rd ed.). Oakland, CA: New Harbinger.

Mruk, C. (2006). *Self-esteem: Research, theory, and practice: Toward a positive psychology of self-esteem* (3rd ed.). New York: Springer.

Niess, M. B., Sedikides, C., & Stevenson, J. (2002). Self-esteem: A behavioural genetic perspective. *European Journal of Personality*, 16, 351–367.

Niess, M. B., Sedikides, C., & Stevenson, J. (2006). Genetic influences on level and stability of self-esteem. *Self and Identity*, 5, 247–266.

Neiss, M., Stevenson, J., Sedikides, C., Kumashiro, M., Finkel, E., Rusbult, C. E., et al. (2005). Executive self, self-esteem, and negative affectivity: Relations at the phenotypic and genotypic level. *Journal of Personality and Social Psychology*, 89, 593–606.

O'Brien, E. J., Bartoletti, M., & Leitzel, J. D. (2006). Self-esteem, psychopathology, and psychotherapy. In M. H. Kernis (Ed.), *Self-esteem issues and answers: A sourcebook of current perspectives* (pp. 306–315). New York: Psychology Press.

Oestrich, I. H., Austin, S. F., Lykke, J., & Tarrier, N. (2007). The feasibility of a cognitive behavioural intervention for low self-esteem within a dual diagnosis inpatient population. *Behavioural and Cognitive Psychotherapy*, 35, 403–408.

Olson, M. A., Fazio, R. H., & Hermann, A. D. (2007). Reporting tendencies underlie discrepancies between implicit and explicit measures of self-esteem. *Psychological Science*, 18, 287–291.

Owens, T. J., & Stryker, S. (2001). The future of self-esteem. In T. J. Owens, S. Stryker, & N. Goodman (Eds.), *Extending self-esteem theory and research* (pp. 1–9). New York: Cambridge University Press.

Pillemer, D. B., Ivcevic, Z., Gooze, R. A., & Collins, K. A. (2007). Self-esteem memories: Feeling good about achievement success, feeling bad about relationship distress. *Personality and Social Psychology Bulletin, 33,* 1292–1305.

Rhodewalt, F. (2006). Possessing and striving for high self-esteem. In M. H. Kernis (Ed.), *Self-esteem issues and answers: A sourcebook of current perspectives* (pp. 281–287). New York: Psychology Press.

Roberts, J. E. (2006). Self-esteem from a clinical perspective. In M. H. Kernis (Ed.), *Self-esteem issues and answers: A sourcebook of current perspectives* (pp. 298–305). New York: Psychology Press.

Robins, R. W., & Trzesniewski, K. H. (2005). Self-esteem development across the lifespan. *Current Directions in Psychological Science, 14,* 158–162.

Rogers, C. (1951). *Client-centered therapy.* New York: Houghton-Mifflin.

Salsali, M., & Silverstone, P. H. (2003). Low self-esteem and psychiatric patients. Part II. The relationship between self-esteem and demographic factors and psychosocial stressors in psychiatric patients. *Annals of General Hospital Psychiatry.* Retrieved February 15, 2009, from http://www.general-hospital-psychiatry.com/content/

Saunders-Ferguson, K., Barnett, R., Culen, G., & TenBroeck, S. (2008). Self-esteem assessment of adolescents involved in horsemanship activities. *Journal of Extension, 46*(2). Retrieved, February, 2, 2009, from http://www.joe.org/joe/2008april/a6p.shtml

Shen, Y., & Armstrong, S. A. (2008). Impact of group sandtray therapy on the self-esteem of young adolescent girls. *Journal for Specialists in Group Work, 33,* 118–137.

Silverstone, P. H., & Salsali, M. (2003). Low self-esteem and psychiatric patients. Part I. The relationship between low self-esteem and psychiatric diagnosis. *Annals of General Hospital Psychiatry.* Retrieved February 15, 2009, from http://www.general-hospital-psychiatry.com/content/

Smelser, N. (1989). Self-esteem and social problems: An introduction. In A. M. Mecca, N. J. Smelser, & J. Vasconcellos (Eds.), *The social importance of self-esteem* (pp. 294–326). Berkeley: University of California Press.

Tafarodi, R. W., & Ho, C. (2006). Implicit and explicit self-esteem: What are we measuring? *Canadian Psychology, 47,* 195–202.

Taylor, T. L., & Montgomery, P. (2007). Can cognitive-behavioral therapy increase self-esteem among depressed adolescents? A systematic review. *Children and Youth Services Review, 29,* 823–839.

Thomas, S., Stegge, H., Bushman, B., Olthof, T., & Denissen, J. (2008). Development and validation of the Childhood Narcissism Scale. *Journal of Personality Assessment, 90,* 382–391.

Trzesniewski, K. H, Donnellan, M. B., Moffit, T. E., Robins, R. W, Poulton, R., & Caspi, A. (2006). Low self-esteem during adolescence predicts poor health, criminal behavior, and limited economic prospects during adulthood. *Development Psychology, 42,* 381–390.

Trzesniewski, K. H., Donnellan, M. B., & Robins, R. W. (2003). Stability of self-esteem across the life span. *Journal of Personality and Social Psychology, 84,* 205–220.

Twenge, J. M. (2006). *Generation me: Why today's young Americans are more confident, assertive, entitled—And more miserable than ever before.* New York: Free Press.

Wachelka, D., & Katz, R. C. (1999). Reducing test anxiety and improving academic self-esteem in high school and college students with learning disabilities. *Journal of Behavior Therapy, 30,* 191–198.

Wanders, F., Serra, M., & de Jongh, A. (2008). EMDR versus CBT for children with self-esteem and behavioral problems: A randomized controlled trial. *Journal of EMDR Practice and Research, 2,* 180–189.

Watson, D., & Clark, L. A. (1984). Negative affectivity: The disposition to experience aversive emotional states. *Psychological Bulletin, 96,* 465–490.

Wood, J. V., Anthony, D. B., & Foddis, W. F. (2006). Should people with low self-esteem strive for high self-esteem? In M. H. Kernis (Ed.), *Self-esteem issues and answers: A sourcebook of current perspectives* (pp. 289–296.). New York: Psychology Press.

Wood, J. V., Giordano-Beech, M., Taylor, K. L., Michela, J. L., & Gaus, V. (1994). Strategies of social comparison among people with low self-esteem: Self-protection and self-enhancement. *Journal of Personality and Social Psychology* 67, 713–731.

Yalom, I. D. (1995). *The theory and practice of group psychotherapy* (4th ed.). New York: Basic Books.

Section *II*

Childhood

*I*n this stage of life and in the ones that follow, growth and development are more complicated than this discussion would indicate. What may be normal at one stage may not be normal at another stage. The development of the self is complex and nonlinear and cannot be separated from context. Dramatic differences exist in how individuals develop and change throughout life and, consequently, in how they evaluate themselves. Until recently, most of the theories of development were based on research with a limited scope using primarily White males. Nevertheless, a general understanding of developmental psychology lays the groundwork for each of the specific issues presented in this book.

Human development occurs across multiple dimensions: biological/physical, cognitive, behavioral, and emotional. Although individual and group differences across race, ethnicity, and gender cannot be overemphasized, this discussion presents information about general development. While age is not a precise gauge, at all stages of development, people must negotiate specific developmental tasks. These tasks arise as a result of a combination of physical maturation and cultural pressures (Havinghurst, 1972).

Rapid changes occur in all dimensions in the first two years of life. Many researchers have found that infants are more competent earlier than previously thought, and that infants' abilities are highly developed at very early ages. For example, infants as young as three months are able to remember their experiences for a few days to a week, indicating that they have some ability in forming internal representations (Bee & Boyd, 2003).

Developing attachment is a key activity with lifelong consequences. By about six months, clear attachment with parents or parent surrogates forms. Secure attachment allows infants to explore their environment with a sense of safety. Initial attachment, when secure, remains stable over time. Securely attached children are more curious, more socially skilled, and have better task approach skills. Genetics play a strong role in basic temperament, influencing security, although environment can modify temperament through attachment experiences.

Self-concept begins to develop in this early period as well. Infants gain awareness of the self as separate from the mother. They learn about both the subjective and the objective self. From the psychosocial developmental view, during the first year, infants must resolve the trust versus mistrust crisis by forming a loving, trusting relationship with the first caregiver (Erikson, 1959/1980). If negotiated successfully, trust forms and leads to an outcome of hope; if not, infants develop a sense of mistrust. Through the second and third years, children must resolve autonomy versus shame and doubt by directing energies toward developing physical skills. Success results in self-control. If autonomy is unduly thwarted, shame and doubt result.

As the infant moves into early childhood (ages 2–6), physical developments slow but remain steady. Language and cognition increase. In the preoperational stage (Piaget, 1926/1930), 18- to 24-month-old children begin to form mental symbols, and by age 4 they are better differentiators of reality across many tasks. During early childhood, peer relationships first become important. However, attachment with parents remains strong even when manifest behaviors indicate otherwise. The influence of family structure in this period strongly affects social and personality development. The family that is not intact, negligent, or abusive has been connected to negative outcomes. Growth in self-concept is significant in this preschool stage, although the child has not yet developed a global sense of self. Children refine their understanding of social roles and learn self-regulation and self-control. Social experiences modify inborn temperament. Gender-related concepts develop, and by age 6, children learn about gender constancy, stability, and appropriateness.

Children in the third to fifth years enter and must resolve Erikson's initiative versus guilt stage. Children instigate greater independence and self-directed activity. Successful resolution of this stage results in direction and purpose. A lack of resolution results in feelings of guilt.

In middle childhood (ages 6 to 12), physical development slows, although neurological brain growth increases (Bee & Boyd, 2003). Children enter Piaget's concrete operational stage. Information processing, spatial perception skill, and selective attention improve. Children are capable of inductive reasoning but have not yet mastered deductive reasoning. Research suggests that although no major changes in information processing capacity exist in this period, there are improvements in speed and efficiency (Bee & Boyd, 2003). Parental influence, although still strong, begins to be supplanted by social relationships. Gender segregation is at its height. School becomes of primary importance both cognitively and socially. From the sixth year until the onset of puberty, children must resolve the Erikson stage of industry versus inferiority. They must manage the many demands of learning new skills. Success results in competence; failure ends in feelings of inferiority and incompetence. Children are now capable of moral reasoning and behavior as well. Self-concept expands to construct a psychological model of the self in which personality and physical traits are added to accomplishments.

Children as early as age 5 are capable of evaluating their accomplishments in terms of competence and self-worth. They begin to differentiate selective self-esteem domains, and "role taking abilities are sufficiently developed to enable them to consider the perceived judgments and reactions of others" (Demo, 2001, p. 137). Between the ages of 5 and 8, self-esteem becomes increasingly well defined.

Children can perceive the difference between the real self—what the child accomplishes—and the ideal self—how the child wishes to do. Children begin the process of judging their worth and competence in the areas of physical appearance, social acceptance, scholastic ability, athletic and artistic skills and behavior, parent relationships, and peer relationships (Harter, 1999; Shavelson & Marsh, 1986). Furthermore, five characteristics—character, personal responsibility, academic ability, athletic ability, and appearance—generalize across race, gender, and socioeconomic status in middle childhood (Pallas, Entwisle, Alexander, & Weinstein, 1991, as cited in Demo, 2001). Children gain increasing awareness of what they excel at and what they do not, and how their family and societal values affect their sense of self-worth. They develop criteria by which to determine what characteristics are most important to them across various domains. Social relationships, life experiences, and expectations placed on them by themselves and significant others all affect behavior and contribute to a growing sense of global self-esteem. Social support of parents, other valued authority figures, and peers is critical as children adopt their opinions toward the self as well as their standards and values through the internalization process. Television and other media play a significant role, too. Depictions of violence, consumerism, and materialism influence self-evaluations (Chaplin & John, 2007).

By the end of this stage, children begin to protect their developing sense of worth by choosing experiences that confirm or support their internalized model of self-evaluation. Once people create an internal self-esteem model, it is not easily changed without great effort.

Whether in physical/biological, cognitive, behavioral, social, or affective areas, when these normal developmental processes and tasks are not successfully negotiated, self-esteem development can be compromised. Myriad problems result. Chapter 3 in this section discusses issues in early elementary school children and the importance of play in self-esteem development. The section continues with a look at three important areas that can negatively impact self-esteem's formation: intrafamilial childhood trauma, parental mental illness, and giftedness.

REFERENCES

Bee, H., & Boyd, D. (2003). *Lifespan development* (3rd ed.). Boston: Allyn & Bacon.

Chaplin, L. N., & John, D. R. (2007). Growing up in a material world: Age differences in materialism in children and adolescents. *Journal of Consumer Research, 34,* 480–493.

Demo, D. H. (2001). Self-esteem in children and adolescents. In T. J. Owens, S. Stryker, & N. Goodman (Eds.), *Extending self-esteem theory and research* (pp. 135–156). New York: Cambridge University Press.

Erikson, E. H. (1980). *Identity and the life cycle.* New York: Norton. (Original work published 1959)

Harter, S. (1999). *The construction of the self.* New York: Guilford Press.

Havinghurst, R. J. (1972). *Developmental tasks and education* (3rd ed.). New York: David McKay.

Piaget, J. (1930). *The child's conception of the world.* New York: Harcourt, Brace, & World. (Original work published 1926)

Shavelson, R. J., & Marsh, H. W. (1986). On the structure of self-concept. In R. Schwarzer (Ed.), *Anxiety and cognition* (pp. 305–330). Hillsdale, NJ: Lawrence Erlbaum Associates.

3

Facilitating Self-Esteem in Elementary School-Aged Children
A Child-Centered Play Therapy Approach

ERIC J. GREEN AND AMIE C. KOLOS

*E*arly school-aged children's development occurs at a rapid pace across physical, emotional, and mental domains. Physical attributes change as the child's body becomes more proportionate and muscle development increases. Fine and gross motor, attention, language, and social skills continue to develop. Young children, ages 3 and up, are encouraged to apply their new physical and mental abilities in pre-school and physical activities. As children reach 5 years of age, (1) social interaction with peers becomes of interest, (2) academic skills such as reading and writing are taught, and (3) children experience success, failure, praise, and frustration.

Young children eventually become better problem solvers but still cannot think logically about abstract events. As memory changes and improves, children develop the capacity to hold multiple pieces of information in working memory simultaneously. They also develop an increased ability to verbalize thoughts and feelings and can be expected to best verbalize autobiographical events. Significant adults in young children's lives encourage language development.

It is during this stage (age 5–7) that developmental theorists emphasize children's understanding of their areas of competence. Erikson posited that during this industry versus inferiority stage, in learning important skills such as teamwork and academic lessons, children practice self-discipline. Once this ability is mastered, children are capable of functioning in a variety of environments, recognizing their interests and strengths as they begin to develop a healthy level of self-esteem.

SELF-ESTEEM IN CHILDHOOD

The development of self-esteem, a complex and critical component of childhood, coincides with the experiences of early school-aged children in (1) academics and evaluation, (2) participation in extracurricular activities and competition, (3) peer relationships and acceptance/rejection, and (4) familial life at home and relationships with parents and significant caretakers. Young children often rate their own self-worth higher than that of their peers (Galambos, Barker, & Krahn, 2006; Robins, Trzesniewski, Tracy, Gosling, & Potter, 2002); however, the inflated view of self is temporary. Increased integration of negative feedback from teachers, parents, and peers, and increased social comparison may be possible contributors to decreased global self-esteem in children as they progress through elementary into secondary school. Furthermore, demographic variables such as gender, socioeconomic status, and ethnicity impact on self-esteem.

In addition to the external feedback and social comparison that assist children in formulating more realistic views of the self, perceived competence in areas of importance significantly impact the development and maintenance of a child's self-esteem (Harter, 1999; Larouche, Galand, & Bouffard, 2008). Children are able to cultivate their self-esteem by attempting and completing activities in elementary school (Dalgas-Pelish, 2006; Searcy, 2007). Self-esteem is fragile and still in its beginning stages of development at the time a child enters elementary school. As they grow and experience new activities both inside and outside of schoolwork, they begin to recognize areas in which they excel. Children as young as five years old differentiate between domains in which they excel and those that cause them difficulty. It is those areas of success that serve as building blocks for positive self-esteem (Marin, Bohanek, & Fivush, 2008).

The presence of social support is also critical as children develop their self-esteem. As infants, children form attachments with primary caregivers, and these caregivers lay the groundwork for self-esteem through acceptance, reasonable expectations for performance, and a respect for autonomy (Bednar, 1995; Marin, Bohanek, & Fivush, 2008). As children relate to their areas of competence, parents often act as the catalyst for continuation in the area, providing overt and subtle approval and support. This parental support may encourage children to engage in the activity more frequently, thus enabling them to continue developing skills and maintaining positive feelings of competence (Bos, Muris, Mulkens, & Schaalma, 2006).

Children are more likely to experience success when seeking out new, extra-familial relationships with peers as they (1) develop an unwavering sense of acceptance from family, (2) feel confident in their ability to meet age-appropriate expectations, and (3) value their own autonomy (Bednar, 1995). Social support from peers is a new, yet significant, experience for children and indicates the initial situations when a child receives acceptance from someone other than a teacher or family member. Children often view a friend as someone who bolsters their self-esteem, celebrating their successes and supporting them after failures (Berndt, 2002). In addition to acting as a support structure, friends also represent newfound social comparison and evaluation for children. An important aspect of friendships at a young age and into adolescence is reinforcement, as children will look to their friends to laugh at jokes and listen to ideas (Berndt, 2002). Such exchanges with friends also allow children to develop perspective-taking skills, equipping them with tools to feel competent in social interactions and succeed when communicating with others.

Children gauge the importance of their successes by (1) observing reactions from their peers, (2) minimizing differences to protect self-esteem and avoid feelings of inferiority, and (3) gaining acceptance into social networks. Children who are rejected by their peers have difficulty developing positive self-esteem and appropriate social skills, sometimes resulting in social isolation (Margolin, 2007). Researchers on bullying have examined peer acceptance and self-esteem, finding that children perceive victims to be targeted because of having a different appearance than their peers (Frisen, Jonsson, & Persson, 2007), and that bullies may suffer from low self-esteem, exhibiting power and control in order to bolster a low view of self.

Determining domains in which one excels and in which one struggles, developing social skills, and seeking approval from peers are developmentally appropriate tasks for children in elementary school. Children with extraordinarily high intelligence are aware of differences from their peers, receiving external validation of these thoughts from teachers and parents. These children's high self-esteem, as a result of their giftedness, is often countered with perceived castigation from peers. Similarly, children who perceive themselves as incompetent in academia or extracurricular activities compare these deficits, whether real or imagined, to the success peers are having in these areas.

Much of the research on self-esteem in children has examined the relationship between low self-esteem and academic difficulties (Marin, Bohanek, & Fivush, 2008), externalizing problems (Donnellan, Trzesniewski, Robins, Moffit, & Caspi, 2005), depression and suicidal ideation (Emler, 2002), and anxiety (Ollendick, Shortt, & Sander, 2008). The prevalence of mental health issues in childhood often predicts later behavioral disturbances as the child progresses through adolescence and adulthood. Despite the fact that behavioral symptoms may be resolved, some researchers recognize the need for improved self-esteem as a primary goal in child psychotherapy treatment (Dalgas-Pelish, 2006).

INTERVENTIONS

The need to belong is primary to a child's growth and acceptance of self and is constantly under assault as children begin to recognize their areas of competence and the way in which others perceive them. These perceptions are internalized and ultimately factor largely into children's perception of themselves and self-esteem. Interventions can be introduced to provide the child opportunities for mastery. The therapist assists children in testing new ideas and skills and uncovering interests and abilities. Through a nonevaluative, therapeutic relationship (i.e., the acceptance of the child's self-expression and the therapist's encouragement of the child's strengths and ability to change), children experience empowerment and a critical opportunity to identify their internal locus of control.

Child-Centered Play Therapy

Play has been utilized as a therapeutic activity with children for more than 50 years. Widely recognized as the developmentally appropriate way to relate to children, play therapy deemphasizes verbal expression and encourages toys to act as the child's words, while play acts as their language (Landreth, 2002; Post, 1999). Child-centered play therapy (CCPT) is a commonly used, empirically supported method of treating children who present with a range of emotional issues. CCPT is derived from Carl Rogers (1965), who conducted therapy in a nondirective, client-centered manner, basing his approach on the belief that all individuals have the innate ability to strive toward growth. Although he believed that the primary goal of all individuals, no matter their age, is to achieve self-actualization, his theory was not addressed in a child population until one of his students, Virgina Axline (1969), began to apply client-centered ideas to her work with children. Through this work, she developed eight basic principles (Axline, 1969, pp. 73–74):

1. The therapist must develop a warm, friendly relationship with the child, in which good rapport is established as soon as possible.
2. The therapist accepts the child exactly as he is.
3. The therapist establishes a feeling of permissiveness in the relationship so that the child feels free to express his feelings completely.
4. The therapist is alert to recognize the feelings the child is expressing and reflects those feelings back to him in such a manner that he gains insight into his behavior.
5. The therapist maintains a deep respect for the child's ability to solve his own problems if given an opportunity to do so. The responsibility to make choices and to institute change is the child's.
6. The therapist does not attempt to direct the child's actions or conversation in any manner. The child leads the way; the therapist follows.
7. The therapist does not attempt to hurry the therapy along. It is a gradual process and is recognized as such by the therapist.
8. The therapist establishes only those limitations that are necessary to anchor the therapy to the world of reality and to make the child aware of his responsibilities in the relationship.

Research on the implementation of such principles has increased in recent years as practitioners have acknowledged the credibility that empirical support provides to a treatment modality. Play therapy research conducted over six decades highlights the benefits that play therapy has for children needing assistance in the areas of self-concept and self-esteem, problem behaviors, cognitive deficits, social skills development, anxiety, plus depressive and trauma-related symptoms, both of which include self-esteem problems. CCPT and its role in facilitating self-esteem have been examined in the literature, with several studies specifically measuring children's views of self. The hypothesis that participation in CCPT will enhance children's self-esteem is derived from the basic components of client-centered therapy. Axline (1969) posited that problems arise when children attempt to fulfill needs that are missing from their environments. It is within an optimal environment, such as the playroom, where children are exposed to acceptance, empathy, and limits, enabling them to focus on their self-actualization and development of self (Johnson, Pedro-Carroll, & Demanchick, 2005). When considering the specific components of client-centered theory, basic acceptance demonstrates to the children that they are a person of worth, a belief that may have diminished as peer evaluation and negative feedback increased. Further, the therapist's sensitive understanding of the child diverges from the typical adult–child interaction that consists of expectations and conditional approval based on completion of tasks (Landreth, 2002). The difference between praise such as "You're picture is really pretty" and a facilitative response such as "You're making that just how you want to," for example, shifts the approval from the adult's subjective evaluation of the picture to acknowledgment of the child's achievement. It is when children can internalize their skills and recognize areas of competence that they begin to accept themselves, a first step to positive self-esteem.

A recent meta-analysis of the play therapy literature found that humanistic, nondirective play modalities, like CCPT, produced larger treatment effects than non-humanistic-directive approaches (Bratton, Ray, Rhine, & Jones, 2005). Of specific interest to this chapter, a review of the literature concluded that CCPT sessions improved self-concept in first graders struggling with reading (Crow, 1990), socially maladjusted second graders (House, 1970), children of domestic violence (Kot, Landreth, & Giordano, 1998; Kot & Tyndall-Lind, 2005), sexual abuse survivors (Scott, Burlingame, Starling, Porter, & Lilly, 2003), and homeless children (Baggerly, 2004). Another study suggested the utility of CCPT as a protector of self-esteem in at-risk children after finding that those who participated in play therapy maintained a higher level of self-esteem, while those in the control group demonstrated significant decreases in view of self (Post, 1999).

Aspects of CCPT have also been implemented in the Primary Mental Health Project, an empirically based program that has been included in over 2,000 elementary schools throughout the world (Cowen, Hightower, Pedro-Caroll, Work, & Wyman, 1996; Johnson, 2002). This program is designed to prevent school adjustment difficulties while fostering children's well-being. By emphasizing children's competencies both in and out of school, the Primary Project seeks to enhance and maximize school adjustment before it becomes a critical variable in a child's maladjustment. Once children are selected for the program, they enter a therapeutic relationship with a trained paraprofessional and begin having weekly play sessions. Like CCPT, the child sets the pace in these sessions while the therapist supports, tracks, and empathizes with the child. Ongoing evaluation of the Primary Project demonstrates its usefulness in decreasing adjustment problems and increasing social skills and competencies in areas of importance, two areas integral in positive selective self-esteem development (for review, see Johnson et al., 2005).

ROLE OF THE THERAPIST

When the play therapist follows Axline's child-centered principles, providing unconditional positive regard, demonstrating empathy and genuineness, allowing the child to lead the play, tracking play behavior, reflecting feelings and content, returning responsibility to the child, encouraging growth, and setting therapeutic limits, the child is provided with the environment necessary to elicit growth and change (Landreth, 2002). Through the accepting nature of the therapist and play-room, children are able to develop a more positive self-concept by assuming greater responsibility for their actions, becoming more self-directing, self-accepting, and self-reliant, engaging in decision-making and coping strategies, and developing an internal source of evaluation. The nonthreatening, accepting CCPT process is also enjoyed by children and perceived as a catalyst for better decision making both at school and at home and increased empathy. Success in these areas results in children's increased feelings of confidence and competence and improves self-esteem (Caroll, 2001; Green & Christensen, 2006).

Because its focus is on viewing the child as unique and worthy of respect, and not based on the therapist's values, past experiences, or preconceived ideas, CCPT adapts well for children with a wide range of diverse backgrounds and presenting problems. CCPT has been successfully adapted to address treatment goals in group settings (Baggerly, 2004; Kot et al., 1998) and with parents' involvement (Bratton, Landreth, Kellam, & Blackard, 2006).

DIVERSITY IN THE DEVELOPMENT OF SELF-ESTEEM IN EARLY SCHOOL-AGED CHILDREN

Professionals have only recently begun to examine the specific ways in which self-esteem and ethnic identity are related, and some have found that discrimination based on one's ethnic group affects the evaluation of one's ethnic identity. Ethnic identity, one type of selective self-esteem, factors into the development of global self-esteem (Verkuyten & Thijs, 2006). The research on self-esteem in minority children is still developing, with (1) most of the published studies comparing the self-esteem of African American children to White children, (2) few studies having examined the self-esteem of children in other racial groups (Twenge & Crocker, 2002), and (3) even less examining self-esteem in multiracial children (Herman, 2004).

Research has consistently shown that African American children demonstrate higher levels of global self-esteem than their White peers. These children report higher domain-specific self-esteem; however, the differences between African American and White children are smaller in this case (Gray-Little & Hafdahl, 2000). The process of developing self-esteem may also be different for children in these two ethnic groups, and it has been suggested that White children's positive ethnic group membership is related to high self-esteem (Davis, Leman, & Barrett, 2007). African American children may rely more on sources other than in-group positivity to develop self-esteem, such as personal competencies (Davis et al., 2007; Verkuyten & Thijs, 2004).

Considerably less research has been done on early school-aged children of other ethnic groups; however, some studies have been published on the self-esteem of Latino children. These studies have generally found that these elementary school-aged children have lower self-esteem than White, African American, and Asian

American children (Carlson, Uppal, & Prosser, 2000; Twenge & Crocker, 2002). One impediment in learning more about the Latino population is the tendency to combine subgroups under the heading *Latino* (Umana-Taylor, Diversi, & Fine, 2002). In an effort to better understand the self-esteem of children who comprise the Latino population, researchers are beginning to examine variables such as the effect of stigma (Twenge & Crocker, 2002) and family structure (Schmitz, 2005).

The self-esteem of Asian American children has received little attention; however, the Asian culture is thought to play a large role in the development of self-esteem in children. As opposed to children of individualistic cultures, who are encouraged generally to think for themselves as unique and above average, Asian children often downgrade their own abilities in an effort to fit in with peers (Steigler & Smith, 1985). However, a recent meta-analysis comparing the self-esteem of ethnic groups across the life span revealed higher self-esteem among Asian American elementary school-aged children than White, African American, and Latino children of the same age (Twenge & Crocker, 2002).

MULTICULTURAL CONSIDERATIONS IN PLAY THERAPY

Before beginning any type of therapy with children, it is crucial that clinicians recognize and understand different ethnic groups' beliefs about counseling (Gil & Drewes, 2005). Voluntary disclosure of problems to an extrafamilial person (i.e., a therapist) is typically inconsistent with many of the social values practiced in families of African American, Latino American, and Asian American descent (O'Conner, 2005). When working with ethnic minority children in particular, a therapist may encounter parents who are hesitant to engage their child in therapy because they believe that their children's problem behaviors are a direct reflection on their family and parenting abilities. Explaining the theoretical underpinnings of nondirective play therapy to parents whose culture emphasizes goal-oriented activities may also be a critical component to their willingness to enter therapy (O'Conner, 2005).

Play therapists must also consider different cultures' views of play, as the cultural environment often largely determines both the time allotted for play and the characteristics of such play. Children who are involved in cultures where the success of the family is dependent on a child's completion of daily chores and responsibilities play considerably less than children whose primary responsibilities involve school and play (Sue & Sue, 2008; Vandermaas-Peeler, 2002). The goals of the play might be different as well. For example, parents of more individualistic cultures may encourage self-expression and uniqueness, while parents of more collectivist cultures may include lessons of humility and harmony in their play. Therapists must remain cognizant of these variables when they are observing and participating in children's play and are encouraged to include culturally diverse toys as a means of both accepting and welcoming children and honoring ethnicity in the playroom (O'Conner, 2005). The child-centered approach facilitates self-esteem in children of diverse cultural backgrounds because of its emphasis on unconditional acceptance of the child and seeing the world from the child's point of view.

CASE STUDY

Joseph is a seven-year-old African American boy who lives in the suburbs of a major northeastern U.S. city. He resides with his biological mother and his four-year-old brother. He has no contact with his biological father, and his mother states there is no family history of psychiatric illness. At the time of treatment, he recently completed second grade and was participating in summer special education classes to better prepare him for the third grade. His school psychologist and mother were in support of his participating in play therapy sessions due to diagnoses of pervasive developmental disorder (PDD), attention-deficit hyperactivity disorder (ADHD), a simple phobia of insects that frequently resulted in panic attacks, and aggressive outbursts in class and at home. Joseph was being treated by a pediatric psychologist and psychiatrist for some of these issues, and he was prescribed Concerta and Klonadine.

Joseph suffered from epileptic seizures shortly after birth, which his mother attributes to some of his developmental delays. He was enrolled in infant and toddler programs in an effort to help him reach his developmental milestones. His mother reports that these programs helped with the development of his gross and fine motor skills, but that he continued to have difficulty with language development. Working with a speech therapist has improved his language capacity, and Joseph is now able to verbally communicate well with his peers. His mother reports that he has difficulty interacting with peers and lacks basic interpersonal skills such as reading social cues or initiating conversations. She reports that he has very few friends and that there have been instances where peers have teased Joseph or convinced him to act inappropriately. Much of Joseph's day was spent in special education classes and with professionals helping him overcome his deficits. His aggressive behaviors resulted in trouble in class and difficulty maintaining friendships. Consequently, she rates his self-esteem as a 4 on a scale of 1 to 10.

His mother reported limiting activities that left him vulnerable to teasing or bullying, structuring his days, and involving him in age-appropriate activities such as soccer in an effort to improve his social skills and motor coordination. When asked to identify Joseph's strengths, his mother described him as "creative," "bubbly and upbeat," and "affectionate." He enjoys pretending, making up stories, and participating in martial arts. His favorite subject in school is reading, and he is well liked by the school staff. Joseph's mother hopes that he will be able to build his self-esteem, "play out" some of his frustrations and worries, and have fun in his play therapy sessions.

Treatment Conceptualization

Many variables were considered when deciding to utilize CCPT with Joseph, including his diagnoses of PDD and ADHD. CCPT showed promise because of its ability to decrease symptoms such as inattention, hyperactivity, explosive anger, emotional withdrawal, and resistance to change (Ray, Schottelkorb, & Tsai, 2007). Children with PDD typically demonstrate social impairments, limited verbal and nonverbal communication, and a restrictive itinerary of interests and activities, also known as preservative play, often relying on others to give directives and point out mistakes. This experience decreases their autonomy and injures their self-esteem in the process (Kenny & Winick, 2000). As opposed to focusing on overcoming deficits, CCPT allows children to discover their strengths and interests, while developing mastery in new areas such as nonverbal communication and symbolic play.

CCPT can enhance Joseph's developing self-esteem by helping him establish control and responsibility over his decisions, broaden his interests, experience a caring relationship, achieve mastery of developmentally appropriate tasks, express feelings such as fear and aggression in balanced formats, and embrace his uniqueness. The emerging literature on CCPT with elementary school-aged African American boys supports these goals. Baggerly and Parker (2005) suggest that the safety and freedom of a child-centered playroom will allow African American boys to embrace their culture, viewing it as a strength as opposed to a social barrier.

Joseph worked with the play therapist weekly for several months. Throughout the first session, Joseph displayed little affect, rarely made eye contact with the therapist, and spoke very little. His choice of toys and the ways in which they were used were limited; he played primarily with one particular action figure, a robot, and pretend food. For the majority of the first session and some of the second session, he alternated between fighting other figures with the robot, and sorting the play food into dinner and dessert piles. He would then retrieve three bowls and ensure that each bowl was allotted an equal share of the meal. He did not share the meal with the therapist; rather, he instructed the therapist on ways to cook the food (e.g., stir the food in the pot). He was disappointed when the session ended and asked to take toys home with him, but seemed satisfied when the counselor assured him they would be in the playroom when he returned the next week. This type of constancy is often calming and reassuring for children with PDD (Kenny & Winick, 2000).

Over the first month, Joseph was excited to return to the playroom for his follow-up sessions and he readily engaged the therapist in each of the activities he chose. When using the robot figure and the pretend food, Joseph played with them in a way different than only the sorting and categorizing he had engaged in during the first session. He made a meal to share with the therapist and narrated a story in which the robot fought other figures. Themes of nurturance and pretend play emerged in his play as he cooked, instructed the therapist on ways to take care of a baby doll, and used dress-up clothes for both himself and the therapist. The therapist emphasized Joseph's selective self-esteem in these instances, responding to choices in the playroom with facilitative responses such as "You know what this baby needs" and "You like cooking."

After the first month, Joseph began to demonstrate some increased confidence. He dumped out entire buckets of toys and disclosed to the therapist that he had stolen stickers in the prior week. The therapist carefully considered boundaries, and ultimately set few limits on his play as he was not destroying property or in danger of hurting himself, and appeared to be testing the safety of both the therapist and the playroom. In response to the disclosure, the therapist reflected his feelings (i.e., "You're feeling bad that you took some stickers out of the playroom") and used facilitative statements to convey that she still valued him. Reflecting his feelings not only conveyed that the therapist still valued him but also modeled perspective taking and insight, skills with which children with PDD sometimes struggle (Kenny & Winick, 2000). This session was also the first in which Joseph made physical contact with the therapist, giving her a hug when he entered the playroom and sitting closely with the therapist on the floor during his play.

By the eighth session, Joseph was demonstrating palpable changes in his behaviors and demeanor in the playroom, out school, and at home. As opposed to the first session, when he played with the pretend food only as it was intended, he was now engaging in more symbolic play and manipulating the toys to use them in new, creative ways. He was also playing with a wider range of the toys, and he no longer sorted them; in fact, he did more disorganizing, mixing up toys from different bins. Interaction between Joseph and the therapist also continued to increase, and by the end of the second month of therapy, he was spontaneously telling the therapist about his days at school and problems with peers while he played. Joseph's confidence had increased; whereas the therapist told him several times in the first two sessions, "In here, that's something you can decide," Joseph no longer looked to the therapist for approval before deciding on an activity. Rather, it appeared that he felt safe and free to make choices himself. He had begun agreeing with the therapist when the therapist made facilitative statements such as "You know how to do that." He would often respond with, "Yes I do," suggesting that he was internalizing the therapist's statements and connecting the positive regard to his strengths and competencies. His attention had also improved; whereas he had initially moved back and forth between activities, he was now able to focus on one task and interact with the therapist while completing it.

Joseph seemed to respond well to the nondirective, child-centered approach administered by the play therapist. After approximately 2½ months, he demonstrated improvements in areas such as decreased preservative play, expression of emotion, confidence and initiative taking, appropriate social interactions (e.g., turn taking), motor coordination (e.g., playing catch with the therapist), symbolic play, and view of self. He responded well to the few limits that were set. He showed signs of increased feelings of basic worth and new confidence in his accomplishments.

CONCLUSION

Child-centered play therapy is one treatment modality that can be used in children's psychotherapy to facilitate self-esteem. Additionally, the tenets espoused by Carl Rogers, Virginia Axline, and Garry Landreth can be used to teach parents and teachers child-centered principles in an effort to facilitate self-esteem, encourage responsibility, engage in autonomy, and set therapeutic limits. As in the case study mentioned in this chapter, CCPT is a multiculturally competent approach to working with diverse children, as it honors the ethnicity of the child through toy selection, accepting the child where he or she is, and working closely with parents to understand cultural variables to optimize the child's growth and ego development.

REFERENCES

Axline, V. (1969). *Play therapy* (rev. ed.). New York: Ballentine Books.

Baggerly, J. (2004). The effects of child-centered group play therapy on self-concept, depression, and anxiety of children who are homeless. *International Journal of Play Therapy, 13*, 31–51.

Baggerly, J. N., & Parker, M. (2005). Child-centered group play therapy with African-American elementary school boys. *Journal of Counseling & Development, 83*, 387–396.

Bednar, R. L. (1995). Family relations and the development of self-esteem in children. In R. L. Bednar & S. R. Peterson (Ed.), *Self-esteem: Paradoxes and innovations in clinical theory and practice* (2nd ed., pp. 339–374). Washington, DC: American Psychological Association.

Berndt, T. J. (2002). Friendship quality and social development. *Current Directions in Psychological Science, 11*, 7–10.

Bos, A. E. R., Muris, P., Mulkens, S., & Schaalma, H. P. (2006). Changing self-esteem in children and adolescents: A roadmap for future interventions. *Netherlands Journal of Psychology, 62*, 26–33.

Bratton, S., Landreth, G., Kellam, T., & Blackard, S. (2006). *Child parent relationship therapy (CPRT) treatment manual: A 10-session filial therapy model for training parents.* New York: Routledge/Taylor & Francis Group.

Bratton, S. C., Ray, D., Rhine, T., & Jones, L. (2005). The efficacy of play therapy with children: A meta-analytic review of treatment outcomes. *Professional Psychology: Research and Practice, 36*, 376–390.

Carlson, C., Uppal, S., & Prosser, E. C. (2000). Ethnic differences and processes contributing to the self-esteem of early adolescent girls. *Journal of Early Adolescence, 20*, 44–67.

Caroll, J. (2001). Play therapy: The children's views. *Child and Family Social Work, 7*, 177–187.

Cowen, E. L., Hightower, A. D., Pedro-Caroll, J. L., Work, W. C., & Wyman, P. A. (1996). *School-based prevention for children at risk: The Primary Mental Health Project.* Washington, DC: American Psychological Association.

Crow, J. (1990). Play therapy with low achievers in reading (Doctoral dissertation, University of North Texas, 1989). *Dissertation Abstracts International, 50*, 2789.

Dalgas-Pelish, P. (2006). Effects of a self-esteem intervention on school-age children. *Pediatric Nursing, 32*, 341–348.

Davis, S. C., Leman, P. J., & Barrett, M. (2007). Children's implicit and explicit ethnic group attitudes, ethnic group identification, and self-esteem. *International Journal of Behavioral Development, 31*, 514–525.

Donnellan, M. B., Trzesniewski, K. H., Robins, R. W., Moffit, T. E., & Caspi, A. (2005). Low self-esteem is related to aggression, antisocial behavior, and delinquency. *Psychological Science, 16*, 328–446.

Emler, N. (2002). The costs and causes of low self-esteem. *Youth Studies Australia, 21*, 45–48.

Frisen, A., Jonsson, A., & Persson, C. (2007). Adolescents' perception of bullying: Who is the victim? Who is the bully? What can be done to stop bullying? *Adolescence, 42*, 749–761.

Galambos, N. L., Barker, E. T., & Krahn, H. J. (2006). Depression, self-esteem, and anger in emerging adulthood. *Developmental Psychology, 42*, 350–365.

Gil, E., & Drewes, A. (2005). *Cultural issues in play therapy.* New York: Guilford Press.

Gray-Little, B., & Hafdahl, A. R. (2000). Factors influencing racial comparisons of self-esteem: A quantitative review. *Psychological Bulletin, 126*, 26–54.

Green, E. J., & Christensen, T. M. (2006). Elementary school children's perceptions of play therapy in school settings. *International Journal of Play Therapy, 15*, 65–85.

Harter, S. (1999). *The construction of the self: A developmental perspective.* New York: Guilford Press.

Herman, M. (2004). Forced to choose: Some determinants of racial identification in multiracial adolescents. *Child Development, 75*, 730–748.

House, R. (1970). The effects of nondirective group play therapy upon the sociometric status and self-concept of selected second grade children (Doctoral dissertation, Oregon State University, 1970). *Dissertation Abstracts International, 31*, 2684.

Johnson, D. B. (2002). *The Primary Mental Health Project: Program development manual.* Rochester, NY: Children's Institute.

Johnson, D. B., Pedro-Caroll, J. L., & Demanchick, S. P. (2005). The Primary Mental Health Project: A play intervention for school-age children. In L. A. Reddy, T. M. Files-Hall, and C. E. Schaefer (Eds.), *Empirically based play interventions for children* (pp. 13–30). Washington, DC: American Psychological Association.

Kenny, M. C., & Winick, C. B. (2000). An integrative approach to play therapy with an autistic girl. *International Journal of Play Therapy, 9*, 11–33.

Kot, S., Landreth, G. L., & Giordano, M. (1998). Intensive child-centered play therapy with child witnesses of domestic violence. *International Journal of Play Therapy, 7*, 17–36.

Kot, S., & Tyndall-Lind, A. (2005). Intensive play therapy with child witnesses of domestic violence. In L. A. Reddy, T. M. Files-Hall, and C. E. Schaefer (Eds.), *Empirically based play interventions for children* (pp. 31–49). Washington, DC: American Psychological Association.

Landreth, G. L. (2002). *Play therapy: The art of the relationship* (2nd ed.). New York: Taylor & Francis Books.

Larouche, M., Galand, B., & Bouffard, T. (2008). The illusion of scholastic incompetence and peer acceptance in primary school. *European Journal of Psychology of Education, 23*, 25–39.

Margolin, S. (2007). Non-aggressive isolated and rejected students: School social work interventions to help them. *School Social Work Journal, 32*, 46–66.

Marin, K. A., Bohanek, J. G., & Fivush, R. (2008). Positive effect of talking about the negative: Family narrative of negative experiences and preadolescents' perceived competence. *Journal of Research on Adolescence, 18*, 573–593.

O'Conner, K. (2005). Addressing diversity issues in play therapy. *Professional Psychology: Research and Practice, 36*, 566–573.

Ollendick, T. H., Shortt, A. L., & Sander, J. B. (2008). Internalizing disorders in children and adolescents. In J. E. Madduz & B. A. Winstead (Eds.), *Psychopathology: Foundations for a contemporary understanding* (2nd ed., pp. 375–399). New York: Routledge/Taylor & Francis Group.

Post, P. (1999). Impact of child-centered play therapy on the self-esteem, locus of control, and anxiety of at-risk 4th, 5th, and 6th grade students. *International Journal of Play Therapy, 8*, 1–18.

Ray, D. C., Schottelkorb, A., & Tsai, M. (2007). Play therapy with children exhibiting symptoms of attention deficit hyperactivity disorder. *International Journal of Play Therapy, 16*, 95–111.

Robins, R. W., Trzesniewski, K. H., Tracy, J. L., Gosling, S. D., & Potter, J. (2002). Global self-esteem across the life span. *Psychology and Aging, 17*, 423–434.

Rogers, C. (1965). *Client-centered therapy.* Boston: Houghton Mifflin.

Schmitz, M. F. (2005, August). *Cultural and acculturation differences in the self esteem of Latino youth*. Paper presented at the annual meeting of the American Sociological Association, Philadelphia, PA. Retreived July 15, 2008, from http://www.allacademic.com/meta/p18711_index.html

Scott, T. A., Burlingame, G., Starling, M., Porter, C., & Lilly, J. P. (2003). Effects of individual client-centered play therapy on sexually abused children's mood, self-concept, and social competence. *International Journal of Play Therapy, 12*, 7–30.

Searcy, Y. D. (2007). Placing the horse in front of the wagon: Towards a conceptual understanding of the development of self-esteem in children and adolescents. *Child and Adolescent Social Work Journal, 24*, 121–131.

Steigler, J. W., & Smith, S. (1985). The self-perception of competence by Chinese children. *Child Development, 56*, 1259–1270.

Sue, D. W., & Sue, D. (2008). *Counseling the culturally diverse: Theory and practice* (5th ed.). New York: John Wiley & Sons.

Twenge, J. M., & Crocker, J. (2002). Race and self-esteem: Meta-analyses comparing Whites, Blacks, Latinos, Asians, and American Indians and comment on Gray-Little and Hafdahl (2000). *Psychological Bulletin, 128*, 371–408.

Umana-Taylor, A. J., Diversi, M., & Fine, M. A. (2002). Ethnic identity and self-esteem of Latino adolescents: Distinctions among the Latino populations. *Journal of Adolescent Research, 17*, 303–327.

Vandermaas-Peeler, M. (2002). Cultural variations in parental support for children's play. In W. J. Lonner, D. L. Dinnel, S. A. Hayes, & D. N. Sattler (Eds.), *Online readings in psychology and culture* (Unit 11, Chap. 3, http://www.wwu.edu/~culture). Bellingham, WA: Center for Cross-Cultural Research, Western Washington University.

Verkuyten, M., & Thijs, J. (2004). Global and ethnic self-esteem in school context: Majority and minority groups in the Netherlands. *Social Indicators Research, 67*, 253–281.

Verkuyten, M., & Thijs, J. (2006). Ethnic discrimination and global self-worth in early adolescents: The mediating role of ethnic self-esteem. *International Journal of Behavioral Development, 30*, 107–116.

4

Effects of Intrafamilial Trauma on the Development of Self-Esteem

MARY C. BURKE AND ALEXANDRIA E. PILECKI

*T*he relationship between the development of self-esteem and trauma in early life is an important one for mental health professionals to understand because the way that our clients think and feel about themselves and the relative safety of the world around them has meaningful implications for mental wellness and quality of life. Despite the importance of this relationship, little research has been done to address the question of the origins of self-esteem or the impact that trauma during early life has on its development. However, counseling theories on personality development and what is known about the psychological sequel to trauma may provide a means for mental health professionals to begin to understand the potentially complex dynamic between the two. What follows is an explanation of trauma, including incidence and clinical indicators, as well as theoretical information from object relations and attachment theory traditions, that may provide a useful framework for thinking about the origins of self-esteem and the impact of trauma on its development.

ISSUES OF CHILDHOOD TRAUMA

Trauma: Definition and Prevalence

Trauma is defined as an experience that threatens one's sense of safety and security and may or may not involve physical harm. Generally, trauma is experienced as either a single or a repeating event that overwhelms an individual's coping mechanisms and interferes with one's ability to integrate and make sense of emotions and thoughts related to the experience. According to the *Diagnostic and Statistical Manual of Mental Disorders IV–TR* (American Psychiatric Association, 2000), a traumatic event is one that involves "actual or threatened death or serious injury, or a threat to the physical integrity of self or others" and one in which "the person's response involved intense fear, helplessness, or horror" (pp. 218–219). A wide variety of experiences can be characterized as traumatic. Examples include naturally occurring or human-made catastrophic events such as dangerous storms and war or interpersonal violence such as intimate partner violence, rape, and emotional or physical abuse.

Unfortunately, children are not immune to traumatic experiences and are often exposed to traumatic stressors, including natural disasters, accidents, and interpersonal abuses such as physical, sexual, and emotional mistreatment and neglect. The limited coping skills characteristic of infants and young children leave them at increased risk for negative outcomes associated with trauma. Childhood trauma has critical and potentially long-lasting implications for individuals directly involved and presents an urgent public health concern. Research has shown that the number of children exposed to trauma other than interpersonal trauma is relatively low in comparison to intrafamilial trauma, such as emotional neglect or abuse, physical abuse, or bearing witness to domestic violence (Spinazzola et al., 2005). Therefore the focus of this chapter will be on intrafamilial neglect and trauma and its impact on the development of self-esteem.

The mistreatment of children, while unfathomable to some, occurs at alarming rates. During federal fiscal year (FFY) 2006 there were approximately 3.6 million referrals made to Child Protective Service (CPS) agencies, involving an estimated 6 million children. Of these, close to 1 million were substantiated cases of child maltreatment (i.e., physical, sexual, emotional abuse and neglect; U.S. Department of Health and Human Services [USDHHS], 2006). This number does not take into account those situations that go unreported, nor does it illustrate the actual number of children at risk for neglect and abuse, which is thought to be close to 3 million. During this same reporting period, 64.1% of victims experienced neglect, 16% were physically abused, 8.8% were sexually abused, 6.6% were psychologically maltreated, and 2.2% were medically neglected. Again for FFY 2006, 51.5% of the child victims were girls and 48.2% were boys. Not surprisingly, the youngest children had the highest rate of victimization, with the rate of victimization inversely related to the age group of the child. The victimization rate was 24.4 per 1,000 children (of the same age group) for the birth to 1 year grouping, 14.2 per 1,000 children (in the same age group) for those in the 1–3 years age group, and 13.5 per 1,000 children for those in the 4–7 years age group (USDHHS, 2006).

Close to 83% of child abuse victims were abused by a parent acting alone or by a parent acting with another person. In cases of child neglect, 86.7% of victims were neglected by a parent (in contrast to someone other than the parent). Parents were the perpetrators of child sexual abuse in 26.2% of the cases, and in 29.1% of the sexual abuse cases, the abuse was perpetrated by a relative other than a parent (USDHHS, 2006).

Child mistreatment is, of course, a problem faced around the world. What is particularly disturbing, however, is that in comparison to other countries with comparable economic resources, the United States (along with New Zealand) has the highest number of child deaths caused by abuse and other forms of maltreatment (UNICEF, 2007). In addition, in a study by the Innocenti Research Center of the United Nations Children's Fund (2007), the United States was ranked one of the two lowest among countries with similar economies in consideration of child and youth well-being. The study used six dimensions to assess well-being: family relationships, health and safety, education, behavior, risk factors, and the subjective sense of well-being of the population of interest.

Another way of understanding the extent to which child neglect and abuse are impacting those in the United States is to think about the associated direct and indirect financial costs on a national level. In 2007 alone, the overall cost (both direct and indirect) of child abuse was $103.8 billion (Wang & Holton, 2007). Direct costs associated with child neglect and abuse include indices such as spending for child welfare services, chronic health problems, mental health treatment, as well as judicial system and law enforcement expenses. Direct costs for the year 2007 were approximately $33.1 billion. Indirect costs include things such as childhood special education, adult mental and physical healthcare, loss of economic productivity to society, and adult criminal activity. It is estimated that indirect costs for 2007 were $70.7 billion (Wang & Holton, 2007).

The Trauma of Child Neglect and Abuse

The issue of neglect during infancy and childhood merits special attention, as it surely plays a role in development generally and in the development of self-esteem specifically. Child neglect is the failure of a caregiver to provide for the basic needs of a child. Basic needs fall into the categories of physical needs (e.g., supervision, shelter, food), medical needs (e.g., medical or psychological care), educational needs, and emotional needs (e.g., inattention to needs for attention and affection, exposure to violence). When engaged in assessment regarding child neglect, clinicians must consider cultural values regarding standards of care as well as the role of socioeconomic status (i.e., to what extent is the neglect of basic needs related to poverty?). Caregivers of a child may be in need of information about caring for a child or more concrete assistance through community agencies. If after appropriate support is provided, the caregiver does not implement different care strategies, then intervention from local child welfare may be necessary.

Child abuse is often associated with an authoritarian style of parenting and is typically divided into three categories: physical abuse, sexual abuse, and emotional abuse. Frequently occurring types of physical abuse include slapping, beating, physically restraining, or otherwise causing the child pain or physical discomfort. This type of abuse may or may not be in response to behavior from the child (e.g., punishment). Child sexual abuse is characterized by inappropriate behaviors by the caretaker that are sexual in nature and occur with or in the presence of the child. Examples include indecent exposure, inappropriate physical touch (e.g., in the genital region), penetration, and sodomy.

Child emotional abuse is typically the most difficult to identify and prove, which can mean that children are left without assistance and utterly alone in their suffering. Emotional abuse is concomitant with other forms of abuse and is a form of child maltreatment involving a pattern of behavior by the caretaker characterized by negative words, behaviors, and indifference. Emotionally abusive caretakers may constantly criticize, belittle, ignore, reject, or dominate the child. Failure to protect a child from exposure to family violence is also a form of emotional abuse. Finally, a caretaker's refusal or inability to connect emotionally to a child, thereby depriving her or him of the need for human connection, is also a form of this type of abuse.

Complex Trauma and Children

The increase in the amount of research being done in the area of child trauma has contributed greatly to our understanding of the long-lasting impact that such trauma can have on development and psychological functioning. This research has informed our perception on some of the possible differences between adult and child trauma with regard to both types of incidence experienced as traumatic and the impact on the psyche. Yet, children's exposure to violence still presents challenges to the current understanding of posttraumatic stress disorder (PTSD) as defined in *DSM IV–TR* (2000). Clinicians must ensure that they are not overrelying on our limited diagnostic system when working with traumatized children. For example, what if the child experiences violence that is characterized as lifelong and there is no identifiable precipitating event or single traumatic incident? Similarly, does violence that does not present as life threatening in a literal sense for a child still qualify as a traumatic experience? Somewhat helpful is that definitions of *traumatic stressors* have grown to include events that fall within the range of normal experience that are capable from the child's perspective, of causing death or injury, or threatening the physical safety of the child or a loved one (American Academy of Child and Adolescent Psychiatry, 1998). This definition takes into account that a child may feel threatened in situations that adults, with more developed cognitive and coping skills, may not experience as threatening.

Trauma reactions exist on a continuum based in part on the characteristics of the victim and the nature of the trauma (Briere & Spinazzola, 2005). One end of the continuum is characterized by less complex reactions that are predominantly single-occurrence, adult-onset traumatic events: one-time trauma events in which the victim is an adult with a normal developmental history, a secure base for attachment, and no other psychological disorders. More complex trauma reactions exist on the other end of the continuum and typically include victims who are more vulnerable at the time of the trauma. This may mean earlier age of onset, multiple incidents, and protracted trauma experience. The nature of the traumatic event in these situations is often interpersonal and invasive, such as with child abuse or rape.

As a result of recognition of the failure of the PTSD diagnosis to fully account for the full range of experiences following trauma, a specific diagnostic category called *complex PTSD* (Herman, 1997) or *disorders of extreme stress not otherwise specified* (DESNOS) has been proposed. This alternative more completely accounts for the experience of patients suffering from a wider range of persistent symptom clusters that are considered more complicated than those in PTSD. Those whose psychological trauma sequel most often fits into this category are those whose trauma experience interrupts formative (i.e., earlier) developmental periods. Such individuals are at increased risk for dysregulation in various interpersonal and intrapersonal domains. Specifically, disorders of extreme stress involve lasting personality changes that are characterized by dysregulation in emotion/affect, behavior, bodily functioning (e.g., somatoform disorders), interpersonal functioning in relationships/attachment, consciousness (e.g., dissociation), self-perception/self-concept, and systems of meaning.

In an effort to create a diagnostic profile that more accurately captures the unique trauma sequel of children, the Complex Trauma Taskforce of the National Child Traumatic Stress Network (van der Kolk, 2005) developed different diagnostic criteria for PTSD in more complex cases (e.g., children exposed to ongoing interpersonal violence). The criteria for developmental trauma disorder (DTD), proposed for the next edition of the *DSM*, include (1) repeated exposure to developmentally adverse interpersonal trauma; (2) triggered pattern of repeated dysregulation in response to trauma cues, including dysregulation in multiple domains; (3) persistently altered attributions and expectancies about self, relationships, and others; and (4) evidence of functional impairment (van der Kolk, 2005).

Children who have experienced violence will react in various ways to protect themselves and to exercise emotional reactions to the trauma. These reactions are often observable through behaviors and fall into categories of externalizing behaviors (e.g., aggression toward other children or toward self, as with sexual acting out) or internalizing behaviors (e.g., depression, withdrawal). Other protective strategies include the emergence of primary or secondary defense mechanisms (see McWilliams, 1999) or dissociation. Symptomology in children that is consequent of abuse is expressed in dysfunction in the educational setting, familial relationships, and relationships with peers.

Dissociative responses to trauma are not specific to any particular type of trauma. However, they are generally thought to be more common in situations of childhood sexual abuse (Freyd, 1996) and are a key diagnostic feature of complex trauma in children. Dissociation can be defined as disruption in a person's psychological integration of experience. In other words, dissociation interrupts "contact" across domains of functioning (e.g., thinking, feeling, emoting, etc.). It begins as a protective factor against feelings and thoughts that seem utterly unbearable. It also exists on a continuum, with one end characterized by normal daydreaming and the other by dissociative disorder that may include depersonalization, psychic numbing, or amnesia regarding details of the traumatic event. Like other protective defense mechanisms, dissociation can become problematic.

CONCEPTUALIZING THE IMPACT OF CHILDHOOD TRAUMA ON DEVELOPMENT AND SELF-ESTEEM

Psychodynamically oriented and attachment theories offer a framework that can be helpful in understanding the potential implications and treatment issues related to childhood trauma and self-esteem issues. These dynamic theories posit that relationships with others form the basis for personality development, and chaotic and abusive familial environments can have deleterious ramifications for children. Trauma expert Judith Herman (1997) has aptly captured the significance of childhood trauma: "Repeated trauma in adult life erodes the structure of the personality already formed, but repeated trauma in childhood forms and deforms personality" (p. 98).

Attachment Theory

Attachment theory gives primacy to the nature of affectional bonds in early life and their impact on human development. According to Bowlby's (1988) attachment theory, it is critical that parents fulfill their obligation to protect and provide security for children. A parent–child relationship characterized by consistent parental sensitivity and emotional availability promotes the child's development of a secure attachment orientation, one that is marked by the internalization of a positive working model of self and others. The secure attachment orientation and positive working model of self are clearly germane to self-esteem. The secure attachment orientation provides the foundation or secure base for future relationships. Specifically, through this positive and integrated sense of self (high or positive self-esteem) and other, securely attached individuals are comfortably able to experience both closeness and separateness in intimate relationships. Conversely, when early parental caregiving is characterized by rejection or more overt abuse, the child is more likely to struggle in relationships with others. The child may develop an insecure attachment orientation and internalize a negative or problematic working model of self (low or negative self-esteem) and other. This may look like a negative self-model (e.g., self as not lovable) or a negative other model (e.g., other as not trustworthy or reliable).

The secure attachment orientation is the foundation from which infants acquire the confidence to explore the world around them (Lieberman & Knorr, 2007). When children lack this secure base, they are unable to master developmental tasks that would increase feelings of competence and contribute to positive self-esteem. Opportunities to develop feelings of competence and accomplishment are seriously limited when a child does not feel adequately secure to explore and master age-appropriate tasks, including the initial development of trust. Trust is the foundation from which a child emerges with the confidence and self-esteem to approach and successfully navigate future psychosocial milestones. The absence of trust and subsequent limitations with regard to exploration preclude the child from developing a sense of control over physical skills and independence, adversely affecting initial formations of the competence component of self-esteem. The quality of children's attachment is the primary indicator of whether they will develop the skills necessary to successfully navigate through stages of psychosocial development. Achievement and accomplishment form the initial groundwork for feelings of competence.

Object Relations Theories

Similarly, object relations theories also give primacy to the nature of early relationships and their impact on development. Within object relations theories (and most psychodynamically oriented theories of personality) the *self* refers to the unique combination of dynamics of the ego and the internal objects that comprise an individual's character and create a sense of identity that is enduring and relatively stable throughout the lifetime (Scharff & Scharff, 2005). Objects can be people (e.g., mother, father, grandparent) or things with which we form attachments (e.g., stuffed animal, a child's blanket). These need-fulfilling objects and the developing child's relationship with them are incorporated into a self, and become the foundational blocks of the self-structure, or personality. Connection with others is the primary means through which personality development, and hence sense of self and self-esteem, occurs. The critical developmental issue is the child's movement from fusion with and dependence on the mother (or other primary caregiver) to a state of increased independence and differentiation. The very emergence of the self is characterized by increasing maturity or sophistication of the infant's relationships with primary objects (e.g., parents, older siblings, other caregivers). Thus, the foundation for the self-structure is thought to be formed early in life and is borne out of our relationships with the primary objects (significant others). Once formed, the foundation for the self-structure (or personality) can be modified; however, one's basic tendency is to seek connection with others (friends, romantic partners) who will reaffirm these early self-object relationships. Modifying or otherwise altering the self-structure does not typically happen easily, although it can be done. The more traumatic one's early self-object relations are, the more rigid and resistant to change the self-structure (personality) becomes.

During the earliest (preverbal) level of development, the caregiver must have an intimate emotional connection with the child in order for subsequent development to proceed in an ideal manner. In particular, the relationship must be characterized by the mother's emotional identification with her baby, who is believed to only have self-knowledge through identification with the mother (i.e., the inability to differentiate between self and other). This relationship is thought to provide the foundation for the infant's secure movement to knowledge of self as separate. If the quality of the preverbal relationship with the mother is not characterized by close emotional identification, then the infant's experience of self as separate may be characterized by fear and anxiety.

In the context of intrafamilial trauma in which the attachment relationship is marred by abuse and neglect, an infant internalizes representations of others as dangerous, self-seeking, and deceitful (Bailey, Moran, & Pederson, 2007). Over time, these representations lead the child to interpret the intentions and actions of others through a lens of distrust and anticipated rejection. This disrupts the development of interpersonal skills and, consequently, peer relationships in which the child would normally experience a sense of belonging, identification, and worth and acceptance. Failure to achieve this developmental task further compromises the child's sense of agency and relational confidence, which in turn negates feelings of competence and worthiness necessary for the development of positive self-esteem.

Emotional abuse and physical or sexual trauma perpetrated by a primary caregiver or other adult figure is characterized by invasion and control of the child rather than the provision of security and the facilitation of optimal growth. The adult actually plays a destructive role that slows or stops the process of building mental structure, sometimes causing the child to split the self into parts that are not able to grow together. The intrapsychic mechanisms that evolve in such an environment are defined by a child's inability to conceptualize the self as separate from external experiences, and all events are inextricably tied to the experience of abuse (Lieberman & Knorr, 2007). On a fundamental level, the child associates her "bad" behavior with the abuse, an association motivated by her need to maintain some semblance of attachment to needed caregivers. "It is not the outside world on which I am dependent that is bad," the child interprets, "it is me." This process of self-blame, eroding a child's self-worth, disrupting the development of positive self-esteem and an integrated personality structure, is referred to as splitting. Splitting is a psychic mechanism that includes both normal developmental processes and defensive strategies (St. Clair, 2000). When a child cannot rely on her caretaker to alleviate such anxieties, and when the caregiver is actually the source of danger, the child's use of splitting results in a fragmented self-structure and can lead to the development of mental health problems (Chapman, Dube, & Anda, 2007). Through the internalization of bad objects, splitting enables the child to experience a temporary sense of control over the badness outside and sense of safety in the environment. The attachment motivation is primary to the child's survival strategy, and splitting serves to defend against fears of attachment figures, fears that threaten annihilation of a child's underdeveloped self-system.

In addition to splitting, children in unsafe environments may make other psychological adaptations in order to preserve a semblance of attachment to their caregiver, including denial, in which the abuse and associated feelings are submerged into the child's unconscious, and rationalization or some other form of minimization (Herman, 1997). Either of these defensive strategies serves to protect the child by allowing her to maintain a sense of connection to the abusive caregiver and a sense of safety and hope for change.

ASSESSMENT CONSIDERATIONS

Children who experience or are otherwise exposed to violence may exhibit maladaptive functioning in multiple domains (i.e., affective, cognitive, behavioral, physiological, and social). Such maladaptive functioning will be observable in the various systems in which they exist (i.e., educational or healthcare environments, community settings, family system, and peer relationships). Children experiencing violence in the home are likely to be identified initially by schoolteachers and medical personnel. It is important to note that low self-esteem related to abuse or neglect may be particularly noticeable in the school setting by both teachers and counselors. Therefore, it is important that these professionals are trained in the signs and symptoms of the various forms of child abuse and neglect as well as in the symptoms of PTSD. Therapists working in the school setting can take steps to provide regular training for teachers in support of identifying child trauma victims.

Assessment of children who have experienced abuse or other intrafamilial violence should be conducted with consideration of the child's developmental stage and include information gathering in all areas or domains of the child's life. When working with this population, it is important to incorporate multiple sources of information, including family interviews, naturalistic observation, parent and teacher rating scales, review of child records (e.g., medical, mental health, school), structured and unstructured interviews, and formal testing. Assessment typically begins with a detailed psychosocial history in order to identify all traumatic events that the child client may have directly experienced or witnessed. The psychosocial history should include information about each child abuse incident, exposure to family or community violence, painful or otherwise traumatic medical procedures, and all other types of traumatic experiences. Interviews with the child should be conducted with the utmost sensitivity, and initial questions should be open-ended and more general and then move toward more specific, close-ended questions. For example, "What is it like at home between mommy and daddy?" and "Do your parents ever get angry with each other?" then "Do your parents ever hit each other?" Children may be resistant to disclosing information about family relationships and dynamics for a number of reasons, the most salient of which are an effort to protect the integrity of the family and perhaps to protect themselves from retribution from violent caretakers. Such resistance should be honored and processed with the child.

When possible, the psychosocial history is supplemented with the use of trauma-specific standardized measures to assist in identifying the types and severity of symptoms the child may be experiencing. When using formal assessment measures, it is critical to ensure that valid information for the measure was obtained from a sample that matches the client's demographic characteristics, in particular with regard to age, sex, cultural background, language, reading level (if client administered), and nature of traumatic stressor.

Trauma, whether acute or characterized by ongoing exposure to traumatic stimuli, can impact the child's lived experience in many domains. Comprehensive assessment in support of treatment planning must take into consideration the secondary problems or changes in the child's life related to the trauma. For example, secondary problems may include changes in composition of the family system, housing, or the school system in which the child participates. The impact of such changes must be assessed and, when relevant, addressed in treatment.

Caregiver support and emotional wellness following a traumatic experience play an important part in the recovery process and can enhance treatment. Specifically, children whose caregivers demonstrate support in the aftermath of a trauma and who are emotionally present and relatively healthy are more likely to move through the event with fewer negative outcomes (American Academy of Child and Adolescent Psychiatry, 1998). In light of this information, it is not surprising that the extent to which those in the familial environment are responsible for the child's trauma also has an impact on the adaptation and recovery process. This is an important consideration in the assessment and treatment process.

INTERVENTION WITH CHILD VICTIMS OF TRAUMA

Integral to the provision of effective treatment of traumatized children are the establishment of safety, connectedness with others, identification of internal states and affect regulation, cognitive restructuring, improved self-concept, and mastery over developmental tasks. Except in cases where the caregiver is the perpetrator of the trauma, professional consensus indicates the importance of including caregivers in the treatment process. However, careful assessment to ensure that both the caregivers' and therapists' own attachment orientations are organized and resolved should be made prior to treatment (Becker-Weidman & Hughes, 2008). Treatment strategies designed to address the needs of young children often incorporate the use of play therapy, whereas approaches for adolescents utilize adult-oriented interventions while addressing the specific challenges faced during this stage of development, such as high-risk behaviors and peer pressure (Vickerman & Margolin, 2007).

Corrective Interpersonal Experience

Fundamental to treatment with traumatized children is the corrective interpersonal experience, the mechanism through which negative models of self and other, including the various domains of self-esteem, and insecure attachment orientation can be reworked. Treatment models such as dyadic developmental psychotherapy (DDT), an evidence-based treatment with its conceptual origins in attachment theory (Becker-Weidman & Hughes, 2008), emphasize the relationships between therapist and child, caregiver and child, and therapist and caregiver as central components to the effective provision of therapy. A core concept of DDT is intersubjectivity, or the reciprocal experience between child and parent that emerges from affective attunement, joint attention and awareness, and congruent intentions (Becker-Weidman & Hughes, 2008). This relationship provides adequate mirroring through which the child's fragmented self-system can begin to take cohesive form.

The importance of directly addressing and reworking the child's attachment orientation relates to the acquisition of competencies delayed by traumatic experience. The attachment, self-regulation, and competency (ARC; Kinniburgh, Blaustein, & Spinazzola, 2005) framework is a comprehensive intervention that emphasizes secure attachment that provides the basic safety and security necessary to achieve domains of competence marred by trauma, including interpersonal, intrapersonal, cognitive, and emotional. Central to a child's response to trauma is deterioration in the ability to regulate internal states (van der Kolk, 2005). As a result of failure in the attachment relationship to provide the secure base from which a child's normative anxieties are assuaged and affective regulation skills develop, traumatized children are overwhelmed with feelings of fear, anger, and a desperate need to be nurtured. It follows that treatment with this population provides a nurturing environment in which a child can practice and acquire affect regulation skills (Kinniburgh et al., 2005; Saxe, Ellis, Fogler, Hansen, & Sorkin, 2005; van der Kolk, 2005; Vickerman & Margolin, 2007).

The ARC framework identifies three primary regulation skills to be addressed in treatment: affect knowledge, expression, and modulation (Kinniburgh et al., 2005). Affect knowledge refers to the ability to be aware of one's own feelings, to understand the relationship between experience and emotional response, and to be able to accurately identify emotional expression in others. Affect expression skills are achieved when a child feels safe enough to communicate feelings. It has been observed that securely attached children learn a broad vocabulary through which to communicate affective and physiological needs and experiences and spend more time doing so than children who lack such attachments (van der Kolk, 2005). Skills related to affect modulation include the ability to both identify changes in internal emotional states and return to a comfortable state of arousal. Development of skills related to affective regulation promotes adjustment to negative working models of self and other that evolved originally in the traumatic environment. Such models are defined by the internalization of negative emotions (e.g., anger, fear, apathy) and responsibility for one's own trauma (self-blame). Adjustment to the working model of self will allow for increases in various domains of self-esteem, which is critical to the overall development of the child.

Play Therapy

Since trauma derails normative development, hindering achievement of age-appropriate tasks and, consequently, a sense of mastery over one's environment, treatment should provide opportunities to successfully achieve developmental tasks. There is a growing body of evidence that suggests that trauma memories are stored in the right hemisphere of the brain (Gil, as cited in Crenshaw & Hardy, 2007). This indicates that traditional talk therapy alone may not be as effective with regard to working through traumatic experience, as the right hemisphere is more responsive to nonverbal strategies, such as the use of play.

Use of play in therapy gives the child opportunities to work through and integrate traumatic events, but it also provides opportunities for fun and relaxation, and supports the child in developing a sense of physical mastery (van der Kolk, 2005). Trauma leads to isolation and impaired abilities to engage in meaningful connections with others. Treatment, then, should also provide opportunities for relationship building with peers, adults, and the community (Kinniburgh et al., 2005). The development of intrapersonal competencies, including positive self-esteem and feelings of self-efficacy, should also be a goal of treatment when working with traumatized children (Crenshaw & Mordock, 2004). A strengths-based perspective is fundamental to effective treatment. Through positive feedback and affirmation, counselors can help children to identify and refine strengths, which contribute to ego development and positive self-esteem.

Similar to the experience of PTSD among adults, retraumatization is a feature of traumatic stress response in children. This relates to compromised abilities to integrate traumatic memories. Failure to integrate these memories results in a state of extended hypervigilance, in which the child responds with fear and anticipated danger to most stimuli, including those that do not actually pose a threat to the child's safety. Essential to the therapeutic process is the facilitation of opportunities for the child to develop a narrative around the trauma in order for it to be assimilated into past memory (Crenshaw & Hardy, 2007). This enables the child to be free from the grip of triggers that replicate feelings associated with traumatic experience.

As a result of failure of the environment to provide opportunities for children to process and understand traumatic experience, many children engage in trauma reenactment in an effort to gain a sense of mastery over this experience (Crenshaw & Mordock, 2004). On an unconscious level, such children are making efforts to assimilate overwhelming experiences into a tangible reality over which they have control. Behavioral manifestations of reenactment, such as seductive actions and aggression toward caretakers or other children, must be understood as attempts on the part of the child to work through overwhelming experiences. Play therapy provides an outlet through which children can reenact experiences safely and, with the help of the counselor, process fragmented memories.

During the initial stage of play therapy, counselors can explain the purpose of therapy and set reasonable boundaries, such as rules against hitting the therapist, that create a secure frame without interfering with the child's ability to experience necessary feelings of personal control and mastery (Crenshaw & Mordock, 2004). The therapeutic context is one in which children can express scary thoughts and feelings in order to make them go away, and choices about play materials and other aspects of how the session is spent are reserved for the child, not the therapist (Crenshaw & Mordock, 2004). Furthermore, the pace of therapy should be dictated by the child's process and creative expressions. The child can maintain a safe distance from traumatic experience, and gradually act out scenarios more specific to the actual trauma (Crenshaw & Hardy, 2007). The importance of allowing the child to determine the pace of therapy cannot be overemphasized. It is as crucial to give the child space to maintain relative distance from painful feelings associated with traumatic experience, as it is to be available and present when the child is ready to address such emotions (Crenshaw & Hardy, 2007). Failure on the part of the therapist to embody such responsiveness will likely replicate the feelings of abandonment experienced by the child during the trauma. Through the process of play therapy, the therapist pays attention to the emergence of posttraumatic play, or scenes in which the child appears to be stuck in the reenactment of events over which he or she has no control (Crenshaw & Hardy, 2007). In this scenario, the therapist can facilitate working through of traumatic experiences by introducing protective characters such as firefighters or police officers into the play sequence (Gil, as cited in Crenshaw & Hardy, 2007).

ATTENTION TO DIVERSITY

Increasingly over the past decade, attention has been given to the role of cultural and individual diversity in the fields of counseling and psychology. As was pointed out by Mascolo (2004), people present themselves in dimensions characterized by both personal and communal representations. Cultural and individual differences may influence the manner in which the trauma is experienced, the type of support received from the child's family and larger community, and the nature of the relationship between the counselor and the child. Culturally responsible care must include attention to issues of diversity, and guidelines for culturally sensitive practice can be found through the American Counseling Association (ACA), the American Psychological Association (APA), and other related helping professions' guidelines.

CASE STUDY

Serena, a six-year-old White female, was brought for counseling by her foster mother following mandated removal from her parents' home almost two weeks ago. Serena and her four-year-old brother are temporarily separated until a more permanent placement where they can be together is secured. According to Serena's teachers, she is consistent in her attendance; however, she has become increasingly withdrawn over the past year. She performs slightly below the expected range for her age and, more often than not, does not complete homework. Serena did not always appear neat and clean, but she did not appear undernourished. On two occasions they observed and reported bruising on Serena's upper arm.

During the first four years of Serena's life, she often moved from caretaker to caretaker (maternal grandmother, paternal aunt, mother, mother and father) while her parents tried to "make ends meet." The couple has been together intermittently for seven years, and during that time, her father was arrested for intimate partner violence at least three times. The arrest of both of Serena's parents for intimate partner violence was the impetus for her removal from the home. Neighbors reported to the police on different occasions that "they were always screaming and fighting with each other and yelling at Serena." Additional information provided by neighbors indicated that both children spent a lot of time unsupervised in the family's home, and that Serena did not seem to have any friends her age. Serena's foster care provider reported that Serena has been soiling the bed linen almost nightly since arriving and that she "doesn't eat a lot." She also indicated that Serena is very quiet, does not interact with the other children in the home, and avoids eye contact with the adult caretakers.

In this case, we see that Serena has been exposed to physical and verbal violence at the hands of primary attachment figures. As discussed earlier, such violence can lead to an insecure attachment orientation and potentially result in the development of negative working models of the self, including complicated or low self-esteem. Furthermore, Serena's ability to achieve normative developmental tasks is compromised. Serena may have internalized negative working models of other, through which she associates interpersonal contact with danger and distrust. It seems that her attachment orientation is insecure and avoidant in that she avoids contact with peers and adults.

From an object relations perspective, we understand that early exposure to intrafamilial trauma can lead to difficulty in future relationships. The failure in Serena's environment to provide consistent, safe attachment relationships may now interfere with her ability to trust and seek out connectedness with others. In a context where Serena was not able to develop a secure attachment orientation, her developmental progress would have also been delayed. She may have lacked the secure foundation from which she could master the initial developmental task of trust, thereby hindering subsequent developmental tasks and the self-esteem necessary to achieve a sense of mastery over her environment. Her school performance may be indicative of failure to achieve feelings of autonomy and initiative, feelings that promote the sense of accomplishment and competence necessary to the formation of positive self-esteem.

Serena's eating habits may be reflective of her defense against taking "in" anymore. Her self-system may be overwhelmed by dangerous stimulation, and limiting her intake of food may be a way to control what she is taking in, in an environment where she has otherwise lacked such control. Soiling the bed at night may be indicative of regression to the age at which trauma began, a point at which Serena would have had no control over urinary and bowel movements.

Serena's experience within her family is further complicated by her role as a caretaker not only for herself but her younger brother, and by the quality of Serena's relationships with the family members with whom she stayed when her parents were working. The therapist must determine if Serena has had nurturing adults in her life with whom she felt particularly close, and if she was exposed to sexual violence personally or through witnessing others, such as her mother, being sexually assaulted.

The therapist's initial task with Serena is to literally create a place (container) where she feels safe from both psychological and physical harm. This can be done by setting a consistent (ideally several times a week) and frequent schedule for counseling. Another equally important task for the therapist is to foster a relationship with Serena. Based on the information available, the relationships through which Serena was to develop her sense of self were not sufficient enough for her to do so, which accounts for at least some of her current symptomology. In order for her development to progress and to increase the likelihood that she is able to have healthy relationships in the future, the therapist must essentially reparent Serena through their relationship. Serena's internal object relations can begin to be restructured through a supportive, safe relationship in which there is appropriate mirroring and a place for Serena to work through confusing feelings. It will also be important for the therapist to remain aware of opportunities within therapy for Serena to have experiences that will enhance both the competency and worthiness components of her self-esteem. With a child Serena's age, this can be through appropriate praise for behavior at school or expression of more difficult (e.g., negative) feelings. In addition, the therapist can use knowledge about the negative object relations that Serena has internalized (and likely is beginning to or has repressed) in order to design specific interventions to enhance related self-esteem domains. The therapist needs to remain mindful to not set up a situation in which Serena begins to seek therapist praise in such a manner that she is compromising or otherwise "submerging" her true self. Play therapy interventions can be used in support of all work with Serena in the context of the safe, supportive relationship with the therapist where issues are also given voice in language that is appropriate for Serena's age.

CONCLUSION

Exposure to traumatic events, especially within the familial context, presents a grave concern for mental health professionals working with children. Witnessing aggression between caregivers as well as experiencing more direct acts of violence (e.g., physical, emotional, and sexual abuse) are recognized for their connection to PTSD and other psychologically problematic sequel. The limited coping skills characteristic of young children render them at increased risk for the negative outcomes associated with traumatic experiences. Of particular focus in this chapter is the impact of trauma on the ability of the child to develop positive self-esteem.

Attachment and object relations theories were used as the backdrop against which the impact of trauma on self-esteem was considered. These theories suggest that deficiencies in self-esteem are consequent of a combination of temperament and childhood experience with caregivers. Child assessment should take into consideration familial and cultural contexts, the developmental stage of the child, and the nature and degree of traumatic stress the child has experienced. All domains of the child's functioning and the impact on self-esteem should be assessed and treatment should consist of interventions that acknowledge the interpersonal and intrapersonal nature of the child's current and future functioning.

REFERENCES

American Academy of Child and Adolescent Psychiatry. (1998). Practice parameters for the assessment and treatment of children and adolescents with posttraumatic stress disorder. *Journal of the American Academy of Child and Adolescent Psychiatry, 37,* 4–26.

American Psychiatric Association. (2000). *Diagnostic and statistical manual of mental disorders* (4th ed., text rev.). Washington, DC: Author.

Bailey, H. N., Moran, G., & Pederson, D. R. (2007). Childhood maltreatment, complex trauma symptoms, and unresolved attachment in an at-risk sample of adolescent mothers. *Attachment and Human Development, 9,* 139–161.

Becker-Weidman, A., & Hughes, D. (2008). Dyadic developmental psychotherapy: An evidence-based treatment for children with complex trauma and disorders of attachment. *Child and Family Social Work, 13,* 329–337.

Bowlby, J. (1988). *A secure base: Parent-child attachments and healthy human development.* New York: Basic Books.

Briere, J., & Spinazzola, J. (2005). Phenomenology and psychological assessment of complex posttraumatic states. *Journal of Traumatic Stress, 18,* 401–441.

Chapman, D. P., Dube, S. R., & Anda, R. F. (2007). Adverse childhood events as risk factors for negative mental health outcomes. *Psychiatric Annals, 37,* 359–364.

Crenshaw, D. A., & Hardy, K. V. (2007). The crucial role of empathy in breaking the silence of traumatized children in play therapy. *International Journal of Play Therapy, 16,* 160–175.

Crenshaw, D. A., & Mordock, J. B. (2004). An ego-strengthening approach with multiply traumatized children: Special reference to the sexually abused. *Residential Treatment for Children and Youth, 21,* 1–18.

Freyd, J. J. (1996). *Betrayal trauma: The logic of forgetting childhood abuse.* Cambridge, MA: Harvard University Press.

Herman, J. (1997). *Trauma and recovery: The aftermath of violence from domestic abuse to political terror.* New York: Basic Books.

Kinniburgh, K. J., Blaustein, M., & Spinazzola, J. (2005). Attachment, self-regulation, and competency: A comprehensive intervention framework for children with complex trauma. *Psychiatric Annals, 35,* 424–430.

Lieberman, A. F., & Knorr, K. (2007). The impact of trauma: A developmental framework for infancy and adulthood. *Psychiatric Annals, 37,* 416–422.

Mascolo, M. E. (2004). The coactive construction of selves in cultures. In M. E. Mascolo & J. Li (Eds.), *Culture and developing selves: Beyond dichotomization* (pp. 79–90). San Francisco: Jossey-Bass.

McWilliams, N. (1999). *Psychoanalytic case formulation.* New York: Guilford Press.

Saxe, G. N., Ellis, H. B., Fogler, J., Hansen, S., & Sorkin, B. (2005). Comprehensive care for traumatized children: An open trial examines treatment using trauma systems therapy. *Psychiatric Annals, 35,* 443–448.

Scharff, J. S., & Scharff, D. E. (2005). *The primer of object relations.* Lanham, MD: Rowman & Littlefield.

Spinazzola, J., Ford, J. D., Zucker, M., van der Kolk, B. A., Silva, S., Smith, S. F., et al. (2005). Survey evaluates complex trauma exposure, outcome, and intervention among children and adolescents. *Psychiatric Annals, 35,* 433–439.

St. Clair, M. (2000). *Object relations and self-psychology: An introduction* (3rd ed.). Belmont, CA: Wadsworth/Thomson Learning.

United Nations Children's Fund (UNICEF). (2007). *Child poverty in perspective: An overview of child well being in rich countries.* Retrieved September 22, 2008, from www.unicef.org/media/files/ChildPovertyReport.pdf

United Nations Children's Fund (UNICEF) Innocenti Research Center. (2007). *Report card 7: Child poverty in perspective.* Retrieved September 22, 2008, from http://www.unicef-irc.org/publications/pdf/rc7_eng.pdf

U.S. Department of Health and Human Services. (2006). *Child maltreatment.* Retrieved September 22, 2008, from http://www.acf.hhs.gov/programs/cb/pubs/cm06/chapter3.htm#types

van der Kolk, B. A. (2005). Developmental trauma disorder. *Psychiatric Annals, 35,* 401–408.

Vickerman, K., & Margolin, G. (2007). Posttraumatic stress in children and adolescents exposed to family violence. II. Treatment. *Professional Psychology: Research and Practice, 38,* 620–628.

Wang, C., & Holton, D. (2007). *Total estimated cost of child abuse and neglect in the United States.* Retrieved September 28, 2008, from www.preventchildabuse.org/about_us/media_releases/pcaa_pew_economic_impact_study_final.pdf

5

Children of Families Affected by a Parental Mental Illness

ELIZABETH A. MELLIN

Many young children live with mothers, fathers, or other caregivers with mental illness. Estimates suggest 26% of adults ages 18 and over experience a diagnosable mental health disorder each year (Kessler, Chiu, Demler, & Walters, 2005), and that between 21% and 23% of children may live in families where at least one parent has a mental illness (Maybery, Reupert, & Goodyear, 2006). The impact of parental mental illness on the psychosocial development of children is well known. Poor developmental outcomes are four to six times more likely among children of families affected by parental mental illness (Nicholson, Cooper, Freed, & Isaacs, 2008). There is an increased risk for children of parents with mental illness (COPMI) to experience mental disorders themselves in adulthood. Mental illness occurs among one-third, temporary mental health concerns are reported by an additional one-third, and one-third do not experience any emotional or behavioral disturbances (Rutter & Quinton, 1984). As suggested by Reupert and Maybery (2007), families affected by parental mental illness may be particularly at risk as a result of associated poverty, social isolation, and marital conflict. Symptoms associated with mental illness among parents can result in implications for self-esteem among young children. Research has clarified that the impact of parental mental illness on parenting skills is associated with the severity of psychiatric symptoms and the amount of community support rather than a specific diagnostic category (Mowbray, Oyserman, Bybee, & MacFarlane, 2002). This chapter identifies issues related to self-esteem among COPMI and discusses community-based, family-centered interventions. A case study is also presented to illustrate key concepts and themes.

SELF-ESTEEM ISSUES AMONG YOUNG CHILDREN OF FAMILIES AFFECTED BY PARENTAL MENTAL ILLNESS

Parents are central figures in the psychosocial development of young children, and distress associated with mental illness can impact parent–child interactions. Several developmental theories (e.g., transactional model of children of depressed mothers, family model of adult and child development and mental health, and determinants of parenting process model) speak directly to the probable influence of mental illness among caregivers on the psychosocial development of young children, including developmental delays, emotional and behavioral problems, and academic and relationship difficulties (Nicholson et al., 2008). Although the social and emotional development of children growing up can be impacted, it is important to note that many parents with mental illness parent well (Smith, 2004), and parenting is an important role in the lives of many individuals with mental illness (Nicholson et al., 2008).

The parenting style of caregivers with mental illness is hypothesized to be the primary mechanism through which parental mental illness impacts children (Nicholson et al., 2008), and may therefore be particularly salient to the development of self-esteem. Coopersmith (1967) emphasized the role of parents in the development of self-esteem among young children, and parental factors such as parenting style have been linked to self-esteem development. According to Cordell (1999), three theories (competence motivation, industry vs. inferiority, and personal agency) provide grounding for the relationship between children and parents in the development of self-esteem. A central focus of each of these theories is the development of an inner sense of capability in children that is often related to parent–child interactions. Baumrind (1971) identified three parenting styles (authoritative, authoritarian, and permissive) that have been the focus of research studies considering the relationship between caregivers and the psychosocial development of children.

Authoritative

Caregivers who parent authoritatively provide children with clear standards and use support to help children meet expectations. Authoritative caregivers establish realistic and firm boundaries without overly controlling their children. This parenting style uses warmth and sensitivity to help support the child. Coopersmith's (1967) description of the development of self-esteem in children supports the critical role of authoritative parenting styles. This can often be observed among parents who respect commitments they make to children (e.g., promises to take them to the park during the weekend), patiently describe new ideas or information (e.g., telling a child why what they did was wrong or right rather than just admonishing or praising), and providing children with opportunities to make choices (e.g., giving a child a choice to complete homework right after school or after dinner; Mruk, 2006). These approaches to parenting often reflect the ability of caregivers to prioritize the needs of children, respect their developing competencies, and value the voice of children. Caregivers who use authoritative approaches to parenting may therefore impact both global and selective self-esteem elements by communicating their children's worth and importance. The overall estimate of general self-worth (global self-esteem) is influenced when parents communicate their valuing of children through warmth and support. Additionally, authoritative parenting styles have been linked to high levels of academic achievement and better social behavior (Nicholl, 2002) that reflect positive parental feedback on children's selective traits. Many caregivers with mental illness parent authoritatively, especially when they have access to quality treatment, have strong family support systems, and are supported by community members and resources.

Authoritarian

Authoritarian caregivers create high or unrealistic demands and offer little emotional support or encouragement (Baumrind, 1971). Children are typically not included in family decision-making processes; threats, criticism, and punishment are strategies frequently employed to enforce rigid rules. Caregivers with mental illness, for example, may experience irritability or significant distress associated with bipolar, depression, or anxiety disorders and react critically or harshly to children. This is evidenced by setting unrealistic or age-inappropriate standards for behavior, such as expecting a very young children to keep everything perfectly organized in their rooms or expecting them to receive A's on every test and homework assignment. Children who are unable to meet these high expectations may be sharply criticized or punished by caregivers with mental illness whose symptoms influence their ability to help support children in achieving more age-appropriate goals. This inability to meet the unrealistic and developmentally incongruent demands of parents may contribute to feelings of unworthiness or lack of acceptance that impact the development of self-esteem. Additionally, lower academic achievement has been associated with authoritarian parenting styles (Nicholl, 2002) and can reflect the influence of this parenting style on the development of selective self-esteem. Consistent punitive responses to normal struggles associated with the learning process can be associated with lower self-evaluations related to the ability to succeed academically.

Permissive

Permissive parenting style has been expanded into two subtypes: indulgent and disengaged (Baumrind, 1991). Indulgent caregivers tend to be overly responsive to the needs of children and do not set clear limits or boundaries, while disengaged caregivers are both unresponsive and nondirective in their interactions with children. Because of limited coping skills, setting limits is often a difficult task for individuals with mental illness. It can result in a cyclical process whereby caregivers believe they are ineffective parents, diminishing their parental self-esteem and leading to more difficulties establishing and supporting clear standards for behaviors (Duncan & Reder, 2000). Clearly defined standards play a critical role in the development of self-esteem among children, and research has consistently demonstrated how overindulgence negatively impacts psychosocial development among children (Mruk, 2006). DeHart, Pelham, and Tennen (2005) suggest that indulgent parenting styles may have a specific impact on self-esteem because, as a result of little guidance and structure at home, children receive mixed messages about their behaviors when they are rejected in other settings (e.g., schools) or contexts (e.g., peer relationships). As Duncan and Reder (2000) also note, self-preoccupation among caregivers decreases parental support or involvement and can result in a lack of emotional availability to children. This disengaged parenting style and indifference from the caregiver can negatively impact self-esteem development in children (Coopersmith, 1967).

Blunted affect, or difficulty reacting emotionally, is also a side effect of many psychotropic medications and may impact on the ability of caregivers to consistently respond to their children. In addition, caregivers with mental illness may be separated from their children for a period of time if they are hospitalized, and this may also disrupt parental support or engagement with children (Smith, 2004). Young children, who are often not educated about mental illness, may not understand the behavior of their caregiver and misinterpret hospitalizations, blunted affect, and parental self-preoccupation as indicators that they are not relevant or important in their families. The lack of boundaries and feedback associated with permissive parenting styles may also impact the sense of self-worth and development of competencies among young children. Children of caregivers who have a permissive-indulgent parenting style may develop an inflated sense of self-worth, while those who grow up in households characterized by permissive-disengaged caregiving may feel that they are not worthy of feedback from others. In both cases, the development of global self-esteem of young children is likely to be influenced. Similarly, the same lack of boundaries or attention associated with this parenting style may communicate to the child that he or she is not able to develop competence in certain areas or that competencies he or she does have are not valued. For example, a young child who is doing well at school may not receive any feedback from her parent about her achievements, and therefore begin to question the value of her academic competency.

Other factors likely influence the experiences of COPMI. The presence of another caregiver, socioeconomic status, race and ethnicity, and support system of the family are also key factors for counselors in understanding the experiences of COPMI. The presence of a caregiver without a mental illness can help moderate the impact of parental mental illness on children (Hall, 1996). Poverty is also associated with mental illness, and economic stress can exacerbate symptoms of mental illness (Nicholson et al., 2008). Children living in low-income families of color where a caregiver is affected by a mental illness may experience more negative developmental outcomes (Costello, Compton, Keeler, & Angold, 2003), perhaps as a result of additional stressors, such as discrimination, lack of access to healthcare, difficulties finding quality housing, and lack of job opportunities (Nicholson et al., 2008). Stigma associated with mental illness among many minority groups may represent an additional barrier to intervention.

The effects of mental illness can clearly impact interactions between parents and children. Understanding the interface between parental mental illness and self-esteem among young children seems particularly relevant because self-esteem seems to be one of the most significant predictors of resiliency among youth (Nicholson et al., 2008). Counselors working with both adults and children should be attune to identifying the impact of caregiver mental illness on children and associated factors such as poverty, social isolation, and marital discord. Helping professionals who primarily work with adults often do not recognize or fail to address the likely mental health needs of children (Gladstone, Boydell, & McKeever, 2006), and counselors must recognize that presenting problems of children are often a reflection of difficulties experienced by families. Identifying young children, therefore, who are growing up with a caregiver who has a mental illness presents an initial challenge to assessment of self-esteem issues among children.

ASSESSMENT OF SELF-ESTEEM

Although children as young as two and three years understand that they are distinct from others and demonstrate basic self-evaluations such as "I am good at coloring," they are not yet able to conceptualize that they have a unique sense of self or articulate their global self-esteem. Selective self-esteem, however, does seem to be expressed by children prior to the age of 8. Children appear to be able to evaluate personal traits and qualities across different situations, such as home and school (Harter, 2006). Selective self-esteem, for example, may be evident in the descriptions young children make about being "the smartest kid in the class" or behaving better than a sibling. These self-evaluations, however, are not always accurate, as young children are cognitively challenged to understand the difference between ideal and actual competence, and they are unable to correctly understand how they are evaluated by important others in their lives (Harter, 2006).

Because young children cannot yet conceptualize global self-esteem, standardized self-report assessment instruments are not normed on children below the age of 8. Therefore, behavioral observations might be the most appropriate approaches for this population. These methods, however, are vulnerable to the subjective interpretations of others. Triangulation (comparing and synthesizing reports from different sources) increases the accuracy of assessment. Counselors, for example, could check their own behavioral observations with other sources, such as caregivers and teachers, to verify the accuracy of initial assessments. Because children do have a sense of their selective self-esteem (although it may be skewed), asking developmentally appropriate, open-ended questions during initial interviews, such as "How would your mother/father/brother/sister describe you?" or "How do you help at home?" may provide some insight about how children evaluate themselves within the context of their family.

Coopersmith (1967) argued that parental self-esteem impacted self-esteem development in young children through social learning processes. Because of the low rates of self-esteem among many caregivers, especially those with mental illness, and the potential impact of caregiver self-esteem on children, assessing the self-esteem of parents with a standardized self-report instrument may be indicated. The Tennessee Self-Concept Scale (TSCS; Roid & Fitts, 1988) includes a specific category for assessing self-concept as it relates to roles within the family and may be particularly applicable to caregivers. Behavioral observations, especially of interactions between caregivers and children, are also useful for assessing parental self-esteem issues. Counselors working with families affected by parental mental illness, for example, may observe how confident the parent appears when giving appropriate directives to children. Because many counselors working with adults who are experiencing mental illness often fail to address parenting concerns (Gladstone et al., 2006), asking open-ended questions about their thoughts and feelings as they relate to their role as parents is a key consideration. Counselors should ask questions such as "What are some of your strengths and needs as a parent?" or "How do you feel about your role as a parent?" to begin to assess and understand the likely intervention needs of families affected by mental illness. Nicholson et al. (2008) emphasize the importance of regularly asking adults with mental illness about their parenting status, hopes and aspirations, and the developmental needs of their children as key best practices for improving assessment of issues associated with families affected by parental mental illness. If practitioners who primarily specialize in working with adults do not believe they are competent to address the parenting roles and needs of individuals they work with, Nicholson et al. (2008) encourage the developing of collaborative relationships with child-serving professionals as a key step toward reducing barriers to treatment.

INTERVENTION STRATEGIES

There is no evidence-based treatment specifically designed to address the needs of young children of families affected by parental mental illness. While there appears to be no systematic, empirically validated approach to intervening with COPMI, there also is a gap in the literature specific to addressing self-esteem issues that are uniquely associated with parental mental illness. Perhaps because self-esteem is developmentally difficult for children to conceptualize before the age of 8 (Harter, 2006), there is a unique challenge in designing, delivering, and evaluating programs that specifically address this issue. Recommendations for best practices based on the comprehensive review of the literature completed by Nicholson et al. (2008) are used here as the basis for general interventions.

Psychoeducation for Parents With Mental Illness

Caregiver mental illness seems to impact self-esteem development primarily through parenting style. While there are a wide variety of parenting programs available, Ackerson (2003) reports that many of these programs fail to meet the unique needs of parents with mental illness, and that instead of focusing solely on parenting skills, increasing parental capacity may best be approached through situating it within the framework of treatment and recovery. This argument is consistent with Nicholson et al. (2008), who recommend directly incorporating the role of parenting into existing treatment approaches. Strategies include (1) psychoeducation about how parental mental illness may impact the development of children, (2) information on how stressors associated with parenting may impact symptoms of mental illness and recovery, (3) guidance on age-appropriate information about mental illness that parents can share with children, and (4) recommendations for local parenting groups. Based on this framework, counselors who are working with adults with mental illness can start a psychoeducational or support group that helps parents better understand the interface between parenting and mental illness and decreases shame or isolation associated with their difficulties in parenting. Practical advice and support from other parents with mental illness can help increase the relevance of information, decrease stigma, strengthen parenting capacity, and improve the self-esteem of the parents, who are self-esteem models to children. Additionally, a peer-to-peer group or peer parental empowerment program such as Families First, Home Start, or Video Home Training (Gerris, Van As, Weis, & Janssens, 1998), which shifts the focus from problems to strengths-based care, can be useful for increasing parenting self-esteem. Clinicians who work with mental illness may wish to collaborate with those who specialize in working with children and families on issues related to increasing parenting capacity within the framework of recovery from mental illness.

Competency Building

Competency is a central developmental task for young children and influences the development of both global and selective self-esteem. Creating opportunities for success with COPMI can be a critical step to improving self-esteem. Both parents and children can benefit from participating in experiences that build a sense of competence (Nicholson et al., 2008). Identifying strengths and areas of personal interest represents a key first step for counselors in helping create opportunities for success. For example, a family may identify that everyone seems to get along when they are involved in a shared purpose. As an initial step toward creating opportunities for success, the counselor may recommend that the family designate one night a week toward playing a game or spending time putting a puzzle together. During the game, both the parents and the children can commit to receiving positive feedback from one another that contributes to their global self-esteem. For selective self-esteem development, the counselor works to identify enjoyable activities that are important to the child. For example, a child in this family might tell the counselor that she loves to dance and is good at it. The counselor can encourage her parents to support her joining an after-school dance troupe. This can create additional opportunities for positive feedback from adults that will contribute to her developing sense of self-worth.

Developmentally Appropriate Education About Mental Illness

It is critical for counselors to deliver age-appropriate information about mental illness to children. Understanding changes in the behaviors of parents may help children avoid blaming themselves or feeling rejected when their mother's or father's symptoms are exacerbated. As noted by Reupert and Maybery (2007), a few psychoeducational programs (e.g., Positive Connections, VicChamps, and SMILES) have been designed to help educate children about parental mental illness, improve self-esteem, increase coping, and create additional social supports.

However, evaluation of each of these programs has primarily been limited to children between the ages of 8 and 13. It is therefore crucial for counselors to create developmentally appropriate psychoeducation about mental illness for younger children, which could include interventions such as storytelling, play therapy, or art therapy. If a counselor is working with several children experiencing parental mental illness, delivering such information in a group format may be indicated. In addition to the value of the information, the group format might create opportunities for children to connect with others and decrease the stigma and isolation that is commonly associated with parental impairment.

Enhancing Social Support

Building the social support network among COPMI will likely improve self-esteem. Social relationships help to validate self-worth, and children should be encouraged to expand their social support networks through participating in community and extracurricular activities. Strengthening connections to other supportive adults, who can act as self-esteem models, in addition to improving the parent–child relationship, can be a key intervention. After-school, mentoring, or other programs that connect youth to positive, responsible adults would likely provide important support and opportunities for children to receive positive feedback from other significant adults that may be critical to their developing sense of worth and competency. Counselors working with COPMI can develop collaborations with local child-serving organizations that provide formal connections between youth and positive adult role models. Foster grandparent programs (Corporation for National and Community Service, 2008), for example, may represent a key opportunity to build the social support network of children of families affected by parental mental illness. In this program, trained adults over the age of 60 are paired with children from lower socioeconomic backgrounds to offer tutoring, help children learn to read, and spend time supporting children. All have the potential to provide opportunities for positive feedback.

CASE STUDY

Maria is a 25-year-old Latina mother of two boys, Antonio (age 7) and Javier (age 5). She has been married to Carlos (age 23) for the past three years. Maria, who was diagnosed with bipolar disorder last year after being hospitalized for a suicide attempt, is attending counseling to help manage her symptoms. Her counselor has not asked about the children even though she is aware Maria is a parent. Maria reports having trouble finding affordable medications; most of them made her feel like she has "no emotions" and resulted in significant weight gain. Consequently, she stopped taking medication approximately six months ago. Since then, her symptoms have worsened. Sometimes, she physically and verbally attacks Carlos in front of the children, and at other times, the children overhear her sobbing in her room or talking to a friend about killing herself. Lately, she has had trouble getting out of bed in the morning. Most days Antonio makes breakfast for Javier before school. Antonio, who is aware that the family has had financial problems since Maria was fired from her job as a nurse last year, worries that his mother is spending too much money. She often tells Antonio that she does not have money to pay the rent and will have to ask the neighbors for help. Maria tells Antonio that this is a secret between the two of them and he should not tell Carlos. Maria also seems to have some rigid rules for the children. They are expected to keep their rooms spotless, and if anything is out of place, Maria reacts by grounding them to their room for a week or threatening to throw out all of their toys. If Antonio or Javier ask questions about their homework or do not get good marks, she is highly critical, often asking them why they do not try harder or ask her for help when they need it. She also appears anxious when the children are away from her, will not let them go to the homes of friends, or play outside after school, for fear they will be hurt and she will not be able to help them. Maria's behavior sometimes seems impulsive, like the time she picked the boys up early from school to take them on a last-minute trip to the beach.

Carlos appears to have more age-appropriate expectations for the children and, despite working 12 hours a day at two part-time jobs, spends time playing with them. He is affectionate with the children and encourages them to do their best. Carlos remembers that before Maria started experiencing symptoms, she seemed to love being a parent and the boys were thriving, but now it seems she has disengaged from her role and does not feel comfortable interacting with the children.

Maria and Carlos have been arguing a lot lately because both their vehicles might be repossessed after she failed to pay the bills. Carlos is especially upset by the recent financial problems they are experiencing. He was saving money to help pay for more expensive medications that might help Maria. Maria's bipolar symptoms contribute to the family's economic stress, which in turn exacerbate her symptoms, leading to a cycle of expenditures, distress, and more expenditures. Before they go to sleep at night, Maria often cries about all the things she is "doing wrong as a parent" and asks Carlos if she should talk to the children about her diagnosis so at least they would understand that she is trying her best.

Prior to Maria's hospitalization, the children noticed that their mother seemed angry and tired all the time and sometimes seemed to have a lot of silly ideas. They are confused by the changes in her behavior and wonder if they did something to make their mother angry. Both boys are struggling at school and with peers. Antonio is repeating the first grade and is very withdrawn from the teachers and other children. When he does interact with peers, his behavior is often aggressive, and he has been in trouble for biting, kicking, and spitting. Although he is an intelligent child, Antonio does not seem to believe in his abilities and frequently gives up easily during new tasks. Javier appears to be more extroverted than Antonio, but is often anxious, inhibited, and tentative in new situations. He clings to others for support when he is scared and, similarly to Antonio, appears hesitant to try new things. Javier has also had trouble making friends and is struggling with basic concepts in his first year of kindergarten. Both Antonio and Javier have been taking on additional responsibilities at home, especially when Maria is depressed.

Both children are struggling with self-esteem issues; their behaviors are timid and inhibited, and their problems in school and with peers reflect selective self-esteem issues associated with their mother's rigid rules and her authoritarian parenting style. Antonio and Javier are both held to age-inappropriate expectations and receive criticism when they were unable to meet them. Maria's mental illness has resulted in some disengagement in her role as a parent because of her hypersomnia, hospitalization for a suicide attempt, and medication side effects. These factors impact both children's sense of self-worth and acceptance.

Although Carlos does not have symptoms of a mental illness, he is not home often and the significant marital problems between Carlos and Maria limit the potential protective factor of having one parent without a mental illness. The family's financial struggles increase the pressures experienced by Maria, Carlos, Antonio, and Javier, and the family has a limited support system. Maria is estranged from her family and Carlos's family lives nearly 1,000 miles away. Neither Maria nor Carlos has close friends, and the children are not engaged in any extracurricular activities. Social resources that could help provide support seem largely nonexistent and add a sense of isolation among each family member. Without opportunities for positive feedback from others, the developing self-esteem of the boys and Maria and Carlos's sense of competence in their ability to manage their roles as parents are compromised. Finally, Maria's counselor is either not comfortable or not competent to address her parenting role concerns, especially in the context of her recent diagnosis of bipolar disorder.

To address the treatment needs of this family, a psychoeducational support group that provides Maria with the opportunity to learn more about the mutual influence between her parental role and recovery from her disorder may be an important intervention. The counselor currently working with Maria should collaborate with another counselor who specializes in working with children to offer some joint sessions that may be useful in addressing some of Maria's concerns about her role as a parent within the context of her recently diagnosed mental illness. A peer-to-peer group or peer parental empowerment program such as Home Start, which shifts the focus from problem to strengths-based care, may be useful for increasing Maria's parenting self-esteem, which, given its influence through social learning and modeling on Antonio and Javier, could also help increase their self-esteem. A family counselor should work with this family and attend to competency building. For example, Maria, Carlos, and the children could identify that the children are both good at and enjoy riding bikes. The counselor could help the family develop a schedule for regular bike riding with one another. During bike rides, the family may find it easier to communicate, and the activity itself may help decrease stress and improve coping skills. In another example, Antonio might identify that he loves to sing and sings well. He can be encouraged to join the choir at a local church. The time spent in an activity that he is good at and in which he will likely receive positive feedback from adults (e.g., Maria and Carlos, choir director, members of the congregation) has the potential to improve his selective self-esteem and may also contribute to his developing sense of global self-esteem. Finally, enhancing the social support resources of the family is critical. Engaging Antonio and Javier in a foster grandparent program, for example, may be a productive intervention. Because the children are both struggling at school, the foster grandparents program may be an excellent intervention for improving their academic performance and offering them ways to evaluate their performance in school through the feedback they receive from others who can become significant adults in their lives. This could be useful in improving their selective self-esteem, and successes in school may help strengthen their developing sense of global self-esteem.

CONCLUSION

There are multiple influences on the self-esteem development of children of families impacted by parental mental illness. Young children, who are developmentally focused on achieving a sense of competence in their roles at home, school, and the community, primarily look to parents for feedback about their value in these areas. Symptoms and experiences associated with parental mental illness, however, can impact the ability of some parents to provide age-appropriate structure and limits for children to explore their developing competencies and to offer feedback that is warm and supportive. Much of the focus on mental illness among adults has failed to acknowledge parental roles, and as a result, to date there are no evidence-based approaches to guide practitioners addressing self-esteem and other issues among families impacted by parental mental illness. Complicating intervention is the cognitive inability for young children to conceptualize global self-esteem or accurately assess selective self-esteem prior to the age of 8, making the design and delivery of evidence-based approaches difficult. More information is needed to address the age-specific needs of young children of families affected by parental mental illness, but in the meanwhile, based on developmental theories and what is known about how parental mental illness impacts development among children, best practice guidelines can help guide the efforts of counselors to improve the self-esteem of young children and their parents.

REFERENCES

Ackerson, B. J. (2003). Parents with serious and persistent mental illness: Issues in assessment and services. *Social Work, 48,* 187–194.

Baumrind, D. (1971). Current patterns of parental authority. *Developmental Psychology, 4,* 1–103.

Baumrind, D. (1991). The influence of parenting style on adolescent competence and substance use. *Journal of Early Adolescence, 11,* 56–95.

Coopersmith, S. (1967). *The antecedents of self-esteem.* San Francisco: W. H. Freeman & Co.

Cordell, A. S. (1999). Self-esteem in children. In C. J. Carlock (Ed.), *Enhancing self-esteem* (3rd ed., pp. 287–376). Philadelphia: Accelerated Development.

Corporation for National and Community Service. (2008). *Foster grandparents.* Retrieved November 2, 2008, from http://www.seniorcorps.gov/about/programs/fg.asp

Costello, E. J., Compton, S. N., Keeler, G., & Angold, A. (2003). Relationships between poverty and psychopathology: A natural experiment. *JAMA, 290,* 2023–2029.

DeHart, T., Pelham, B. W., & Tennen, H. (2006). What lies beneath: Parenting style and implicit self-esteem. *Journal of Experimental Social Psychology, 42,* 1–17.

Duncan, S., & Reder, P. (2000). Children's experience of major psychiatric disorder in their parent: An overview. In P. Reder, M. McClure, & A. Jolley (Eds.), *Family matters: Interfaces between child and adult mental health* (pp. 83–95). New York: Routledge.

Gerris, J. R. M., Van As, N. M. C., Wels, P. M. A., & Janssens, J. M. A. M. (1998). From parent education to family empowerment programs. In L. L'Abate (Ed.), *Family psychopathology: The relational roots of dysfunctional behavior* (pp. 401–426). New York: Guilford.

Gladstone, B. M., Boydell, K. M., & McKeever, P. (2006). Recasting research into children's experiences of parental mental illness: Beyond risk and resilience. *Social Science & Medicine, 62*, 2540–2550.

Hall, A. (1996). Parental psychiatric disorder and the developing child. In M. Gopfert, J. Webster, & M. Violette (Eds.), *Parental psychiatric disorder: Distressed parents and their families* (pp. 17–41). New York: Cambridge University Press.

Harter, S. (2006). The development of self-esteem. In M. H. Kernis (Ed.), *Self-esteem issues and answers: A sourcebook of current perspectives* (pp. 144–150). New York: Psychology Press.

Kessler, R. C., Chiu, W. T., Demler, O., & Walters, E. E. (2005). Prevalence, severity, and comorbidity of 12-month DSM-IV disorders in the national comorbidity survey replication. *Archives of General Psychiatry, 62*, 617–627.

Maybery, D. J., Reupert, A. E., & Goodyear, M. (2006). *Evaluation of a model of best practice for families who have a parent with a mental illness.* Unpublished evaluation report retrieved November 3, 2008, from http://www.quantifyingconnections.com/COPMIpage.htm

Mowbray, C., Oyserman, D., Bybee, D., & MacFarlane, P. (2002). Parenting of mothers with a serious mental illness: Differential effects of diagnosis, clinical history, and other mental health variables. *Social Work Research, 26*, 225–240.

Mruk, C. J. (2006). *Self-esteem research, theory, and practice: Toward a positive psychology of self-esteem* (3rd ed.). New York: Springer.

Nicholl, W. G. (2002). Working with families: A rationale for school counseling programs. In L. D. Miller (Ed.), *Integrating school and family counseling: Practical solutions* (pp. 31–49). Alexandria, VA: American Counseling Association.

Nicholson, J., Cooper, J., Freed, R., & Isaacs, M. R. (2008). Children of parents with mental illnesses. In T. P. Gullotta & G. M. Blau (Eds.), *Family influences on childhood behavior and development: Evidence-based prevention and treatment approaches* (pp. 231–265). New York: Routledge/Taylor & Francis Group.

Reupert, A., & Maybery, D. (2007). Families affected by parental mental illness: A multi-perspective account of issues and interventions. *American Journal of Orthopsychiatry, 77*, 362–369.

Roid, G. H., & Fitts, W. H. (1988). *Tennessee Self-Concept Scale: Revised manual.* Los Angeles: Western Psychological Services.

Rutter, M., & Quinton, D. (1984). Parental psychiatric disorder: Effects on children. *Psychological Medicine, 14*, 853–880.

Smith, M. (2004). Parental mental health: Disruptions to parenting and outcomes for children. *Child and Family Social Work, 9*, 3–11.

6

Fostering Healthy Self-Esteem in Gifted and Talented Students

MICHELLE C. MURATORI

Since competence and achievement are thought to be integral elements of self-esteem and are intertwined with an evaluation and awareness of self-worth, one might wonder why this text is devoting a chapter to exploring the self-esteem needs of a population that appears to be very competent and high achieving. In fact, one reason often cited by teachers for not advancing a bright student who needs to be academically accelerated is that it will upset other kids and "diminish the self-esteem of other students" (Colangelo, Assouline, & Gross, 2004, p. 9). The self-esteem of the gifted and talented student does not seem to be factored into the equation, yet experts in gifted education acknowledge how painful it is for these students to be thwarted, discouraged, and diminished (Davidson, Davidson, & Vanderkam, 2004). To possess ability and to feel power they are never allowed to use becomes traumatic for some of the ablest students. It is critical for society to pay attention to the needs of academically talented children. By jeopardizing their self-esteem, we all pay a price; high ability and low self-esteem can be a dangerous combination. At the very least, by failing to develop their own talents, able individuals miss the opportunity to reach their potential, and society is robbed of an amazing contribution or discovery that could have been made, but sadly never came to fruition. At the very worst, pathological distortions of the self, whether deflated or excessively inflated, can lead highly able persons to commit unspeakable acts, putting themselves or others in harm's way.

This chapter sensitizes the reader to issues and factors that are believed to impact the self-esteem of gifted students. It identifies strategies that practitioners can use to assist these students in developing the skills to realistically appraise themselves academically, socially, and emotionally, and build healthy self-esteem. Ways to promote tolerance and greater understanding among educators and others who interact with academically talented learners are also discussed.

SELF-ESTEEM ISSUES OF ACADEMICALLY TALENTED STUDENTS

Blessing and Curse of Being Gifted

Characteristics often associated with giftedness may have a positive or negative effect on one's self-esteem. Research on the social and emotional well-being of academically talented students does not support the notion that these students are psychologically more at risk than students of average ability. Nevertheless, problems such as underachievement, boredom, unhealthy perfectionism, and succumbing to the effects of peer pressure are predictable when needs for academic achievement and intellectual peers are unmet. Neihart (1999) has suggested that psychological outcomes for gifted children and adolescents may be positive or negative, depending on three factors that interact synergistically: one's personal characteristics (e.g., self-perceptions, temperament, and life circumstances), one's type of giftedness, and one's fit with his or her educational placement.

Underachievement among the gifted remains a topic of great concern to gifted education specialists and others who interact with these students. Underachievement can be described as a discrepancy between expected and actual performance (Peterson & Colangelo, 1996). It can become an insidious and chronic problem that may go unnoticed by teachers until the pattern is well established and difficult to reverse. Highly able students who earn above average or even excellent grades in school, yet exert little, if any, effort, are clearly not working to their potential and are not being afforded the opportunity to develop good study habits, work habits, and time management skills (Rimm, 2003).

Unhealthy or maladaptive perfectionism is problematic for some gifted students. Like self-esteem, perfectionism is a construct that has a rich conceptual history (Rice & Dellwo, 2002). Although often viewed as a negative and debilitating problem, which it certainly can be, perfectionism may also manifest in a more adaptive form, in which high personal standards and organization significantly correlate with positive affect, academic performance, and adjustment (Rice & Dellwo, 2002). According to Rice and Dellwo (2002), "adaptive perfectionists hold themselves to high expectations but do not worry excessively about meeting those expectations" (p. 194). Coopersmith (1967) believed that individuals with high self-esteem have confidence in their perceptions and judgments and view themselves as being capable of resolving their own problems. It seems fair to suggest that adaptive perfectionists generally demonstrate self-acceptance and self-respect (Rosenberg, 1979) and have a strong sense of global self-esteem. While they strive to do their best, they do not view their imperfections or shortcomings (actual or perceived) as a negative reflection of their worthiness as human beings, which may explain why they respond to minor setbacks in an adaptive or constructive manner rather than being immobilized by them.

Rice and Dellwo (2002) claim that perfectionism of the maladaptive type is characterized by "excessive concerns about making mistakes, doubts about one's behavior, and the experience of one's parents as being excessively critical" (p. 189). These researchers speculate that maladaptive perfectionists internalize the image of their critical parents and eventually the image of themselves as undesirable, lacking clear goals and direction, and having a pervasive sense of not being good enough. Experiencing such great internal stress, Horney (1950) believed that these individuals might become alienated from their real selves. While under favorable conditions, they might channel their energies into realizing their potentialities, individuals who are alienated from their real selves "shift the major part of [their] energies to the task of molding [themselves], by a rigid system of inner dictates, into [beings] of absolute perfection" (Horney, 1950, p. 13). As Horney (1950) indicated, "nothing short of godlike perfection" (p. 13) could fulfill these individuals' idealized images of themselves and satisfy their pride in the "exalted attributes" (p. 13) that they believe they have, could have, or should have.

Ablard and Parker (1997) discovered that parents whose achievement goals for their academically talented children emphasized high performance (high grades and test scores) were more inclined to observe dysfunctional perfectionism in their children than parents who encouraged their able children to learn for the sake of understanding. Unfortunately, dysfunctional perfectionism can lead some gifted students to underachieve because they refuse to submit work that they deem less than perfect (Pyryt, 2004). Whether or not maladaptive perfectionists' grades suffer as a result of their unrealistic expectations of themselves, the emotional turmoil they experience is cause for concern, as it can pave the path for clinical depression to ensue (Pyryt, 2004). Since feedback from the external world contributes to feelings of acceptance and worth (or lack thereof), gifted students who suffer from low self-esteem may internalize the notion that they are worth only as much as their latest achievement, leading them to rarely feel satisfied with themselves for more than a fleeting moment. Being recipients of conditional positive regard by their parents or teachers (the opposite of what Carl Rogers [1959] envisioned as being an essential ingredient of a caring, nurturing, and growth-promoting relationship), it should come as no surprise that these students have a limited capacity for positive regard for themselves, and possibly for others as well.

Although one may be tempted to help maladaptive perfectionists lower their standards to relieve their stress and sense of inadequacy, Ashby and Rice (2002) suggest that lowering standards is not the solution. Another team of researchers conducted a series of four studies to test their hypothesis that experiencing success leads to raising standards, which in turn helps to maintain performance-related esteem by augmenting perceptions of competence (Eidelman & Biernat, 2007). Their findings across studies support their claim that success prompts standards to be raised. Participants in one of Eidelman and Biernat's studies "reported that they would feel better meeting a high standard by a small margin than meeting a low standard by a large margin" (2007, p. 759). Without question, fostering healthy self-esteem in able students often must include educational interventions aimed at creating greater (albeit not overwhelming) academic challenges and facilitating intellectual curiosity, a vital part of who these students are.

Many academically talented students seem to be satisfied with their peer relationships and seem to adjust well socially as anecdotal and empirical research suggest; however, some do not adjust as well (Muratori, 2003; Muratori, Colangelo, & Assouline, 2003) due to factors that may be by-products of their giftedness. In addition to developing problems associated with being underchallenged in school, some gifted students develop asynchronously. These students may lack social maturity despite being far more advanced academically than their chronological peers, or they may not have developed the fine motor skills to communicate their complex thoughts on paper. Asynchronous development can manifest in any number or combination of ways (e.g., between or within the academic, social, emotional, or biological/physical domains of functioning). The great disparity that exists between students' relative strengths and weaknesses (a reflection of their uneven development) may exacerbate feelings of low self-efficacy in their weaker areas. Moreover, if students place much importance on a particular skill or ability that they lack competence in, whether it be social skills, motor skills, or otherwise, their negative self-evaluation in that specific context (selective self-esteem) may affect their global self-esteem to a greater degree than would be the case if the skill or ability was of less significance to them.

Other gifted students may possess an abundance of talents, in fact, so many that they have difficulty maintaining focus and committing to goals. Although multipotentiality may appear to be "a problem one would gladly suffer, it is a significant problem for gifted students" (Colangelo, 2003, p. 377). Since feedback from significant others plays a critical role in shaping self-esteem, multitalented students who continually receive praise and encouragement from their parents and teachers might feel tremendous pressure to live up to the praise and not disappoint them. This can become a source of distress for students when they feel pulled in too many directions and have to make difficult decisions about their educational and career paths, extracurricular activities, balance between academics and social lives, and management of their schedules. Setting limits with themselves and others may prove to be the most formidable task of all!

Another common characteristic of gifted individuals is that they perceive the world with great intensity, sometimes overwhelming themselves and others around them. These intensities, or overexcitabilities, may find expression in one or more of the following domains: psychomotor, intellectual, imaginational, sensual, and emotional (Tieso, 2007). Like riding in a car that lacks shock absorbers, gifted students who have a heightened sensitivity to the stimuli surrounding them tend to have a keener awareness than their average-ability counterparts of the figurative bumps and potholes, which sometimes cannot be avoided in life. Although great sensitivity is an asset and may inspire one to create amazing works of literature or art or make groundbreaking discoveries in science or mathematics, it can also feel like a burden to gifted persons and may impact their self-esteem. At a time when peer acceptance is becoming increasingly important, being acutely aware of feeling different may intensify a gifted student's feelings of loneliness.

Complicating matters exponentially, some gifted learners are burdened with having a learning or other disability. Just as their giftedness may mask their disability to some extent, their disability may mask their giftedness, leaving others with an inaccurate picture of who they are as learners. Because their academic/cognitive profiles tend to be very complicated, "with so many pieces of contradictory behavior to sort out" (Mills & Brody, 2002, p. 1), educators may be ill-equipped to serve them, especially if the gifts and disabilities remain unidentified

(Assouline, Nicpon Foley, & Huber, 2006). Very bright students who are doubly exceptional may be "on a downward spiral of falling grades, diminishing motivation, and increasing behavioral or emotional problems" (Mills & Brody, 2002, p. 1). These problems might include low self-esteem, depression, anxiety, and acting out in ways that require disciplinary action. According to Brody and Mills (2004), "although any child with a learning disability can develop these problems, gifted children appear to be more prone because of their increased sensitivity, confusion caused by their ability to do many things easily while struggling with other tasks, and the assignment of negative labels (e.g., lazy)" (p. 78).

In schools lacking a culture that embraces academic achievement, some gifted students feel compelled to hide their intellectual gifts so as to avoid negative reactions from other students, teachers, or other school personnel who appear to misunderstand them. These students may unfortunately internalize the message that it is not acceptable for them to be who they truly are, which may damage their global self-esteem. Even if these students find other ways to draw positive attention to themselves (e.g., through sports or social clubs), they are at risk of downplaying the importance of their intellectual gifts, which in both the short term and long run may be detrimental to their self-esteem and may prevent them from maximizing their potential.

In response to the tendency of gifted students to camouflage their academic achievements in school, Geake and Gross (2008) posed the provocative question, "What internal process prevents us from celebrating precocious intellect as enthusiastically and publicly as we highlight precocious athletic or musical talent?" (p. 218). While one may partially attribute this to Western society's hostility toward *intellectual* elites, the authors claim "the problem is intensified by the stereotypic view of gifted students that holds they are arrogant, overconfident, and self-centered" (Geake & Gross, 2008, p. 218). Although some gifted students do exhibit behaviors that are off-putting to others, possibly due to a lack of maturity, one must be mindful of the fact that some students with average abilities are arrogant, overconfident, and self-centered. In actuality, research has shown that "as a group, gifted children tend to be socially and emotionally more mature than their age mates" (Robinson, 2004, p. 61).

The challenge of developing one's academic talent in an unsupportive culture may be magnified for gifted students of color and other gifted minority students. The underrepresentation of these students "in gifted and talented education (GATE) programs has been a well-documented concern for several decades" (Worrell, 2007, p. 23). While efforts have been and continue to be made in recruiting culturally, linguistically, and ethnically diverse students into school-based programs and supplemental academic programs for gifted students, more attention needs to be focused on retention. So what precludes gifted minority students from getting involved and remaining active in special programs for the gifted? Negative peer pressures have hindered African American students from wanting to participate; students of color are often accused of acting White if they excel in school (Ford, 2000; Ogbu, 2003). Other hindering factors include being teased by African American peers, having a weak or negative racial identity, feeling isolated from the majority of other students in the program who typically are not ethnic minorities (Moore, Ford, & Milner, 2005) and who are suspected of viewing them as inferior, and distrusting White people and their institutions (Ogbu, 2003). Unquestionably, poor parental involvement contributes to the underrepresentation of African American students in gifted programs as well (Moore et al., 2005).

Exacerbating the problem, some educators have adopted a deficit view of African American students, believing they "are 'deprived' or 'disadvantaged' and 'lack' what it takes to be high achievers…. These assumptions perpetuate the lack of opportunity for some students to achieve at high levels and negatively affect their motivation" (Swanson, 2006, p. 12), setting the stage for low self-esteem to develop. Although much of the literature on gifted minority students has focused on African Americans, it is worth noting that Latino American and Native American students encounter formidable barriers as well (Moore et al., 2005).

Each of the aforementioned issues/factors obfuscates gifted children's academic, social, and emotional needs, and with each added layer of complexity, students are less likely to feel understood and may not have the insight into why they feel different. A major concern is that if the needs of gifted students go unrecognized, these students will be hindered from developing a strong self-concept.

While some students harness their feelings of being different in productive ways, demonstrating resilience, others may not have the inner or external resources to overcome injuries to their self-esteem. To gain a more nuanced picture of self-esteem issues in this population (which is composed of several subpopulations of gifted students), it is important to consider the implicit and explicit messages that are often conveyed to gifted learners not only by adults and age peers, but through policies, which may have an impact on their global and selective self-esteem.

No Child Left Behind—Except the Gifted

"Not every child has an equal talent or an equal ability or an equal motivation, but they should have an equal right to develop their talent and their ability and their motivation" (Kennedy, 1963). Those words, spoken eloquently by John F. Kennedy decades ago, are extremely relevant today for gifted and talented students throughout the nation. Fast-forwarding to more recent times, the stated purpose of the No Child Left Behind Act, introduced during the George W. Bush administration, is "to close the achievement gap with accountability, flexibility, and choice, so that no child is left behind" (U.S. Department of Education, 2002, Sec. 1). Perhaps when introduced, this initiative seemed to be a step forward, in theory at least; however, under so much scrutiny and pressure to increase standardized test scores for accountability, many educators have overlooked the needs of gifted students and instead have invested their time and energy into helping the less able acquire rote skills and factual knowledge to avoid designation as a failing school (Tieso, 2007).

While students of all ability levels surely would benefit from having individualized educational plans that are tailored to their unique needs, one might argue that curricular flexibility and access to alternative and supplemental educational options are *essential* for gifted and talented students. Yet despite ample evidence that acceleration-based interventions are effective, in terms of both educational outcomes and cost,

America's school system keeps bright students in line by forcing them to learn in a lock-step manner with their classmates. Teachers and principals disregard students' desires to learn more—much more—than they are being taught. Instead of praise and encouragement, these students hear one word— no. When they ask for a challenge, they are held back. When they want to fly, they are told to stay in their seats. Stay in your grade. Know your place. It's a national scandal. And the price may be the slow but steady erosion of American excellence. (Colangelo et al., 2004, p. 1)

INTERVENTION STRATEGIES

Given the myriad issues that can affect gifted children, it seems virtually impossible to describe one intervention strategy that would be effective for most or all of them. For instance, even within the same school, an African American gifted female may face different pressures than her male counterpart. A profoundly gifted 12-year-old child who may be ready for college courses in certain subjects will most certainly have different academic, social, and emotional needs than a moderately gifted 12-year-old who is one grade level above age peers. Two gifted students who have virtually the same academic profiles (e.g., strong mathematical and verbal reasoning abilities) may differ in any number of ways (in terms of level of self-esteem or insight, the presence or absence of learning disabilities or mental health issues, overexcitabilities/intensities, family dysfunction, socioeconomic status, etc.), making it impractical to counsel them using the same specific strategy. In lieu of offering a narrowly defined approach that may be too constricting given the diverse needs of these students, I will describe a general framework that counselors can use in a flexible manner, which includes the following components: (1) a comprehensive assessment, including the use of standardized testing; (2) the modification of educational strategies to accommodate the student's need for greater academic challenge, if necessary; and (3) the use of strategies to enhance the student's social and emotional development and, in particular, the student's self-esteem.

Since empathy is the cornerstone of effective counseling, professionals who counsel the gifted, whether in a school, community-based, or private practice setting, should draw upon their empathy and clinical assessment skills to gain a clear and comprehensive understanding of the gifted students' concerns and self-esteem needs. In some cases, a multipronged approach may need to be implemented, which involves the participation of the students' school counselors, teachers, and parents (and of course, the students themselves).

Encourage the Use of Standardized Testing and Other Assessments

Since the social and emotional adjustment of intellectually advanced students is inextricably linked to their academic adjustment, counselors working with them may need to incorporate standardized ability tests into their assessment protocol if the student hasn't already been tested. An important caveat is that using grade-level assessments with this student population will not give counselors the most accurate information about the students' abilities because the tests tend to be too easy for them. An effective strategy is to have them participate in a regional talent search program, which entails taking an above-grade-level standardized test (e.g., taking the SAT, designed for high school juniors or seniors, as a seventh or eighth grader) to assess their verbal and mathematical reasoning abilities. For instance, two seventh grade students who earn scores in the 99th percentile in math on a grade-level test may earn dramatically different scores on a harder exam, for example, the SAT math, in which the ceiling is raised. Indisputably, a student who earns 780 out of a possible 800 on the SAT math has substantively different learning needs (in terms of level and pace) than one who earns a score of 500. Since the early 1970s, the talent search model pioneered by the late Dr. Julian C. Stanley has been highly successful and has revolutionized the way that academic talent is identified and nurtured (Olszewski-Kubilius, 2004; Stanley, 2005).

For students who may be twice exceptional or have more complex learning needs, additional testing may be necessary (Assouline et al., 2006). Professionals who are unfamiliar with the needs and characteristics of intellectually advanced children and adolescents will need to refer or run the risk of misdiagnosing them. For instance, behavior that is commonly associated with attention-deficit disorder or attention-deficit hyperactivity disorder may actually be a by-product of a student's giftedness (Webb et al., 2005).

To revisit the issue of multipotentiality, academically talented students who are proficient in many areas of endeavor may have difficulty committing to a single educational or career path (Colangelo, 2003). As one gifted student who entered college early stated, "If I choose this path, what does it mean that I've given up another path forever?" (Muratori, 2003, p. 116). Forfeiting educational and career options can be a major source of stress for these individuals. Thus, these students may gain more clarity about their future direction by taking a battery of vocational assessments, which might include a personality inventory such as the Myers–Briggs Type Indicator (MBTI), a survey of values, and an interest inventory (e.g., one of the Holland instruments).

Gifted students may benefit from the use of self-esteem assessments discussed in Chapter 1. In addition, the Multidimensional Self Concept Scale (MSCS; Bracken, 1992) can be used with gifted students and is psychometrically sound. Depending on the presenting issue, whether it is existential depression, to which some gifted students succumb, perfectionism, or some other manifestation of distress, other relevant inventories or assessments can be incorporated into the counseling process. Many academically precocious students enjoy testing and problem solving, so acquiring information about themselves may be of tremendous value and interest to them.

Ensure the Level of Academic Challenge Is Appropriate

As mentioned, curricular flexibility in the classroom and access to alternative and supplemental educational options are essential for gifted and talented students if they are to feel good about themselves. Academic acceleration, in its 18 forms (see Southern & Jones, 2004, for a full description), and countless available enrichment opportunities provide able students with choices today that were not available when the talent search model was first implemented. These options make it possible for able students to create educational plans that are tailored to their unique needs. For example, middle school students with extremely high math reasoning abilities and average verbal reasoning abilities may need to be accelerated in math only. In the event it is unfeasible to attend the more advanced math class at the high school for one period a day, students could enroll in the math class through an online or distance education program. Before these options are pursued, they might look into the possibility of studying the material independently under the supervision and guidance of a faculty member.

A variety of supplemental educational opportunities, including academic summer programs, local math circles, book clubs, academic competitions (e.g., geography and spelling bees, science fairs), online academic communities, volunteer and internship programs, and so forth, may be pursued, not only to augment the students' academic programs, but to bring students with similar interests and passions together socially.

Enhance the Student's Social and Emotional Development

Placing students in an academic environment that exposes them to like-minded peers has proven to be beneficial to many gifted students, and appears to increase their self-esteem. One academically talented teenager who accelerated his entry into college through a special program designed for young entrants put it most eloquently:

> High school was the flat, black-and-white landscape of Dorothy Gale's Kansas. Simon's Rock was the wonderful Land of Oz, in color. Instead of being ashamed of my curiosity about what was going on over the rainbow, I could wear that curiosity proudly and openly. I left a culture that promoted ignorance and traded it for a culture that promoted learning. (Olszewski-Kubilius, 1998, p. 231)

Although most gifted students are neither interested nor ready to enter college full-time at a younger-than-typical age, they tend to fare well socially when they take courses with others who are intellectually at a similar level. As mentioned, enrichment programs outside of school can also provide students with the much needed exposure to intellectual peers. These programs give students who feel isolated from their peer groups at school the opportunity to practice social skills with other bright students who get their jokes and share similar interests. They afford students who often feel marginalized the opportunity to get the kind of feedback from peers they need in order to feel a healthy sense of self-worth and acceptance. The following comment was made by the parent of an exceptionally able middle school student who attended a rigorous academic summer program:

> I actually think the social aspects of this experience outweigh the academic. My rather detached, loner child came back with a core circle of friends (of both genders) that he continues to exchange email with. His experience of being a normal kid at camp has given him a new confidence in forming relationships back home.... This social agility is something that he NEVER had before. He's

never been normal and he's never really reached out socially before…. This program has been transformational. It was eye-opening to be surrounded by kids like him.

Bolstering his self-esteem, this boy's positive summer experience restored his faith that compatible peers, with whom he could authentically connect, did exist. Although a temporary decline in academic and general self-concept can be expected for many gifted students while attending academic summer programs due to social comparison effects, their self-concepts tend to be restored to their original status after the students return to school (Robinson, 2004). Moreover, in the case of able students who behave arrogantly because they buy into the notion that their intellectual giftedness gives them license to treat their peers condescendingly and insensitively, participating in a summer program may be precisely what they need to reign in their egos and appraise themselves more realistically. Learning that some other students are equally as able, if not abler, than they may be a difficult yet important life lesson. One might argue that it is better to learn this lesson at a younger age when the stakes are relatively low and before the problem gets way out of hand.

Students with deficits in their social skills may need more intensive intervention. Social skills training, which may involve role playing and learning effective strategies, can lead students to receive more positive feedback from others, which in turn may boost their confidence in social situations.

ROLE OF THE COUNSELOR

A major task of the counselor is to ensure that the gifted student's academic needs are appropriately met. In many cases, simply facilitating an educational intervention may result in greater academic, social, and emotional satisfaction. School counselors who understand the needs of gifted students are in a position to play a major role in helping their colleagues work more effectively with them. As an advocate for gifted students, the school counselor can assist able learners by placing them in appropriately challenging courses (which sometimes requires a bit of creativity) and pointing them in the direction of supplemental resources that may reenergize their love of learning.

Cognizant of the potential problems that can occur when gifted students' needs are not met, school counselors can take a proactive stance and look for signs that indicate an intervention is needed. These signs might include depressed affect, low motivation, eating disorders, sleep disorders, underachievement, boredom, social isolation, or disruptive behaviors, to name a few. They could also develop a seminar or workshop for the school administrators and teachers to disseminate information about the needs of these students and to create a culture at the school that is more accepting and tolerant of high academic achievement. If school personnel fail to establish such a culture, it is likely that the students will hold negative attitudes toward their gifted peers.

Group work in a school setting, community mental health setting, or a private practice is another venue for addressing the self-esteem needs of these students.

Exploring topics that are relevant to giftedness (e.g., multipotentiality, perfectionism, asynchronous development, overexcitabilities/intensities) may help these students gain greater insight into themselves and establish a support network. Bibliotherapy is another effective strategy to use since many gifted learners are avid readers, and "books can be used to increase students' motivation and engagement, to increase students' achievement, and to improve their sense of self" (Ford, 2000, p. 235). This approach to self-understanding may appeal to able students who are not eager to participate in a group, yet certainly could be used in conjunction with group work quite effectively. Ford (2000) has pointed out how powerful multicultural literature can be for gifted Black students, in that it can serve as a catalyst for social action, for helping them appreciate their similarities and differences with others, and for increasing their cultural awareness and sensitivity.

Depending on the nature and severity of his or her issues, the student may need individual counseling. In some cases, family counseling may be called for. Whether the issue is directly related, peripherally related, or entirely unrelated to their intellectual giftedness, students should seek counseling if problems begin to interfere with functioning at home or at school and cause distress. Clinicians may need to help some gifted clients develop better coping mechanisms for dealing with their emotional intensities or debilitating perfectionism and rigidity. They may need to assist them in developing more realistic perceptions of their academic and personal strengths and weaknesses. Clinicians may need to help them work through anxiety or depression, which may be caused by any number of stressors and exacerbated by their extreme sensitivity. These students may need assistance in sorting out interpersonal problems with peers or family members, finding meaning in life or coping with existential themes, developing better organizational skills or social skills, or in working out a host of other problems. Regardless of what is burdening these children, clinicians must remember that the gifted, like those who are not intellectually gifted, need support and compassion. High ability does not make them immune from experiencing problems faced by those who are less able. The gifted child may feel devastated by the death of a family member or pet, parents' marital problems, or the loss of a valued relationship.

Like educators, practitioners who doubt their own intellectual abilities may feel intimidated at times working with children who demonstrate such astonishing abilities. Thus, it is crucial for them to be vigilant in monitoring themselves for countertransference reactions and to deal with their feelings appropriately (e.g., in supervision or personal counseling if the need arises). Furthermore, because many gifted students demonstrate an impressive level of competence in certain areas of their functioning, counselors must not fall into the trap of expecting too much of them in areas in which they may be less competent or able. By developing realistic standards and expectations with regard to these clients, counselors will be able to effectively model healthy behaviors and attitudes, which in turn may help their gifted clients appraise themselves more realistically and accept themselves for being the perfectly imperfect yet extraordinary individuals that they are.

CASE STUDY

Dylan, 11, had exceptional mathematical reasoning abilities (earned SAT math score of 720 as a seventh grader), yet demonstrated disturbing behavioral patterns and showed little interest in school. Dylan is a student who easily could have fallen through the cracks of the educational system. According to his mother:

> Several times Dylan actually skipped school by hiding in a bathroom, reading books the entire day. While I was able to compel him to physically attend school by driving him there personally, he had mentally "dropped out" and saw it as a waste of time that actually diminished the time he had to study and learn. He clearly yearned for a more challenging environment. Dylan said, "I would rather die than have to go to school next year." Last year he was exhibiting signs of social isolation. Dylan refused to go to the lunchroom or recess, where he felt that no one understood him.

Fortunately, due to his mother's persistence to seek out resources to help her son and an appropriate educational intervention, Dylan made a "dramatic transformation" over a period of several months. His mother recently reported, "He is no longer the child who showed signs of depression and a lack of interest in school. Instead, he is happy, cheerful, socially engaged and demonstrates excitement about learning." She attributed his remarkable progress to the implementation of the individualized educational plan that, at last, satiated his need for more advanced course work and resulted in him feeling understood and accepted by others.

Dylan's asynchronous development or unevenness across domains of functioning (e.g., taking accelerated math and science yet needing to be tucked in at night by his parents) created challenges for this remarkably talented student and his parents who were relentless in their pursuit to help him. After consulting with a counselor at the Johns Hopkins University Center for Talented Youth (CTY) and having Dylan participate in CTY's talent search, Dylan's parents met with the school guidance counselor to discuss the need to drastically modify his school program. Initially hesitant to endorse the proposed modifications, the counselor agreed to read the literature on acceleration and, fortunately, after realizing how stellar Dylan's SAT math score was for a student so young, had a change of heart.

Dylan's school counselor advocated on his behalf and, after getting the permission of the principal, arranged for him to take his math and science courses online, where he could proceed at a pace that was appropriate for his abilities. Within three months, he completed algebra II, geometry, and honors chemistry, and the challenge reignited his love of learning. Meanwhile, at his middle school, he remained with his age mates in his other courses, where the level of instruction was commensurate with his verbal reasoning abilities (SAT critical reading score of 490), and he developed a better attitude. During the summer, he participated in a CTY summer program and took an accelerated physics course.

By exposing him to challenging educational opportunities that engaged him in the learning process and led him to experience the intrinsic rewards of high achievement and competence, Dylan's self-esteem improved, and not surprisingly, his social relationships seemed to fare better as well. He learned to get along better with his school classmates, but developed his best friendships with other highly able peers that he met at CTY who validated his self-worth. Dylan made changes with his parents' and counselor's support that enabled him to find a social group that satisfied his needs for friendship and implement a new educational plan that was well matched to his intellectual needs, reinforcing both his selective and global self-esteem. Although no additional interventions seemed necessary at that time, his counselor remained committed to monitoring his adjustment and touching base with Dylan's parents on a regular basis.

CONCLUSION

It appears to be part of the human condition to need affirmation in order to feel good about ourselves and our place in the world. Gifted children may feel the extra burden of being different from their nongifted peers, and the extent to which they feel a sense of belongingness and acceptance by others may have a powerful effect on their self-esteem. While counselors should be careful to avoid attributing all problems these students encounter to their giftedness, they should be aware of the unique challenges to which these students are vulnerable and of the strategies that may help them develop a healthy sense of self.

REFERENCES

Ablard, K. E., & Parker, W. D. (1997). Parents' achievement goals and perfectionism in their academically talented children. *Journal of Youth and Adolescence, 26,* 651–667.

Ashby, J. S., & Rice, K. G. (2002). Perfectionism, dysfunctional attitudes, and self-esteem: A structural equations analysis. *Journal of Counseling & Development, 80,* 197–203.

Assouline, S. G., Nicpon Foley, M., & Huber, D. H. (2006). The impact of vulnerabilities and strengths on the academic experiences of twice-exceptional students: A message to school counselors. *Professional School Counseling, 10,* 14–24.

Bracken, B. A. (1992). *Multidimensional Self Concept Scale: Examiner's manual.* Austin, TX: Pro-Ed, Inc.

Brody, L. E., & Mills, C. J. (2004). Linking assessment and diagnosis to intervention for gifted students with learning disabilities. In T. Newman & R. J. Sternberg (Eds.), *Students with both gifts and learning disabilities* (pp. 73–93). New York: Kluwer Academic/Plenum.

Colangelo, N. (2003). Counseling gifted students. In N. Colangelo & G. A. Davis (Eds.), *Handbook of gifted education* (3rd ed., pp. 373–387). Boston: Allyn & Bacon.

Colangelo, N., Assouline, S. G., & Gross, M. U. M. (2004). *A nation deceived: How schools hold back America's brightest students* (Vol. I). Iowa City, IA: The Connie Belin & Jacqueline N. Blank International Center for Gifted Education and Talent Development.

Coopersmith, S. (1967). *The antecedents of self-esteem.* San Francisco: W. H. Freeman & Co.

Davidson, J., Davidson, B., & Vanderkam, L. (2004). *Genius denied: How to stop wasting our brightest young minds; What you and your school can do for your gifted child.* New York: Simon & Schuster.

Eidelman, S., & Biernat, M. (2007). Getting more from success: Standard raising as esteem maintenance. *Journal of Personality and Social Psychology, 92,* 759–774.

Ford, D. Y. (2000). Multicultural literature and gifted black students: Promoting self-understanding, awareness, and pride. *Roeper Review, 22,* 235–241.

Geake, J. G., & Gross, M. U. M. (2008). Teachers' negative affect toward academically gifted students: An evolutionary psychological study. *Gifted Child Quarterly, 52,* 217–231.

Horney, K. (1950). *Neurosis and human growth: The struggle toward self-realization.* New York: W.W. Norton & Company.

Kennedy, J. F. (1963, June 11). Radio and television report to the American people on civil rights at the White House in Washington, DC. Boston: John F. Kennedy Presidential Library and Museum.

Mills, C. J., & Brody, L. E. (2002). The doubly exceptional child: A principal's dilemma. *Streamlined Seminar, 20,* 1–2.

Moore J. L., III, Ford, D. Y., & Milner, H. R. (2005). Recruitment is not enough: Retaining African American students in gifted education. *Gifted Child Quarterly, 49,* 51–67.

Muratori, M. C. (2003). *A multiple case study examining the adjustment of ten early entrants.* Unpublished doctoral dissertation, University of Iowa, Iowa City.

Muratori, M., Colangelo, N., & Assouline, S. (2003). Early entrance students: Impressions of the first semester of college. *Gifted Child Quarterly, 47,* 219–238.

Neihart, M. (1999). The impact of giftedness on psychological well-being: What does the empirical literature say? *Roeper Review, 22,* 10–17.

Ogbu, J. U. (2003). *Black American students in an affluent suburb: A study of academic disengagement.* Mahwah, NJ: Lawrence Erlbaum Associates.

Olszewski-Kubilius, P. (1998). Early entrance to college: Students' stories. *Journal of Secondary Gifted Education, 10,* 226–247.

Olszewski-Kubilius, P. (2004). Talent searches and accelerated programming for gifted students. In N. Colangelo, S. G. Assouline, & M. U. M. Gross (Eds.), *A nation deceived: How schools hold back America's brightest students* (Vol. II, pp. 69–76). Iowa City, IA: The Connie Belin & Jacqueline N. Blank International Center for Gifted Education and Talent Development.

Peterson, J. S., & Colangelo, N. (1996). Gifted achievers and underachievers: A comparison of patterns found in school files. *Journal of Counseling & Development, 74,* 399–407.

Pyryt, M. (2004, June). Helping gifted students cope with perfectionism. *Parenting for High Potential,* 10–14.

Rice, K. G., & Dellwo, J. P. (2002). Perfectionism and self-development: Implications for college adjustment. *Journal of Counseling & Development, 80,* 188–196.

Rimm, S. B. (2003). Underachievement: A national epidemic. In N. Colangelo & G. A. Davis (Eds.), *Handbook of gifted education* (3rd ed., pp. 424–443). Boston: Allyn & Bacon.

Robinson, N. M. (2004). Effects of academic acceleration on the social-emotional status of gifted students. In N. Colangelo, S. G. Assouline, & M. U. M. Gross (Eds.), *A nation deceived: How schools hold back America's brightest students* (Vol. II, pp. 59–67). Iowa City, IA: The Connie Belin & Jacqueline N. Blank International Center for Gifted Education and Talent Development.

Rogers, C. (1959). A theory of therapy, personality and interpersonal relationships as developed in the client-centered framework. In S. Koch (Ed.), *Psychology: A study of science: Formulations of the person and the social context* (Vol. 3, pp. 184–256). New York: McGraw Hill.

Rosenberg, M. (1979). *Conceiving the self.* New York: Basic Books.

Southern, W. T., & Jones, E. D. (2004). Types of acceleration: Dimensions and issues. In N. Colangelo, S. G. Assouline, & M. U. M. Gross (Eds.), *A nation deceived: How schools hold back America's brightest students* (Vol. II, pp. 5–12). Iowa City, IA: The Connie Belin & Jacqueline N. Blank International Center for Gifted Education and Talent Development.

Stanley, J. C. (2005). A quiet revolution: Finding boys and girls who reason exceptionally well mathematically and/or verbally and helping them get the supplemental educational opportunities they need. *High Ability Studies, 16*, 5–14.

Swanson, J. D. (2006). Breaking through assumptions about low-income, minority gifted students. *Gifted Child Quarterly, 50*, 11–25.

Tieso, C. L. (2007). Overexcitabilities: A new way to think about talent? *Roeper Review, 29*, 232–239.

U.S. Department of Education. (2002). *No Child Left Behind Act of 2001.* Retrieved February, 25, 2009, from http://www.ed.gov/policy/elsec/leg/esea02/beginning.html#sec1

Webb, J. T., Amend, E. R., Webb, N. E., Goerss, J., Beljan, P., & Olenchak, F. R. (2005). *Misdiagnosis and dual diagnoses of gifted children and adults: ADHD, bipolar, OCD, Asperger's, depression, and other disorders.* Scottsdale, AZ: Great Potential Press.

Worrell, F. C. (2007). Ethnic identity, academic achievement, and global self-concept in four groups of academically talented adolescents. *Gifted Child Quarterly, 51*, 23–38.

Section *III*

Adolescence

A dolescence progresses in stages. Early adolescence begins with the first physical changes of puberty, which can occur as early as 10 but generally occur between the ages of 12 and 14. Middle adolescence is considered to be approximately ages 14 to 16–17; late adolescence occurs from approximate ages 17 to 20. The transition from primary to secondary school is a period of anxiety for many children as they face different life and social experiences; major physical, biological, and cognitive changes; and emotional distress.

Although parental attachment, when secure initially, remains strong, primary relationships once based mainly on family shift to peers who exert greater influence on social behavior and moral development. Whereas same-sex peer relationships were the norm in childhood, most adolescents now develop opposite-sex friendships and socialize in mixed-gender groups. Social comparison increases and can affect both selective and global self-esteem. The range of significant others grows to include valued peers and, for some, revered adults outside the family circle. Adolescents become less secure and more unsure of themselves as they struggle with their place in the greater community. They base their selective self-esteem on the opinions and reactions of peers far more frequently than before. The internalized self-evaluation developed in early childhood comes into question as the discrepancy between the child's ideal self and the actual self becomes clearer through more experiences and with increased cognitive ability. With new introspection and greater self-consciousness, many adolescents become overly self-critical (Harter, 1999), some excruciatingly so. Physical appearance, athletic competence, romantic attractiveness, sexual identity and behavior, academic performance, and job skill competence are a few of domains that affect self reevaluations.

Most scholars support the idea that self-esteem decreases in early adolescence, with substantial declines in academic motivation and achievement and sense of self-worth (Baldwin & Hoffman, 2002; Robins & Trzesniewski, 2005). Body image and other problems of puberty play a significant role in this decrease (Robins & Trzesniewski, 2005). Girls experience steeper drops in self-esteem than boys, perhaps due to the American "masculine bias" (Bee & Boyd, 2003). The groundbreaking report from the American Association of University Women, *How Schools*

Shortchange Girls (1992), presented research showing that girls who once felt good about themselves and their abilities lose significant levels of self-esteem as they move toward and through adolescence. Furthermore, although boys' self-esteem does decrease, it seems to be consistently higher than girls' throughout high school (Chubb, Fertman, & Ross, 1997).

To state that all children experience plummeting self-esteem, however, would not be accurate. Research suggests that approximately one-third of adolescents have consistently high self-esteem or experience modest increases between sixth and eighth grades. Thus, many adolescents are more content with themselves than is assumed (Demo, 2001). Some researchers have found stability in self-esteem in teen years, "supporting a view of adolescence as a period of development, growth, maturation, increased cognitive sophistication, improved reasoning skills, broadening self-understanding, and rising self-acceptance" (Demo, 2001, p. 140).

Some of this stability may be accounted for by gender and ethnic differences. In a three-year study of early adolescence, Adams, Kuhn, and Rhodes (2006) found that girls' self-esteem was lower than boys' for Latinos and European Americans, but not for African Americans. Self-esteem among European Americans was moderately high in sixth grade but dropped sharply by eighth grade. Self-esteem in African American and Latino adolescents was stable, with the former showing high self-esteem levels and the latter showing low self-esteem levels across the three years. Nevertheless, approximately one-fifth of adolescents experience steep drops in self-esteem at this time (Hirsch & DuBois, 1991, as cited in Demo, 2001). Asian Americans tend to have lower personal self-esteem than European White Americans (Rhee, Chang, & Rhee, 2003).

Adolescents progress into Piaget's (1926/1930) formal operational stage, during which they learn to think in abstract concepts and with logic. They now develop the ability for deductive reasoning and metacognition. They are able to think in if–then relationships, and thus begin to question their earlier socialization, debate previously assumed premises about standards and values, and self-reflect in ways they could not earlier. Moral development becomes more sophisticated as adolescents struggle with various moral and ethical dilemmas (see Kohlberg, 1976; Gilligan, 1982). However, not all individuals exhibit this higher level of thinking, and even those who develop the capability do not use it consistently.

Adolescents enter Erikson's (1959/1980) identity versus role confusion life stage. If children successfully negotiated conflicts in earlier stages, they are able to work on answering the "Who am I?" question in a search for identity. They must resolve how to be an authentic self and how to share one's identity with others. They must develop their sense of identity about gender roles, ethnicity and race, occupation, politics, and religion or spirituality. When parents allow children to appropriately explore their own identities, this stage is more likely to be resolved successfully. When parents require and push their children to unreasonably conform to their own beliefs and standards, the result is role confusion. Successful resolution of this stage results in capacity for fidelity and devotion. Marcia (1980) extended Erikson's work to include two key elements: a crisis in decision making followed by a commitment to new standards, roles, and values. Old choices are reexamined and new ones emerge in what is often a period of intense upheaval.

With an increased cognitive ability, examination of the self-concept becomes more focused yet more abstract. Locus of control is highly correlated with self-esteem. Begun in childhood, it solidifies in adolescence as children move toward a less external locus of control for each year of high school (Chubb et al., 1997). The relationships between and among the external environment, internal personal factors, and behavior operate together to influence belief in the ability to exercise control over the self and one's circumstances (Bandura, 1997). Those with an outer locus of control attribute behaviors and outcomes to external events—chance, fate, or powerful others—whereas those with an inner locus attribute them to their own personal attributes and efforts. People with low self-esteem tend to exhibit a greater degree of outer locus of control.

Individuals in whom self-esteem was lower in childhood undergo more difficulties in adolescence, experiencing feelings of inadequacy in many domains. While strong family support has a positive effect on self-esteem, adolescents with inadequate family support suffer poorer mental health, delayed social development, and worse overall well-being (Baldwin & Hoffman, 2002). A range of problems, such as substance abuse, depression, eating disorders, emotional and psychological disorders, and many more, emerge. This section addresses only a few of the many possible issues: attention-deficit hyperactivity disorder (ADHD), eating disorders, and at-risk adolescents, with emphasis on violent behavior and teen pregnancy. The latter discusses the conflicting and often puzzling results about self-esteem as a factor in adolescent at-risk behaviors. The final two chapters in this section consider the case of self-esteem in African American males and females. Although quite a bit of research suggests that these adolescents have higher self-esteem than their European White, Latino, and Asian counterparts, the factors that contribute to the difference and discussions of what self-esteem issues look like in African Americans shed some light on possible strategies and interventions.

REFERENCES

Adams, S., Kuhn, J., & Rhodes, J. (2006). Self-esteem changes in the middle school years: A study of ethnic and gender groups. *Research in Middle Level Education, 29,* 1–9.
American Association of University Women Educational Foundation and National Education Association. (1992). *The AAUW report: How schools shortchange girls.* Washington, DC: Author.
Baldwin, S. A., & Hoffman, J. P. (2002). Dynamics of self-esteem: A growth-curve analysis. *Journal of Youth and Adolescence, 31,* 101–113.
Bandura, A. (1997). *Self-efficacy: The exercise of control.* New York: W.H. Freeman & Co.
Chubb, N. H., Fertman, C. I., & Ross, J. L. (1997). Adolescent self-esteem and locus of control: A longitudinal study of gender and age differences. *Adolescence, 32,* 113–129
Demo, D. H. (2001). Self-esteem in children and adolescents. In T. J. Owens, S. Stryker, & N. Goodman (Eds.), *Extending self-esteem theory and research* (pp. 135–156). New York: Cambridge University Press.
Erikson, E. H. (1980). *Identity and the life cycle.* New York: Norton. (Original work published 1959)

Gilligan, C. (1982). *In a different voice: Psychological theory and women's development.* Cambridge, MA: Harvard University Press.

Harter, S. (1999). *The construction of the self.* New York: Guilford Press.

Kohlberg, L. (1976). Moral stages and moralization: The cognitive developmental approach. In T. Lickone (Ed.), *Moral development and behavior: Theory, research, and social issues* (pp. 31–53). New York: Henry Holt.

Marcia, J. E. (1980). Identity in adolescence. In J. Adelson (Ed.), *Handbook of adolescent psychology* (pp. 159–187). New York: Wiley.

Piaget, J. (1930). *The child's conception of the world.* New York: Harcourt, Brace, & World. (Original work published 1926)

Rhee, S., Chang, J., & Rhee, J. (2003). Acculturation, communication patterns, and self-esteem among Asian and Caucasian American adolescents. *Adolescence, 38,* 749–768.

Robins, R. W., & Trzesniewski, K. H. (2005). Self-esteem development across the lifespan. *Current Directions in Psychological Science, 14,* 158–162.

7

Assessment and Treatment of Self-Esteem in Adolescents With ADHD

GINA RICHMAN, TANA HOPE, AND STEPHANIE MIHALAS

C hildren progress through myriad changes during adolescence. These changes include becoming more peer focused in determining how to judge whether their behavior is socially acceptable and morally correct. Adolescents constantly compare and contrast their behavior with that of their peers and determine their self-worth based on the feedback they receive. An adolescent who carries the diagnosis of attention-deficit hyperactivity disorder (ADHD) is using a comparison group of normative peers rather than other peers with ADHD to make self-statements of worth in forming their self-concept. As a function of these differences, adolescents with ADHD can develop a very negative view of themselves, one that is filled with self-deprecation.

DEVELOPMENTAL STAGES OF SELF-ESTEEM

Self-esteem is formed throughout a person's life as events are recorded and evaluative interpretations of each event are made. Memories are stored of each of these events, and as new events occur, one draws from previous experience when deciding how to respond. A child's self-esteem begins to form from the first years of life and takes shape from experiences a child is exposed to and his or her reactions to those experiences. A child who is praised and nurtured through these early experiences will have the foundation to develop positive self-esteem because of the successful evaluation by others. A child who is criticized, discouraged from trying, punished for failure, or ridiculed is more likely to develop an unhealthy self-esteem and begin questioning his or her competency and worthiness. Boden, Fergusson, and Horwood (2008) found relationships between low self-esteem and a range of

behaviors, including mental illness, substance abuse, social and adjustment problems, high levels of anxiety, and suicidal ideation and attempts. These findings suggest that self-esteem plays an extremely important role in how adolescents judge
the quality of their lives.

ADHD AND SELF-ESTEEM

Adolescents with ADHD have a greater likelihood of suffering from low self-esteem
for many reasons, including having more difficulty with authority figures, poor
peer relationships, lack of motivation and effort to succeed, poor self-monitoring,
greater parental conflict, increased academic difficulty, and feelings of hopelessness and depression (Conners & Jett, 2001). As children with ADHD transition to
adolescence and look more to their peers for approval and affiliation, it becomes
an endless cycle of attempts, failures, and negative self-esteem that overwhelms
the lives of these adolescents. Compounding the problem is that comorbidity with
other disorders occurs in most children diagnosed with ADHD, including oppo-
sitional/defiant disorder, language disorders, tic disorder, anxiety disorders, and
mood disorders (Hill & Van Haren, 2005).

Studies have revealed that adolescents with ADHD experience decreases in
the degree of involvement in school activities and academics, as well as increases
in emotional instability and school-related behavior problems. These behaviors are
often predictive of subsequent behavioral issues, including substance abuse, delinquency, teen pregnancy, and an increase in high school dropout rates (Dryfoos,
1990, 1998). A longitudinal study conducted by Edbom, Lichtenstein, Granlund,
and Larsson (2006) assessed the relationship between ADHD and self-esteem
with adolescent twins. The results indicated that there was a long-term relationship between ADHD symptoms as reported by parents at ages 8 and 13 and low
scores in measures of self-reported self-esteem at 13 years of age. Tarter, Blackson,
Brigham, Moss, and Caprara (1995) found that hyperactivity predicted low self-
esteem leading to social withdrawal and substance use disorder in adolescents
aged 12 to 14.

Thus, adolescents with ADHD appear to have behavioral characteristics that
place them at higher risk of having poor self-esteem. Adolescents may not be as
forgiving in their evaluation of a peer with ADHD when that peer exhibits negative behaviors. Given this type of negative peer evaluation, it is not a surprise
that teens with ADHD view themselves in pessimistic ways and underestimate
their self-worth. Events in adolescence can have a significant impact on later adult
behaviors, and high self-esteem serves as a source of resiliency or positive adaptation, and low self-esteem results in the development of a wide range of maladaptive
responses to the issues of adolescence (Boden et al., 2008). Therefore, the need for
early treatment is paramount so that self-esteem problems are not pervasive across
the life span.

ASSESSMENT

The assessment of self-esteem generally occurs within a comprehensive psychological evaluation when a client presents with symptoms, including depression, anxiety, poor peer relations, and ADHD (Adler, Stewart, & Psychosocial Working Group, 2004). As one part of the comprehensive psychological evaluation, the assessment of self-esteem can be accomplished through the use of psychological questionnaires (see Chapter 1). Common to most comprehensive psychological evaluations of adolescents are clinical interviews with multiple informants (e.g., adolescents, caregivers, and teachers), direct observation of the behaviors, completion of questionnaires to screen for emotional and behavioral difficulties, and testing to rule out learning difficulties. Because self-esteem has been shown to be related to family functioning, assessment should include caregivers' style of parenting, their emotional well-being, and goodness of fit between adolescent temperament and educational and home environments.

While family functioning and parenting style can be assessed via clinical interview and observation during the therapy session, questionnaires such as the Beck Depression Inventory-II (BDI-II; Beck, Steer, & Brown, 1996) and Parenting Stress Index (PSI-3; Abidin, 1995) can be administered to further assess emotional well-being of parents. In addition, assessing goodness of fit between an adolescent's temperament and his or her educational setting necessitates communication with teachers and observation of the child's classes. Limitations imposed on therapists by managed care agencies often prohibit therapists from directly working with school personnel. In these situations, therapists may rely on contact with teachers via phone and receiving questionnaires by mail.

When considering ADHD, attention should also be given to obtaining the caregiver's report of the adolescent's behavior across multiple settings, age of onset of difficulties, and teacher report. Common questionnaires used in the assessment of ADHD include ADHD Rating Scales-IV (DuPaul, Power, Anastopoulos, & Reid, 1998), Conners' Parent Rating Scale–Revised (CPRS-R; Conners, 1990), Conners' Teacher Rating Scale–Revised (CTRS-R; Conners, 1990), Conners-Wells' Adolescent Self-Report Scale (CASS; Conners & Wells, 1997), and the Vanderbilt ADHD Diagnostic Parent and Teacher Scales (Wolraich, Feurer, Hannah, Baumgaertel, & Pinnock, 1998). A child who presents with ADHD as the primary diagnosis should have, in addition to questionnaires specific to ADHD, a variety of broad screening measures included in their diagnostic interview due to the high comorbidity rate of ADHD with other psychological problems, such as anxiety, depression, and oppositional defiant behavior.

INTERVENTION STRATEGIES

Once an adolescent is given a primary diagnosis of ADHD, clinicians should tailor a multicomponent treatment plan that targets the specific emotional and behavioral deficits identified in the evaluation. Additionally, modality of treatment should be flexible, including those participants necessary to obtain change (e.g., family therapy, individual therapy, collaboration with school personnel, and consultation with pediatrician). Imbedded within this treatment, the therapist should target for change those areas of life identified as problematic that are thought to influence self-esteem, such as symptoms related to anxiety, depression, or ADHD; classroom placement and quality of interactions in school; caregivers' style of parenting; parent–child communication; family functioning; and the adolescent's social skills.

School and Treatment

To address classroom placement, the therapist serves the role of a consultant. As a consultant, a therapist contacts teachers, mental health staff, and administrators to ensure that the student is appropriately placed according to the Individual Education Plan (IEP) or 504 regulations. The therapist also assumes the role of assisting to develop behavioral intervention plans, accommodations, and modifications that allow the teacher to present educational materials in an environment that most closely matches the student's academic needs, interactional style, and temperament. The school counselor can provide individual or group instruction to increase social skills and self-esteem (Vlam, 2006) or increase anger management, coping, and stress management strategies (Lopez, Olaizola, Ferrer, & Ochoa, 2006) in conjunction with having the primary focus of therapy in the outpatient therapeutic setting. To assist in the generalization of skills taught by the school counselor, the classroom teacher can encourage the process by matching the child to appropriate peers in small group settings where the student can practice the skills taught while the teacher unobtrusively assists the social and academic interaction, thereby setting the child up for success. This humanistic approach to learning fosters improved self-esteem through social and academic success. Additionally, the teacher can administer any accommodations and modifications listed within a child's IEP/504 plan, focusing on accomplishments instead of mistakes and failures. For example, a paper can be graded based on items completed instead of all items on the worksheet. Similarly, a child can be asked to complete only the odd- or even-numbered items, thereby increasing the likelihood of their success. Finally, Wolter, DiLollo, and Apel (2006) suggest that school-based speech therapists may utilize narrative therapy when addressing comorbid language-literacy deficits and poor self-esteem. Creating this socially and educationally supportive environment affords the student the opportunity for increased success by emphasizing the student's strengths and maintaining his or her self-esteem (Foley, 2007).

Family and Treatment

Style of parenting can be addressed through therapy sessions with the primary caregivers. To maintain the hierarchy of the family and prevent the adolescent from sabotaging treatment, it is suggested that the adolescent not attend initial therapy sessions. To assist in increasing self-esteem, parenting sessions should emphasize increasing parents' social support of their child (LaBarbera, 2008); increasing parents' positive affect and warmth toward their child, especially for girls (Ojanen & Perry, 2007; Rudy & Grusec, 2006); limiting excessive control of their child, especially for boys (Ojanen & Perry, 2007); increasing authoritative parenting over permissive, authoritarian, or neglectful parenting (Milevsky, Schlechter, Netter, & Keehn, 2007); and educating parents on the need for goodness of fit between their parenting style and their adolescent's temperament (Foley, 2007) and current difficulty of low self-esteem. To increase parents' support of their child, the parents and child can construct a list of those activities or events that are most valued by the child. For example, while one child may value participating in sports or other after-school activities, other children may value being able to visit with classmates on the weekend, carrying a cell phone, or having solid academic success. Parents can promote self-esteem by encouraging their adolescent to use a problem-solving approach to reach the desired goal. Problem solving with the entire family will allow the adolescent the opportunity to receive positive and constructive feedback on his or her cognitive processing and decision making. This interactional style creates a naturally reinforcing environment for the adolescent, thus promoting enhanced self-esteem and family cohesion.

Issues of poor parent–child communication and family functioning can be addressed through family therapy. By reducing family conflict and increasing cohesion, an adolescent is more likely to value and appreciate the family unit, thereby increasing one's sense of worth and acceptance. Due to the possible reciprocal effect between self-esteem and family functioning (Vandeleur, Perez, & Schoebi, 2007), it is suggested that the adolescent's self-esteem and other reported symptoms be addressed through multiple modalities of treatment (e.g., individual or group therapy) during the process of family therapy. To assist in improving self-esteem, family therapy should focus on restructuring the family system to create a solid hierarchy with appropriate boundaries, reinforce the use of good parenting strategies, teach basic communication and problem-solving strategies, and increase mutual trust and empathy between family members. Individual or group therapy can reinforce what is taught within the family therapy session while utilizing cognitive-behavioral therapy to directly address features of poor self-esteem, such as cognitive distortions and negative self-talk. Instruction in social skills, daily life coping skills, and assertiveness training or anger management skills is often warranted (Impett, Sorsoli, Schooler, Henson, & Tolman, 2008).

ADHD and Treatment

In considering ADHD as an exemplar disorder for the purpose of this discussion, in addition to the aforementioned suggestions, treatment consideration should also be given to utilizing a standard form of treatment known to be effective with ADHD, such as behavioral family therapy. Specifically, instruction in organization, planning, and study skills is often necessary (Conners & Jett, 2001). Care should be taken that parents are not overprotecting or lowering their expectations of their adolescent (Sanders, 2006), and that teachers and others have not labeled the adolescent, thereby increasing their social rejection (Gentschel & McLaughlin, 2000). Working together, educators and parents can develop an educational plan that takes into consideration the most optimal conditions under which the adolescent can thrive. This will likely include a curriculum that matches the individual's instructional level and result in the adolescent achieving academic competence and self-worth. Moreover, parents should endeavor to establish household routines and structure to ensure that the adolescent has a sense of achievement and competence in the home environment as well. The adolescent's pediatrician should be consulted as to the appropriateness of stimulant medication as part of treatment, and the family and adolescent should be educated on the role of medication to ensure acceptance of medication management. Last, group therapy has been shown to be an effective therapeutic strategy in improving social skills, applying anger management techniques, and learning impulse control (Hansen, Meissler, & Ovens, 2000).

UNDERSTANDING SELF-ESTEEM IN DIVERSE CONTEXTS

It is important to consider the role that diversity plays in the development and maintenance of a healthy sense of self-esteem. Differences based on ethnicity and gender are two common clinical considerations in work with any population.

Ethnicity Considerations

There is a growing percentage of minority adolescents living in the United States (see McLoyd, 1998), and ethnic differences in self-esteem during adolescence have been highlighted by numerous researchers. For example, African American adolescents often report higher self-esteem than their Asian or Latino peers, which is often attributed to a higher sense of group autonomy. They report a sense of camaraderie among one another at school, in the neighborhood, and at spiritual settings (Chapman & Mullis, 2000). Asian Americans, on the other hand, typically report the lowest self-esteem compared to other minority adolescents, which is attributed to their self-perceptions of unattractiveness and peer discrimination (Rosenbloom & Way, 2004; Way & Chen, 2000). Further, the Asian American community may place a lower priority on enhancing self-esteem among youth than the Latino and African American communities (Sodowsky, Kwan, & Pannu, 1995).

Peer victimization based on ethnic discrimination also has been linked to adolescents' self-esteem, specifically ethnic self-esteem (Verkuyten, Kinket, & Van der Wiele, 1997). Moreover, ethnic self-esteem has been found to mediate the relationship between discrimination and global self-worth (Verkuyten & Thijs, 2006). Ethnic self-esteem is how an adolescent feels about his or her own racial or ethnic group and includes one's evaluation, belongingness, and sense of interdependence to a particular group. Given the realities of discrimination, fostering a healthy sense of ethnic self-esteem is of critical importance. However, the question remains, "How does the clinician help build an adolescent's self-esteem despite discrimination that may take place at school, in the neighborhood, or on the playground?"

One of the most important factors revealed in the research is that family support provides the greatest encouragement for self-esteem over time (Greene & Way, 2005). When an adolescent has a supportive family, one that is involved in his or her activities (e.g., sports, academics), he or she develops a strong connection of being surrounded by loving and nurturing adults, and consequently is more likely to develop highly positive morale and enhanced self-esteem. Family involvement in extracurricular activities that provides consistent, positive, and affirming feedback to the adolescent is essential to increasing self-esteem. Through the course of family therapy, a therapist can help families develop strong bonds, maintain open communication, and effectively manage conflict. Moreover, parents can learn how to minimize unnecessary daily hassles that can be stressors to adolescents. Therapeutic family interventions have support in the literature to enhance self-esteem and improve adolescent development (Seidman, Lambert, Allen, & Aber, 2003).

Other interventions to consider when working with minority adolescents and families to improve adolescents' self-esteem include parental engagement in supervision/monitoring, teen engagement in extracurricular activities and commitment to engage in spiritual growth, parents' and teachers' dedication to high academic standards, and teen involvement in a study group (Wright, 2000). These interventions, while basic, are keystone concepts that enhance self-esteem by fostering competence in valued domains of life.

Gender Considerations

Gender differences in self-esteem are also important considerations in clinical work with adolescents because societal pressures link physical appearance to global self-worth. Substantial research shows that compared to females, males tend to report higher self-esteem throughout all stages of adolescence, while females' self-esteem continues to decline throughout adolescence. Interestingly, many females tend to outperform males academically but perceive themselves as academically inept compared to males (Bouffard & Couture, 2003). A recent study conducted by Ahmavaara and Houston (2007) found that boys' confidence in intelligence was mediated by self-esteem, such that boys consistently had higher perceived levels of intelligence than females, albeit true levels of intelligence predicted by standardized assessments did not show that males were more intelligent. Interestingly, males have more academic problems within the school setting, such as higher rates of retention, placement in special education, and dropping out of school, than females (see Raffaele Mendez, Mihalas, & Hardesty, 2006). Thus, it seems clear that self-esteem does not necessarily serve as a buffer against problematic issues.

For females in middle school, considerable stressors such as relational victimization, sexual harassment, and body image have been well documented in the literature; however, based on the research and our clinical experience, the main locus that is frequently affected by low self-esteem in many adolescent females, and that is overlooked by clinicians, is in the academic arena. Females receive gender-stereotyped messages through the media and larger culture about what they can and cannot do academically (e.g., science and math). Clinicians can advocate for females to take part in programs that emphasize female empowerment through the math and sciences, such as Operation SMART and Expanding Your Horizons (Raffaele Mendez et al., 2006). Clinicians may also engage in cognitive-behavioral therapy (CBT) techniques to challenge male-dominated gender role mental models that families and adolescents may firmly hold. Techniques that could be used include Socratic dialogue and test of evidence (TOE). CBT may be a useful therapeutic tool because it would alleviate the cognitive dissonance females have between what they would like to explore and the limited access to these aspirations as a function of societal pressures and concomitant self-esteem issues that continue to hold them back from their dreams.

While academics and employment are two variables affected by self-esteem for females, males and females are equally affected by body image and physical appearance (Seidah & Bouffard, 2007). This strong finding suggests that clinicians cannot overlook that males also are consumed with societal pressures to both lose and gain weight. Males in the Seidah and Bouffard (2007) study who reported body dissatisfaction also reported lower competence in all social domains (e.g., friendships with peers, family relations) and felt less capable academically. Practitioners should be self-aware of their own gender biases when working with males, as to not make the assumption that the male patient is not body-conscious. The clinician should probe for issues of anorexia, bulimia, and other *DSM–IV* diagnoses related to weight, as this is a predominant issue in the adolescent development phase for *both* males and females.

ADHD Considerations

Adolescents with ADHD have an immature appraisal system because of the widely held belief that ADHD is partially accounted for by the limbic system within the frontal lobe. Therefore, when adolescents with ADHD appraise other children, they often make negative and inaccurate attributions about themselves and others. Moreover, they often become depressed more easily because they project blame or often dislike the fact that they must take medication. Consequently, their self-esteem is directly affected by depression and the negative thoughts that become widely held beliefs. Let us consider adolescent females with ADHD. They may have a more difficult time upholding friendships than normative adolescent females, and thus their self-esteem is heavily compromised. For example, Thurber, Heller, and Hinshaw (2002) found that females with ADHD responded more negatively and aggressively to hypothetical vignettes. Additionally, this same sample of females also predicted the actions of other hypothetical peers to respond in aggressive and negative ways. Alternatively, comparison females expected that peers would respond in a prosocial manner. The fact that the experimental group made hostile attribution biases may be attributed to the fact that many adolescents with ADHD have fewer friends and are oftentimes rejected in peer settings because of their aggressive behavior (Zalecki & Hinshaw, 2004). The result is that their self-esteem tends to waver and fluctuates frequently.

Clinicians could work closely with females who have been diagnosed with ADHD to ensure they have the proper social skills to make and maintain friends. Second, clinicians may help the adolescent work through problems and issues utilizing the social problem-solving process or other systematic methods so that the adolescent can develop a strategy of solving problems in a way that does not result in haphazard or erroneous assumptions. Finally, the clinician can involve the patient in a group comprised of adolescent girls to socialize the patient and provide direct feedback on attribution biases and friendship-making skills.

Another interesting issue that faces the clinical community actually pertains to parents of ADHD adolescents. The research indicates that children are best treated by a combination of psychopharmacological treatment and therapy. However, parental ethnic perceptions of treatment effectiveness become important and may play an important part in building and maintaining rapport with a family. Dosreis and colleagues (2003) found that 63% of non-White and 29% of White parents reported that counseling was the best form of treatment for ADHD, and that 59% of White parents preferred medication over counseling compared to 36% of non-White parents ($p < .01$). However, in this particular study, all parents reported that medication had no improvement in self-esteem. This study has implications for the practitioner because it suggests ethnicity may be important to take into consideration when providing psychoeducational, psychotherapeutic, and psychopharmacological treatment options to parents who are requesting assistance for the adolescent with ADHD.

CASE STUDY

Sarah was a 13-year-old Asian American female when she presented for an evaluation. Her parents reported that she was eight years old when she was diagnosed with ADHD. Sarah's mother stated that she initially became concerned about Sarah's behavior six years ago when she consistently blamed her friends for things that went wrong rather than taking any responsibility. When Sarah was held accountable, she would become aggressive toward her parents. She was unable to sustain friendships, and at school had trouble with poor attention span and "annoying" behavior toward classmates, including talking loudly and making inappropriate comments. Sarah complained to her parents that she was never invited to classmates' birthday parties or sleepovers. Sarah told her parents that she was sure her classmates were leaving her out of social events because she looked different than her friends. She began making negative self-statements and withdrawing from family social events and extracurricular activities. After obtaining a diagnosis of ADHD, Sarah began a medication protocol and received school consultation services to address the behavioral problems in the classroom. Current concerns reported by the family include withdrawal, sleep difficulties, low academic achievement, and poor self-image. Her parents report that Sarah's ADHD symptoms are effectively managed by her stimulant medication. In retrospect, at the time of diagnosis, the treatment plan did not address intrapsychic factors (e.g., self-esteem issues, psychoeducation, possible comorbid depression, and anxiety) that would be pervasive during Sarah's adolescence and adulthood.

Assessment

To address the specific current concerns, the clinician conducted a full assessment, including clinical interviews (e.g., parents alone, Sarah alone, and the entire family). This type of comprehensive interview format allows the clinician to obtain guarded information and observe the family dynamics. After the clinical interviews, specific assessment instruments were chosen based on the information presented.

The instruments chosen in this case for Sarah included the Children's Depression Inventory (CDI; Kovacs, 1992), Culture-Free Self-Esteem Inventories (CFSEI-3; Battle, 2002), and the Conners-Wells' Adolescent Self-Report Scale (CASS; Conners & Wells, 1997). This battery allowed for the evaluation of depression, academic abilities, self-esteem in a culture-free context, as well as assessing Sarah's continued difficulties with ADHD. The instruments chosen for Sarah's parents included the Parenting Stress Index (PSI-3; Abidin, 1995) and the Conners' Parent Rating Scale–Revised (CPRS-R; Conners, 1990). This battery allows for the evaluation of parental stress, parent–child dysfunctional interaction, parents' perception of the challenging nature of parenting the child, as well as assessing the difficulties associated with ADHD. As the family did not report any significant school-based difficulties, the clinician did not feel that it was imperative to contact the school at this time. Based on assessment results, the therapist determined that Sarah's primary diagnosis was major depression, single episode. Additionally, based on the CFSEI-3, she is suffering from self-esteem problems. Her parents both scored above the 90th percentile on the total stress index of the PSI-3, suggesting the necessity for family therapy.

Treatment

The modality of treatment chosen to address the family's concerns included a combination of individual and family therapy. Family therapy included sessions with the parents and family sessions. Within the context of individual therapy, the focus of treatment was on Sarah's perception of her physical attractiveness and ethnic identity. Suggestions during treatment included engaging in activities with culturally similar peers and open dialogue about her cognitions around her ethnicity. While Sarah is not openly reporting any conflict with peers around her ethnicity, oftentimes in therapy, minority adolescents begin to disclose cognitive dissonance between who they are and norms set by dissimilar peers. This treatment plan is suggested specifically for this stage of development, as adolescents are simultaneously striving for a sense of identity, group cohesion, and positive feedback from others. Thus, therapy can focus on teaching Sarah social skills through modeling and opportunities for practice. This approach will increase the likelihood of the generalization of these skills with peers and enhance her sense of self-esteem. Additionally, this stage of adolescence is typically marked with secrecy from adults, thereby increasing the time it may take for the therapist to build rapport and the patient to disclose personal information.

Therapy with Sarah's parents included psychoeducation about adolescent development, self-esteem, and comorbid depression and ADHD. This format of therapy afforded Sarah's parents the foundation to understand their daughter's behavior and provide support outside of the therapeutic setting. To protect rapport and ensure that Sarah understands the limits of confidentiality, the therapist spoke with her about the focus of the parent-only sessions.

Within some cultures, encouragement of self-esteem is not always communicated clearly by parents to their children. Our family therapy sessions focused on engaging the parents in making positive-praise statements about Sarah. The therapist modeled these authentic praise statements to Sarah. To assist the parents in conveying their concerns and expectations to her, the second focus of family therapy sessions included problem-solving and communication skills training. Issues of concern were selected in a graduated process from least conflicting to most conflicting to be discussed while learning and maintaining appropriate boundaries, using nonblaming statements, staying focused on the current concern, and working toward a solution. By beginning with a problem of minimal emotional impact, the family was able to more easily focus on the communication skills rather than on the emotional charge of the specific underlying problem.

CONCLUSION

This chapter highlights the complexities adolescents with ADHD face in their social, emotional, and academic development. Of particular importance is the preservation of self-esteem through this challenging period of growth. Factors such as poor peer relationships, greater parental conflict, increased academic difficulty, and feelings of hopelessness and depression are examples of potential areas of increased concern for these adolescents. It is therefore imperative that professionals take into consideration the many facets of treatment, including individual, family, and school-based interventions, when working with adolescents that present with low self-esteem.

REFERENCES

Abidin, R. R. (1995). *Parenting Stress Index* (3rd ed.) Lutz, FL: Psychological Assessment Resources, Inc.

Adler, N., Stewart, J., & Psychosocial Working Group. (2004). *Self-esteem*. Retrieved September 23, 2008, from http://www.macses.ucsf.edu/Research/Psychosocial/notebook/selfesteem.html

Ahmavaara, A., & Houston, D. M. (2007). The effects of selective schooling and self-concept on adolescents' academic aspiration: An examination of Dweck's self-theory. *British Journal of Educational Psychology, 77*, 613–632.

Battle, J. (2002). *Culture Free Self-Esteem Inventories* (3rd ed.). Austin, TX: Psychological Assessment Resources, Inc.

Beck, A. T., Steer, R. A., & Brown, G. K. (1996). *Beck Depression Inventory* (2nd ed.). San Antonio, TX: The Psychological Corporation and Harcourt Brace & Company.

Boden, J. M., Fergusson, D. M., & Horwood, L. J. (2008). Does adolescent self-esteem predict life outcomes? A test of the causal role of self-esteem. *Development and Psychopathology, 20*, 319–339.

Bouffard, T., & Couture, N. (2003). Motivational profile and academic achievement among students enrolled in different schooling tracks. *Educational Studies, 29*, 19–38.

Chapman, P. L., & Mullis, R. L. (2000). Racial differences in adolescent coping and self-esteem. *Journal of Genetic Psychology, 161*, 152–160.

Conners, C. K. (1990). *Conners' Rating Scales* (rev.) [Long and short for teachers, parents, and adolescents]. Toronto: Multi-Heath Systems Inc.

Conners, C. K., & Jett, J. L. (2001). *Attention deficit hyperactivity disorder (in adults and children): The latest assessment and treatment strategies*. Kansas City: Compact Clinicals.

Conners, C. K., & Wells, K. C. (1997). *Conners-Wells' Adolescent Self-Report Scales*. Toronto: Multi-Health Systems, Inc.

Dosreis, S., Zito, J. M., Safer, D. J., Soeken, K. L., Mitchell, J. W., & Ellwood, L. C. (2003). Parental perceptions and satisfaction with stimulant medication for attention-deficit hyperactivity disorder. *Developmental and Behavioral Pediatrics, 24*, 155–162.

Dryfoos, J. G. (1990). *Adolescents at risk: Prevalence and prevention*. New York: Oxford University Press.

Dryfoos, J. G. (1998). *Safe passage: Making it through adolescence in a risky society*. New York: Cambridge University Press.

DuPaul, G. J., Power, T. J., Anastopoulos, A. D., & Reid, R. (1998). *ADHD Rating Scales-IV: Checklists, norms and clinical interpretation*. New York: Guilford.

Edbom, T., Lichtenstein, P., Granlund, M., & Larsson, J. (2006). Long-term relationships between symptoms of attention deficit hyperactivity disorder and self-esteem in a prospective longitudinal study of twins. *Acta Paediatrica, 95*, 650–657.

Foley, M. (2007). School-age temperament: Implications for school nurses. *Journal for Specialists in Pediatric Nursing, 12*, 128–131.

Gentschel, D. A., & McLaughlin, T. F. (2000). Attention deficit hyperactivity disorder as a social disability: Characteristics and suggested methods of treatment. *Journal of Developmental and Physical Disabilities, 12*, 333–347.

Greene, M. L., & Way, N. (2005). Self-esteem trajectories among ethnic minority adolescents: A growth curve analysis of the patterns and predictors of change. *Journal of Research on Adolescence, 15*, 151–178.

Hansen, S., Meissler, K., & Ovens, R. (2000). Kids together: A group play therapy model for children with ADHD symptomatology. *Journal of Child and Adolescent Group Therapy, 10*, 191–211.

Hill, B. A., & Van Haren, J. (2005). *The AD/HD book: Answers to parents' most pressing questions*. New York: The Penguin Group.

Impett, E. A., Sorsoli, L., Schooler, D., Henson, J. M., & Tolman, D. L. (2008). Girls' relationship authenticity and self-esteem across adolescence. *Developmental Psychology, 44*, 722–733.

Kovacs, M. (1992). *Children's Depression Inventory (CD): Manual*. Toronto: Multi-Health Systems, Inc.

LaBarbera, R. (2008). Perceived social support and self-esteem in adolescents with learning disabilities at a private school. *Learning Disabilities: A Contemporary Journal, 6*, 33–44.

Lopez, E. E., Olaizola, J. H., Ferrer, B. M., & Ochoa, G. M. (2006). Aggressive and nonaggressive rejected students: An analysis of their differences. *Psychology in the Schools, 43*, 387–400.

McLoyd, V. C. (1998). Changing demographics in the American population. Implications for research on minority children and adolescents. In V. C. McLoyd & L. Steinberg (Ed.), *Studying minority adolescents: Conceptual, methodological, and theoretical issues* (pp. 3–20). Mahwah, NJ: Lawrence Erlbaum Associates.

Milevsky, A., Schlechter, M., Netter, S., & Keehn, D. (2007). Maternal and paternal parenting styles in adolescents: Associations with self-esteem, depression and life-satisfaction. *Journal of Child and Family Studies, 16*, 39–47.

Ojanen, T., & Perry, D. G. (2007). Relational schemas and the developing self: Perceptions of mother and of self as joint predictors of early adolescents' self-esteem. *Developmental Psychology, 43*, 1474–1483.

Raffaele Mendez, L., Mihalas, S. T., & Hardesty, R. (2006). Gender differences in academics. In G. G. Bear & K. M. Minke (Eds.), *Children's needs III: Development, prevention, and intervention* (pp. 553–565). Bethesda, MD: NASP University Press.

Rosenbloom, S. R., & Way, N. (2004). Experiences of discrimination among African American, Asian American, and Latino adolescents in an urban high school. *Youth and Society, 35,* 420–451.

Rudy, D., & Grusec, J. E. (2006). Authoritarian parenting in individualist and collectivist groups: Associations with maternal emotion and cognition and children's self-esteem. *Journal of Family Psychology, 20,* 68–78.

Sanders, K. Y. (2006). Overprotection and lowered expectations of persons with disabilities: The unforeseen consequences. *Work, 27,* 181–188.

Seidah, A., & Bouffard, T. (2007). Being proud of oneself as a person or being proud of one's physical appearance: What matters for feeling well in adolescence? *Social Behavior and Personality, 35,* 255–268.

Seidman, E., Lambert, L. E., Allen, L., & Aber, J. L. (2003). Urban adolescents' transition to junior high school and protective family transactions. *Journal of Early Adolescence, 23,* 166–193.

Sodowsky, G. R., Kwan, K. K., & Pannu, R. (1995). Ethnic identity of Asians in the United States. In J. G. Ponterotto, J. M. Casas, L. A. Suzuki, & C. A. Alexander (Eds.), *Handbook of multicultural counseling* (pp. 123–154). Thousand Oaks, CA: Sage.

Tarter, R., Blackson, T., Brigham, J., Moss, H., & Caprara G. V. (1995). The association between childhood irritability and liability to substance use in early adolescence: A 2 year follow-up study of boys at risk for substance abuse. *Drug and Alcohol Dependence, 39,* 253–261.

Thurber, J. R., Heller, T. L., & Hinshaw, S. P. (2002). The social behaviors and peer expectations of girls with attention deficit hyperactivity disorder and comparison girls. *Journal of Clinical Child and Adolescent Psychology, 31,* 443–452.

Vandeleur, C. L., Perrez, M., & Schoebi, D. (2007). Associations between measures of emotion and familial dynamics in normative families with adolescents. *Swiss Journal of Psychology, 66,* 5–16.

Verkuyten, M., Kinket, B., & Van der Wielen, C. (1997). The understanding of ethnic discrimination of preadolescents. *Journal of Genetic Psychology, 158,* 97–112.

Verkuyten, M., & Thijs, J. (2006). Ethnic discrimination and global self-worth in early adolescents: The mediating role of ethnic self-esteem. *International Journal of Behavioral Development, 30,* 107–116.

Vlam, S. L. (2006). Research to reality: Applying findings to practice. *Journal of School Nursing, 23,* 299–300.

Way, N., & Chen, L. (2000). The characteristics, quality, and correlates of friendships among African American, Latino, and Asian American adolescents from low-income families. *Journal of Adolescent Research, 15,* 274–301.

Wolraich, M. L., Feurer, I. D., Hannah, J. D., Baumgaertel, A., & Pinnock, T. Y. (1998). Obtaining systematic teacher reports of disruptive behavior utilizing DSM-IV. *Journal of Abnormal Child Psychology, 26,* 141–152.

Wolter, J. A., DiLollo, A., & Apel, K. (2006). A narrative therapy approach to counseling: A model for working with adolescents and adults with language-literacy deficits. *Language, Speech, and Hearing Services in Schools, 37,* 168–177.

Wright, M. A. (2000). *I'm chocolate, you're vanilla: Raising healthy black and biracial children in a race-conscious world.* San Francisco: Jossey-Bass.

Zalecki, C. A., & Hinshaw, S. P. (2004). Overt and relational aggression in girls with attention deficit hyperactivity disorder. *Journal of Clinical Child and Adolescent Psychology, 33,* 125–137.

8

Body Image, Eating Disorders, and Self-Esteem Problems During Adolescence

ANN JACOB SMITH

Adolescence is a border between childhood and adulthood. Like life on all borders, it is teeming with energy and fraught with danger.

—**Mary Pipher (1994)**

A dolescence is a time defined by its intense changes, a dramatic storm of physical, emotional, cognitive, and social development. Research suggests that self-esteem declines in early adolescence, particularly for females who report significantly lower rates of self-esteem and higher rates of depressed mood (Kearney-Cooke, 1999). Harter (2006) hypothesizes that this decline is most likely due to negative body images that emerge during pubertal changes. Physical appearance, in particular, contributes to self-esteem during the teenage years, and teenagers' perceptions of their attractiveness are the single, strongest predictor of adolescent self-esteem.

Typically, the physical changes associated with puberty begin between the ages of 9 and 12 in females, and 10 to 14 in males. Hormonal changes stemming from the pituitary gland lead to rapid and sometimes dramatic weight and growth spurts. As females experience the physical changes brought on by puberty (breast development, increase in height, development of body hair, and menarche), body fat percentages increase in ranges from approximately 16% to 26%, in just a few years. Males experience an increase in body hair, deepening of the voice, broadening of the shoulders, growth of the external genital areas, and increase in height and muscle mass. For both sexes, sexuality, romantic interest, and the importance of peer acceptance increase.

As biological processes transform the body, cognitive and emotional shifts also occur. Once self-confident children become self-conscious and introspective teenagers (Harter, 2006). This budding self-consciousness may further become a destructive tool for self-criticism and guilt. Emotional development plays a tremendous role in the building of self-concept. Although hormones can be blamed for emotionally volatility, negative emotions are more likely to be rooted in relationship stress with family and peers, or academics (Lin et al., 2008).

RELATIONSHIPS WITH PEERS AND PARENTS

Prior to the onset of puberty, relationships are largely based around family and same-sex friendships. By early adolescence, adolescent boys and girls report decreasing attachment to their parents and begin to interact in opposite-sex friendships and mixed-gender socializing. Social groups become a safe place where the adolescent can break away from the family and experience acceptance and security. While adolescent friendships can be both intense and volatile, they also provide the perception of a secure environment through which the adolescent can experiment with new expressions of identity and behaviors. The benefits of adolescent friendships are profound, teaching conflict resolution, compassion, empathy, and the giving and receiving of social feedback. Peer acceptance is critical, and interactions with peer groups can have a significant positive or negative effect on self-esteem (Anderson & Olnhausen, 1999).

Yet much of an adolescent's identity is shaped by parental relationships and significant events in the family's history (divorce, death, illness, or economic difficulties). Parental expectations set the standard for what behaviors are considered good enough. These expectations are explicitly expressed or implied through parental behavior, and cover most areas of the adolescent's life. Relationships with parents during adolescence, while often infused with conflict, are critically important to the development of self-esteem and positive body image.

Self-scrutiny and social evaluation also increase awareness of culture, race, and economics. As adolescents wrestle with personal identity and self-definition, they turn away from parents and, in many cases, turn toward ethnic roots for confirmation and identity. For many teenagers, this begins the process of ethnic or racial identity development, which is influenced by parents' ethnic socialization and by interaction with peers of diverse backgrounds (Hill, Bromell, Tyson, & Flint, 2007). Teenagers support their ethnic identity through the selection and exclusion of peers and activities. This tendency toward ethnic peer grouping and conformity is often viewed as an implicit norm in high school (Riera, 2004). Economic differences permeate adolescent culture through choices of clothing, cars, technology, and other material goods indicative of wealth. For those with access to money, it is a means of taking control of their lives and using material goods as a means of self-expression; those without spending money feel self-conscious and may choose peer groups based on financial status (Riera, 2004).

BODY IMAGE

Given all the rapid changes occurring both internally and externally, it is not surprising that much of adolescence for both males and females is spent in front of the mirror, preoccupied with others' perceptions of their body and the overwhelming desire to fit in. Generally, body perceptions measured during adolescence are markedly different depending on gender, with males being less negatively affected than females. The onset of problematic eating behaviors and body dissatisfaction in females has been closely linked to those growth spurt periods when hormones stimulate natural increases in body weight and fat (Sinton, Davison, & Birch, 2005). In general, females tend to be dissatisfied with their bodies, to the point that some refer to female negative body perceptions as a normative experience in our culture (Phillips, 2003).

Body image studies show that of all age groups, adolescents have the strongest physical appearance orientation and the most negative self-evaluations of appearance. At a time when body and mind are undergoing massive transformations, female adolescents particularly seem to have a hyperfocus on appearance and distorted body image concerns. Although teenage boys do suffer with body esteem issues during early adolescence, teenage females (typically White, but with increasing frequency among all races and ethnicities) are disproportionately affected by disorders related to eating, shape, and weight. In comparison to boys, physical development for girls can often be a more negative experience, associated with lower self-esteem, lower academic self-perceptions, depression, body dissatisfaction, and eating disorders (Kearney-Cooke, 1999).

ROLE OF POPULAR CULTURE ON BODY IMAGE AND SELF-ESTEEM

Experts in the field of development and body image describe a theoretical orientation known as developmental contextualism. In this model, thoughts and feelings about the body are seen as products of socialization that result from others' reactions to one's appearance. This feedback informs an adolescent's cognitive and emotional development involving the body; teenagers who perceive themselves as physically unattractive tend to have poor self-evaluations, and thus lower self-esteem, while those with positive body images tend to rate themselves more competently, with higher reported self-esteem (Lerner & Steinberg, 2004). Physical appearance directly links with self-esteem, as feedback from peers, schools, parents, and other adults informs an adolescent's perception of body attractiveness.

Adolescents' role models and ideals drift from family of origin toward peer groups and popular culture. The social influences of popular culture are societal norms that are passed on to the general public through the mass media. Today, adolescents living in the United States have broad access to the mass media of television, movies, music, magazines, and the Internet. In fact, a longitudinal study looking at media use during adolescence found that the average adolescent spends over 40 hours per week engaged with some form of media (Roberts & Foehr, 2004).

Brown and Strasburger (2007) suggest that the media have an impact on sex, drugs, aggressive behavior, academic success, obesity, eating disorders, and suicide. Professionals cannot underestimate the influence of this powerful force. Many experts in the field of eating disorders have implicated mass media as the "pusher" of unrealistic body ideals, which are then internalized by its young consumers. Teenagers are the primary audience of the popular media; both teenage girls and boys strongly believe that the mass media influences their body image, with increased exposure leading to worsening body image scores (Elgin & Pritchard, 2006; Polce-Lynch, Myers, Kliewer, & Kilmartin, 2001).

As the main consumers of popular media and the most vulnerable to its pressures, teenagers often see the underweight and physically fit body ideals depicted in the mass media as the standard against which they judge attractiveness, beauty, and wealth. Today, Western society's thin standard is increasingly difficult to reach, and so intolerant of fat that the urge to diet in females may begin as early as age 6 (Gardner, Stark, Fiedman, & Jackson, 2000). Exposure to thin media images lowers the domain of self-esteem focused specifically on appearance (Ip & Jarry, 2008).

SELF-ESTEEM AND OVERWEIGHT ADOLESCENTS

Those same images in popular culture driving females of normal development toward body dissatisfaction have an even greater consequence for those adolescents who are overweight. Both males and females report severe low self-esteem issues arising from their overweight status (Viner et al., 2006). Neumark-Sztainer, Wall, Story, and Fulkerson (2004) found that weight teasing by family, body dissatisfaction, and dieting/unhealthy weight control behaviors strongly and consistently predicted overweight status in teenagers.

It is not surprising that overweight adolescents suffer from low self-esteem. In a study examining peer perceptions of obese classmates, they were consistently rated by their peers as socially withdrawn, less physically attractive, less athletic, and more apt to be sick, fatigued, and absent from school (Zeller, Rieter-Purtill, & Ramsey, 2008). For both sexes, physical appearance self-esteem decreases as body mass index (BMI) increases. Further, obese female adolescents demonstrate increasingly lower levels of self-esteem as they mature. By early adolescence, those obese children with lower levels of self-esteem report significantly higher rates of sadness, loneliness, and nervousness and were more likely to smoke tobacco or consume alcohol (Strauss, 2000).

ADOLESCENT EATING DISORDERS AND SELF-ESTEEM

Depression, suicide, delinquency, and eating disorders are among some of the problems associated with low self-esteem in youth (Kearney-Cooke, 1999). In a study looking at a group of male and female adolescents ages 12–15, the lowest self-esteem scores were in the domains of romantic appeal and physical appearance

(French, Perry, Leon, & Fulkerson, 1996). Zerbe (1995) connects a "shaky self-esteem," mainly focused on appearance, with the development of eating disorders. She describes the process by which an adolescent girl "thwarted in following her own goals [will] receive powerful positive reinforcement for attaining and maintaining society's goals" (p. 102).

Evidence suggests strong associations between low self-esteem levels and risk for eating disorders, particularly in females. Although studies tend to vary in their method of evaluating self-esteem (global vs. selective domains), they agree that, particularly in adolescence, low self-esteem is a risk factor for the development of eating disorders and body dissatisfaction. Silverstone (1992) stated that low self-esteem is prerequisite to developing an eating disorder.

Eating disorders are fairly uncommon. The mean prevalence of anorexia nervosa in adolescents from Western Europe and the United States is 0.3%, and 1% for bulimia nervosa (Hock & van Hoeken, 2003). Although these numbers may not sound alarming, eating disorders are known to have the highest mortality rates of any of the psychiatric disorders in females, with a shocking standard mortality rate of 10.5 (Birmingham, Sue, & Hlynsky, 2005). Moreover, there is evidence that partial syndrome eating disorders, subclinical eating disorders, or eating disorders not otherwise specified may affect a much larger population. In one study, 56% of ninth grade females and 28% of ninth grade males reported at least one method of disordered eating (Croll, Neumark-Sztainer, Story, & Ireland, 2002).

Low self-esteem and perfectionism have been isolated as two of the highest risk factors for the development of eating disorders (Furnham, Badmin, & Sneade, 2002). Further, low self-esteem has been associated with poor response to treatment and relapse (Fairburn, 2008). Studies repeatedly show associations between low self-esteem and eating disorders, as well as increased risk of suicidal ideation (even in subclinical eating disorders) and multiple health compromising behaviors, including substance abuse and cigarette smoking. Unfortunately, even successful treatment of eating disorders has not been shown to improve self-esteem levels back to normal. While low self-esteem levels do improve with remission of symptoms, they rarely return to a normative level, which puts recovered adolescents at risk of relapse (Daley, Jimmerson, Heatherton, Metzger, & Wolfe, 2008).

GENDER AND MULTICULTURAL ISSUES RELATED TO BODY IMAGE AND SELF-ESTEEM

In general, eating disorders and the factors that contribute to eating disorders (body image dissatisfaction and eating disturbance) are most common among White female adolescents (Wildes, Emery, & Simmons, 2001). However, disordered eating is showing an increase among all social classes and ethnic groups in the United States and other nations. In fact, there appears to be only one ethnic group protected from Western society's thin ideal: African American teenage girls, whose self-esteem does not appear to be as heavily focused around appearance and shape or weight as it is for White teenage girls. A large epidemiological study found that African American girls appear to have higher and more stable self-esteem and greater satisfaction with their physical appearance than White girls (Brown et al., 1998). Almost uniformly, studies report that African American adolescent females participate in less dieting behavior, feel less pressure to be thin, and tend to report a more positive body image than White females (Malloy & Herzberger, 1998). One prevalent theory is that African American females have a strong sense of racial identity that serves as a protective factor, insulating physical appearance self-esteem through the rejection of White cultural ideals (Altabe, 1998; Negy, Shreve, Jensen, & Uddin, 2003).

Nevertheless, the past few years have seen a significant increase in the development of eating disorders in adolescent females of other races and ethnicities (Miller & Pumariega, 2001), who often report dieting behavior and eating disorder symptomology similar to White females. In fact, one study found that, regardless of ethnicity or gender, adolescents who participate in dieting behaviors tend to experience difficulties with body dissatisfaction, self-esteem, and depression similar to those of White females; males and females with a higher degree of acculturation tend to participate in weight control behaviors (Cachelin & Regan, 2006). Non-White adolescent females who follow cultural standards similar to those of White females tend to report similar body dissatisfaction and weight concerns in all measures of weight and body satisfaction (Altabe, 1998). Greater identification with popular culture tends to be related to the level of acculturation, low self-esteem, and a powerful need for societal acceptance (Gowen, Hayward, Killen, Robinson, & Taylor, 1999). Highly acculturated Asian American adolescent girls also reported significantly greater perfectionism scores, and specifically, body perfectionism.

An increasing number of males across different ethnicities also engage in weight control behaviors, with a growing percentage of males being admitted to inpatient eating disorder treatment facilities (Braun, Sunday, Huang, & Halmi, 1999). A recent study (Chao et al., 2008) found that both Latino and African American male adolescents reported more weight control behaviors than White males, perhaps due to a higher rate of obesity in Latinos, and a strong emphasis on athletic performance in Black adolescent males.

ASSESSMENT OF SELF-ESTEEM IN ADOLESCENTS

Assessment Tools

Researchers have long encouraged the use of a multidimensional approach to the study of self-esteem in adolescents. Their reasoning is that "young adolescents judge their self-worth on a variety of dimensions, including competence in physical appearance, social acceptance by peers, scholastic and athletic abilities or behavioral conduct." Valid and reliable assessment tools experiencing widespread use in the research literature include Shape and Weight Based Self-Esteem Inventory (Geller, Johnston, & Madsen, 1997, pp. 5–24), Harter Self-Perception Profile for Adolescents (Harter, 1988), and Body-Esteem Scale for Adolescents and Adults (Mendelson, Mendelson, & White, 2001). Each of these assessments breaks down self-esteem by dimensions or domains that are appropriate for adolescents.

Using Cognitive–Behavioral Skills for Assessment

For school counselors, who have greater access to the adolescent's everyday world, assessment of self-esteem can be made through observations from parents and teachers, written stories or poems, responses to interview questions, as well as pen-and-paper assessment tools (Brooks, 1992). Family counselors can also use family interviews to gather information about an adolescent's inner world and self-image. Fairburn (2008) offers clinical suggestions for assessing an individual's self-esteem. His interest is in determining whether the individual suffers from "core low self-esteem," a predictor of poor outcomes in eating disorder treatments. If core low self-esteem is present, Fairburn suggests a modified treatment path to address the low self-esteem more directly. Questions that will help to quantify global self-esteem without using a written assessment tool are to first ask the client how they define self-esteem (as noted earlier, there is little understanding of the actual definition), then ask the client, based on their definition of self-esteem, to rate their own on a Likert scale from 1 to 10. With younger adolescents, the counselor might be even more concrete by saying, "Compared to most of the kids your age, would you say your satisfaction with yourself, in general, is higher, the same, or lower?" The counselor can be more specific about the area, both high and low, in perceived selective esteem, saying, for example, "On a scale from 1 to 10, how satisfied are you with your body or appearance?" and "On a scale from 1 to 10, how satisfied are you with your academic performance?" Clients can be asked to compare their different domains of self-esteem and discuss the normalcy of differing levels of satisfaction among the varying domains. By quantifying areas of higher esteem, cognitive methods can help the client recognize that lower esteem in one area does not have to generalize to a global feeling of low self-esteem. Once clients have perspective regarding their own specific domains of low self-esteem, the counselor can begin targeting the areas of low self-esteem more directly.

MAKING A CASE FOR PREVENTION

Traditionally, eating disorder prevention programs have focused on eating disorder behaviors and symptoms. Treatment of self-esteem issues, particularly in early adolescence, may be the least harmful and most beneficial means of preventing eating disorders. In 2002, O'Dea and Abraham developed an eating disorder prevention program for both adolescent females and males focused on self-esteem. According to the authors, traditional programs are rarely effective in improving body image and eating behaviors and have even been shown to "glamorize and normalize eating disorders, and provide information on dangerous methods of weight control" (p. 44). Approximately 500 students ages 11–14 from both public and private schools participated in a nine-week program seeking to identify positive aspects of self, rather than communicating negative messages about dieting and weight control behaviors. It included coping with stress, challenging stereotypes and media ideals, learning how to positively self-evaluate and build one's self-esteem, asking for positive feedback from others, and improving relationship and communication skills. Students were also encouraged to work outside the program with family and friends, in order to learn how to elicit positive feedback from those who mattered in their lives. The intervention had a positive effect on low core self-esteem in adolescents who were considered to be at increased risk for eating disorders. Body dissatisfaction improved, and less emphasis was placed on physical appearance and social acceptance. This approach suggests that through exercises meant to improve global self-esteem, adolescents can become more resilient and resistant to the pressures from media, culture, and peers that encourage dieting and abnormal weight loss behaviors.

INTERVENTIONS TARGETING LOW SELF-ESTEEM IN ADOLESCENCE

If an adolescent has already developed an eating disorder, the interventions given in this section are not adequate, or appropriate, to treat a life-threatening disorder with high mortality rates. However, for the adolescent who does not yet have an eating disorder diagnosis, but who may be experiencing family problems, adjustment problems to school, relationship difficulties with peers, depression, anxiety, or other such disorders, the following interventions and preventative strategies may be useful for improving self-esteem, and thus potentially preventing the onset of a devastating, and potentially lethal, eating disorder. Because self-esteem has consistently been shown to be a risk factor predicting eating disorders, it is logical to target self-esteem as a means of preventing eating disorders.

Enhancing Global Self-Esteem

Parents, mentors, teachers, and counselors can aid in the development of self-esteem by encouraging teenagers to take responsibility for their mistakes, learning to be persistent, and developing a sense of self-responsibility and family responsibility (Everly, 2009). Didion (1968) stated it beautifully: "Character—the willingness to accept responsibility for one's own life—is the source from which self-respect springs." This sense of responsibility, both for self and to family, creates an overall feeling of competence and self-respect, both of which contribute to overall self-esteem. Global self-esteem can be enhanced when adolescents develop a sense of responsibility by making a personal contribution to their world (school, home, and neighborhood). For example, the counselor can encourage an adolescent client to participate in or initiate a community-based project that reflects an area of passion and concern, such as volunteering at the humane society, cooking dinner for the family once per week, tutoring younger children, or other contributory activities (Brooks, 1992). Each has the potential for achievement and increased competence.

Creating an environment where the adolescent has greater control can boost global self-esteem. A counselor can help the adolescents and their families create opportunities for them to make choices and decisions. Examples might include choosing the charity that the family sponsors, deciding where the family will go on vacation, or determining where and how he or she will study. Just as negative commentary and criticism contribute to low self-esteem, positive feedback can positively influence adolescent self-esteem.

Moreover, interventions targeting low self-esteem should begin early. The longer an adolescent lives with low self-esteem, the more difficult it becomes to change. School counselors or clinicians who conduct outreach activities at middle and high schools are in the unique position of being able to "strike while the iron is cold." These counselors have the opportunity to be proactive about pursuing adolescents who might be deemed at risk for low self-esteem and eating disorders, and conduct interventions before behavioral symptoms develop.

Cognitive–Behavioral Interventions

Cognitive–behavioral therapy has been shown to be successful in improving self-esteem and preventing depression in adolescence. Fairburn (2008) warns the clinician about poor eating disorder treatment outcomes for those who have "core low self-esteem." In his treatment manual, he goes over the basic tenets of cognitive–behavioral therapy (CBT), including the initial educational portion of CBT that involves teaching the participant about cognitive "distortions" that contribute to low self-esteem. Treatment involves self-awareness and active self-talk to refute negative thought patterns that lead to low self-esteem. Some examples of the distortions challenged through CBT include discounting positive self-qualities, paying selective attention to only negative feedback, setting higher standards for one's self than ever would be imposed on others, and over-generalizing any experience of nonsuccess as proof of a pattern of failure; at the same time, CBT teaches problem-solving skills, emotional control, and divergent thinking (Fairburn, 2008). The counselor may focus on one aspect of a student's personal competence, such as sense of humor and optimism, and challenge the adolescent to recognize attributes and talents outside of her appearance that serve in positive self-definition. Counselors then typically include some method of self-monitoring thoughts and behaviors outside of treatment.

Acceptance and Mindfulness Interventions

A recent movement emanating from a CBT foundation is acceptance and commitment therapy (ACT). This movement shows promise in improving self-esteem in adolescents. ACT involves experiential exercises, metaphors, behavioral tasks, and homework to develop psychological flexibility. For adolescents who are still bridging the gap between concrete and formal operational thinking, the use of metaphors and experiential learning is both appropriate and necessary.

ACT emphasizes acceptance, or "taking a stance of non-judgmental awareness and actively embracing the experience of thoughts, feelings and bodily sensations as they occur" (Hayes & Stroshal, 2004, p. 7). Adolescents commit to behavioral change processes and learn to tolerate intense feelings or bodily sensations without experiencing threat or needing to act. For example, someone with an eating disorder may be experiencing critical internal voices giving out negative body image messages regarding specific parts of their bodies. ACT would help that individual learn to accept that those voices are in attendance, but to commit to the long-term goal of not acting on those voices. With each refusal to engage in eating disordered behaviors, despite the internal voices, individuals gain a sense of accomplishment and confidence that they are in control. This sense of control translates into greater self-efficacy and self-esteem.

BEHAVIORAL INTERVENTIONS

Exercise has been positively correlated with high self-esteem in children and adolescents. Specifically, higher physical activity at ages 9 and 11 years predicted higher self-esteem at ages 11 and 13 years, respectively, controlling for covariates. Positive effects of physical activity on self-esteem were most apparent at age 11 and for girls with higher BMI (Schmalz, Deane, Birtch, & Davison, 2007). Thus, counselors should encourage healthy levels of physical activity in order to boost self-esteem levels. In overweight adolescents, the counselor should work to find a weight management program with more emphasis on exercise than on restriction of calories.

Other prevention programs have utilized mindfulness-based interventions to assist in both stress management and body awareness (Daubenmeri, 2005; Scime & Cook-Cottone, 2008). Yoga and meditation are effective tools for reducing anxiety and teaching methods of self-soothing. Diaphragmatic breathing techniques, progressive muscle relaxation, and meditation reduce anxiety and offer the adolescent skills that will benefit him or her throughout life.

BODY ESTEEM INTERVENTIONS

Because this chapter focuses on eating disorders in youth, the area of body esteem will be addressed more specifically. As discussed earlier, females, in particular, tend to put a heavy emphasis on body esteem during the teenage years. Therefore, counselors working with adolescents need a toolbox of strategies to address body esteem more specifically. Traditionally, these interventions have been known as body image interventions; improving a young female's perceptions of her own body is to increase body esteem. Therefore, these terms will be used interchangeably throughout this section. Strategies for body esteem improvement include the reduction of problematic behaviors that decrease body esteem, or improvement of body esteem through cognitive and behavioral interventions.

Reducing Behaviors That Impair Body Esteem

Body checking is a phenomenon that has just recently begun to be discussed in treatment literature. Shape checking occurs so frequently that many individuals with eating disorders are not even aware that they do it (Fairburn, 2008). Body or shape checking is the process of repeatedly checking one's body, often using unusual methods. These checking behaviors serve to continually reinforce negative body image. Such behaviors include self-measurement of areas of low body esteem and comparing one's body, shape, or eating habits with others'. The obvious example of checking behavior that involves measurement would be the scale, but there are multiple ways adolescent females with lower body esteem use that may go unnoticed. Some examples of body checking can include measuring legs, waist, and wrists using tools such as hands or tape measures, or using visual cues to see bones, such as the clavicle or hip bones. Educating the client about body checking and destructive comparative thinking patterns is the first task of the counselor (Fairburn, 2008).

If clients are aware that they engage in these behaviors, but are not aware of how often they do it, a useful exercise is to have clients chart their body checking behaviors using a self-monitoring tool. After gaining awareness of the frequency of body checking behaviors, the counselor and client together can strategize the best means of terminating the negative feedback loop. This might include throwing out the scale or tape measure, covering the full-length mirror for several weeks, or putting a rubber band on the wrist as a reminder not to measure wrists. For comparative thinking patterns, clients are also asked to monitor checking and record how often comparative thoughts occur. Once clients' awareness of comparative thinking has been raised, they are encouraged to challenge comparative thoughts and redirect thinking toward positive messages about the body.

Part of altering an adolescent's cognitive framework is encouraging a focus on balancing all domains of self-esteem, while lowering the importance placed on physical appearance. If interventions fail to decrease the level of importance placed on physical appearance, the counselor should work to boost the value given to other areas of self-esteem where the adolescent feels more competent (Kirsh et al., 2007).

Interventions to Improve Body Esteem

Concurrent to reducing problematic behaviors that reduce body esteem, the counselor should also be using strategies to improve body esteem. Counselors should inquire about areas of neutrality or satisfaction and encourage clients to focus on them when confronted with intrusive thoughts about areas of negative body esteem.

During adolescence, clothes play a large role in both reflecting and reinforcing body esteem. What types of clothes encourage positive body esteem should be determined, and clients can be encouraged to wear these clothes often while avoiding the clothes that reduce their body esteem. A counselor can often tell how clients feel about their body by noticing how they are dressed. Often, sessions can begin with an observation about clothes, which leads into an active discussion about body image on that day. If clients are undergoing treatment that requires weight regain, it is particularly important to address body esteem, and work with the client to challenge negative body image while improving body esteem with positive affirmations, distraction techniques, and flattering clothes.

INTERVENTIONS WITH FAMILY

Practitioners should make every effort to include families in their treatment. In the past, particularly when working with eating disordered clients, parents were seen as "the problem" and therapeutic work rarely included family. However, the most recent evidence-based studies have shown that parental involvement in treatment results in quicker recoveries, fewer relapses, and stronger family communication going forward (Lock, le Grange, Agras, & Dare, 2001).

Therapeutic work with the family is critical for an accurate assessment of the problem. Including the family in therapy provides a glimpse into the family dynamic that may be fostering or creating problems, and is more likely to result in interventions that are effective in impacting the entire system. Initially when a counselor begins individual treatment with the teenager, adolescents may be reluctant to pull family into sessions. Adolescents often do not want to reveal their difficulties to their parents, perhaps fearing disappointment or an invasion of privacy. A skilled therapist can reassure the adolescent that the purpose of including the family in treatment is to improve family communication and elicit the support of the family to help the adolescent overcome his or her presenting problem. Reassurance that personal information revealed in therapy will not be divulged typically appeases a reluctant teenager's fears.

Teaching Empathy and Appreciation for Differences

The relationship between self-esteem problems and family may stem from a mismatch in the temperamental characteristics of parent and child. Teenagers often perceive the tension or frustration of a parent with a different temperament and feel that they are disappointing the parent or failing to live up to the parent's expectations (Brooks, 1992). Counselors can facilitate understanding and more productive family functioning through educating families about a mismatch in temperament, and teaching parents to be more empathic, understanding, and appreciative of their child's unique needs and style, while shifting their expectations toward a direction more reflective of their child's personality and temperament (Brooks, 1992). Often, by counselors simply pointing out the difference in temperament, a parent who has perceived their child's behaviors as "wrong" or in need of correction can begin to appreciate their child's "different" behaviors as part of the unique characteristics that make up a growing individual.

Adjusting Family Communication Related to Weight and Shape

Negative body image in females, in particular, has been linked to negative parental comments (particularly fathers), or family criticism, about their child's shape and weight. Those who perceive parents as critical of their appearance or weight rate their family support poorly on surveys and tend to report lower global self-esteem (Taylor et al., 2006). While parents need to be open and communicative with their adolescent children, negative or teasing comments regarding the adolescent's weight can also greatly impact a teenager's body image and self-esteem

(Keery, Boutelle, van den Berg, & Thompson, 2005). Parents can help to boost body esteem, in particular, by making positive, accepting comments regarding their child's appearance and weight and discouraging their teenager from negative comments regarding their own shape, or the shape of their peers. Also, by modeling intolerance for critical comments related to body shape or weight, in general, adults can greatly influence the emphasis adolescents place on appearance and shape.

Practitioners can encourage changes at home that can lower the risk of eating disordered behaviors, increase self-esteem, and result in a closer relationship with parents. Recommendations include minimizing food rules and negative discussions about food; minimizing negative commentary about their child's or their own (parents') bodies or weight; providing healthy food options; offering meals at regular, structured mealtimes; and making mealtime positive family time (Loth, Neumark-Sztainer, & Croll, 2009). In general, adolescents who reported more frequent family meals, a high priority placed on eating meals together, a positive atmosphere at family meals, and a more structured family meal environment were less likely to engage in disordered eating (Neumark-Sztainer et al., 2004). If a school counselor is facilitating a prevention program, parents can be included in a structured, positive feedback exercise *unrelated to appearance*, which has been shown to significantly improve overall self-esteem and enhance body esteem (O'Dea & Abraham, 2000).

ROLE OF THE COUNSELOR

Practitioners have the ability to enhance and expand adolescents' self-esteem through the process of developing the therapeutic relationship, and the acceptance and positive regard that accompany a strong bond between counselor and client. Through acceptance, adolescents experience a sense of worthiness and importance that they may not have experienced before.

Depending on the context in which the counselor is seeing an adolescent, different interventions can be utilized to boost self-esteem. For those counselors who see adolescents presenting for the first time with depression or anxiety, this is an opportunity to address low self-esteem issues in a way that may prevent further pathology. If a counselor is offering individual or family therapy to an adolescent who has already developed an eating disorder or obesity, improving self-esteem will be only one aspect of the multiple interventions necessary to aid in recovery. Eating disorder treatment will be more effective overall if therapists include interventions targeting a deemphasis of appearance-related self-esteem and an increase in self-esteem related to other aspects of the adolescent's life. Whether working with the family to improve appearance-focused dialogue (including reducing negative comments), conducting prevention programs through the schools, or facilitating a life skills group, counselors serve a critical role in the development of healthy self and body esteem.

CASE STUDY

Alana is an attractive 16-year-old, wealthy, White Jewish teenager living in Washington, DC. She is a star soccer player and straight A student at a prestigious private school. This client is the daughter of a well-known physician and a stay-at-home mother raising her and her three siblings. Alana was referred for counseling by her soccer coach, as her negative mood and drastic weight loss were noticed by both teammates and teachers. Alana's current weight is lower than expected for her height, but has not dropped below the 85% threshold that is used in the classification of anorexia nervosa. During the assessment it is evident that Alana suffers from low self-esteem and disordered eating. She does not meet full criteria for an eating disorder, but she has begun to restrict her intake by excluding certain food groups from her diet. Her body esteem is extremely poor, with Alana reporting that she is a "fat pig" and "hates" her body.

A family assessment showed some communication problems, not only between Alana and her parents, but also between her mother and father. The family spent little time together. The father worked long days and rarely made it home for dinner. The mother was extremely thin herself, with a long history of dieting and restricting. She was exhausted and angry with the father for his lack of participation in the family's day-to-day life. The entire family seemed to overemphasize thinness and physical fitness. Both parents had extremely high expectations of Alana's grades and performance in soccer, and Alana's academics and athletics exempted her from any household responsibilities. Alana stated, "All they care about is my grades and if I'm winning at soccer. They didn't even notice I had lost weight, because it wasn't on my report card."

The counselor began working with Alana to help her improve her body image and stop restricting her food intake to lose weight. She helped the parents work through changing their schedules to accommodate family dinners every night and coached them on the appropriate language to use with regard to weight and shape. They were encouraged to begin giving Alana greater responsibilities around the house, including regular household chores and being in charge of her dog. Their tendency to criticize their children when they were less than perfect was challenged and extinguished through many painful and difficult family sessions. The counselor worked alone with Alana's parents to help them work together to ensure one or both of them ate breakfast and dinner with Alana every day. Alana's parents were encouraged to reduce their pressure on academics and sports and to focus more on spending time together, and reconnecting in their marriage.

The counselor worked with Alana to improve her self-esteem by expanding her view of herself to include her friendships, her spiritual life, a strong relationship with her grandparents, and her love of animals. By deemphasizing the importance of the selective self-esteem domains of Alana's appearance and performance, and by focusing on helping Alana have a more balanced view of herself, the counselor was able to help Alana improve her self-esteem, stop restricting her intake, stop hating her body, and avert the onset of an eating disorder.

CONCLUSION

Low self-esteem in adolescents is a risk factor for multiple health-threatening problems. Particularly for young females, a struggling self-esteem is a significant risk factor for eating disorders. While diagnosed eating disorders only affect a small proportion of teenagers in the United States and Western world, subclinical problems, disordered eating patterns, and abnormal weight loss methods plague a much wider segment of Western society's youth.

Counselors have a unique and important opportunity to intervene before such problems become lethal eating disorders, which are extremely difficult to treat successfully and suffer abysmal relapse and recovery rates. Through appropriate assessment and intervention, counselors can help adolescents improve self-esteem and balance out cultural messages about appearance and body ideals, while navigating the storm of adolescence healthily.

REFERENCES

Altabe, M. (1998). Ethnicity and body image: Quantitative and qualitative analysis. *International Journal of Eating Disorders, 23*, 153–159.

Anderson, J. A., & Olnhausen, K. S. (1999). Adolescent self-esteem: A foundational disposition. *Nursing Science Quarterly, 12*, 62–67.

Birmingham, C., Sue, J., & Hlynsky, J. (2005). The mortality rate from anorexia nervosa. *International Journal of Eating Disorders, 38*, 143–146.

Braun, D. L., Sunday, S. R., Huang, A., & Halmi, K. A. (1999). More males seek treatment for eating disorders. *International Journal of Eating Disorders, 25*, 415–424.

Brooks, R. B. (1992). Self-esteem during the school years. Its normal development and hazardous decline. *Pediatric Clinics of North America, 39*, 537–550.

Brown, J. D., & Stasburger, V. C. (2007). From Calvin Klein to Paris Hilton and MySpace: Adolescents, sex and the media. *Adolescent Medicine, 18*, 484–507.

Brown K. M., McMahon, R. P., Biro, F. M., Crawford, P., Schreiber, G. B., Similo, S. L., et al. (1998). Changes in self-esteem in black and white girls between the ages of 9 and 14 years. The NHLBI Growth and Health Study. *Journal of Adolescent Health, 23*, 7–19.

Cachelin F. M., & Regan, P. C. (2006). Prevalence and correlates of chronic dieting in a multi-ethnic U.S. community sample. *Eating and Weight Disorders, 11*, 91–99.

Chao, M., Pisetsky, E. M., Dierker, L. C., Dohn, F., Rosselli, F., May, A. M., et al. (2008). Ethnic differences in weight control practices among U.S. adolescents from 1995 to 2005. *International Journal of Eating Disorders, 41*, 124–133.

Croll, J., Neumark-Sztainer, D., Story, M., & Ireland, M. (2002). Prevalence and risk and protective factors related to disordered eating behaviors among adolescents: Relationship to gender and ethnicity. *Journal of Adolescent Health, 31*, 166–175.

Daley, K. A., Jimmerson, D. C., Heatherton, T. F., Metzger, E. D., & Wolfe, B. E. (2008). State self-esteem ratings in women with bulimia nervosa and bulimia nervosa in remission. *International Journal of Eating Disorders, 41*, 159–163.

Daubenmeri, J. J. (2005). The relationship of yoga, body awareness, and body responsiveness to self-objectification and disordered eating. *Psychology of Women Quarterly, 29*, 207–219.

Didion, J. (1968). *Slouching towards Bethlehem: Essays.* (pp. 145). New York: Farrar, Straus, & Giroux.

Elgin, J., & Pritchard, M. (2006). Gender differences in disordered eating and its correlates. *Eating and Weight Disorders, 11*, e96–e101.

Everly, G. S. (2009). *The resilient child: Seven essential lessons for your child's happiness and success.* New York: DiaMedica Publishing.

Fairburn, C. (2008). *Cognitive behavior therapy and eating disorders.* New York: Guilford Press.

French, S. A., Perry, C. L., Leon, G. R., & Fulkerson, J. A. (1996). Self-esteem and change in body mass index over 3 years in a cohort of adolescents. *Obesity Research, 4*, 27–33.

Furnham, A., Badmin, N., & Sneade, I. (2002). Body image dissatisfaction: Gender differences in eating attitudes, self-esteem, and reasons for exercise. *Journal of Psychology, 136*, 581–596.

Gardner, R. M., Stark, K., Fiedman, B. N., & Jackson, N. A. (2000). Predictors of eating disorder scores in children ages 6 through 14: A longitudinal study. *Journal of Psychosomatic Research, 49*, 199–205.

Geller, J., Johnston, C., & Madsen, K. (1997). The role of shape and weight in self-concept: The shape and weight based self-esteem inventory. *Cognitive Therapy and Research, 21*, 5–24.

Gowen, K. L., Hayward, C., Killen, J. D., Robinson, T. N., & Taylor, C. B. (1999). Acculturation and eating disorder symptoms in adolescent girls. *Journal of Research on Adolescence, 9*, 67–83.

Harter, S. (1988). *Manual for the Self-Perception Profile for Adolescents.* Denver, CO: University of Denver.

Harter, S. (2006). The development of self-representations in childhood and adolescence. In W. Damon & R. Lerner (Eds.), *Handbook of child psychology* (6th ed., pp. 506–561). New York: Wiley.

Hayes, S., & Stroshal, K. D. (Eds.) (2004). *A practical guide to acceptance and commitment therapy.* New York: Spring Science and Business Media, Inc.

Hill, N. E., Bromell, L., Tyson, D. F., & Flint, R. (2007). Developmental commentary: Ecological perspectives on parental influences during adolescence. *Journal of Clinical Child Adolescent Psychology, 36*, 356–366.

Hock, H., & van Hoeken, D. (2003). Review of the prevalence and incidence of eating disorders. *International Journal of Eating Disorders, 34*, 383–396.

Ip, K., & Jarry, J. L. (2008). Investment in body image for self-definition results in greater vulnerability to the thin media than does investment in appearance management. *Body Image, 5*, 59–69.

Kearney-Cooke, A. (1999). Gender differences and self-esteem. *Journal of Gender Specific Medicine, 2*, 46–52.

Keery, H., Boutelle, K., van den Berg, P., & Thompson, J. (2005). The impact of appearance-related teasing by family members. *Journal of Adolescent Health, 37*, 120–127.

Lerner, R. M., & Steinberg, L. (2004). The scientific study of adolescent development: Past, present and future. In R. Lerner & L. Steinberg (Eds.), *Handbook of adolescent psychology* (2nd ed., p. 1). New York: Wiley.

Lin, H. C., Tang, T. C., Yen, J. Y., Ko, C. H., Huang, C. F., Liu, S. C., et al. (2008). Depression and its association with self-esteem, family, peer and school factors in a population of 9586 adolescents in southern Taiwan. *Psychiatry Clinical Neuroscience, 62*, 412–420.

Lock, J., le Grange, D., Agras, W. S., & Dare, C. (2001). *Treatment manual for anorexia nervosa: A family-based approach.* New York: Guilford Press.

Loth, K. A., Neumark-Sztainer, D., & Croll, J. K. (2009). Informing family approaches to eating disorder prevention: Perspectives of those who have been there. *International Journal of Eating Disorders, 42*, 146–152.

Malloy, B. L., & Herzberger, S. D. (1998). Body image and self-esteem: A comparison of African-American and Caucasian women. *Sex Roles, 38*, 631–643.

Mendelson B. K., Mendelson, M. J., & White, D. R. (2001). Body-esteem scale for adolescents and adults. *Journal of Personality Assessment, 76*, 90–106.

Miller, M. N., & Pumariega, A. J. (2001). Culture and eating disorders: A historical and cross-cultural review. *Psychiatry, 64*, 93–110.

Negy, C., Shreve, T. L., Jensen, B. J., & Uddin, N. (2003). Ethnic identity, self-esteem, and ethnocentrism: A study of social identity versus multicultural theory of development. *Cultural Diversity and Ethnic Minority Psychology, 9*, 333–344.

Neumark-Sztainer, D., Wall, M., Story, M., & Fulkerson, J. A. (2004). Are family meal patterns associated with disordered eating behaviors among adolescents? *Journal of Adolescent Health, 35*, 350–359.

O'Dea, J. A., & Abraham, S. (2000). Improving the body image, eating attitudes and behaviors of young male and female adolescents: A new educational approach that focuses on self-esteem. *International Journal of Eating Disorders, 28*, 43–57.

Phillips, S. (2003). Adolescent health. In I. B. Weiner (Ed.), *Handbook of psychology* (Vol. 9, pp. 465–486). New York: Wiley.

Pipher, M. (1994). *Reviving Ophelia: Saving the selves of adolescent girls* (p. 292). New York. Random House.

Polce-Lynch, M., Myers, B. J., Kliewer, W., & Kilmartin, C. (2001). Adolescent self-esteem and gender: Exploring relations to sexual harassment, body image, media influence and emotional expression. *Journal of Youth and Adolescence, 30*, 225–244.

Riera, M. (2004). *Uncommon sense for parents with teenagers* (rev. ed.). Berkeley, CA: Celestial Arts.

Roberts, D. F., & Foehr, U. G. (2004). *Kids and media in America.* Cambridge, UK: Cambridge University Press.

Schmalz, D. L., Deane, G. D., Birch, L. L., & Davison, K. K. (2007). A longitudinal assessment of the links between physical activity and self-esteem in early adolescent non-Hispanic females. *Journal of Adolescent Health, 41*, 559–565.

Scime, M., & Cook-Cottone, C. (2008). Primary prevention of eating disorders: A constructivist integration of mind and body strategies. *International Journal of Eating Disorders, 41*, 134–142.

Silverstone, P. H. (1992). Is chronic low self-esteem the cause of eating disorders? *Medical Hypotheses, 39*, 311–315.

Sinton, M., Davison, K. K., & Birch, L. L. (2005, April). *Evaluating the association between girls' reactions to pubertal development and girls' risk for body dissatisfaction and disordered eating.* Paper presented at the annual meeting of the Academy for Eating Disorders, Montreal, Canada.

Strauss, R. S. (2000). Childhood obesity and self-esteem. *Pediatrics, 105*, e15.

Taylor, C. B., Bryson S., Celio Doyle, A. A., Luce, K. H., Cunning, D., Abascal L. B., et al. (2006). The adverse effect of negative comments about weight and shape from family and siblings on women at high risk for eating disorders. *Pediatrics, 118*, 731–738.

Viner, R. M., Haines, M. M., Taylor, S. J., Head, J., Booy, R., & Stansfeld, S. (2006). Body mass, weight control behaviours, weight perception and emotional well being in a multiethnic sample of early adolescents. *International Journal of Obesity, 30*, 1514–1521.

Wildes, J. E., Emery, R. E., & Simons, A. D. (2001). The roles of ethnicity and culture in the development of eating disturbance and body dissatisfaction: A meta-analytic review. *Clinical Psychology Review, 21*, 521–551.

Zeller, M. H., Reiter-Purtill, J., & Ramey, C. (2008). Negative peer perceptions of obese children in the classroom environment. *Obesity, 16*, 755–762.

Zerbe, K. J. (1995). *The body betrayed. A deeper understanding of women, eating disorders, and treatment.* Carlsbad, CA: Gurze Books.

9

At-Risk Adolescents
Self-Esteem, Youth Violence, and Teen Pregnancy

DAVID A. CRENSHAW AND JENNIFER LEE

At-risk youth can suffer various forms of devaluation, assaults on their dignity and self-esteem that are at the core of deep, invisible emotional wounds that can result in violent acts or risky sexual behavior. To adequately address the complicated emotional underpinnings to youth violence requires careful exploration of the blows to their self-worth and sense of humanity.

Teenage girls at risk for early pregnancies may in some cases be seeking acceptance, resulting from invisible wounds of rejection, low self-esteem, and lack of belonging, although these are only some of the multiple influences that contribute to teen pregnancies. Youth violence and teen pregnancy are presented in this chapter as examples of self-esteem issues in at-risk adolescents.

YOUTH VIOLENCE AND SELF-ESTEEM

Assaults on the self-esteem of our youth can lead in extreme cases to a demoralizing cycle that culminates in violent behavior. These assaults on the self-esteem of adolescents often span a spectrum of devaluation. Devaluation takes many forms and is defined as "a process that strips a person or a group of dignity and a sense of worth" (Hardy & Laszloffy, 2005, p. 35).

Abandoned, neglected, or abused infants and children, regardless of race, gender, or class, will suffer devaluation that may in some cases leave lasting scars. It is crucial, however, that we not assume lasting scars because there are numerous exceptions, and the strength and resilience of children to overcome a harsh beginning in life should never be underestimated. Nevertheless, the powerful unavoidable message to these children is that they were rejected to one degree or another by their primary caretakers, usually the biological parents. The resulting wounds can be aggravated further when some of these children are placed in foster care and moved from one family or one out-of-home placement to another. The authors know from their extensive work in the foster care system of children who by the time they were eight years old lived in as many as 14 different temporary foster homes. Each failed placement inflicts a still deeper blow to their sense of worth as human beings. We can't emphasize enough that these wounds are not inevitable, particularly in the sense of leaving lasting scars. It is not, however, the norm or always possible for children who suffer repeated rejection by the caretakers in their early life to achieve a positive outcome. The resilience of some children in the foster care system, compared to others, may be due to differences in positive and affirmative feedback from significant others in their lives.

A child born poor, regardless of color or gender, will suffer devaluation that is likely to impact global self-esteem. Such children will quickly learn when they enter school that the clothes they wear are not up to the style and tastes of the more affluent children, and they realize early on that they are marginalized in their social group. Growing up in poverty can have a devastating impact. Even when reaching adulthood, no matter what degree of success they achieve, some will in the inner recesses of their psyche still feel poor. These adults may feel undeserving of their success, particularly if members of their family, parents, and siblings are still mired in the poverty that marred their childhood.

Children who are bullied, taunted, scapegoated, or experience social rejection from peers suffer greatly not only during childhood but also into their adult lives. Garbarino (2006) noted that social rejection is a kind of "psychological malignancy." He observed that in every culture, studies have concluded that children who are habitually socially rejected in childhood do not fare well in life. Although there are exceptions, social acceptance and belonging is one of our most basic human needs and directly impacts global self-esteem because the denial of positive feedback from peers can negate feelings of self-worth and acceptance. Conversely, the child development literature repeatedly shows that positive social adjustment in childhood is one of the most robust predictors of successful adjustment as adults.

Devaluation is especially salient for U.S.-non-dominant-culture, at-risk youth. Children of color find it difficult to negotiate development, particularly in the adolescent years, without internalizing to some degree self-hatred reflecting the sense of being "second class" in a White male-dominant culture (Hardy & Laszloffy, 2005; Liang & Fassinger, 2008). Studies have shown an inverse relationship between racism and both self-esteem and life satisfaction among African American students and adults (Broman, 1997; Jackson et al., 1996). Studies of the effects of racism on Asian Americans revealed that perceived racism adversely affects community as well as social well-being, depression, and psychological distress (Lee, 2003), quality of life (Utsey, Chae, Brown, & Kelly, 2002), and subjective competence (Ying, Lee, & Tsai, 2000). To the extent that devaluing attitudes of the dominant culture are internalized by children of color, it will negatively impact their global sense of self.

Research on Violence and Self-Esteem

The research on the relationship of self-esteem to violence yields conflicting results. Some of the variation in results may be due to methodological problems in measuring self-esteem by relying on self-report measures, but cultural influences may play a role as well. In addition, selective self-esteem, for example, may be bolstered by reinforcement from peer subgroups when engaging in antisocial behavior such as bullying or substance abuse, but selective or contingent self-esteem tends to be less stable than global self-esteem. What is valued in the peer group may be devalued by parents and teachers, but for some adolescents the evaluation by peers will carry more weight than feedback from adults.

To illustrate these conflicting findings, a study by Kunchandy (2008) found that low self-esteem in urban African American youth was related to an increased number of aggressive acts. In a study of the effects of self-esteem on substance abuse, however, Ostrowsky (2008) found that low self-esteem and depression were not associated with either increased alcohol use, use of marijuana, or violent behavior. In fact, with older adolescent girls, high self-esteem was associated with increased violence. This latter finding may partly be explained by a separate ethnographic study of female youth in two poverty-stricken inner-city neighborhoods that found establishing a reputation through violence provided the adolescent girls with a measure of security as well as a sense of mastery, status, and self-esteem (Ness, 2005). In other words, toughness and ability to fight may have led to high selective self-esteem due to the reinforcement of the subculture and the survival value of such skills in the inner city. This finding, however, may not reflect true high global self-esteem but compensatory self-esteem.

Some of the confusion in the literature may be explained by Sandstrom and Jordan (2008). They pointed out that researchers have relied on explicit measures of self-esteem, thus conflating two distinct types of positive self-regard: secure self-esteem (characterized by high levels of explicit and implicit self-esteem) and defensive self-esteem (characterized by high levels of explicit but low levels of implicit self-esteem). Sandstrom and Jordan tested the hypothesis that children with high levels of defensive, but not secure self-esteem would engage in higher levels of aggressive behavior. In their study, 93 children completed measures of both explicit and implicit self-esteem. Teachers assessed children's level of physical and relational aggression in the school setting. As predicted, there was a positive association between explicit self-esteem and aggression when levels of implicit self-esteem were low, but not when levels of implicit self-esteem were high.

A study by Benda and Corwyn (2002) on the effects of abuse on child and adolescent violence found that in a study of 1,031 participants (13–18 years old), self-esteem, attachments to female caretakers, and father's education were inversely related to violence. Suicide attempts were found to be positively related to violence, but only in the group 15 years of age and younger. Attachment to father, beliefs, and religiosity were inversely related to violence, whereas frustration and alienation were positively related to violence in both younger and older adolescents.

One of the most insidious forms of devaluation is child abuse and neglect. Greenburg and Paivio (1997) studied the core emotions of childhood abuse survivors.

They found that the core maladaptive affects were shame and fear/anxiety. Shame and fear/anxiety were coupled with two basic views of self: feelings of worthlessness and a sense of the self as weak. Feelings of worth and competence are core components of global self-esteem, and the lack of competence may be linked to the view of the self as weak. In addition, maladaptive core feelings of shame were linked to the "bad me" sense of self, and fear was linked with the "weak me." Greenburg and Paivio also found that rage can be a core maladaptive feeling, especially when there has been exposure to violence. They concluded that rage is often closely linked to fear and connected to an underlying sense of vulnerability. Greenburg (2002) explained that destructive anger and rage typically derive from a history of witnessing or suffering violence and typically lead to serious relationship problems that can take the form of the insecure/ambivalent attachment patterns.

The research of Main and Cassidy (1988) revealed how early the impact of abuse and exposure to violence can impair relationships with others. In studying the responses of abused and disadvantaged toddlers to distress in same-age peers, they found that not a single child who was abused showed concern in response to the distress of an age mate. Rather, the abused toddlers often reacted to the distress of an age mate with disturbing behavior patterns, such as physical attacks, fear, or anger. Three of the abused toddlers alternatively attacked and sought to comfort their peers in distress. By contrast, disadvantaged but nonabused toddlers in this seminal study responded to the distress of age mates with simple interest, concern, empathy, or sadness. The abused children showed a critical deficit in capacity for empathy, and that is a crucial factor in breaking the cycle of violence.

The problem of youth violence is multidetermined and defies linear explanations. Schwartz and DeKeseredy (2008) pointed out that a strategy to solve the problem of interpersonal violence by focusing on the private problems of individuals is doomed to failure. A major source of devaluation in our culture is the prevailing attitudes toward girls and women. Schwartz and DeKeseredy noted the powerful impact of social forces that leads to more societal outrage toward the mistreatment of dogs than is typically elicited in response to violence toward women. If we are to progress in solving the problem of youth violence, children need to grow up in a society where the same intensity of outrage accompanies acts of violence toward women.

TEEN PREGNANCY AND SELF-ESTEEM

Data from the U.S. Centers for Disease Control and Prevention (CDC; 2008) reveal that about one-third of girls in America become pregnant before the age of 20. According to a survey conducted by the Guttmacher Institute (2006), approximately 750,000 females between the ages of 15 and 19 become pregnant each year. With the highest rates among developed countries, teenage pregnancy remains a significant threat to adolescent health in the United States (CDC, 2008).

Teenage pregnancy rates in the United States were recently at their lowest levels in 30 years, showing a 36% decrease compared to peak pregnancy rates in 1990 (Guttmacher Institute, 2006). Research suggests that increased abstinence and contraceptive practices may account for the decrease (Santelli, Lindberg, Finer, &

Singh, 2007). However, a more recent report found that the steadily declining teen pregnancy rates in the United States may be ending, with rates increasing from 40.5 births per 1,000 teenage girls in 2005 to 41.9 births per 1,000 in 2006, the most recent year of available data (CDC, 2008).

The problem of teenage pregnancy has been further inflamed by recent media reports by *Time* magazine (Kingsbury, 2008) on an alleged "teenage pregnancy pact" at Gloucester High School in Massachusetts, where 17 teenage girls became pregnant, a rate four times higher than that of the previous year. School officials revealed that the girls, all under the age of 16, made an agreement to get pregnant on purpose and raise their babies together. Searching for the culprit had many people speculating about the girls' need to belong to counteract feelings of social isolation and low self-esteem, the influence of peer pressure, the impact of broken families, and the lack of parental supervision and family support. The incident remains under investigation at the time of this writing, leaving many questions unanswered, yet it underscores the persistence of teenage pregnancy as a national health issue.

Research on Teenage Pregnancy and Self-Esteem

Conventional wisdom suggests that low self-esteem and poor self-image in girls lead to more sexual risk-taking behaviors, such as unprotected sex and multiple sexual partners, thereby increasing the risk of unplanned pregnancies and contracting sexually transmitted diseases. If prevention efforts focus on increasing teenage girls' self-esteem levels, they will engage less in risky sexual behaviors, thereby reducing the rates of teenage pregnancy. However, the extant literature on the relationship between self-esteem and adolescent pregnancy remains inconclusive. While some researchers found significant correlations between low self-esteem and teenage pregnancy, others found significant correlations in the opposite direction, and still others found marginal or no association between the variables.

Hockaday, Crase, Shelley, and Stockdale (2000) conducted a prospective study to examine factors that contribute to pregnancy in a sample of pregnant adolescents ($n = 452$) and a nonpregnant comparison group ($n = 373$). Results indicated that pregnant adolescents were more likely than the comparison group to have lower self-esteem, and engage more in risk-taking behaviors such as alcohol use and early sexual activity. Pregnant adolescents were also more likely to have lower educational expectations, mothers with fewer years of education, and more traditional attitudes about women's familial roles.

In a longitudinal study by Ethier et al. (2006), the relationship between psychological factors and sexual behavior was studied in a sample of sexually active female adolescents. The researchers found that early sexual activity and history of risky sexual partners were related to lower self-esteem, and lower self-esteem predicted increased risk of unprotected sex six months later. However, the study was limited by its focus on sexually active individuals and retrospective reports. It is unclear whether the same girls had lower self-esteem before initiating sex, leaving the causal relationship between self-esteem and subsequent sexual behavior still in question.

In contrast to the aforementioned studies, Medora and von der Hellen (1997) found no significant differences in self-esteem levels between pregnant teens, teen mothers, and the control group consisting of nonpregnant and nonparenting teens. The mean scores, as measured by the Bachman Self-Esteem Scale, were slightly higher for the pregnant teens and teen mothers than for the control group. Similarly, Robinson (1994) investigated the relationship between self-esteem, sexual behaviors, and teen pregnancy, and found no significant differences in self-esteem levels between sexually active and nonsexually active females, or between pregnant adolescents and their nonpregnant peers. Most pregnant teens in this sample lived in rural environments, and most were in their last trimester of pregnancy. The author posits that a positive self-concept fostered by community values and family acceptance may help the pregnant teens adapt to their situation.

Limitations of the Research

Although research studies have investigated the potential relationship between self-esteem and sexual behavior, causation has not been established, and the determinants of sexual behavior among adolescents remain unclear. Boden and Horwood (2006) point out significant limitations in the literature, the most important being the exclusion of social and contextual factors that contribute to self-esteem development and risky sexual behavior. The authors explain that low self-esteem tends to be more common in individuals who experience multiple disadvantages, such as socioeconomic deprivation, family dysfunction, and exposure to abuse, factors that are related to sexual risk-taking behavior. In their 25-year longitudinal study, the relationship between self-esteem, later risky sexual behavior, and its consequences among adolescents was examined. Results showed that lower self-esteem at age 15 was related to increased risk of unprotected sex, more sexual partners, and greater risk of pregnancy. However, after adjusting for potential confounding variables, such as family functioning, family socioeconomic background, child abuse, and individual characteristics, the relationship was nonsignificant. The authors conclude that the effects of self-esteem on sexual behavior and pregnancy were modest, and suggest that contextual factors may be more important determinants of risky sexual behavior than direct effects of self-esteem. Their findings illuminate a general process in which the development of low self-esteem and increased sexual risk taking unfolds within the psychosocial context of the individual.

Another explanation of the inconsistent findings across studies in the teen pregnancy literature may be the lack of clarity and imprecise definitions of self-esteem. As this book suggests, self-esteem as a construct includes both global and selective components, with the latter having varying significance to the self. This fluctuating self-attitude depends on experience and role-defining characteristics, thereby making the construct difficult to define and measure reliably across studies. Differentiating between global and selective self-esteem elements, identifying the underlying factors, and understanding the relationship between these components would be an important strategy to clarify the inconsistent results among studies.

Overall, similar to the existing literature on self-esteem and violence, the literature on self-esteem and teen pregnancy is inconclusive. The complex relationship likely involves a wide range of interacting variables, underscoring a need for pre-vention efforts that target contextual factors rather than individual characteristics in isolation.

INTERVENTION STRATEGIES FOR AT-RISK ADOLESCENTS

Intervention Strategies for Adolescents at Risk for Violence

It is hard to overstate the devastating impact of social rejection and isolation that often accompanies victimization of children on self-esteem, however it is defined or measured.

Overall, the authors adhere primarily to a relational therapy orientation and believe that just as the woundedness of youth stems largely from strained or frac-tured relationships, healing also takes place in a relational context of safety, trust, warmth, and genuineness. In addition, strengths-based and competency-based approaches to child, adolescent, and family therapy are particularly relevant to intervening with potentially violent youth suffering from low self-esteem. Currie (2004), in a sociological study of contemporary youth, found that a crucial turning point in the lives of at-risk youth was learning how to care about themselves—to view themselves as people of value, who really matter. This turning point was facilitated by "charismatic adults" (Brooks & Goldstein, 2004), defined as adults from whom adolescents can gather strength. Charismatic adults retained faith in the youth and saw strength and virtue in them.

Brooks (1993) urged therapists and parents to look for "islands of competence" in youth. Hardy and Laszloffy (2005) advocated a similar approach. They urged therapists to honor "badges of ability" in youth. The therapeutic focus becomes one of identifying two or three of the youngster's best abilities and encouraging pride in the ownership of these talents. It speaks to enhancing salient positive selective self-esteem domains. Validating the abilities of these youngsters is one of the more effective interventions with potentially violent young people (Crenshaw & Garbarino, 2007). Typically, these talents and abilities are a hidden dimension in the lives of violent youth, along with their unspeakable sorrow (Crenshaw & Garbarino, 2007). The opportunities for children of color, children of poverty, chil-dren with special needs, and children whose sexual orientation is nonheterosexual to receive validation of their talents are more limited than they are for children of the majority cultural and middle- and upper-class socioeconomic groups. This intervention is often overlooked because it is so simple and straightforward that it is not seen as a potent tool in turning around the lives of disenfranchised teens.

A recent study of a strengths-based approach with adolescents showed good results in preventing substance abuse (Tebes et al., 2007). Adolescents receiving the positive youth development after-school program in an urban setting were sig-nificantly more likely to view drugs as harmful at program exit, and exhibited sig-nificantly lower increases in alcohol, marijuana, other drug use, and any drug use one year after beginning the program. The use of a strengths-based approach in residential treatment has shown positive results in terms of enhancing children's treatment and education along with decreasing numbers of safety holds and need for out-of-classroom supports (Kalke, Glanton, & Cristalli, 2007). The strengths-based approach has shown promise in engaging families as well as improving treatment outcome for youth in residential treatment programs (Nickerson, Salamone, Brooks, & Colby, 2004). Six case studies of youth at risk highlighted the practical details of implementation of a strengths-based approach (Cristantiello, Crenshaw, & Tsoubris, 2008). It is likely that all of the mentioned strengths-based approaches increase the sense of worth, competence, and achievement, and provide opportunities for positive feedback from others that contribute to global self-esteem, and to a selective sense of self-esteem when specific strengths are validated.

In view of the growing theoretical and empirical support for strengths-based approaches with at-risk youth, a number of specific interventions have been developed that can be used in individual, group, or family therapy. One such intervention is the Ballistic Stallion, a projective drawing and storytelling strategy that can be used with preteens and adolescents (Crenshaw, 2006, 2008). The intervention is a three-part strategy that includes the therapist telling the story of the Ballistic Stallion, followed by a drawing exercise, and then the preteen or adolescent telling a story in response to the original story. The story features 12-year-old Sally, who undertakes what appeared to be an impossible task of riding a stallion that no one else was able to ride, thus prompting her father to want to sell the horse. Sally was able to achieve her goal just in time to prevent the sale of the horse. The story then is followed by directives for the youngster to draw the Ballistic Stallion and, even more relevant to the theme of this chapter, to then tell a story of a triumph of their own. The teens are told to tell a story about a time when they overcame the odds, when they were able to accomplish something that appeared to be impossible, perhaps something that no one else felt they could do, but they did it. It is emphasized that it need not be something as dramatic or heroic as riding a stallion in the story, but a time when they felt justly proud because they were able to face and overcome a difficult challenge. This strategy is a way of bringing into sharp focus the strength, talents, courage, and determination of the child. Strengths identified are located in the client and are not dependent on the continuing presence of the therapist in the teen's life. Focusing on such strengths and qualities in the adolescent will contribute to selective self-esteem by increasing their sense of worthiness, competency, and achievement when specific skills or qualities are highlighted.

Another specific tool for focusing on the competency and strength of teens is a variation of the Heartfelt Feelings Coloring Card Strategies (HFCCS) that were developed with two primary domains: the expressive and the relational (Crenshaw, 2008). The *expressive* component is used as a psychoeducational tool to teach younger children to identify feelings and develop a vocabulary for expressing a range of emotions. The *relational* domain, however, can be used with older children and adolescents to explore key interpersonal relationships. The everyday heroes is one of the relational strategies that specifically focus on strengths. This tool can be used in individual, group, or family therapy. The cards are printed in the form of greeting cards and are published by the Coloring Card Company (www.coloringcardcompany.com). The teen is asked to draw in the heart shape printed on the front of the card a personal everyday hero or heroine. Everyday heroes don't usually hit home runs on national TV or get awarded medals for brav-ery, but they might stand up for a friend, admit when they are wrong, do the right thing when it is unpopular, and be heroic in countless other ways that "fly under the radar." When they have drawn their "everyday hero or heroine," they are then asked to write on the inside of the greeting card a note to the person they picked. The final step is to ask them to identify if in some way they have been an everyday hero to someone or if someone in their family has been one even if not recognized by others. Family everyday heroes can serve as positive sources of identification for the teen. Everyday heroes also offer opportunities for strengthening global self-esteem, and by validating specific qualities such as courage or determination, this task can also increase selective self-esteem.

A nontraditional intervention that has received some empirical support is mar-tial arts training (Blowers, 2007). High-risk adolescents improved from baseline measurements in self-esteem and a less favorable attitude toward violence. High-risk no-training comparison group peers did not show the same degree of positive change. It could be that the martial arts training contributed to the adolescents' sense of competence and achievement.

Prevention Strategies for Adolescents at Risk for Pregnancy

Researchers advocate the need for more comprehensive efforts to prevent teenage pregnancy, aside from those focused on enhancing self-esteem, to include psycho-logical, social, and interpersonal factors (Ethier et al., 2006). Some suggest that self-esteem needs to be reconceptualized to expand the view that low self-esteem causes maladaptive behaviors to a more comprehensive understanding that takes into account economic, family, and personal difficulties. Boden and Horwood (2006) recommend that interventions focus on improving the psychosocial condi-tions within which individuals develop. The following prevention strategies are examples of teenage pregnancy prevention programs that target the problem from multiple levels—individually, interpersonally, and systemically.

Robin et al. (2004) reviewed adolescent sexual risk reduction programs aimed at decreasing the risk of teenage pregnancy and enhancing psychosocial determinants. The authors cite Safer Choices, a two-year school-based program shown to be effec-tive in reducing the frequency of unprotected sex among high school students (Coyle et al., 1999). The multicomponent program has a unique focus on systemic change within the school and the influence of the environment on adolescent behavior. The program components include school organization, curriculum and staff devel-opment, peer resources and school environment, parent education, and school–community linkages. Results showed that the program had a positive impact on numerous psychosocial variables, including knowledge, self-efficacy for condom use, normative beliefs and attitudes regarding condom use, perceptions about risk, and parent–child communication. Although Safer Choices was not successful at delay-ing the onset of sex or decreasing the number of sexual partners, it was effective in promoting contraceptive use, thereby reducing the frequency of unprotected sex.

Competence-based interventions aimed to elevate educational values and academic success may also help adolescents delay sexual activity and delay childbearing in young girls. These strategies are based on the "status failure" explanation that adolescents with low educational ability and aspirations may be more likely to become pregnant and drop out of school, whereas adolescent girls with higher educational aspirations are less likely to engage in sexual activity and will intentionally delay pregnancy to pursue their goals (Hockaday, Crase, Shelley, & Stockdale, 2000). Youth interventions geared toward enhancing integral elements of self-esteem such as competence and academic success have shown promise in reducing sexual risk behavior (Robin et al., 2004). The Teen Outreach Program and the Seattle Social Development Program are two such competence-based programs.

The Teen Outreach Program is a resiliency-based intervention that integrates volunteer community service with classroom discussions about future life options to reduce the risk of teen pregnancy and academic failure. Results of one study showed that high school students in the experimental group had significantly lower rates of teen pregnancy, school suspensions, and academic failure than students in the control group (Allen, Philliber, Herling, & Kuperminc, 1997). An important feature of the program is that it does not explicitly focus on the specific problem behaviors it aims to prevent. Instead, it enhances the individual's competence in decision making, managing emotions, and positive interactions with peers and adults, all elements in healthy self-esteem. The program also helps students establish autonomy, while fostering a sense of connection with significant others. The effectiveness of the intervention points to the potential value in looking beyond micro-skills development to target a wider range of developmental tasks of adolescence.

The Seattle Social Development Project is another youth resiliency program, developed for elementary school students. The program, based on the social development model, promotes school and family bonding, academic success, and social competence to decrease health risk behaviors through various methods, including teacher training, parent training, and social competence training for children (Hawkins, Catalano, Kosterman, Abbott, & Hill, 1999). The main hypothesis suggests that strong bonds of attachment and commitment to school can protect against problem behaviors, while carving a developmental path toward positive academic outcome and fewer risky behaviors later in adolescence. Results of one study by Hawkins and colleagues (1999) showed that students in the experimental group, who received the intervention in first through sixth grades, were less likely to report being sexually experienced, having multiple sex partners, and being pregnant or causing pregnancy by age 18 than the control group. Experimental group participants also reported more commitment and attachment to school, less misconduct, and better academic achievement than control group participants.

In another longitudinal study, the long-term effects of the Seattle Social Development Project on sexual behavior and pregnancy were examined (Lonczak, Abbott, Hawkins, Kosterman, & Catalano, 2002). Results found that the intervention group reported significantly fewer sexual partners and more condom use during last intercourse than the control group. Female participants were significantly less likely to become pregnant and experience birth by 21 years of age. The study provided further support for the promotion and development of critical components of self-esteem, including social bonding, academic achievement, and social competence in preventing risky sexual practices and unwanted pregnancies in early adulthood.

CASE STUDY

Nicole, at 15 years old, was a new transfer student. She had a long history of behavioral problems and was labeled a "troublemaker" in her previous school, a label that she wore like a badge in her new school.

Nicole's behavioral records from elementary school showed numerous suspensions for physical fights with students and verbal altercations with teachers. Although of average IQ and academic ability, she showed little interest in her academics and often refused to do work. She had a mild learning disability. Since Nicole was unable to control herself in mainstream classes, she was placed in remedial classes with more structure and individualized attention. Nicole became increasingly disrespectful toward her teachers and constantly provoked her peers. She did not see herself as similar to the other kids, and mocked them for their apparent shortcomings. During this time, Nicole was diagnosed with oppositional defiant disorder. Her several previous therapists identified her tendency to defend against her perceived weaknesses with acting-out behaviors. Nicole was known to instigate other students, and appeared to look for trouble wherever she could find it.

Nicole's behavioral problems began at the age of 8, at the time of her parents' divorce. Shedding outward appearances and defensive postures, Nicole was a vulnerable girl who was struggling with her family's disintegration. Her father was battling alcohol and drug addiction, and her mother was unable to care for her, leaving Nicole in the care of her maternal aunt. The multiple losses and rejections made Nicole feel that her only hope for survival was to fend off others, refuse their help, and prove that she was strong enough to take care of herself.

When her disruptive behaviors showed no signs of abating, she was enrolled in a special school for youth with behavioral problems, which exacerbated her problems. She refused to go to school and became increasingly angry and defiant. Her aunt, quickly running out of resources, made a frantic call to Nicole's father, now clean and sober, and insisted that Nicole live with him.

After Nicole transferred schools when she moved in with her father, her behavioral problems continued and she again was placed in a remedial classroom. She received numerous detentions weekly for being defiant and disrespectful to everyone. Nicole received in-school and out-of-school suspensions every month; she wasn't afraid to push the limits and "show who's boss." Her behavior appeared to be indicative of defensive self-esteem.

She was referred to school-based therapy at the start of the academic year based on the urging of her father and special education personnel. When Nicole met with her therapist for the first time, she barely uttered a word. She had an overly confident demeanor, hardly made eye contact, slouched in her chair, and provided one-word answers. She stated that the only reason she showed up was because the school and her father "forced" her. She was distrustful and briefly alluded to a past incident when a previous therapist broke her confidence.

The process of therapy and rapport building was very slow, but Nicole consistently showed up for her appointments. As she grew to trust her therapist, she voluntarily talked about an incident at school, usually one that led to a detention or a suspension. Over time, she was able to reflect on her actions and think about how she could have handled the situation differently. Although Nicole was labeled a "bad kid" and perceived as dangerous, she never acted violently toward others in her new school and appeared incapable of hurting others. She received detentions mostly for verbal outbursts and inappropriate behaviors in the classroom.

In therapy, Nicole expressed her disdain toward school. She had long-standing plans to drop out when she turned 16. She had internalized the negative projections that she was "stupid" and that she "would never amount to anything" but had a strong internal drive to prove everyone wrong. She wanted to open her own restaurant and become a successful entrepreneur.

With kids like Nicole, it's critical to find those "islands of competence." For Nicole, it was her hard work ethic. She loved working her part-time job at a local restaurant, always being on time for her shifts and putting extra effort into her work responsibilities. She also had a boyfriend who she deeply cared for. When her boyfriend expressed his desire to drop out of school, Nicole was furious and insisted that he graduate. When the discrepancy about her own educational path was pointed out, she just shrugged her shoulders and looked away.

In her new school, Nicole found that there were many adult role models who wanted to help her. One of the school counselors scheduled time to have breakfast with Nicole once a week before school. The time together became a sacred and special ritual. Nicole became friendly with the other counselors and secretaries, and occasionally stopped by during her lunch period, just to say hello. Nicole also took her therapist's suggestions that she come see her whenever she felt she was getting out of control and asked to be excused from class if she was on the verge of acting out. Her therapist attended all meetings with Nicole at the request of her father, her guidance counselor, the dean of students, or her teachers. She gradually got the message that no one was giving up on her, and these adults slowly joined her group of significant others.

Over the course of the year, Nicole received fewer detentions and she was able to apply the skills she learned in therapy to help manage her anger. She slowly stopped seeing the school administrators as enemies and more as her allies. She learned that in consultation with her father, the school was looking out for her best interest and wanted to find the best possible fit for her educational needs. Halfway through the school year, Nicole decided that she would enroll in a few mainstream classes, and eventually proved that she could keep up with the work. At the end of the year, after experiencing a few successes, Nicole decided that she wanted to stay in school and graduate. The therapist celebrated her decision, and asked if she would share the news with the other counselors and secretaries with whom she was close. When Nicole told them of her plans to graduate, they were overjoyed. With this positive feedback, perhaps for the first time in her life, she felt competent. She was willing to take proactive measures to create her own destiny, rather than react against a label that was forced upon her.

Nicole's emerging awareness of her own self-worth was aroused by an increasing sense of competence and achievement in her academic work. These integral elements of selective self-esteem held particular significance for Nicole based on her past experiences and perceived failures. The positive feedback she received for her accomplishments was coupled with the affirmation and strong emotional bonds she forged with significant adult figures. Attending to the selective self-esteem components including social competence, academic achievement, and a genuine sense of connection to others may have boosted Nicole's global level of self-esteem. No one can be talked into good self-esteem, but the experience of being considered worthy of the unfailing commitment and caring of others can be a powerful emotionally corrective experience, and so it was for Nicole.

CONCLUSION

This chapter has explored the contributions of low self-esteem in increasing the vulnerability of teens to two of the most potentially devastating hazards to our young people: youth violence and teen pregnancy. While self-esteem, both global and selective, is a complex tapestry of contributing threads that lead to these risks, its role must be carefully considered and evaluated. While the jury is still out on how exactly low self-esteem contributes to the complex pathway leading to youth violence or teen pregnancy, it is clear that a basic need of all human beings is acceptance and belonging, and that is a basic component of global self-esteem. When those basic needs are frustrated, the risk for a variety of adverse outcomes increases. The chapter also discussed intervention and prevention strategies as well as a detailed case study in which relational, empathic healing played a crucial role.

REFERENCES

Allen, J. P., Philliber, S., Herling, S., & Kuperminc, G. P. (1997). Preventing teen pregnancy and academic failure: Experimental evaluation of a developmentally based approach. *Child Development, 64,* 729–742.

Benda, B. B., & Corwyn, R. F. (2002). The effect of abuse in childhood and in adolescence on violence among adolescents. *Youth & Society, 33,* 339–365.

Blowers, J. G. (2007). Impact of an after-school martial arts program on at-risk students. *Dissertation Abstracts International: Section B: The Sciences and Engineering, 68,* 1913.

Boden, J. M., & Horwood, L. J. (2006). Self-esteem, risky sexual behavior, and pregnancy in a New Zealand birth cohort. *Archives of Sexual Behavior, 35,* 549–560.

Broman, C. L. (1997). Race-related factors in life satisfaction among African Americans. *Journal of Black Psychology, 23,* 36–49.

Brooks, R. (1993). *The search for islands of competence.* Paper presented at the Fifth Annual Conference of CHADD, San Diego.

Brooks, R., & Goldstein, S. (2004). *Raising resilient children: Fostering strength, hope, and optimism in your child.* New York: McGraw-Hill.

Centers for Disease Control and Prevention. (2008). *Teen pregnancy fact sheet.* Atlanta, GA: Author. Retrieved September 16, 2008, from http://www.cdc.gov/reproductivehealth/AdolescentReproHealth/

Coyle, K., Basen-Engquist, K., Kirby, D., Parcel, G., Banspach, S., Harrist, R., et al. (1999). Short-term impact of Safer Choices: A multicomponent, school-based, HIV, other STD, and pregnancy prevention program. *Journal of School Health, 69,* 181–188.

Crenshaw, D. A. (2006). *Evocative strategies in child and adolescent psychotherapy.* Lanham, MD: Jason Aronson.

Crenshaw, D. A. (2008). *Therapeutic engagement of children and adolescents: Symbol, play, drawing and storytelling strategies.* Lanham, MD: Jason Aronson.

Crenshaw, D. A., & Garbarino, J. (2007). The hidden dimensions: Profound sorrow and buried human potential in violent youth. *Journal of Humanistic Psychology, 47,* 160–174.

Cristantiello, S., Crenshaw, D. A., & Tsoubris, K. (2008). Diamonds in the rough: A strengths-based approach to healing. In D. A. Crenshaw (Ed.), *Child and adolescent psychotherapy: Wounded spirits and healing paths* (pp. 63–78). Lanham, MD: Jason Aronson.

Currie, E. (2004). *The road to whatever: Middle-class culture and the crisis of adolescence.* New York: Metropolitan Books.

Ethier, K. A., Kershaw, T. S., Lewis, J. B., Milan, S., Niccolai, L. M., & Ickovics, J. R. (2006). Self-esteem, emotional distress and sexual behavior among adolescent females: Interrelationships and temporal effects. *Journal of Adolescent Health, 38,* 268–274.

Garbarino, J. (2006, March 22). *Words can hurt forever.* Daniel Kirk Memorial Lecture at Marist College, Poughkeepsie, NY.

Greenburg, L. S. (2002). *Emotion-focused therapy: Coaching clients to work through feelings.* Washington, DC: American Psychological Association.

Greenburg, L. S., & Paivio, S. C. (1997). *Working with the emotions in psychotherapy.* New York: Guilford.

Guttmacher Institute. (2006). *U.S. teenage pregnancy statistics: National and state trends and trends by race and ethnicity.* New York: Author.

Hardy, K. V., & Laszloffy, T. (2005). *Teens who hurt: Clinical interventions to break the cycle of adolescent violence.* New York: Guilford Press.

Hawkins, J. D., Catalano, R. F., Kosterman, R., Abbott, R., & Hill, K. G. (1999). Preventing adolescent health-risk behaviors by strengthening protection during childhood. *Archives of Pediatrics and Adolescent Medicine, 153,* 226–234.

Hockaday, C., Crase, S. J., Shelley, M. C., & Stockdale, D. F. (2000). A prospective study of adolescent pregnancy. *Journal of Adolescence, 23,* 423–438.

Jackson, J. S., Brown, T. N., Williams, D. R., Torres, M., Sellers, S. L., & Brown, K. (1996). Racism and the physical and mental health status of African Americans: A thirteen-year national panel study. *Ethnicity and Disease, 6,* 132–147.

Kalke, T., Glanton, A., & Cristalli, M. (2007). Positive behavioral interventions and supports: Using strengths-based approaches to enhance the culture of care in residential and day treatment education environments. *Child Welfare Journal, 86,* 151–174.

Kingsbury, K. (2008, June 18). Pregnancy boom at Gloucester High. *Time.* Retrieved September 28, 2008, from http://www.time.com/time/world/article/0,8599,1815845,00.html

Kunchandy, E. M. (2008). The relationship between self-esteem and aggression in urban African American youth. *Dissertation Abstracts International: Section B: The Sciences and Engineering, 68,* 6314.

Lee, R. M. (2003). Do ethnic identity and other-group orientation protect against discrimination for Asian Americans? *Journal of Counseling Psychology, 50,* 133–141.

Liang, C. T., & Fassinger, R. E. (2008). The role of collective self-esteem for Asian Americans experiencing racism-related stress: A test of moderator and mediator hypotheses. *Cultural Diversity and Ethnic Minority Psychology, 14*, 19–28.

Lonczak, H. S., Abbott, R. D., Hawkins, J. D., Kosterman, R., & Catalano, R. F. (2002). Effects of the Seattle Social Development Project on sexual behavior, pregnancy, birth, and STD outcomes by age 21. *Archives of Pediatrics and Adolescent Medicine, 156*, 438–447.

Main, M., & Cassidy, J. (1988). Categories of response to reunion with the parent at age 6: Predictable from infant attachment classifications and stable over a 1-month period. *Developmental Psychology, 24*, 415–426.

Medora, N. P., & von der Hellen, C. (1997). Romanticism and self-esteem among teen mothers. *Adolescence, 32*, 811–824.

Ness, C. D. (2005). Finding the aggression in girls' violence. *Dissertation Abstracts International: Section A: Humanities and Social Sciences, 66*, 1978.

Nickerson, A. B., Salamone, F. J., Brooks, J. L., & Colby, S. A. (2004). Promising approaches to engaging families and building strengths in residential treatment. *Residential Treatment for Children & Youth, 22*, 1–18.

Ostrowsky, M. K. (2008). Extending Khantzian's self-medication hypothesis: An examination of low self-esteem, depression, alcohol use, marijuana use, and violent behavior. *Dissertation Abstracts International: Section A: Humanities and Social Sciences, 68*, 739.

Robin, L., Dittus, P., Whitaker, D., Crosby, R., Ethier, K., Mezoff, J., et al. (2004). Behavioral interventions to reduce incidence of HIV, STD, and pregnancy among adolescents: A decade in review. *Journal of Adolescent Health, 34*, 3–26.

Robinson, R. B. (1994). The relation between self-esteem, sexual activity, and pregnancy. *Adolescence, 29*, 27–35.

Sandstrom, M. J., & Jordan, R. (2008). Defensive self-esteem and aggression in childhood. *Journal of Research in Personality, 42*, 506–514.

Santelli, J. S., Lindberg, L. D., Finer, L. B., & Singh, S. (2007). Explaining recent declines in adolescent pregnancy in the United States: The contribution of abstinence and improved contraceptive use. *American Journal of Public Health, 97*, 150–156.

Schwartz, M. D., & DeKeseredy, W. S. (2008). Interpersonal violence against women: The role of men. *Journal of Contemporary Criminal Justice, 24*, 178–185.

Tebes, J. K., Feinn, R., Vanderploeg, J. J., Chinman, M. J., Shepard, J., Brabham, T., et al. (2007). Impact of a positive youth development program in urban after school settings on the prevention of adolescent substance use. *Journal of Adolescent Health, 41*, 239–247.

Utsey, S. O., Chae, M. H., Brown, C. F., & Kelly, D. (2002). Effect of ethnic group membership on ethnic identity, race-related stress, and quality of life. *Cultural Diversity and Ethnic Minority Psychology, 8*, 366–377.

Ying, Y., Lee, P., & Tsai, J. L. (2000). Cultural orientation and racial discrimination: Predictors of coherence in Chinese American young adults. *Journal of Community Psychology, 28*, 427–442.

10

Promoting the Self-Esteem of Adolescent African American Males

DERYL F. BAILEY AND MARY BRADBURY-BAILEY

One key opens one lock; but when it comes to working with adolescents, count
on there being lots of locks!

—Anonymous

*H*aving counseled adolescent African American males for the past 30 years,
this quote typically comes to mind when we listen to yet another parent,
teacher, or administrator share their frustration with the undeveloped
academic and social potential of a particular young man. Their frustration stems
from the harsh reality they know exists for too many young African American
males who end up in special needs classes rather than gifted classes, in-school or
out-of-school suspension, and prison rather than college. And while this negative
reality may be our catalyst for action, it is the other side of the coin that needs to be
our constant focus—the "human wealth" losses from not developing the intellectual, emotional, and social potential that lies within adolescent African American
males. So why does this quote come to mind as we work with this population?
Simply because one size does not fit all—and the ideas and research regarding
self-esteem and adolescent African American males exemplify this fact. So if we
are interested in promoting the self-esteem of adolescent African American males,
then we need to understand that our approach must be multifaceted, developmental, and comprehensive.

For adolescent African American males, practitioners, educators, and community
leaders often respond with programs dedicated to the building of positive self-esteem
only to be disappointed with the program's mixed results. To fully understand the
construct of self-esteem for adolescent African American males, adults interested in
changing the educational and life trajectories for this population should begin with
reviewing and understanding identity development models and their relationship to
self-esteem, since the two seem intertwined for this age group.

TRADITIONAL IDENTITY DEVELOPMENT THEORIES

Traditional identity development theories suggest that one's self-esteem may lower as the individual moves from childhood to early adolescence; during this time period, children enter school and begin to compare themselves to others, resulting in feelings of inferiority and self-criticism. As a part of their self-development, their assessment of personal strengths and weaknesses due to academic and social interactions becomes a part of their educational routine and challenges their self-esteem. During middle and late adolescence, self-esteem can be further impacted by the contradictions that mark identity development during this time period. Examples include adolescents' need to gain independence from adults while increasing their dependence on peer interactions, and their need to demonstrate unique personal characteristics while at the same time feeling part of a group (Cobb, 2001; McDevitt & Ormrod, 2002).

UNDERSTANDING COMMON MISCONCEPTIONS

While traditional identity development theories provide insight into normative behaviors for adolescents, researchers mainly collected data on middle-class White students; thus, any conclusions made concerning self-esteem for adolescent African American males should also consider research related to culturally specific issues as well as racial identity development. Without these considerations, several misconceptions could be made regarding the self-esteem of adolescent African American males and, as with most misconceptions, can have a negative impact on the effectiveness of programs targeting this population.

The most common misconception concerning self-esteem and adolescent African American males assumes that poor academic and social performance in school directly corresponds to low or poor self-esteem. However, the opposite is true with most African American male students who score high on measures of global esteem despite poor performance in school. Some researchers (Ogbu & Davis, 2003; Steele, 1997) cite academic disidentification as a possible explanation in that African American students, especially males, do not see the logic of identifying with a system that seems more committed to their failure than their success. Furthermore, studies revealed an interesting relationship between self-esteem and adaptive skills for African American males—high self-esteem scores typically equated with low adaptive skills (Blash & Unger, 1995; Gaskin-Butler & Tucker, 1995; Tucker, 1999; Tucker & Herman, 2002). This information could prove to be critical in the development of appropriate programs and interventions aimed at the success of adolescent African American males.

While planning interventions, well-intentioned educators, counselors, mental health professionals, and community leaders may make the mistake of focusing on the negative impact of poverty, poor academic performance, minimal access to healthcare, and the constant struggle against institutional racism rather than focusing on the overwhelming resiliency of adolescent African American students. Focusing on the negative often leads to victimization and a sense of futility, especially for adolescent African American males, who have often been referred to as an "endangered species" (Boyd, 2007; Jones, 2007; Pluviose, 2006). Researchers who are not naïve to the myriad problems faced by African American students, but choose to focus instead on the resiliency demonstrated by this population, recommend programs and interventions that are developmental, comprehensive, and culturally specific, with a focus on self-empowerment (Blash & Unger, 1995; Gaskin-Butler & Tucker, 1995; Obiakor & Beachum, 2005; Tucker, 1999).

Finally, the "rugged individualism" often linked with positive self-esteem for members of the dominant culture should not necessarily be prescribed to adolescent African American males. Establishing relationships and maintaining the integrity of those relationships far outweigh the importance of individualism for these young men. For example, after a program implements a special trip, the positive experiences and the memories will be more closely tied to how the young men experienced the trip with their peers than to any sights or landmarks; they will remember their interactions with people they met as a part of the trip rather than the historical facts and figures presented. Thus, collective self-esteem takes precedence over individual self-esteem (Bailey & Bradbury-Bailey, 2007; Luhtanen & Crocker, 1992; Sue & Sue, 2003).

CULTURALLY RELEVANT RESEARCH

With these misconceptions pervasive in the educational and mental health communities, not only is the effectiveness of special programs and interventions minimized, but participating adolescent African American males are usually seen as "defective" if they do not demonstrate the necessary improvements or change. To prevent the negative impact of misconceptions as well as the "misreading" of adolescent African American males, programs or interventions with the goal of enhancing the global and selective self-esteem for this population should have a good understanding of additional developmental tasks, racial identity development theories and models, and self-empowerment theories. In addition, White program staff must understand their own racial identity development and how their development may influence their interactions with adolescent African American males. The following sections represent an overview of research related to these topics.

Initially, identity development for adolescent African Americans was based on traditional theories, but later researchers added developmental tasks for minority adolescents due to their own experiences with racism. For African Americans, the challenges of adolescent development become multiplied because of historical and social factors arising from institutional racism. Facing the negative impact of racism on a daily basis can easily erode feelings of competence and worthiness; for many adolescent African Americans males, this reality can translate into feelings of low self-esteem. According to Crawley and Freeman (1993), the interaction of these factors during this critical time period can result in additional developmental tasks for students of color that must be realized for the formation of a healthy identity. These tasks are most directly influenced by race, ethnicity, and culture. These additional developmental tasks may include those listed in Table 10.1.

TABLE 10.1   Additional Developmental Tasks for Students of Color

Age	Additional Developmental Tasks
Early school age	Incorporation of racial labels into evolving self-concept
	Recognize, identify, and label social inconsistencies
Middle school age	Recognize and develop skills for negotiating multiracial environments and bicultural experiences, each containing mixed and contradictory messages
	Enhance and deepen skills for handling social inconsistencies, e.g., racism, discrimination, prejudice
	Forge an appropriate and healthy identity in the face of racism, discrimination, prejudice
	Fine-tune sensing and judging skills to screen out or transform negative racial/color images and messages
Puberty	Refine healthy identity that transforms and transcends societal messages of inferiority, pathology, and deviance based on color, race, and culture
	Strengthen skills for negotiating bicultural and multiracial environments

Source: Adapted from Crawley and Freeman (1993).

Racial Identity Theory

Eventually, models for racial/cultural identity development became the prominent feature of cross-cultural counseling. Evidence suggests a connection between the development of a healthy racial identity and positive self-esteem. To fully understand self-esteem as a component of identity development, counselors, educators, mental health professionals, and community leaders should be familiar with the stages of racial identity for African American males and their implications on self-esteem. Early work by both Cross (1987) and Phinney (1989) proposed several stages specifically related to identity development unique to minority cultures; the two models are contrasted in Table 10.2.

While these models became the foundation for racial/cultural identity development, further research (Cross, 1995; Sue & Sue, 2008) revealed that each stage actually contains multiple contrasting identities as a function of race salience. Race salience is "the degree to which race is an important and integral part of a person's approach to life" (Cross, as cited in Sue & Sue, 2008, p. 237). Refining his original model, Cross (1995) proposed that the preencounter stage could yield one of two contrasting identities, including preencounter assimilation or preencounter anti-Black, with the former demonstrating a low salience for race with self-esteem tied to other factors, and the latter reflecting low self-esteem and high self-hatred. Cross (1995) redefined the internalization stage as one of three identities, each of which is characterized by Black self-acceptance equated to high levels of self-esteem: "Black nationalist (high Black positive race salience), biculturalist (Blackness and fused sense of Americanness), and multiculturalist (multiple identity formation, including race, gender, and sexual

TABLE 10.2   Racial Identity Development Models

Cross's Model	Stage Description	Phinney's Model	Stage Description
Preencounter	Individual's identity is tied to the dominant culture as a result of low self-esteem and high self-hatred	Unexamined ethnic Identity	Individual does not equate his or her ethnic background as a part of his or her identity
Encounter	After experiencing racism, the individual becomes aware and celebrates cultural values	Ethnic identity search	As the individual adds experiences to his or her life, he or she begins to examine values unique to his or her culture
Immersion	Cultural values become more meaningful; stronger identification of personal culture and rejection of dominant culture	Achieved ethnic identity	Individual appreciates, practices, and depends on personal cultural values as an integrated part of his or her identity
Internalization	Individual's identity fulfilled with acceptance of personal cultural values for himself or herself as well as others		

Source: Adapted from Harris, 1995; Kroger, 2000.

orientation" (as cited in Sue & Sue, 2008, p. 238). In all these models, progressing through these stages as part of one's identity development correlates directly to increasing levels of self-esteem. For adolescent African American males, to value and embrace their racial identity can greatly enhance both global and collective self-esteem.

Atkinson, Morten, and Sue (1998) proposed the racial/cultural identity development model that has broader applications beyond adolescent African Americans, but may still be useful to the practitioner as he or she develops programs and interventions geared to this population. Briefly, the stages include (Sue & Sue, 2008):

1. Conformity: Minorities prefer dominant cultural values.
2. Dissonance and appreciating: Minorities experience either racism personally or a contradiction to dominant views or racism and begin to question their judgment of themselves, their peers, and the dominant culture.
3. Resistance and immersion stage: Minorities begin to reject dominant cultural values while accepting their culture's values and norms.
4. Introspection: Minorities begin to subjectively balance judgment based on an individual's actions after feeling the psychological drain of anger against the dominant culture, and begin to see the need to reach out to members of all groups.

5. Integrative awareness: Minorities begin to understand that an apprecia-tion for diversity represents a lifelong journey and they exhibit a more positive self-image.

Again, being able to embrace one's racial identity frees the individual to appreciate the strength gained from having to fight racism on a daily basis; this strength could easily translate into a more positive self-esteem.

Self-Empowerment Theory

Given the current climate of institutional racism that adolescent African Americans must face (Tucker, 1999; Tucker & Herman, 2002), we and several other researchers suggest incorporating the self-empowerment theory (SET) when working to promote the self-esteem for adolescent African American males. SET advocates developing an internal sense of control and influence in reaching desired life goals.

> SET postulates that behavior problems and academic failure, as well as proso-cial behavior and academic success, are significantly influenced by levels of (a) self-motivation to achieve academic and social success, (b) perceived self-control over one's behavior and academic success, (c) self-reinforcement for engaging in social and academic successful behaviors, (d) adaptive skills for life success, and (e) engagement in successful behaviors. (Tucker & Herman, 2002, p. 766)

Implementation of SET should involve multiple aspects of the adolescent's life, including school, community, and parents. This becomes necessary because institutional racism sends a consistent message through the school and the larger community that challenges both academic and social self-esteem for adolescent African American males. Self-empowerment becomes a tool that can allow these young men to resist the impact of these negative messages and instill feelings of self-worth and competence.

White Racial Identity Development

To successfully work with adolescent African American males, White practitioners need to know their own racial identity status; their status determines how much they understand the impact of White privilege and the pervasive effects of racism. Helms (1995) identified six racial identity statuses, as identified in the Table 10.3.

When programs and interventions specific to adolescent African American males yield minimal results relative to measurements of improvement, program staff may blame program participants rather than examining their own motiva-tions and interactions as well as the appropriateness of components of the program and interventions. Institutional racism and the ripple effect of White privilege are so embedded in our society that many Whites are unaware of racism's existence, and thus, its negative impact on the healthy development of adolescent African American males.

TABLE 10.3   White Racial Identity Development

Status	Description	Possible Impact
Contact	Oblivious to racism and its impact on people of color; minimal experience with students of color	Will not appreciate cultural differences while imposing their own dominant cultural values
Disintegration	Become conflicted over examples of the two standards that exist for Whites vs. people of color	Begin to become uncomfortable with their "whiteness" and may experience feelings of guilt
Reintegration	Rather than dealing with the conflict from the previous stage, become self-absorbed in the superiority of their own socioracial group (Italian, Irish, German, etc.)	Will believe that students of color are totally responsible for their own failures and need to stop making excuses
Pseudoindependence	Due to some painful encounter, the individual begins to acknowledge the significance of cultural differences as well as their own biases	May want to help students of color, but still expect them to incorporate characteristics unique to the dominant culture
Immersion	Personally assesses their biases, stereotypes, involvement in racist actions or institutions as well as how they have benefitted from White privilege	Will be more focused on changing themselves and other Whites rather than changing the students of color
Autonomy	Aware of their own whiteness by understanding their role in racism and privilege; understand and appreciate cultural differences; seek diversity in their relationships	When dealing with students of color, constantly assess their interactions and work relative to cultural sensitivity and the expression of dominant cultural values

Source: Adapted from Helms (1995, as cited in Sue & Sue, 2008).

INTERVENTION STRATEGIES

Based on culturally relevant research, programs and interventions with the goal of having a positive impact on the global and selective self-esteem of adolescent African American males should (1) understand identity development and, consequently, how self-esteem may differ for this group; (2) use the main tenets of the self-empowerment theory; and (3) be aware of their own racial identity development and its potential impact on their work with students of color.

Objectives

Program developers should incorporate the following objectives:

1. Select staff based on cultural sensitivity and their experience working with adolescent African American males
2. Offer intensive training for all staff that will be developing the program or intervention
3. Offer intensive training for all staff that will be working directly with participants
4. Training should include:
   a. Acknowledgment of misconceptions and how they can interfere with the development and implementation of any program or intervention
   b. Review of additional developmental tasks for adolescent African American males and their impact on self-esteem
   c. Review of racial identity theories and models and their connection to self-esteem
   d. Analysis of staff members' own racial identity development and how their "current stage" could impact the development or implementation of the program or intervention
   e. Improvement in understanding for the need of a program or intervention that is both developmental and comprehensive
   f. A review of the self-empowerment theory and the importance of self-empowerment as a means of enhancing self-esteem for this population
5. Develop a program that incorporates an understanding of adolescent development for African American males that includes a knowledge of additional developmental tasks and racial identity development theories and models
6. Develop a program that works on adaptive skills that can improve both academic and social performance for participants, allowing for self-empowerment
7. Develop a program that represents a comprehensive support model that involves personal, family, and community aspects as participants work to improve academic, social, and personal performance

Interventions that incorporate these program objectives will have a greater chance of impacting self-esteem in the hopes of changing the educational and life trajectories of adolescent African American males. The following section describes a successful program that has been developed and implemented based on these objectives.

Programs That Work—Project: Gentlemen-on-the-Move

Project: Gentlemen-on-the-Move (PGOTM), one component of Empowered Youth Programs (EYP), represents a developmental and comprehensive program dedicated to enhancing the self-esteem of adolescent African American males by intentionally creating an environment that encourages academic and social potential. Developing this potential promotes both academic and collective self-esteem by using the peer group as its vehicle. Building feelings of competence and self-worth relative to academics and tying academics to future career goals represent two primary goals for PGOTM members. PGOTM has evolved into a peer group that values education; students new to PGOTM find themselves surrounded with a new set of peers committed to high academic standards, evoking the power of collective self-esteem to realize academic self-esteem. Statistics for program participants show lower rates in absenteeism, classroom behavior issues, discipline referrals, and failed classes than for nonparticipants. In addition, program participants demonstrate increased academic rigor by completing more advanced academic courses, as well as higher rates of passing academic courses, high school graduation, and acceptance into postsecondary institutions (Bailey, 2003; Bailey, Bradbury-Bailey, Hopkins, & Sims-Browning, 2009). The design of PGOTM seeks to promote self-esteem for this population through an exploration and understanding of both academic and social self-domains.

Exploring and Understanding the Academic Self

Too often, adolescent African American males feel alienated in the educational system and rarely experience feelings of self-worth and competence relative to academics. To counter the negative messages associated with low academic self-esteem and performance, PGOTM members participate in a variety of activities that reverse this trend by establishing clearly defined academic goals, developing and nurturing positive academic habits, fostering a sense of camaraderie between members relative to academics, and maintaining a connection between home, school, and program staff. These activities are the Saturday Academy, college tours, and fall and spring exam lock-ins.

Saturday Academy During the Saturday Academy, PGOTM members participate in group and individual academic counseling sessions (academic advisement) that provide each member with opportunities to develop an academic portfolio. The development of the academic portfolio allows for the addition of individual self-esteem to collective self-esteem as it relates to academic potential. As a part of the academic portfolio, PGOTM members complete the following:

1. Long-term academic goals that include at least two colleges they would like to attend as well as a list of necessary academic requirements for each school, including SAT/ACT scores and grade point averages (GPAs)
2. A six-year academic plan that maps out the four years of high school as well as the first two years of college and stresses the completion of college prep courses and advanced placement courses necessary to attend and be successful in college
3. Short-term academic and social goals for each semester based on the six-year academic plan

The academic counseling sessions also afford members the opportunity to discuss problems associated with academics as they arise, share their academic successes and disappointments with the group, and experience support from both peers and the academic counselor as they strive to meet both short-term and long-term academic goals. Both the academic counseling sessions and academic portfolio send consistent messages to PGOTM members that personalize the value of academics, allowing them to include academics as an important component of their identity.

Part of the feedback given during academic counseling sessions comes from EYP's Academic Monitoring Forms (AMFs). Program participants' teachers complete these forms in the middle of each grading period as a way to monitor academic progress on a more consistent basis. Information from the AMFs can be easily communicated to parents as well. This four-way communication between teachers, program staff, parents, and PGOTM members relative to their academic and social progress represents yet another consistent message to PGOTM members concerning the importance of the academic self—a message that comes from the significant adults in their lives. Even though adolescents crave independence from significant adults as part of their identity development, they still require acknowledgment of their progress if an area in their life is to be incorporated as part of their self-worth.

Other components of the Saturday Academy that boost academic self-esteem include group and individual tutoring sessions and academic rotations that focus on verbal and math skills specifically related to the SAT. Building core skills in the academic arena increases feelings of academic competence for PGOTM members, which could translate into increased levels and salience of academic self-esteem. Because the Saturday Academy mainly depends on the use of groups, a close connection between collective and academic self-esteem can also be established. Group and individual tutoring sessions are dedicated to supporting program participants as they attempt more challenging academic courses (i.e., advanced college prep and advanced placement). Sessions include study skills, test-taking strategies, and time management as well as specific work on course content. The decision to dedicate the academic rotations to the improvement of SAT verbal and math skills stems from achievement gap data provided the Education Trust (2003, 2006). Program participants complete a practice test and then work in small groups to "teach each other" the solutions to math problems or explain the reason for selecting a particular answer in the verbal section; teachers and graduate students monitor group work and only guide students to solutions if no one in the group can figure out the "why" of an answer. This allows program participants to become both academic team members and academic leaders as they take ownership of their learning. This approach uses the power of collective self-esteem to foster the importance of academic self-esteem for PGOTM members while also increasing levels of academic competence in areas that have been historically weak for this population.

College Tours   As a way to affirm the goal-setting and six-year plan portions of the academic counseling sessions, program participants visit a variety of college campuses each year. If they participate in the program for all four years of high school, they will have toured a combination of postsecondary institutions, including private and state-supported historically black colleges (HBCs), predominantly White institutions varying in size and location, and two-year transfer schools.

Fall and Spring Exam Lock-Ins   These are intensive exam preparations for standardized state tests and teacher-prepared final exams. Like other academic components of PGOTM, the lock-ins weave a close connection between collective self-esteem and academic self-esteem while giving members the opportunity to increase levels of academic competence. Program participants are "locked in" a local high school the weekend prior to state tests and teacher-prepared final exams and participate in a series of individual and group study sessions as well as competitive quiz sessions. Study sessions closely follow the model of the Saturday Academy tutoring sessions so that program participants are familiar with the routine. Preliminary results indicate that exam lock-in participants score significantly higher on state standardized tests than nonparticipants (Bailey et al., 2009).

Exploring and Understanding the Social Self   Given the additional developmental tasks and issues associated with navigating racial identity development for adolescent African American males, PGOTM dedicates time to promoting self-empowerment through analysis of problems and issues specific to their age group and the development and practice of skills to overcome them. Dealing with racist incidents on a consistent basis without developing a healthy racial identity can result in feelings of victimization for adolescent African American males; these feelings can lower self-worth and render the individual powerless in his or her efforts to overcome the negative impact of such incidents. During the self-discovery (also known as the leadership rotation) portion of the Saturday Academy, group leaders (teachers and graduate students) help PGOTM participants work through sessions that explore topics related to personal and social challenges, including social skills, anger management, leadership skills, and career exploration. These sessions allow the young men to develop adaptive skills necessary for success in a variety of situations that may or may not be working in their favor. Working in small groups, PGOTM members participate in scenarios, discuss personal experiences and related examples, and design solutions to potential problems. Since group identification represents an important part of their identity development, having a positive group to identify with and discuss relevant issues represents a powerful tool for promoting self-esteem for program participants.

CASE STUDY

Curtis, currently a junior in high school, has been a member of PGOTM since eighth grade. His mother works for the local school district as a classroom teacher and enrolled her son in the program because of his poor academic performance, which steadily declined throughout middle school in spite of both punitive action and promises of rewards. Furthermore, Curtis was much larger than other students his age, which often led to teasing from them. He exhibited lack of control, resulting in negative responses to such incidents, which, of course, led to increased time spent in both in-school and out-of-school suspensions.

Initial interviews and preassessments revealed no connection between academic performance and feelings of self-worth for this student; in middle school, Curtis performed only enough to be moved to the next grade and accomplished little. This resulted in achievement gaps in the areas of reading and math that naturally hindered his academic progress in high school. To be honest, we were surprised when Curtis returned to the program after his initial meeting, and even more surprised when he returned the next year, because his story does not represent either an immediate or gradual transformation, as with many of our other participants, but instead a constant battle fought by program staff, his mother, his coaches, and his teachers. But the battle for Curtis to see his academic and social potential was finally realized last semester, when he jubilantly called us to inform us that he had passed all his classes, was making progress in his "credit recovery" class, and intended to play football next year.

Several events immediately came to mind after his phone call that after reflection may have aided in this transformation. First, four years of constant communication between and constant "nagging" from program staff, teachers, coaches, his mother, and even other PGOTM participants provided a consistent message of Curtis's academic value and his responsibility to his family and community to develop that academic potential. Although Curtis received positive feedback from those who had become significant to him, until Curtis internalized the value of academics as part of his self-worth, there was no need of excellence. Second, during one particular college tour, PGOTM students were allowed to briefly shadow a college student; Curtis happened to be paired with a very academic female who served as a strong self-esteem model. She introduced Curtis to one of her study teams, which also happened to be mostly females, as part of the shadowing experience. After returning to the bus, Curtis immediately asked me, "Are all the women in college smart like that? And that pretty?" I remember my affirmative answer, resulting in a curious, thoughtful look that remained on his face for most of the ride home. Finally, his positive relationship with his coaches and our communication with them relative to his academic and social performance have also contributed to increased levels of competence and self-worth.

CONCLUSION

Working with adolescent African American males can be a challenge, but given their underdeveloped potential to contribute to their communities and society at large, it is a challenge that needs to be accepted. Program developers and staff members who seek to enhance self-esteem for adolescent African American males must be willing to investigate the issues of this population and their own biases and misconceptions before beginning this work. Doing so will allow them to increase their effectiveness in working with adolescent African American males.

REFERENCES

Atkinson, D. R., Morten, G., & Sue, D. W. (Eds.). (1998). *Counseling American minorities* (5th ed.). Boston: McGraw-Hill.

Bailey, D. F. (2003). Preparing African American males for postsecondary options. *Journal of Men's Studies, 12*, 15–24.

Bailey, D. F., & Bradbury-Bailey, M. E. (2007). Promoting achievement for African American males through group work. *Journal of Specialists in Group Work, 32,* 83–96.

Bailey, D. F., Bradbury-Bailey, M. E., Hopkins, E., & Sims-Browning, L. (2009). *A preliminary investigation of the effect of an intensive exam preparation initiative on the exam performance of high school African American students.* Unpublished manuscript.

Blash, R. R., & Unger, D. G. (1995). Self-concept of African American male youth: Self-esteem and ethnic identity. *Journal of Child and Family Studies, 4,* 359–373.

Boyd, H. (2007). It's hard out here for a Black man. *Black Scholar, 37,* 2–9.

Cobb, N. J. (2001). *Adolescence: Continuity, change, and diversity* (4th ed.). Mountain View, CA: Mayfield Publishing.

Crawley, B., & Freeman, E. (1993). Themes in the life views of older and younger African American males. *Journal of African American Men Studies, 1,* 15–29.

Cross, W. E. (1987). A two-factor theory of Black identity. In J. Phinney & M. Rotheram (Eds.), *Children's ethnic socialization* (pp. 117–133). Newbury Park, CA: Sage.

Cross, W. E. (1995). The psychology of nigrescence: Revising the Cross model. In J. G. Ponterotto, J. M. Casas, L. A. Suzuki, & C. M. Alexander (Eds.), *Handbook of multicultural counseling* (pp. 93–122). Thousand Oaks, CA: Sage.

The Education Trust. (2003). *African American achievement in America.* Retrieved February 13, 2006, from http://www2.edtrust.org/NR/rdonlyres/9AB4AC88-7301-43FF-81A3EB94807B917F/0/AfAmer_Achivementpdf

The Education Trust. (2006). Yes we can: Telling truths and dispelling myths about race and education in America. *Assessment, Accountability, and Reform.* Retrieved May 3, 2008, from http://www2.edtrust.org/EdTrust/Product+Catalog/main.htm#assessment

Gaskin-Butler, V. T., & Tucker, C. M. (1995). Self-esteem, academic achievement, and adaptive behavior in African American children. *Educational Forum, 59,* 234–243.

Harris, H. W. (1995). Introduction: A conceptual overview of race, ethnicity, and identity. In H. W. Harris, H. C. Blue, & E. H. Griffith (Eds.), *Racial and ethnic identity: Psychological and creative expression* (pp. 1–14). New York: Routledge.

Helms, J. E. (1995). An update of Helm's White and people of color racial identity models. In J. G. Ponterotto, J. M. Casas, L. A. Suzuki, & C. M. Alexander (Eds.), *Handbook of multicultural counseling* (pp. 181–191). Thousand Oaks, CA: Sage.

Jones, S. J. (2007). *The State of Black America 2007: Portrait of the Black male.* Silver Spring, MD: Beckham Publications Group.

Kroger, J. (2000). *Identity development: Adolescence through adulthood.* Thousand Oaks, CA: Sage.

Luhtanen, R., & Crocker, J. (1992). A collective self-esteem scale: Self-evaluation of one's social identity. *Personality and Social Psychology Bulletin, 18,* 302–318.

McDevitt, T. M., & Ormrod, J. E. (2002). *Child development and education.* Upper Saddle River, NJ: Pearson Education.

Obiakor, F. E., & Beachum, F. D. (2005). Developing self-empowerment in African American students using the comprehensive support model. *Journal of Negro Education, 74,* 18–29.

Ogbu, J. U., & Davis, A. (2003). *Black American students in an affluent suburb: A study of academic disengagement.* Mahwah, NJ: Lawrence Erlbaum Associates.

Phinney, J. S. (1989). Stages of ethnic identity development in minority group adolescents. *Journal of Early Adolescence, 9,* 34–49.

Pluviose, D. (2006). Black, Hispanic male crisis focus of higher ed summit. *Diverse Issues in Higher Education, 23,* 22.

Steele, C. (1997). A threat in the air: How stereotypes shape intellectual identity and performance. *American Psychologist, 52,* 613–629.

Sue, D. W., & Sue, D. (2003). *Counseling the culturally different: Theory and practice* (4th ed.). New York: John Wiley & Sons.

Sue, D. W., & Sue, D. (2008). *Counseling the culturally diverse: Theory and practice* (5th ed.). Hoboken, NJ: John Wiley & Sons.

Tucker, C. M. (1999). *African American children: A self-empowerment approach to modifying behavior problems and preventing academic failure.* Needham Heights, MA: Allyn & Bacon.

Tucker, C. M., & Herman, K. C. (2002). Using culturally sensitive theories and research to meet the academic needs of low-income African American children. *American Psychologist, 57,* 762–773.

11

Self-Esteem of African American Adolescent Girls

BARBARA HERLIHY AND ZARUS E. P. WATSON

Multiple forces operate continuously and reciprocally to shape the self-esteem systems of African American adolescent girls. In addition to all the normal developmental issues associated with adolescence, they must deal with daily experiences of marginalization based on their race/ethnicity and gender. These developmental and environmental factors present African American girls with significant challenges to developing and internalizing positive self-esteem (Diller, 2007).

The self-esteem of African American adolescent girls has received little attention in the counseling literature (Adkinson-Bradley & Sanders, 2006). Much of the research on this population has been problem focused, centering on issues such as low academic achievement and school failure, premature sexuality, teen pregnancy, substance abuse, deviance, and identity confusion. This problem-centered perspective seems to have fostered an assumption that African American girls must suffer from a diminished sense of self-worth and low self-esteem. Yet, numerous studies have indicated that African American adolescent females have positive self-esteem.

To understand how so many African American girls manage to maintain high self-esteem in the face of daily experiences of "quadripartite discrimination" (Adkinson-Bradley & Sanders, 2006) associated with their race, gender, age, and (often) economic class, it must be recognized that self-esteem is a complex construct. As Chapter 1 explained, it is at once global and comprised of specific elements that fluctuate over time and across circumstances. Thus, many African American girls may have high global self-esteem and positive self-esteem in some respects and in some situations, but have low self-esteem related to other components of the self and in different circumstances. For example, Martinez and Dukes (1991) studied the joint effects of race and gender on the self-esteem of 7th to 12th graders. They found that being African American and female was associated with lower scores on perceived intelligence, but also that African American females became generally more satisfied with themselves as they passed through their high school years. Martinez and Dukes concluded that culture may help to insulate the self-esteem of African American girls from the bombardment of negative messages they receive from the larger society. Thus, the mediating or "buffering" effect of cultural variables must be considered in any attempt to understand the self-esteem systems of this population.

In this chapter, we first explore forces that shape the self-esteem of African American adolescent girls at the societal, institutional, and familial levels. Next, we discuss the efficacy of individual, group, and family counseling approaches with this client group. Finally, we present the case study of Jessica, a 14-year-old African American girl whose story illustrates how multiple forces can interact to influence self-esteem. We conclude by suggesting counseling strategies and interventions that might be used successfully with Jessica and other African American adolescent females.

INFLUENCES ON SELF-ESTEEM

Societal Forces: Racism and Sexism

African American girls develop their self-esteem from a position of marginalization in American society. Experiences with racism and sexism are pervasive forces in their daily lives (Sanders & Bradley, 2005). When African American girls are judged in comparison to White, middle-class standards, behaviors that are culturally acceptable are often mislabeled as deviant rather than as normative, adaptive, and self-affirming. These girls are keenly aware of such judgments. As one young girl stated, "Society sees African American females as always getting pregnant and all that kind of thing and being on welfare" (Shorter-Gooden & Washington, 1996, p. 469).

Issues of race and racism become particularly salient for African American girls when they enter adolescence, due to changes in school groupings and broader participation in the social environment (Diller, 2007). They do not begin to segregate in their social and school interactions until adolescence, when they may gravitate naturally to other African American girls to the exclusion of their White peers. These peer groups may adopt an "oppositional stance" that arises from the anger and resentment felt in response to their growing awareness of the systematic exclusion of African Americans from full participation in American society (Diller, 2007). In Tatum's (1997) view, for African American girls, joining with their peers for support in the face of the stressor of racism is a positive coping strategy that serves a protective function and insulates their self-esteem. Their "boisterous" and "confrontational" behavior can be seen as self-affirming and as a way to manage their devalued race and gender status (Stevens, 1997).

Some writers assert that race and gender are equally important in the development of the self-esteem of African American girls, while others believe that gender is a less salient variable than race. Even if gender is not the primary identity for African American girls, their gender adds to their subordination in a White male-dominated society (Hansen, Gama, & Harkins, 2002) and must be considered as it interacts with race to influence self-esteem.

Although gender role expectations have become more flexible in recent decades, societal norms for masculinity and femininity remain firmly embedded in our collective psyche. Gender awareness appears in children as young as two years old, and by middle childhood their knowledge about gender roles is well established (Worell & Remer, 2003). Gender role expectations do vary by culture, however. Much has been written about the strength and resiliency of African American women, and mothers model these traits and inculcate them in their adolescent daughters (Porter, 2000b). Such modeling can have a positive effect on self-esteem, but it also can create burdensome expectations. African American girls are socialized to believe that strength, persistence, and direct expression of anger are both positive and functional (Sanders & Bradley, 2005); however, this perpetuates an image that their stressors and mental health needs can be ignored because they are able to cope with life's difficulties (Porter, 2000b).

When African American girls are not being judged by their behavior, they are being evaluated by their level of physical attractiveness (Adkison-Bradley & Sanders, 2006). For adolescent girls, physical attractiveness is a selective component of self-esteem that is heavily weighted and is influenced by their judgments of how they measure up to societal ideals. African American girls can be as obsessed with their appearance as their White counterparts. For example, as Robinson-Wood (2009) notes, many Black females "spend an inordinate amount of time, psychic energy, and money on the monumental issue of hair" (p. 197). Nonetheless, the media and the beauty industry devalue their appearance by lauding a "Eurocentric masculinist aesthetic" (Hill-Collins, 1990) that includes a thin body, light or white skin color, and angular facial features (Sanders, 1997; Sanders & Bradley, 2005). Traditional African features such as "nappy" or kinky hair texture, darker skin and eye color, and wide facial features are deemed unattractive and inferior by mainstream culture (Jackson & Greene, 2000; Sanders, 1997). Even the fashion and beauty magazines that are targeted toward African Americans seem to send mixed messages about physical attractiveness. When we leafed through a recent issue of *Essence,* we saw positive portrayals of full-figured women such as Queen Latifah and Jennifer Hudson. However, the African American models in advertisements for clothing and makeup, while not all light-skinned, had rail-thin bodies and angular facial features, such as aquiline noses. When these images of attractiveness are left unchallenged and are internalized by African American girls, the self-worth component of their self-esteem is negatively affected.

African American adolescent girls have been found to have more positive body images than their White counterparts (Belgrave, Chase-Vaughn, Gray, Addison, & Cherry, 2000). They seem to experience less social pressure to be thin and report higher levels of self-esteem and more confidence in their attractiveness than White girls (Eccles, Barber, Jozefowicz, Malenchuck, & Vida, 1999). However, with greater exposure to mainstream cultural pressures, African American girls are as likely as their White peers to feel dissatisfied with their weight and to diet excessively (Emmons, 1992). It would be erroneous to assume that eating disorders are rare among this population. Emmons found that African American adolescent females were more likely than any other race and gender group she examined to use laxatives as a dieting strategy. Recently, attention has been drawn to the high incidence of obesity among African American girls. Although poor nutritional habits that are embedded in certain cultures may be one contributing factor, Robinson and Ward (1991) suggest that obesity among African American females may be a quick-fix resistance strategy to combat daily experiences of racism and sexism.

School

Messages from the larger society are continually reinforced by its institutions, including its schools, which are of primary importance for adolescents. The alarming school dropout rate among African American boys has been well documented, and attention to academic underachievement has been directed toward girls in general, largely leaving African American adolescent females out of the dialogue. Studies of sex differences have demonstrated clearly that schools treat boys and girls differently. A 1992 study entitled "How Schools Shortchange Girls" (cited in Pipher, 1994) captured public attention with its report that boys do better and feel better about themselves as they move through school, while the self-esteem of girls and their scores on standardized achievement tests decline. With respect to race differences, lack of academic achievement may be indicative of a reluctance on the part of African American adolescents to "act White" or "sell out" to the dominant culture. The self-esteem of these adolescents has been shown to be less influenced by school achievement or school failure than White adolescent self-esteem (Hare, 1985; Lay & Wakstein, 1985).

There is ample evidence that females in general, and African American adolescent females in particular, are underrepresented in the academic areas of math and science. Even high-academic-performing African American girls do not often choose to pursue areas of study considered to be nontraditional. In recent years, researchers have linked this phenomenon of nonengagement by African American adolescent females in math and science to a lack of confidence and self-esteem rather than to inability or poor academic performance (Ahia, 2006). The schools may do little to eliminate or mitigate this self-defeating mind-set (Porter, 2000a; Weiler, 1997). For example, an African American girl who achieves an A grade in physics may feel proud of her achievement. However, she may not necessarily feel competent to pursue a career in physics, if the message conveyed by school personnel is that her performance is an isolated event not typical for her peer group.

A large percentage of African American adolescent females arrive at their secondary schools educationally underprepared, although they may have the innate ability to be successful academically if they could be successfully engaged. Unfortunately, school personnel tend to focus on their inappropriate behavior. In a need to overcompensate toward stereotypical attitudes regarding their race, African American girls can manifest behaviors "associated with powerlessness and hopelessness relative to their ability to become scholars" (Adkinson-Bradley & Sanders, 2006, p. 81). Behaviors that are labeled as aggressive, defiant, and unmotivated can be explained by their perception that they are invisible unless they are loud and act out. Gender role stereotyping may contribute to these behaviors, in that African American girls may resist the imposition of dominant-culture ideals of femininity by being loud and aggressive toward males and educational personnel (Taylor, Gilligan, & Sullivan, 1995). Teachers, administrators, and even school counselors often fail to understand these behaviors as a manifestation of frustration, resentment, and anger mired in a context of social oppression within which their low levels of self-esteem become a normative outcome.

As young African American females approach early adulthood, they must make decisions that will significantly influence their future quality of life. What they choose to study as adolescents will have a significant effect on their possible career. For some, ill-informed choices of study are just the beginning of a marginalization process that can proceed along a lifelong path on the bare periphery of society. Identity foreclosure, which is a commitment to decisions after little or no exploration, can occur when pervasive negative social messages are internalized. Hauser and Kasendorf (1983) found that African American adolescents exhibited considerable foreclosure, stabilizing their identities early with a premature closing off of possibilities in terms of image of self and future accomplishments. For African American girls, identity foreclosure can have significant social and educational repercussions. Some girls (especially those from low-socioeconomic-status [SES] families), given their lack of self-confidence and self-esteem necessary to pursue alternative life paths, may deliberately become pregnant, seeking the traditional role of mother as the only rite of passage into adult womanhood (Porter, 2000a). Others, internalizing messages of academic incompetence learned in the school environment, may fail to explore career possibilities that require education beyond high school.

Without doubt, the educational environment becomes a central place for learning and self-evaluation during adolescence. Sanders and Bradley (2005) suggest that, in the minds of some African American adolescent girls, schools function more like educational hospices—places where they go to die spiritually, academically, and emotionally because expectations for them are limited or nonexistent. With consequences so dire, it is crucial for schools to address the academic underachievement and perceptions of restricted career choice among this population.

Family

African American families and White families are more alike than they are different, and they are as diverse in their structures. Although there are significant commonalities that link all African Americans as a community, there is a great deal of variance in how these families perceive and react to their realities (Parham & Brown, 2003). Keeping these cautions in mind, it is important to recognize that African American families do influence the developing self-esteem of their daughters in some culturally specific ways.

The family can act as a buffer between African American adolescents and society's negative evaluations of them, thus becoming a source of healthy self-esteem (Norton, 1983). Racial socialization of children by their families helps to mitigate the negative effects of racist discrimination (Fischer & Shaw, 1999). Parents who address racism and prejudice directly and help their children identify with their own race can strengthen the ability of their daughters, when they reach adolescence, to resist institutional racism and increased peer pressure to act White.

This buffering effect may operate differently with respect to gender, as compared to race. Families provide models of gender-appropriate behavior for their daughters, and African American fathers may gender-type their daughters to a greater degree than do White fathers (Price-Bonham & Skeen, 1982). Many African American mothers promote assertiveness and independence as a means of encouraging self-protection skills to combat racism (Cauce et al., 1996), but may out of necessity push daughters into the role of "parental child" (Diller, 2007). In African American families, girls often undertake adult responsibilities such as household duties and the care of younger siblings at an early age (Sue & Sue, 2003).

Wright (1998) believes that parental closeness is another important factor in supporting African American adolescent girls' developing self-esteem; to the extent that parents can be present and emotionally involved in their daughters' daily lives, there is a greater likelihood for the development of positive self-esteem. This closeness is difficult to maintain in low-SES families, when fathers are absent due to the cycle of poverty and racism, and when single-parent mothers are torn between having to earn a living and being available for their daughters.

It is important to emphasize adaptive strategies within the African American family. These include an extended generational system of parenting, in which the parent role is distributed across several generations living in the home (Diller, 2007), creation of a "buffer zone" between children and societal stereotyping and discrimination, and socialization for racial pride. That African American girls have made healthy adjustments within this society often is "a reflection of an active socialization process that takes place within their families to prepare their members to confront institutional barriers" (Greene, 1994, p. 23). Messages sent by adolescent girls' immediate environments at home can mitigate those of the broader society and provide a basis for the internalization of positive self-esteem (Norton, 1983).

COUNSELING INTERVENTIONS

Adolescents, in general, are often reluctant to seek help, partially because of the perceived threat to their developing self-esteem (Cauce et al., 2002). African American youth, in particular, "do not come to counseling willingly" (Sue & Sue, 2003). They are likely to be resistant to counseling for a number of reasons. Their peers are very important to them, and their perceptions of the social stigma attached to counseling can have an important influence. Their reluctance might relate to the tendency of African American youth to turn to family members when they are experiencing a problem, rather than to "out-group members" who are not part of their social network (Offer, Howard, Schonert, & Ostriv, 1991). When African American adolescent girls can be engaged in counseling, we believe that individual, small group, and family counseling all can be effective in addressing the multiplicity of their self-esteem issues.

School counselors are an obvious source of individual counseling assistance for African American girls. We would advise school counselors to avoid focusing primarily on "symptoms" such as poor grades and acting out behaviors in school. Instead, they should listen and remain nonjudgmental, and engage students from a questioning stance. Through active listening and taking the time to get to know these adolescent girls, counselors may be able to form a therapeutic alliance and introduce counseling strategies such as narrative therapy, bibliotherapy, and journaling. Additionally, group counseling and support groups have long been regarded as a treatment of choice for African American girls (Adkinson-Bradley & Sanders, 2006). Finally, family therapy is recommended for its focus on the family system, which remains a powerful influencing force for most adolescents. Structural family therapy has been advocated for African American adolescents because it focuses on alterations in family structure that have resulted from stressful life events (Sykes, 1987), is short-term and goal-oriented, and accounts for the impact of external forces on the family.

CASE STUDY

Jessica, age 14, is a light-skinned African American ninth grader at a public high school with a predominantly ethnic minority student population. Until this year, Jessica had attended a selective all-girls private academy where 85% of the students were White and where her academic performance had been in the A to B range and her conduct exemplary. Although Jessica started out well at her new school, her grades have declined to a present C/D level. Her conduct in the classroom also has deteriorated, and she now rarely participates in discussions. At the beginning of the school year, Jessica had inquired about joining the track team. She was a star on the track team at her old school. Currently, she seems to have dropped all interest in track or any other after-school activities.

Jessica's teachers note that she has attached herself to a certain clique of students who sit in the rear of the classroom. This group of African American girls is viewed by teachers as being overly preoccupied with boys and clothing, and not academically inclined or underachievers. These girls have been observed in the hallways taunting and even physically pushing around other girls whom they label as "eggheads" who "think they are better than everyone else." Although Jessica was once the target of such abuse, she has become attached to this group, occasionally cutting class. She has been reprimanded for acting disrespectfully toward teachers. One of her teachers characterizes her behavior as "oppositional-defiant."

Ms. Adams, the school counselor, has asked Jessica's mother to meet with her to discuss Jessica's school performance and behavior. Jessica's mother, a research librarian at the large state university, states that Jessica's behavior also has begun to change at home, noting behavioral changes—including sullenness, noncooperation, irritation with her younger brothers, and under-the-breath mumbling when requests are made—when she and her husband first separated. Her behaviors have gotten worse since the divorce was finalized and Jessica's father moved out of the household. Her father visits every other weekend and tends to spend most of his time with Jessica's younger brothers, on her mother's insistence. As she puts it, "I don't know how to raise men." She surmises that Jessica probably wants more time with her father, but as a girl and the oldest, "Jessica has things that need doing."

Jessica's mother adds that her daughter's poor behavior is even more troubling because she needs to depend on Jessica to help with her brothers and with the upkeep of the house. She says, "I know that it has been difficult for Jessica. Her father isn't around much and she had to leave her friends and go to a school where she knows no one. I had to move her to the public school or sell the house. We saved and fought too hard to get this house in this neighborhood. If you came to our street, you would notice that there aren't too many people of our persuasion around." Jessica's mother adds that she herself has always been academically inclined and an overachiever, and so has Jessica. "I used to call her junior—after me. I was the first one in my family to go to college, let alone earn a master's degree. If Jessica's grades don't improve, she isn't going to have a chance in life."

Discussion

Jessica seems to have become "a different person" since she started the ninth grade. She has experienced significant changes in her family situation and school environment that affect her academic performance, school behavior, peer relationships, and the ways she interacts with adults. At age 14, she is likely experiencing rapid changes in the physical, affective, and cognitive domains that affect her self-esteem. Possible counseling issues with Jessica include academic, behavioral, social, familial, and developmental concerns. Any successful counseling intervention will need to consider these multiple levels of Jessica's functioning.

Individual Counseling

To the extent that Jessica sees Ms. Adams as representative of the adults in her school environment who judge her negatively, Jessica may view her with resentment and mistrust. If she perceives that she is being referred for counseling against her wishes and that she does not need assistance, as is the case with many adolescents (Fitzpatrick & Irannejad, 2008), it will be difficult for Ms. Adams to engage her in the counseling process.

When Ms. Adams first meets with Jessica, she might ask Jessica to describe her feelings about counseling and what she thinks counseling is, and how she is feeling about her life in general. If Jessica is typical of many African American adolescent girls, she may be unlikely to talk directly about herself or about specific personal issues. She may make statements like, "I want to go back to the school I attended last year. All the people here have attitude." Or, she might say, "Some girls are having a tough time not fitting in, but I'm doing okay."

Narrative therapy might prove effective with Jessica, as it will allow her to give voice to her experiences and feelings in a medium that she perceives as less threatening than the traditional speaking dyad. If Jessica likes to read, bibliotherapy is very successful with many African American girls (Adkinson-Bradley & Sanders, 2006) and might be employed to help buttress Jessica's self-esteem. A healing narrative like *The Color Purple* (Walker, 1982) might be empowering for Jessica; she could experience herself as a strong and resilient protagonist (Semmler & Williams,

2000). Such exposure to competent role models might help to buttress Jessica's own sense of competence and have a positive effect on her self-esteem.

If Jessica enjoys writing, journaling might be another nonthreatening means for her to express herself and assign meaning to her experiences at school and at home. Ms. Adams may be able to discern and reflect back to Jessica any themes that emerge from these expressions, perhaps such as Jessica's feelings of powerlessness and lack of control over changes in her life.

It is vital that Jessica have an active role in formulating any counseling goals that may be set. Adolescents are very concerned with issues of independence and self-determination and are especially sensitive to having goals imposed on them by others (Fitzpatrick & Irannejad, 2008). If Jessica comes to see counseling as a process that can increase rather than diminish her self-esteem (Vogel, Wester, & Larson, 2007), she may become actively engaged in the process. Then, she and Ms. Adams can direct their focus to working on more concrete, behavioral goals.

On the other hand, Jessica may remain unresponsive to Ms. Adams' attempts to engage her in individual counseling. Other approaches that could be efficacious in helping Jessica include group counseling and family counseling.

Group Counseling

Group counseling and support groups have long been regarded as a treatment of choice for African American girls (Adkinson-Bradley & Sanders, 2006). Ms. Adams could initiate psychoeducational groups with the goal of assisting not only Jessica, but other girls who attend the school as well. Jessica will not feel singled out for counseling if such groups are a routine component of the school's guidance curriculum. Ms. Adams will need to give careful forethought to the composition of these groups. No single group should be comprised solely of Jessica and her current clique, as the members would tend to use the group as a forum for reinforcing each other's attitudes and behaviors. A group that includes Jessica, some members of her peer group, and at least an equal number of girls in the school who are targets of their taunting could provide opportunities for all participants to benefit from the power of collective feedback. Girls who may be reticent to express themselves in a one-on-one conversation with an adult often are more assertive and verbose in a group with their peers.

Adkinson-Bradley and Sanders (2006) describe a 10-week psychoeducational and life preparation group for adolescent African American girls. It includes a number of activities that could be incorporated into Ms. Adams' groups. Topics for bibliotherapy and journaling assignments are targeted toward defining self-esteem, writing as preparation for a successful academic year, expanding vocational and educational choices, identifying personal strengths, conflict resolution, and practicing coping strategies for stressful situations—all of which are pertinent to Jessica's current needs. For example, a "Her Story" session that features historical contributions of African American women could help Jessica identify role models of success as scientists, scholars, astronauts, and leaders of nations. This could help her and her peers to reframe their view of academic success as acting White. A session could focus on finding mentors within the school. Jessica might approach the track coach, if the coach is amenable to serving as a mentor. Jessica could be asked to share her skills and knowledge by serving as the coach's assistant, as an entrée to reengaging her in an extracurricular activity at which she can excel. This Afrofemcentric (African-female-centered) perspective seems ideal for assisting girls like Jessica to feel validated and empowered and to enhance their self-esteem.

Family Counseling

Jessica's mother and the family should be referred for family counseling. There is little doubt that Jessica's school behaviors and decline in academic performance are in some ways a reflection of and reaction to the changes in her family. During a divorce and in its initial aftermath, parents may shift their attention away from their children and onto themselves, for financial, emotional, or social support reasons, leaving the children to feel unwanted, confused, and resentful. Jessica seems to be acting out some of these feelings. Family counseling will provide a venue for her to raise her concerns without being labeled the "identified patient" in the family system.

Although Jessica's parents may not have intended any of their postdivorce adjustments in the family to be punitive toward Jessica, she may perceive that her education is less important than that of her brothers because they remain at the private academy while she has been forced to go to a public school. She may also perceive herself as less important to her father, who now spends the majority of his family time with the boys. She may resent her additional household responsibilities and care of her younger brothers. The role flexibility the family is displaying is a strength, particularly for African American families under stress (Boyd-Franklin, 1989), yet it is having negative repercussions for Jessica. The family therapist may help the parents to see the situation through Jessica's eyes and to make some minor adaptations. For instance, a family agreement might be made that Jessica and her father will have a regularly scheduled father–daughter day every other week. Jessica's mother appears to be distracted by the responsibilities of single parenting and financial pressures. In counseling sessions when these distractions are set aside, she may be able to refocus on the importance to Jessica's development of the mother–daughter relationship. As a well-educated and successful career woman, she is a potent self-esteem role model for Jessica. In family counseling sessions, both of Jessica's parents can be encouraged to express to Jessica that she is important to them and is a valued member of their family system. This positive feedback from the two most significant adults in her life might help to increase Jessica's feelings of self-worth and acceptance.

Jessica's family has many other strengths that can be used as building blocks in counseling. They value education, have provided their children with a home in a desirable neighborhood, and appear to have been effective in creating a buffer zone between their children and the prejudice and discrimination in the larger world. Until this year, Jessica was a successful student and a track star at the private academy where African American students were in the distinct minority. Now she is in a public school with a large ethnic minority population and has surrounded herself with a small circle of friends who are also African American. Rather than view this with concern, Jessica's parents can be helped to see it as part of a normal developmental process.

At age 14, Jessica may be at a crucial point in her development. Through individual or group counseling, or both, the school counselor can be instrumental in helping Jessica regain her social and academic self-esteem. Through family counseling, Jessica's parents may be better able to continue to provide her with a buffer zone against the challenges of racism and sexism that she will continue to encounter and to reinforce her growing self-esteem.

CONCLUSION

The self-esteem systems of African American adolescent girls are complex and are influenced by multiple forces, both developmental and environmental. In this chapter, we explored the social influences of racism and sexism in the larger society, factors in the school environment, and the role of the family. The case study of Jessica was presented as a means to illustrate how counseling interventions such as individual, group, and family counseling might help strengthen the global and selective self-esteem of African American adolescent females.

REFERENCES

Adkison-Bradley, C., & Sanders, J. L. (2006). Counseling African American women and girls. In C. C. Lee (Ed.), *Multicultural issues in counseling: New approaches to diversity* (3rd ed., pp. 79–91). Alexandria, VA: American Counseling Association.

Ahia, C. E. (2006). A cultural framework for counseling African Americans. In C. C. Lee (Ed.), *Multicultural issues in counseling: New approaches to diversity* (3rd ed., pp. 57–62). Alexandria, VA: American Counseling Association.

Belgrave, F. Z., Chase-Vaughn, G., Gray, F., Addison, J. D., & Cherry, V. R. (2000). The effectiveness of a culture- and gender-specific intervention for increasing resiliency among African American preadolescent females. *Journal of Black Psychology, 26*, 133–147.

Boyd-Franklin, N. (1989). *Black families in therapy*. New York: Guilford Press.

Cauce, A. M., Domenenech-Rodriguez, M., Paradise, M., Cochran, B. N., Shea, J. M., Srebnik, D., et al. (2002). Cultural and contextual influences in mental health help seeking: A focus on ethnic minority youth. *Journal of Consulting & Clinical Psychology, 70*, 44–55.

Diller, J. V. (2007). *Cultural diversity* (3rd ed.). Pacific Grove, CA: Thomson Brooks/Cole.

Eccles, J., Barber, B., Jozefowicz, D., Malenchuck, O., & Vida, M. (1999). Self-evaluation of competence, task values, and self-esteem. In N. G. Johnson, M. C. Roberts, & J. Worell (Eds.), *Beyond appearance: A new look at adolescent girls* (pp. 53–84). Washington, DC: American Psychological Association.

Emmons, L. (1992). Dieting and purging behavior in Black and White high school students. *Journal of the American Dietetic Association, 92*, 306–312.

Fischer, A. R., & Shaw, C. M. (1999). African Americans' mental health and perceptions of racist discrimination: The moderating effects of racial socialization experiences and self-esteem. *Journal of Counseling Psychology, 46*, 395–407.

Fitzpatrick, M. R., & Irannejad, S. (2008). Adolescent readiness for change and the working alliance in counseling. *Journal of Counseling & Development, 86*, 438–445.

Greene, B. (1994). African American women. In L. Comas-Diaz & B. Greene (Eds.), *Women of color: Integrating ethnic and gender identities in psychotherapy* (pp. 10–29). New York: Guilford.

Hansen, L. S., Gama, E. M. P., & Harkins, A. K. (2002). Revisiting gender issues in multicultural counseling. In P. B. Pedersen, J. G. Draguns, W. J. Lonner, & J. E. Trimble (Eds.), *Counseling across cultures* (5th ed., pp. 163–184). Thousand Oaks, CA: Sage.

Hare, B. R. (1985). Stability and change in self-perception and achievement among Black adolescents: A longitudinal study. *Journal of Black Psychology, 11*, 29–42.

Hauser, S. T., & Kasendorf, E. (1983). *Black and white identity formation*. Halabar, FL: Kreiger.

Hill-Collins, P. (1990). *African American feminist thought: Knowledge, consciousness, and the politics of empowerment*. New York: Routledge.

Jackson, L. C., & Greene, B. (2000). *Psychotherapy with African Americans: Innovations in psychodynamic perspectives and practice*. New York: Guilford Press.

Lay, R., & Wakstein, J. (1985). Race, academic achievement, and self-concept of ability. *Research in Higher Education, 22*, 43–64.

Martinez, R., & Dukes, R. L. (1991). Ethnic and gender differences in self-esteem. *Youth & Society, 22*, 318–338.

Norton, D. G. (1983). Black families' life patterns, the development of self and cognitive development of black children. In G. J. Powell, J. Yamamoto, A. Romero, & A. Morales (Eds.), *The psychosocial development of minority children* (pp. 275–306). New York: Burnner/Mazel.

Offer, D., Howard, K. I., Schonert, K. A., & Ostriv, E. (1991). To whom do adolescents turn for help. Differences between disturbed and non-disturbed adolescents. *Journal of American Academy of Child and Adolescent Psychiatry, 30*, 623–630.

Parham, T. A., & Brown, S. (2003). Therapeutic approaches with African-American populations. In F. D. Harper & J. McFadden (Eds.), *Culture and counseling: New approaches* (pp. 81–98). New York: Allyn & Bacon.

Pipher, M. (1994). *Reviving Ophelia: Saving the selves of adolescent girls*. New York: Balantine.

Porter, R. Y. (2000a). Understanding and treating minority youth. In J. F. Aponte & J. Wohl (Eds.), *Psychological intervention and cultural diversity* (2nd ed., pp. 167–182). Needham Heights, MA: Allyn & Bacon.

Porter, R. Y. (2000b). Clinical issues and intervention with ethnic minority women. In J. F. Aponte & J. Wohl (Eds.), *Psychological intervention and cultural diversity* (2nd ed., pp. 183–199). Needham Heights, MA: Allyn & Bacon.

Price-Bonham, S., & Skeen, P. (1982). Black and White fathers' attitudes toward children's sex roles. *Psychological Reports, 50*, 1187–1190.

Robinson, T. L., & Ward, J. V. (1995). African American adolescents and skin color. *Journal of Black Psychology, 21*, 256–274.

Robinson-Wood, T. L. (2009). *The convergence of race, ethnicity, and gender: Multiple identities in counseling*. Upper Saddle River, NJ: Pearson.

Sanders, J. L. (1997). My face holds the history of my people and the feelings in my heart: Racial socialization and evaluations of facial attractiveness of preadolescent African-American girls. *Dissertation Abstracts International, 57*, 7760B (UMI No. 9716998).

Sanders, J. L., & Bradley, C. (2005). Multiple lens paradigm: Evaluating African American girls and their development. *Journal of Counseling & Development, 83*, 299–304.

Semmler, P. L., & Williams, C. B. (2000). Narrative therapy: A storied context for multicultural counseling. *Journal of Multicultural Counseling and Development, 28*, 51–62.

Shorter-Gooden, K., & Washington, N. C. (1996). Young, Black, and female: The challenge of weaving an identity. *Journal of Adolescence, 19*, 465–475.

Stevens, J. W. (1997). African American female adolescent identity development: A three-dimensional perspective. *Child Welfare, 76,* 145–172.

Sue, D. W., & Sue, D. (2003). *Counseling the culturally diverse: Theory and practice* (4th ed.). New York: Wiley & Sons.

Sykes, D. K. (1987). An approach to working with Black youth in cross cultural therapy. *Clinical Social Work Journal, 15,* 260–270.

Tatum, B. D. (1997). *Why are all the Black kids sitting together in the cafeteria?* New York: Basic Books.

Taylor, J. M., Gilligan, C., & Sullivan, A. M. (1995). *Between voice and silence: Women and girls, race and relationship.* Cambridge, MA: Harvard University Press.

Vogel, D. L., Wester, S. R., & Larson, L. M. (2007). Avoidance of counseling: Psychological factors that inhibit seeking help. *Journal of Counseling & Development, 85,* 410–422.

Walker, A. (1982). *The color purple.* New York: Washington Square.

Weiler, J. (1997). *Career development for African-American and Latina females.* ED410369, ERIC/CUE Digest 125, ERIC Clearinghouse on Urban Education.

Worell, J., & Remer, P. (2003). *Feminist perspectives in therapy: Empowering diverse women* (2nd ed.). New York: Wiley & Sons.

Wright, M. A. (1998). *I'm chocolate, you're vanilla: Raising healthy black and biracial children in a race-conscious world.* San Francisco: Jossey-Bass.

Section *IV*

Young Adulthood

*I*n young adulthood, as in every life stage, development does not necessarily proceed uniformly. Although there is lack of consensus, based on observable regularities, most researchers say the chronological age range for young adulthood begins at approximately 18–20 and continues until 40. Because the potential for self-esteem issues occurs in the progression from adolescence to adulthood, this section deals primarily with the earlier part of this range. The 20–30 transition from adolescence to young adulthood involves biological, physical, cognitive, and social changes that affect psychological changes (Levinson, 1978, 1996).

Primary aging—the inevitable, normal aging process—differs from secondary aging—the variations in aging resulting from the environment that include social class, health habits, and possible diseases (Bee & Boyd, 2003). In general, adults are at their peak throughout young adulthood, physically and mentally. Athletic skill that depends on speed, strength, or gross motor coordination increases early in the decade and then declines. Athletic skill that depends on endurance increases throughout the decade and then begins to decline. Gradual weight gain begins and continues through middle age (Berk, 2006). Losses begin to occur in this period. The rate of decline across the adult life span varies substantially through a combination of primary and secondary aging factors. Differences include health habits, genetics, social support including intimate relationships, sense of control, and acute and chronic stressors.

Cognitive development increases into early adulthood. The brain has reached a stable size by age 21, although a brain spurt may occur in the mid to late 20s (Bee & Boyd, 2003). Some scholars propose that Piaget's theory falls short, that a postformal operational stage exists in adulthood. This dialectical thought (Basseches, 1984) is characterized by relativistic thinking, the ability to tolerate contradictory evidence and ambiguity, and subjective, contextual reasoning. Although not all adults reach this stage, those that do recognize that truth depends upon circumstances and varies by situation, multiple explanations are possible depending upon point of view, problems do not have single solutions, and no one explanation is necessarily accurate.

People in early young adulthood pursue decisions about education, work, and relationships. Although those in the earliest part of young adulthood are relatively independent from social roles and expectations, they begin to construct a "dream" image of who they will be in the adult world and go about bringing the dream to fruition throughout young adulthood (Levinson, 1978) through the processes of acquisition and consolidation.

As adolescents leave secondary school they make choices about future training and work. They either begin work in the private sector or in the military, or seek higher education opportunities, often delaying significant relationships. Only about one-third of young adults attend college full time directly after secondary school graduation, and many drop out later, usually temporarily. The college experience varies greatly, with nontraditional students more common than traditional ones. Females have a higher graduation rate than males. Underrepresented in higher education institutions, African American students drop out at higher rates than Whites, Asian Americans, Latino Americans, or Native Americans (National Center for Educational Statistics, 1997, as cited in Bee & Boyd, 2003). African American students who do complete college have a strong sense of racial identity and persistence.

Most young adults enter into a phase of stability and do not experience dramatic turmoil in their self-concepts as they progress into the later phase of this stage (Donnellan, Trzesniewski, Conger, & Conger, 2007), although processes differ for men and women. Individuals pursue and establish occupational role identity whether or not they seek higher education, vocational, or on-the-job training. Men, even today, tend to have a more stable career development trajectory, whereas women's career development is more likely to accommodate home and childcare responsibilities, thus extending their career development trajectory into middle age. Women who choose home and family over career may delay occupational aspirations and behaviors until later young adulthood or middle age.

Early young adults enter Erikson's (1959/1980) intimacy versus isolation stage and must successfully resolve the ability to form and sustain deeply personal relationships by the time they reach 30–40 years of age. Although intimacy is not the same as sexuality, sexual activity usually increases during the 20–30 year stage, and sexually transmitted diseases are more prevalent than at any other life stage. Intimate partner abuse and sexual violence is significant; alcohol and drug abuse is typically a contributing factor. Most individuals gain the ability to seek a satisfying, sexually intimate relationship that ends in the commitment for marriage or cohabitation and ultimately parenthood. Successful resolution of this stage results in the capacity for devotion and fidelity. If they have not previously resolved the identity stage in adolescence, individuals are not likely to develop mature relationships and may retreat into isolation. For women, however, the self is not separated from the interactions with others (Jordan, Kaplan, Miller, Stiver, & Surrey, 1991; Miller, 1986). Relatedness rather than autonomy is a key component of identity, and identity is resolved through connection to others. Throughout adulthood, mutual empathy is the hallmark of maturity and impacts growth through connections with others.

Career and work continue to be a major focus throughout the entire young adulthood stage. Additional roles in social and community activities occupy some people as well. For those who are parents, family roles are of primary importance. People develop the capacity and skill to manage multiple responsibilities but also experience greater levels of stress. The social clock—the internalized sense that major life milestones must be reached in a specific, prescribed time period—plays a significant part in shaping adulthood (Neugarten, 1968). People reevaluate life roles at transition points of approximately 30 and again at approximately 40–45 and work on changing structures that never did or no longer fit them (Levinson, 1978). Overall, what began as turmoil in adolescence settles into maturity and stability by the end of young adulthood. Changes in personality "tend to reflect increasing levels of maturity and adjustment, as indicated by higher levels of conscientiousness and emotional stability" (Robins & Trzesniewski, 2005, p. 159).

Evidence suggests that mean levels of global self-esteem rise from adolescence to young adulthood, although individual changes in selective, domain-specific self-esteem vary (Donnellan et al., 2007). Self-esteem increases gradually during young and middle adulthood and shows remarkable stability from earlier levels. Those whose self-esteem was high in childhood and adolescence will continue to have relatively high self-esteem in young adulthood, and the gender gap remains about the same, with males experiencing higher levels than females (Robins & Trzesniewski, 2005). The capacity to relate in positive ways to others increases self-esteem in women, whereas independence and lack of personal involvement and emotion indicate higher self-esteem for men at this stage of life; high-self-esteem men seem to value successful assertiveness and high-self-esteem women value helping their female friends (Harter, 1999).

Self-esteem is at once stable and changing in adulthood, depending upon differences in its conceptualization as a state or a trait phenomenon. "To characterize self-esteem as entirely trait-like may obscure the fact that changes can and do occur in response to various experiences and interventions. Similarly, to characterize self-esteem as entirely state-like obscures the degree to which self-esteem is consistent over time, linked to highly stable individual-difference constructs such as personality traits, predictive of long-term life outcomes, and moderately heritable" (Trzesniewski, Donnellan, & Robins, 2003, p. 217). Certainly, selective, even global, self-esteem can decrease if the dream image created in late adolescence and early adulthood is not established. This discrepancy between the ideal and real self, as in earlier stages, can negatively impact feelings of worth and competence when accomplishments do not match goals. If the magnitude of the discrepancy is great, maladjustments can result, although they may also serve as adaptive motivators (Harter, 1999). For those in whom self-esteem is unstable and vulnerable at earlier life stages, problems in early adulthood can exacerbate already existing mental health issues. New problems can arise as people progress through the young adult years when multiple life roles and stressors overwhelm overburdened lives. For those who have been socialized to believe that they must pursue perceived success in all areas equally, or for those for whom the American ideal of success has been out of reach because of marginalization, low self-esteem can impact on emotional well-being and happiness. This section discusses only a few circumstances in which self-esteem can be a significant factor during the first part of early adulthood: the special issues of young women, sexuality, and with alcohol and other drug (AOD) use. We again find conflicting and puzzling results in AOD and its association with self-esteem.

REFERENCES

Basseches, M. (1984). *Dialectical thinking and adult development*. Norwood, NJ: Ablex.

Bee, H., & Boyd, D. (2003). *Lifespan development* (3rd ed.). Boston: Allyn & Bacon.

Berk, L. E. (2006). *Development through the lifespan* (4th ed.). Boston: Allyn & Bacon.

Donnellan, M. B., Trzesniewski, K. H., Conger, K. J., & Conger, R. D. (2007). A three-wave longitudinal study of self-evaluations during young adulthood. *Journal of Research in Personality, 41,* 453–472.

Erikson, E. H. (1980). *Identity and the life cycle*. New York: Norton. (Original work published 1959)

Harter, S. (1999). *The construction of the self*. New York: Guilford Press.

Jordan, J. V., Kaplan, A. G., Miller, J. B., Stiver, I. P., & Surrey, J. L. (1991). *Women's growth in connection: Writings from the Stone Center*. New York: Guilford Press.

Levinson, D. J. (1978). *The seasons of a man's life*. New York: Knopf.

Levinson, D. J. (1996). *The seasons of a woman's life*. New York: Knopf.

Miller, J. B. (1986). *Toward a new psychology of women* (2nd ed.). Boston: Beacon Press.

Neugarten, B. L. (1968). Adult personality: Toward a psychology of the life cycle. In B. L. Neugarten (Ed.), *Middle age and aging* (pp. 137–147). Chicago: University of Chicago Press.

Robins, R. W., & Trzesniewski, K. H. (2005). Self-esteem development across the lifespan. *Current Directions in Psychological Science, 14,* 158–162.

Trzesniewski, K. H., Donnellan, M. B., & Robins, R. W. (2003). Stability of self-esteem across the life span. *Journal of Personality & Social Psychology, 84,* 205–220.

12

Young Women and Self-Esteem

BRANDON HUNT

T ransitioning from adolescence into adulthood is a major developmental task that involves becoming more independent and forging new relationships. Given the relational nature of women (Miller, 1986), it is no surprise that the self-esteem of young women can be affected by this transition. The focus of this chapter is on helping young women successfully navigate the transition from adolescence into adulthood, and includes a group-based intervention designed to enhance their self-esteem.

DEVELOPMENTAL STAGES FOR YOUNG WOMEN

Life span development involves the physical, cognitive, emotional, and social changes people experience throughout their lifetime. At the early adult stage, physically, women have transitioned out of puberty and are still exploring their identities as sexual human beings, even if they are not engaged in sexual behavior. For the most part, their physical development is complete, and many young women are at the peak of their physical abilities. Cognitively, young adults are more fluid in their interpretations of events and situations. Rather than using concrete thinking, they use their own experiences to weigh all aspects of a situation before they make a decision. They begin to move from dualistic thinking, which focuses on good and bad, right and wrong, to multiple thinking that is relativistic, which allows them to view the world as less absolute. This developmental change requires more critical thinking, as well as an ability to tolerate and process through ambiguous situations. During this transition time, young women begin to make independent decisions related to relationships, finances, and education and work. As a result, they may also begin to experience adult stressors—related to that push for independence— they may not be prepared to handle due to their maturity level and because they have not learned skills to manage stress effectively (Donnellan, Trzesniewski, & Robins, 2006; Feldman, 2006). Socially, young women are sorting out their identity

191

and defining how they view themselves as people and as women. They have begun to individuate from their parents or guardians and are more connected to and identify with their peer group, reflecting their strong need to maintain a sense of connection with other people. This need to feel connected to others is one of the hallmarks of women, whereas men are driven by a need to be independent and autonomous (Gorbett & Kruzek, 2008; Josephs, Markus, & Tafarodi, 1992). Young women may also experience overt or covert sexism as well as unwanted sexual attention, and they use their support systems to help them make decisions about how to respond to such experiences.

In addition to developmental changes, young women also experience changes in life roles and life events. One life event is engaging in romantic and sexual relationships with the personal and societal expectation that women will find a life partner. Depending on their level and stability of self-esteem, young women may engage in risky behaviors as a way to find a romantic partner. For women who are lesbian or bisexual, this life stage involves coming out to themselves and other people, as well as exploring the implications of being a member of a sexual orientation minority. At this time young women also begin to think about whether and when to have children, which can raise concerns about fertility and childbearing. A second life event is navigating the beginning stages of establishing and maintaining a career, which may involve higher education. A third life event is developing financial independence.

SELF-ESTEEM ISSUES AND NEEDS FOR YOUNG WOMEN

Transitioning into adulthood is a time ripe with challenges and possibilities, involving gains and losses that can ignite feelings of inadequacy and powerlessness as people negotiate new roles and new expectations in unfamiliar terrain. For young women, the transition into adulthood can lead to an increased level of self-consciousness and discomfort as they begin developing a cohesive sense of self as an independent and autonomous person while continuing to value and engage in interpersonal relationships. It is this tension between independence and putting relationships with other people first in their lives that can have a negative effect on their self-concept and self-esteem (Sanchez & Kwang, 2007). The higher young women's self-esteem, the more able they are to cope with these changes in a positive, flexible, self-confident, and self-affirming manner (Carlock, 1999; Orth, Robins, & Roberts, 2008).

Although research shows that state self-esteem is relatively stable over time, trait self-esteem can increase and decrease throughout the life span, depending on changes in the social environment and the person's level of maturity. There is a decline in self-esteem during adolescence, which may be a result of biological changes related to puberty and cognitive changes that lead to more abstract thinking, with adolescent self-esteem dropping twice as much for girls as for boys. In adulthood self-esteem gradually begins to rise again (Impett, Sorsoli, Schooler, Henson, & Tolman, 2008; Robins, Trzeniewski, Tracy, Gosling, & Potter, 2002).

In terms of relationships with others, young women create more fluid boundaries, experience stronger emotional connections to other people that get deeper over time, and express a stronger need for family cohesion and connectedness than young men (Gorbett & Kruzek, 2008). As girls age, they begin to lose their sense of power and trust in themselves as they become more attuned to societal attitudes toward women. They become more aware of society's expectations that they work to maintain strong and positive connections with others, regardless of the cost to them, and that they should value relationships over their own needs. At the same time, young women have an increased need for validation from others, whether it is family, close friends, partners, or other people in their lives. They also seem to have a wider scope of significant others whose perceived evaluations matter to them. Within these relationships, the opinions of certain people are more important and can have a greater effect on women's self-esteem, but all relationships are viewed as an integral part of their individual identity. In several studies people with higher self-esteem reported receiving a high level of approval from people in their lives, in addition to personally feeling competent in life areas they believed were important, compared to people with lower self-esteem (Harter, 2006).

Josephs et al. (1992) found that women with high self-esteem had a greater sense of connection and interdependence with other people than women with low self-esteem. For women, "self-esteem may depend not only on 'doing a job well' or 'being a person of worth,' but also on fostering and sustaining relationships" (p. 400). Not receiving validation or receiving negative feedback from others can result in lower self-esteem, and can reinforce existing negative self-esteem, since women's sense of self is predicated on having strong and lasting positive relationships. Sometimes this desire for belonging comes at a cost as young women feel pressure to put their needs aside to avoid conflicts in their relationships (Impett et al., 2008). Bepko and Krestan (as cited in Carlock, 1999) refer to this as the *code of goodness*. Not living up to this code can have a negative effect on their self-esteem—particularly since young women are aware of the importance society places on them putting their relationships first—leading to feelings of shame and low sense of worth when they try to put themselves first.

Young women may feel the need to censor their own thoughts and feelings, even their behaviors, to maintain their relationships. In a longitudinal study of 183 adolescent girls, Impett et al. (2008) found that "girls who reported the highest levels of authenticity [being their true selves] experienced the greatest gains in self-esteem" (p. 729) over a five-year period of time, noting that for girls and women positive self-esteem was strongly related to the ability to be authentic and to be their true selves in relationships. Given the importance women place on relationships, as well as the value society places on women maintaining the code of goodness, young women need to find ways to be authentic in their relationships so that they can maintain a strong sense of self while also being present for other people. Positive self-esteem, particularly social self-esteem, helps young women to develop strong and validating personal relationships with friends and family, intimate romantic relationships, and professional relationships with school and work colleagues (Gorbett & Kruczek, 2008; Impett et al., 2008).

In terms of romantic relationships, young women put a great deal of effort into finding and maintaining intimate partnerships. Holland (as cited in Sanchez & Kwan, 2007) interviewed college women and found that participants spent much of their time either discussing, actively pursuing, or engaging in romantic relationships. This need to be engaged in romantic relationships is a driving force for young women, and Sanchez and Kwan (2007) noted that women rated increased self-esteem as a benefit of being in a romantic relationship.

The transition into young adulthood can lead to loneliness and a decreased sense of belonging as young women physically and developmentally separate from parents, other family members, and friends, and begin to develop new support systems and relationships. For some young women, the inability to develop new relationships as well as changes within existing relationships can lead to *acting in* behaviors, where they internalize negative feelings and engage in self-destructive behaviors. This idea of acting in rather than acting out, as males do, reflects the code of goodness where young women take care of others at their own expense (Carlock, 1999). Problems associated with acting in behaviors include disordered eating, risky sexual behavior, alcohol and other drug overuse and abuse, involvement in abusive intimate relationships, engaging in self-injurious behavior, and problems in school or the workplace (Azzarto, 1997; Impett et al., 2008; Liang, Tracy, Taylor, & Williams, 2002).

Young women with low self-esteem are susceptible to depression and anxiety (Liang et al., 2002). Young women may also be overly sensitive to rejection and criticisms, particularly if those experiences support their already negative sense of themselves as inadequate and incompetent (Liang et al., 2002; Orth et al., 2008). Young people with low self-esteem often seek reassurance from others to the point of excess, which can result in rejection by the very people they seek reassurance from; they tend to seek out negative feedback from partners as a way to reinforce their negative sense of self; and their low self-esteem leads them to avoid social interactions, reinforcing their negative sense of self because they do not receive the social support and validation they want and need (Orth et al., 2008). Furthermore, young adult women tend to have a large number of people they consider to be their significant others.

ASSESSING SELF-ESTEEM IN YOUNG WOMEN

Given the importance young women place on relationships, using an interview protocol is a good way to assess self-esteem because of the necessity of interaction between client and counselor. Questions can be designed to address global and selective self-esteem. In terms of global self-esteem, counselors can accurately define self-esteem and ask clients to rate themselves, discussing how the clinical definition fits with the clients' own definition of self-esteem. Counselors can ask clients how their sense of self and their self-esteem has affected their life choices to date, including discussion about the clients' childhood perceptions of who they would become as women, exploring the influences family, friends, their community, and society had on them. Additional topics that address global self-esteem include the messages clients received from parents and other adults about the role and worth of women in society; how they think other women their age perceive themselves; and what clients want for themselves, and believe they are worthy of attaining, in the next 5, 10, and 20 years. Given the importance of relationships to women, counselors can ask clients about their role and satisfaction in their relationships with others, particularly people they view as significant, and how those relationships affect their sense of self and their self-esteem. Each of these topics not only provides information about the clients' level of global and selective self-esteem, but can be a starting place to help clients explore internal and external messages they received about their worth as females and how those messages made life easier or more challenging for them in developing their own self-identity and self-esteem.

With regard to selective self-esteem, counselors can ask clients to talk about qualities, traits, and abilities they believe are personal strengths and weaknesses and how they affect their self-esteem. During this discussion, counselors should determine whether these qualities, traits, and abilities are important to their clients, since higher self-esteem has been linked to people feeling competent in life areas that were salient to them. If a woman does not believe she has strong athletic abilities, for example, that will not have a negative effect on her self-esteem if being athletic is not important, or has a lower weighted value, to her. On the other hand, performing poorly during a marathon may have a negative effect on a young woman who values her long-distance running ability. Clients can also be asked about specific situations where they felt undervalued or unappreciated and what events or interventions helped them feel better, or worse, about themselves, particularly focusing on relationships that may have helped or hindered the situation.

INTERVENTION STRATEGIES

Societal pressure, particularly from significant others, to consistently and effectively meet the needs of others—the code of goodness—can result in young women engaging in behaviors that may cause them emotional and physical harm, reinforcing their belief that they are not worthy or capable of being loved. Learning to focus on their own needs and wants allows young women to engage in more balanced and equal relationships that support their sense of belonging as well as a positive sense of self. Increasing opportunities for young women to engage in positive and supportive relationships, in both structured and natural settings, can increase and maintain self-esteem, particularly selective self-esteem, because it gives them a chance to validate and be validated by others in domains important to them. Because young women view their relationships as an integral part of who they are, engaging in productive and supportive relationships increases their sense of self-worth. As Liang et al. (2002) noted, the "*quality and nature* of women's relationships may be more meaningful than ... [their] *quantity or structure*" (p. 273).

In a study of 296 female college students, Liang et al. (2002) found that relational quality predicted self-esteem and belonging, with stress being the strongest predictor of low self-esteem and loneliness. Being in strong and supportive relationships helps women develop coping skills and strategies, increase their support systems, and develop emotional resiliency. In addition, women prefer relationships that involve mutual disclosing of personal and intimate information, as well as empathy. It is these factors that support the use of a psychoeducational group format to enhance and support the self-esteem of young women transitioning into adulthood. Strong relational skills not only empower women individually and in their relationships, but they increase the women's sense of worth and validation, and support their need for strong and authentic connections with other people (Liang et al., 2002).

There are a number of counseling techniques and strategies that increase self-esteem. Individual counseling can be the treatment of choice initially for young women whose self-esteem is so low that they are threatened by the group setting. The counselor can work to assist these young women by acting as a positive self-esteem model, offering noncontingent positive regard, and serving as an accepting significant other.

Designing a Self-Esteem Psychoeducational Support Group

The intervention described here uses several techniques and strategies discussed by Mruk (2006b), including a group format, modeling positive feedback and acceptance from group members and the counselor, and "natural self-esteem moments" (Mruk, 2006a, p. 166). The interactive psychoeducational group consists of five 2-hour sessions, preferably occurring once a week with the same members attending all five sessions. As Mruk (2006b) recommends, it is helpful to do a brief telephone screening to determine whether the group format is appropriate.

The goals of the psychoeducational group are (1) to help young women become more realistic, more accepting, and less critical in their evaluations of themselves; (2) to help them engage in fewer potentially self-harming behaviors; and (3) to support participants in becoming more aware of their positive qualities and attributes (Wood, Anthony, & Foddis, 2006). The group consists of three phases. The first phase is the identity phase, where participants begin to explore and become aware of their self-perceptions and beliefs about self, as well as how they affect their self-esteem. The second phase involves an increased awareness of personal strengths and weaknesses. The final phase is the nurturance phase, where participants begin to integrate this new self-awareness into their thoughts, behaviors, and self-identity (Mruk, 2006b). Although the intervention is designed for a group, activities can be used in individual counseling as well.

Psychoeducational Group Structure and Activities

During Week 1, which addresses the identity phase of self-esteem enhancement, participants become acquainted with each other and the group facilitator, which sets the stage for the work to come in future sessions. It is important that participants agree on a set of group rules and expectations, since this begins to create a safe and supportive environment. Being in relationships is important to young women, and feeling valued and validated leads to increased self-worth, so taking the steps necessary to create a safe group environment should not be overlooked and may need to be revisited in future sessions.

In the first session participants learn about self-esteem and how self-esteem and self-worth have an effect on their sense of self. The facilitator also provides an overview of the phases of the group and how weekly activities complement the purpose of the group. Participants can engage in activities designed to help them get to know each other and talk about what they hope to gain from being in the group. One activity, which addresses cognitive aspects of selective and global self-esteem, involves each participant naming two women she believes have strong self-esteem, and talking about how those women might describe experiences in their lives that helped them develop strong self-esteem. Participants can select women they know or famous women (real or fictional). Group members discuss the role interpersonal relationships played in these women's lives, particularly in terms of challenges they may have faced and how their relationships helped them to stay strong and become successful. Group members can then create a list of the qualities and life experiences all or most of these women possess that can be morphed into one woman who would serve as a self-esteem role model.

At the end of the first session, the facilitator introduces the idea of participants journaling their experiences during the five-week group and beyond. Journaling can help young women express their thoughts and feelings, particularly as they negotiate the development life tasks expected of them. The facilitator provides topics for group members to write about each week. For example, to address global self-esteem, participants can write about how their childhood and adolescent experiences led them to who they are today, particularly in terms of their confidence and sense of self, or they can journal what they remember about how women in their current age bracket were described when they, the clients, were children. Group members can also write about particular life experiences or situations where they felt they were successful, or failed in some way, to address competence in selective self-esteem domains.

The counselor should stress the importance of group members being as honest and specific as they can so that when they look back on their writing over the duration of the group they get a clear sense of life experiences and events that affected their self-esteem, including ways they might have used the information they learned in the group to handle the situation differently. The facilitator, along with the group members, can make the decision whether to have participants talk about their journaling experiences each week, have the counselor review the journals each week and give written feedback, or encourage journal writing but not make it a required part of weekly discussions. As Vonk (2006) discovered, participants who received written comments from psychologists in an online diary study had increased self-esteem that remained high four months after the study ended, compared to a control group and a treatment group that wrote in the online diary but received no written comments. These findings support the idea of having the counselor write comments on the journals, but having members discuss their journal entries may also be helpful. Mruk (2006b) recommends providing journals to participants since it can motivate people to actually keep a journal.

During Week 2, which continues the identity phase, participants begin to explore how their life experiences influence their self-esteem. Based on the education and discussion that occurred during Week 1, this exploration occurs as group members assess their support network during a life phase of their choosing (i.e., as an adolescent, as a young adult, or both) using an exercise adapted from Carlock (1999). Group members draw a circle, placing themselves in the circle, then noting all the people they view as strong supports as lines coming out from the circle, almost like rays from the sun. The people identified can be family, friends, romantic partners, co-workers, or classmates—anyone the women view as part of their support system. For each person identified, group members draw a line with an arrow at one or both ends of the line. The length of the line represents the level of support received in terms of encouragement, acceptance, honest opinions, respect, and validation, with a shorter line meaning stronger support. The arrow at the end of the line represents whether the support comes to the women, goes from the women, or both. After the diagrams are completed, members explain their diagram to the group and talk about what it was like to complete the activity. This activity addresses cognitive and affective elements of selective and global self-esteem. It is helpful with this population because group members have the opportunity to explore their interpersonal relationships in a supportive setting that can serve to validate their experiences.

During Week 3, which moves into the increased awareness phase of self-esteem enhancement, participants create two collages. The counseling work occurs as participants engage in producing and then discussing their collages, since the women will talk with and support each other as they create their collages. On one collage, participants use pictures and words from magazines and newspapers to provide content that represents messages young women receive about who they are supposed to be and their own personal responses to these messages. In other words, the participants identify how those messages have affected their present sense of self. On the other collage, group members use words and pictures to note their strengths, positive qualities, and achievements to date. Since the activity can bring up negative feelings for some participants as they explore their negative self-perceptions, the counselor may find it necessary to be even more supportive during this activity, encouraging participants not to use the collage as a way to focus on their negative qualities and failures. Once finished, participants share their collages with other group members and the facilitator, talking about what they represent to them and what it was like to engage in the activity. This activity addresses the cognitive and affective elements of global self-esteem.

Weeks 4 and 5 address the nurturance phase of self-esteem enhancement. Mruk (2006b) described an activity that can be used in Week 4 to address the cognitive and affective elements of self-esteem enhancement. Participants write a list of 10 positive attributes or qualities they possess, and then share the list with the rest of the group. While the activity may seem simple, much of the group work occurs when participants who are unable to come up with 10 qualities share what that experience is like and receive feedback from other group members about their strengths and abilities. At this point the members have begun to establish trusting relationships with each other, and they can help members who are struggling by suggesting positive qualities they see in each other. It is helpful if the facilitator starts the activity by providing realistic examples, perhaps even sharing examples of what she or he might write on her or his list, and allowing participants adequate time to complete the task before discussing their lists and processing the experience (Mruk, 2006b).

During the final meeting, participants process what the group experience was like for them and how they believe they changed for the positive as a result of being in the group. Several activities could be incorporated into this session, depending on the needs and wishes of the group. Members could write a note to each woman, describing her strengths and contributions to the group. Another option would be to have participants write a list of two self-esteem-related goals they hope to achieve in the next six months or the next year, as well as specifics on how they hope to reach those goals. Activities of this type address cognitive and affective elements of selective and global self-esteem, and completing these tasks in a group setting supports and reinforces women's needs to be in supportive relationships.

ROLE OF THE COUNSELOR

When working with young women with self-esteem concerns, it is important that counselors are accepting, supportive, realistic, and appropriately challenging for two reasons. First, they serve as models of strong self-esteem for many of their clients, and second, the interpersonal nature of counseling provides clients with another positive and significant relationship in which they can explore their thoughts, feelings, and beliefs about themselves and the world they live in and receive affirmative feedback from.

One important role for counselors is to help young women set realistic boundaries and engage in healthy behaviors. The counseling relationship can provide another way for young women to explore and express their authentic selves and see themselves as competent and capable women. Counselors can provide accurate and honest feedback, and educate young women about future developmental changes and how to manage upcoming transitions in ways that support and enhance their self-esteem. Focusing on strengths and coping strategies that have worked for clients in the past can help them find alternative options for dysfunctional or destructive strategies they may be currently using, such as engaging in risky sexual behavior or abusing alcohol and other drugs as a way to feel good about themselves. Counselors can also serve as a consistent source of support in an honest, caring, and nonjudgmental way, while helping clients identity other people and supports that exist in their lives to increase their social support network.

Although men and women can be effective when working with clients with self-esteem issues and concerns, female counselors can serve as strong and confident role models for young women. This may be particularly true in a group format where counselors serve as models by sharing their own experiences of growing up female, being careful about when and how they use self-disclosure.

OUTCOME EVALUATION

Given the nature and format of the group intervention, counselors can perform process and outcome evaluations. Process evaluation includes a check-in at the beginning or end of each meeting to see how the women perceive participation affecting their self-esteem and sense of self-worth. For outcome evaluation, participants could complete a self-esteem assessment measure before they begin the group, at the end of the 5 weeks, and then again 6 months and 12 months after the group ends, to evaluate how their self-esteem increased as a result of participating in the group. Group members could be taught how to complete and evaluate the assessment themselves, or the counselor could send out the instruments for the participants to complete at the appropriate times and then provide written feedback that points out their growth and increased self-esteem. (See Chapter 1 for a list of suitable instruments.)

CASE STUDY

Katie is a 20-year-old White woman who was urged to go to the university counseling center by her dormitory resident advisor after she talked with her about being treated for a sexually transmitted disease. Katie went for an intake and was referred to individual counseling for eight sessions, which is the upper limit of sessions students can receive on campus. During the intake Katie expressed concerns about being in counseling, saying she was worried she would be "a bad patient" and that she did not want to "waste the counselor's time" with her "trivial problems."

In the first session Katie focused on her family and childhood. She said her parents, who have been married for 24 years, are both very involved with their careers (her mother is a family physician and her father is a certified public accountant), and that "they have very high expectations" that she will be successful in her career and in her life, although she said that did not "matter" to her. She said she knows her parents love her, but "they are not the kind of people who give a lot of praise" because they believe she should be successful for herself and not to receive praise. In the first session it was apparent Katie did not receive the level of support and validation necessary for adolescent girls to develop a strong sense of self. She expressed not being able to talk with her parents, and feeling like she should be able to solve her problems on her own without "burdening" other people.

Katie is an only child and said she has been a "latchkey kid" since she was 11 years old, noting there were few children in her neighborhood growing up, and most of them were boys. She said she had a few close girl friends until she entered 10th grade. At that time, she said her friends started to exclude her from group activities and she found "hate notes" in her locker (there were six or seven notes total over the course of nine months) that said she was a "loser" and that "no boy would ever like her." She never learned who wrote the notes, but she thinks it may have been some of her friends. Katie said those events led her to being "obsessed" about not being as likable or attractive as other girls, who were starting to date boys and get into committed relationships. She dated casually in high school but said it was mostly going out with groups of people, and she did not engage in any sexual activity beyond kissing. Katie said her parents encouraged her to study hard and not to be so concerned about making more friends and finding a boyfriend, which was contrary to the message young women receive about society's expectations that they work to maintain strong and positive connections with others.

The counselor allowed Katie to decide what she wanted to talk about in session, using empathy and validation statements to encourage her to tell her story on her own terms. This approach gave Katie control over what she wanted to talk about, allowing her to take care of her own needs while providing opportunities for her to begin to develop a relationship with the counselor. When asked what she wanted to gain from counseling, Katie said she wanted to "feel better" about herself and learn "how to trust people" besides her family.

Katie started the second session saying she wanted to talk about her current experiences, rather than her childhood. She talked about being a good student who earned primarily As, just like in high school. She said she wanted to become a physical therapist and that maintaining a high grade point average was important for her to get into graduate school. Her global self-esteem was high, but she struggled with selective self-esteem regarding her relationships with peers. Katie was confident about her ability to be successful in school, and her problems revolved around finding people with whom she felt comfortable. She said she wasn't able to nurture relationships with her peers, although she expressed wanting to feel more connected to the other young women she described as casual friends. She also wanted to find a boyfriend who would treat her well.

When Katie entered college she found that using alcohol helped her to feel more confident in social situations around her new peers, particularly boys. This behavior is not uncommon for young women with low self-esteem who are struggling to expand their self-identity in a new situation. During her third year of college, Katie began to drink heavily (five to seven drinks in an evening) and engaged in casual sexual relationships with boys she met at parties in the hopes of finding a boyfriend and feeling like she fit in. She said all of her friends did this and she did not want them to think she was a "baby" if she did not "drink and hook up." Katie said she only "went home with boys three or four times," and stopped the behavior toward the end of the fall semester to focus more on her coursework.

Over the next summer Katie had her first serious relationship, dating Adam for several months. She broke up with him when she learned he was dating another girl at the same time he was seeing her. Although breaking up with Adam was an example of Katie's strong sense of self because she was taking care of herself, her perspective was that if she had been "a better girlfriend," then Adam would not have cheated on her. Although some of her friends tried to talk with her about the breakup, Katie said she did not talk with them because she was embarrassed Adam had cheated on her and she did not want them to "feel sorry" for her or laugh about her behind her back. Katie said she started drinking again heavily six weeks ago to deal with her sadness, and that it was "easier" for her to have sex with different boys every weekend so she would not get her "heart broken again." She was embarrassed that she acquired a sexually transmitted disease and said she would "be more careful next time."

Katie's selective self-esteem regarding relationships, particularly with romantic partners, was very low, and she had a hard time letting her friends support her. The counselor worked with Katie to help her reframe her breakup with Adam so she could see that she was really taking steps to care for herself by ending the relationship, similar to how she cared for herself as a child when her parents were at work and she was home alone. Katie and her counselor explored what Katie believed she deserved in a partnered relationship, what qualities she looked for in a partner, and what qualities she believed she brought to an intimate relationship. They also began to explore what Katie believed she deserved in a friendship, and how she could start to open up more with her friends so that she did not feel so alone. This exploration continued for the next two sessions as Katie learned how to think of herself as strong and supportive in a romantic relationship and friendships. At the end of the second session the counselor talked with Katie about attending a psychoeducational self-esteem support group, in addition to individual counseling, to help her learn ways to improve her self-esteem in terms of finding and maintaining supportive relationships. Katie agreed to attend a six-week group that was starting at the Center for Women Students.

In the third session Katie said she had "hooked up with a boy" she met in a bar and talked about how angry and disgusted she was with herself because she had promised herself she would not do that again. She had asked several friends to watch out for her, but when the time came to leave the bar, she refused to leave with them. Now she was worried they would not want to stay friends with her. Katie and the counselor spent the session talking about what led to her decision to go home with the young man, the role alcohol played in her decision, and what she might have done differently if she had not been drinking. They also role played how she might talk with her friends about what happened and her concerns that they would not want to remain her friend.

During the fourth session Katie talked about a situation where she decided not to go home with a man she met in a bar, even though she had been drinking, and how she felt about that decision. She thought it was fine for women to engage in casual sexual relationships if that was their choice, but she wanted to make the decision when she was sober and had time to think about what that behavior would mean for her. Because she wanted to be in a committed relationship, she made the decision to change her behavior by not drinking excessively and then hooking up with men. Over the remaining sessions Katie and her counselor continued to talk about her sense of self in relation to other people, and she began to experiment with sharing more of her concerns and problems with her friends. She viewed her counselor as a positive self-esteem model of a woman who could take care of her own needs while also caring for other people, and the validation and support Katie received in counseling helped her begin expressing her feelings and concerns with her close friends without worrying as much about what they would think of her if they knew about her insecurities. She also started to share some of her concerns with her parents, and role played with her counselor how to ask her parents for more verbal support and praise. The work Katie did in individual and group counseling helped her feel more confident about herself and what she had to offer other people, and her self-esteem about her ability to engage in relationships with close friends and potential partners began to increase, while its salience was not as heavily weighted. She also began to show evidence of increasing the importance of the academic domain of her selective self-esteem.

CONCLUSION

The significance of being involved in supportive and validating relationships and the positive effects they have on young women's self-esteem cannot be underestimated. Engaging in and maintaining healthy relationships increases their sense of self-worth and helps them avoid engaging in potentially harmful behaviors like alcohol and other drug overuse and abuse, disordered eating, and sexual acting out. As a result of internal and external expectations, young women must work to maintain a balance between taking care of themselves and meeting the needs of others. If that balance is disrupted, young women with low self-esteem focus on doing what other people want and need, often at their own expense. Individual and group counseling can provide young women with low self-esteem the tools they need to begin to feel confident and secure and to realize their authentic and true potential.

REFERENCES

Azzarto, J. (1997). A young women's support group: Prevention of a different kind. *Health & Social Work, 22,* 299–305.

Carlock, C. J. (1999). *Enhancing self-esteem.* Philadelphia: Accelerated Development.

Donnellan, M. B., Trzesniewski, K. H., & Robins, R. W. (2006). Personality and self-esteem development in adolescence. In D. K. Mroczek & T. D. Little, *Handbook of personality development* (pp. 285–309). Mahwah, NJ: Lawrence Erlbaum Associates.

Feldman, R. S. (2006). *Development across the life span* (4th ed.). Upper Saddle River, NJ: Pearson Prentice Hall.

Gorbett, K., & Kruczek, T. (2008). Family factors predicting social self-esteem in young adults. *The Family Journal: Counseling and Therapy for Couples and Families, 16,* 58–65.

Harter, S. (2006). The development of self-esteem. In M. J. Kernis (Ed.), *Self-esteem issues and answers: A sourcebook of current perspectives* (pp. 144–150). New York: Psychology Press, Taylor & Francis Group.

Impett, E. A., Sorsoli, L., Schooler, D., Henson, J. M., & Tolman, D. L. (2008). Girls' relationship authenticity and self-esteem across adolescence. *Developmental Psychology, 44,* 722–733.

Josephs, R. A., Markus, H. R., & Tafarodi, R. W. (1992). Gender and self-esteem. *Journal of Personality and Social Psychology, 63,* 391–402.

Liang, B., Tracy, A. L., Taylor, C. A., & Williams, L. A. (2002). Mentoring college-age women: A relational approach. *American Journal of Community Psychology, 30,* 271–288.

Miller, J. B. (1986). *Toward a new psychology of women* (2nd ed.). Boston: Beacon Press.

Mruk, C. J. (2006a). Changing self-esteem: Research and practice. In M. J. Kernis (Ed.), *Self-esteem issues and answers: A sourcebook of current perspectives* (pp. 164–169). New York: Psychology Press, Taylor & Francis Group.

Mruk, C. J. (2006b). *Self-esteem research, theory, and practice: Toward a positive psychology of self-esteem* (3rd ed.). New York: Springer.

Orth, U., Robins, R. W., & Roberts, B. W. (2008). Low self-esteem prospectively predicts depression in adolescence and young adulthood. *Journal of Personality and Social Psychology*, 95, 695–708.

Robins, R. W., Trzesniewski, K. H., Tracy, J. L., Gosling, S. D., & Potter, J. (2002). Global self-esteem across the life span. *Psychology and Aging, 17*, 423–434.

Sanchez, D. T., & Kwang, T. (2007). When the relationship becomes her: Revisiting women's body concerns from a relationship contingency perspective. *Psychology of Women Quarterly, 31*, 401–414.

Vonk, R. (2006). Improving self-esteem. In M. J. Kernis (Ed.), *Self-esteem issues and answers: A sourcebook of current perspectives* (pp. 178–186). New York: Psychology Press, Taylor & Francis Group.

Wood, J. V., Anthony, D. B., & Foddis, W. F. (2006). Should people with low self-esteem strive for high self-esteem? In M. J. Kernis (Ed.), *Self-esteem issues and answers: A sourcebook of current perspectives* (pp. 288–296). New York: Psychology Press, Taylor & Francis Group.

13

Self-Esteem and Sexuality
An Exploration of Differentiation and Attachment

FRANCESCA G. GIORDANO AND LEE COVINGTON RUSH

RELATIONSHIP BETWEEN
SELF-ESTEEM AND SEXUALITY

S elf-esteem issues have been linked to a variety of sexuality problems in adults and couples, including difficulties with sexual desire, love, and intimacy. The interaction between sexuality and self-esteem can be seen from many different perspectives. While self-esteem appears as a variable in the literature of adolescent sexual development, it seems to be regarded differently when applied to adult sexual development. This change may stem from adolescent sexuality literature being influenced by the sexuality education and developmental psychology, in which concepts such as self-esteem development play a clear practical and conceptual role. For example, in the adolescent sexuality literature, low self-esteem is indicated as a predictor of risky behaviors such as sexual promiscuity and related behaviors (Spencer, Zimet, Aalsma, & Orr, 2002). Sex education programs often use self-esteem building activities to promote positive sexual decision making and to decrease risk-taking behaviors in adolescents (Sexuality Information and Education Council of the United States [SIECUS], 2008). Positive self-esteem is seen as a foundation on which healthy sexuality is built.

When the relationship between sexual functioning and problems associated with sexuality, including issues such as intimacy and love, and self-esteem is considered in adults, the focus is often shifted to the individual self, and seen as much more clearly influenced by early psychodynamic thinking and family therapy theory literature. In consequence, concepts such the self-in-context, self-differentiation, and attachment play a much stronger role in the conceptual understanding of how self-esteem impacts healthy sexual behaviors. Healthy sexual functioning and intimacy skills are seen, in adults, as the key to relationship satisfaction. Positive self-definition is the component linking sexual interactions to self-esteem (Lieser, Tambling, Bischof, & Murry, 2007). However, global self-esteem tends to be emphasized. The "self" in self-esteem thus becomes a much more complex component in intimacy, relationship satisfaction, and love. When treating intimacy problems, relationship issues are often seen as the global self-esteem component. Although the sexual self is only one aspect of the overall self, it is sometimes efficient to link global self-esteem and adult sexual relationships. However, the sexual self is only one portion of the whole self, and as a result, aspects of it (such as body image and attachment issues) can also be evaluated and treated separately as aspects of selective self-esteem. Additionally, certain selective self-esteem issues become problematic, for example, when defining sexual dysfunction by the standards of performance and evaluation and associating the results with global self-esteem. Furthermore, the multidimensional self includes multiple identities in which culture plays a significant role.

A more global concept of the relationship between self-esteem and adult sexuality suggests that when individuals enter adulthood they already have a self-concept that influences their sexual behaviors in highly complex ways. Factors that build or damage self-esteem play a role in the overall context in which sexual behaviors occur. For example, healthy adults need to involve themselves in intimacy without losing a sense of individual identity. The literature often sees traditional concepts such as competence and achievement as obstacles to the development of the healthy sense of self needed for intimacy. Mikulincer and Goodman (2006) connect concepts such as self-esteem to attachment, suggesting that healthy sexuality is a capacity of the self that allows performance-based sexual behaviors to result in feelings of competence and achievement that serve to build self-esteem, rooted in strong attachment bonds and supported by a solid self (Schnarch, 1997). Sexuality that has an emphasis on behavioral successes, such as orgasm and erectile performance, tends to "miss the point" or even damage sexually intimate relationships (Schnarch, 1997). It should be noted that sexual self-esteem, "the positive regard and capacity to experience one's sexuality in a satisfying and enjoyable way" (Snell & Papini, 1989, p. 256), has been linked to an individual assessment of sexual competence and skill (Smith, 2007). However, for this discussion, issues of self-in-context, differentiation, and attachment are emphasized in the conceptual framework that underlies the activities within this chapter.

CONCEPTUAL FRAMEWORK: ROLE OF SELF-ESTEEM IN HEALTHY SEXUALITY

An adult's awareness of the roots of their sexual problems is often traced back to their experiences as an adolescent. In adolescence, as social skills develop, developmental changes impact body awareness and image, and sexual experimentation and behaviors begin to integrate. Many of these experiences can be tied to the sexual problems of adults. As a result, adolescence is the reasonable place to begin examining sexual problems rooted in self-esteem. It is how adults remember and reexperience meaningful adolescent sexual experiences that pave the way to their adult sexual relationships. Adults seem to very clearly understand that their inability to develop sexually satisfying relationships is connected to their comfort with intimate connections with others. Many relationship therapists suggest that adult intimate relationships can be used to overcome problems rooted in solid-self issues and those of attachment.

Therefore, we see the influence of self-esteem issues on sexual problems in adults to be threefold. First, they result from sexual experiences in adolescence and their influence on self-esteem. Second, the implications of self-esteem to sexual issues in adults are better conceptually understood through attachment and understandings of the solid self. Finally, neither of these influences on self-esteem can be understood in any depth without understanding the role of culture.

SELF-ESTEEM AND THE ROLE OF CULTURE

In discussing the intersection of self-esteem, sexuality, and culture, as they relate to other than majority constructs, Chow provides a notation that may serve as an instructive place to start our discussion:

> Race and ethnicity are thus coterminous with sexuality, just as sexuality is implicated in race and ethnicity. To that extent, any analytical effort to keep these categories apart from one another may turn out to be counterproductive, for it is their categorical enmeshment—their categorical miscegenation, so to speak— that needs to be foregrounded. (Chow, 2002, as cited in Asher, 2007, pp. 6–7)

There appears to be scant research on the implications self-esteem and sexuality from a cultural context, perhaps due in part to these otherness *positionalities*. For example, multicultural researches, such as McGoldrick, Giordano, and Garcia-Preto (2005) and Sue and Sue (2003), in discussing persons from collectivistic cultures, especially Asian Americans, Asian Indians, and African Americans, tend to reference the sensitivity with which one may attempt to discuss issues regarding sex and sexuality. This reticence in relationship to sexuality has, it seems, much to do with cultural constructs framed on modesty, attending to private issues within the family, not bringing shame upon the family, and cultural indictments against same-sex identities. Further complicating these issues, Asher (2007) maintains that the general focus of multiculturalism has been viewed in terms of race and culture with limited attendance to sexuality. These constraints notwithstanding, much of the research that has emerged relating to cultural others articulates the intersection between self-esteem and sexuality, similar to the general theories related to the majority culture, though in many instances in combination with other or additional variables. In proceeding with this discussion, there are two important caveats: The connections between ethnic identity, self-esteem, and adjustment are at this point inconclusive, and a number of critics question whether Western models of sexual identity are even applicable in discussing nonmajority cultures (Frable, 1997).

Of the extant research, sexuality, sexual behavior, and self-esteem issues related to African American men and women have focused on cultural standards of sexual attractiveness. Wade (2003) maintained that the efficacy of the evolutionary theory regarding African Americans' adaptations in relationship to self-perceptions of attractiveness and self-esteem has not yet been fully examined. Wade found that self-esteem and sexual attractiveness for African American women were predicated on their skin tone and, more precisely, their acceptance or nonacceptance of it. Much research explicates the internalized oppression of many African Americans and the intersection of skin color and self-esteem, emerging from Western constructs of beauty. For African American men, self-esteem was predicated on their physical and sexual attractiveness. Thus, for African American men, skin tone seems not to affect issues of self-esteem.

A factor that may have particular consequences for African American males in regards to their self-esteem is what Franklin (1999) refers to as their *invisibility syndrome*. This syndrome "is presented as a way to explain the intrapsychic struggle for personal identity by African American men … particularly in cross-racial circumstances, and how these experiences obscure genuine identity and promote inherent stress related to their management" (Franklin, 1997, as cited in Franklin, 1999). *Invisibility*, in this instance, is defined as "an inner struggle with the feeling that one's talents, abilities, personality, and worth are not valued or even recognized because of prejudice and racism" (Franklin, 1999, p. 761). Thus, from this construct, it is proposed that the African American male's self-esteem is both degraded and eroded. The consequence of this invisibility syndrome according to Wyatt (1999) may include less responsibility in dealing with unwanted sexual outcomes, may foster false or misleading notions of African American men's sexual anatomy and prowess, and may include multiple sexual exploits. All these sexually related behaviors are seen then as efforts to prop up the masculine self, while concurrently seeking to enhance the lowered self-esteem. In considering the multiple contexts of African American sexuality, Parmer and Gordon (2007) cogently noted: "We cannot view African American sexuality without considering how forces of the past have shaped the continued process of changing behavior and practices" (p. 195).

The intersection of sexuality, self-esteem, and culture is of consequence in framing any discussion on these issues. It is also apparent that the direct influence of cultural *otherness* on sexuality and self-esteem is an area in need of further study. The impact of oppression and racism on the definition of the self and on self-esteem and healthy sexuality should be considered when exploring the nature of the solid self. Many adults are also aware of the impact of multiple identities on their sense of self, which further complicates this already complex picture.

ADOLESCENT SEXUAL DEVELOPMENT

Adolescence is the time when we are most keenly aware of the development of our sexual selves, and where sexual experiences usually most influence our developing self-esteem. Sexuality educators suggest that for adolescents to successfully complete their sexual development, they must also develop positive self-image

(SIECUS, 2008). The connection between self-esteem and healthy sexual development has been made by others; Selverstone (1989) suggests that one of the four important tasks of adolescents is the development of a unique identity, and that sexual behaviors may be key to that development. He suggests that as adolescents experience themselves as sexual beings, make decisions, and learn to relate in a sexual way, the insights they gain about themselves can help develop a sense of independence, foster directedness, and build positive self-worth. These experiences and behaviors lead to the development of a sexual self as one aspect of selective self-esteem.

This link between sexual behaviors and decisions in adolescence influences sexual orientation and the core development of the sexual self. Butler (1991), in her critique of the social construction of gender and the impact of performance theory on gender development, suggests that sexual behaviors and the social context in which they occur have a powerful effect on the development of the self. This may be especially true in adolescence and in our adult recollection, in telling stories of our sexual escapades for the reactions of others. It is not only the behaviors themselves and their direct consequences, but the reactions of those around us that form our sense of self and enhance or damage our self-esteem.

Timing and Decision Making Regarding Sexual Behaviors

Timing of sexual behaviors and the capacity to cope with the effects of sexual activity have been connected to self-esteem. The link between self-esteem and sexuality behaviors in adolescents seems influenced by peer context. Meier (2007) found that girls who have sex at younger ages than their peers (in relationships that subsequently ended) were more likely to experience decreased self-esteem. Adolescents who develop solid decision-making and critical-thinking abilities fare much better, as do those who can evaluate the pressures of the social norm without being peer-pressured into sexual behaviors. Spencer et al. (2002), investigating the early initiation of sexual intercourse, found a relationship suggesting that there might be a negative effect on self-esteem for girls and a positive effect for boys. Noll, Trickett, and Putnam (2000) found that adolescent girls seek romantic partners chiefly for emotional support and self-esteem building. Often the shame and guilt experienced around early sexual choices can have long-term self-esteem implications (SIECUS, 2008). It seems clear that peer context—positive opinions and feedback—is of critical importance to self-esteem enhancement.

Body Image

Sex forms an inappropriate focus of identity development when adolescents define themselves by level of sexual attractiveness. Lessons about body image are one of the six course areas that should be covered in human development/sexuality education curricula (SIECUS, 2008). While linkage of self-esteem, body weight, and size is especially troubling for girls, it also seems to be problematic for boys and the development of masculinity. Internalized negative body images and low self-esteem can be intensified, for boys as well as men, by positions of power in adult life, as a result of men's minimal opportunities to accept the vulnerability of their physical selves and emotions (Seidler, 2007). The relationship between body image and self-esteem is well documented and has been seen to have its greatest impact on the development of selective characteristics of self-esteem. Sanchez and Kwang (2007) found that body shame can affect overall feelings of relationship confidence and global self-esteem. The conflict between reality and expectation leading to low self-esteem, impotence, and sexual dysfunction is often connected to the physical changes associated with aging (Sharpe, 2003), and the root of this connection is found in adolescence.

Sexual Communication/Boundaries

The ability to develop communication and social skills related to sexual behaviors and choices is linked to self-esteem. It seems to affect the development of a sense of personal power and self-efficacy. Healthy sexual relationships are consensual, non-exploitive, honest, mutually pleasurable, safe, and protected (Conklin, 2007). When adolescents experience sexual relationships with these factors, improved self-esteem results. Decision making, about what type of information to share with whom, is one aspect of developing healthy sexual boundaries. Adolescence is when individuals begin developing the communication skills needed to discuss intimate information with others.

Sexual Coercion/Violence

Experiences of sexual violence or coercion—whether sexual abuse/incest, stranger rape, date rape/dating violence, or unwanted sexual activity—happen during adolescence; their effects on self-esteem and sexual development are especially devastating. Sexual violence often creates toxic shame, which in turn damages self-esteem and impedes healthy sexual development. Dating violence seems to be pervasive during the teen years. Prior victimization negatively affects judgment of risk, a phenomenon to which adolescent girls are especially vulnerable, and drinking habits increase this further. While boys are also victims of sexual violence, they may be more affected as perpetrators of sexual coercion. College women are often victims of unwanted or coerced sexual activity. Feeling responsible for impaired judgment, self-blaming, and a sense of shame are some ways in which the consequences of sexual violence/coercion damage self-esteem.

Cultural Factors

In reviewing culturally diverse adolescents, an emphasis can be found on the influence of parents as communicators of positive cultural self-esteem messages. Parents may be especially influential in limiting sexual risk-taking behaviors. Turner, Kaplan, and Badger (2006) alert us that most of the research related to adolescent self-esteem has been on White adolescents. The limited research thus far suggests that the self-esteem of Latina girls is lower than the self-esteem of both White and African American girls. In their study, Turner et al. (2006) found that among Latina girls (Puerto Rican and Dominican), the positive communications patterns (identified as empathic understanding) between these girls and their mothers tended to enhance the girls' self-esteem. In tandem, other studies have proposed that these positive communication patterns not only enhance these girls' self-esteem, but also diminish risky sexual activity. Liebowitz, Castellano, and Cuellar (1999) found that among Mexican American youth, both male and female, the main indicator for the absence of sexual activity related to the "child's perception of parent-child congruity of sexual values … [and] with the second best predictor being [the] child's educational goals" (p. 477). In this study, the youths' self-esteem or communication patterns were not correlated with sexual abstinence. The authors propose that self-esteem may be a more complex independent variable, as self-esteem for adolescents can be conceptualized in varying ways, such as by ethnicity or appearance. Similarly, Mandara, Murray, and Bangi (2003), in examining the sexual activity of African American adolescents, found that self-esteem factors were not mediators in terms of the sexual activity of these youth. Rather, their study concluded that it is parental monitoring of African American girls that mediated their sexual activity, and that these girls' self-esteem may not be contingent on sexual activities. For African American boys, factors related to the African American male culture may intersect with and encourage youthful sexual activity.

ADULT SELF-ESTEEM CONCEPTS AND THEIR EFFECTS ON SEXUALITY

Differentiation

Schnarch (1997), perhaps more than any other sexuality therapist, has emphasized the important role differentiation of self has on sexual pleasure and intimacy in adults, establishing adult eroticism as more a function of emotional maturation than physiological responsiveness. Taking his ideas from Bowen's (1978) solid self, Schnarch's model of adult sexuality is based on an honest understanding of how past and present experiences affect the core self; an awareness of current feelings, thoughts, and behaviors; and a self open to genuine feedback. Such a self is truly erotic and helps to sustain self-esteem. He encourages "eyes open" orgasm among couples, moving from other-validation to self-validation during intimate encounters. In this sense, intimate sex derives from the development of adult autonomy and ego strength. Schnarch suggests that sex experienced with self-validation does not depend on the positive feedback from others—feedback that may often be disingenuous. Adults able to have healthy, open, and clear communication with each other are able to have increased levels of intimacy and sexual pleasure; they can be fully present during sexual interactions and be aware of each other's solid self. Mature adult experiences with truly intimate sex are seen to enhance self-esteem and the overall relationship. Smith (2007) connects this understanding of "good sex" to well-being, competence, autonomy, and relatedness.

Attachment

The three types of attachment styles (secure, anxious, and avoidant) have an effect on romantic love and the habitual patterns of relational expectations, emotions, and behaviors. These styles are rooted in early life experiences, and affect sexuality through adults' responses to intimacy and vulnerability. Schnarch's work, addressed in the previous section, describes how the healthy secure attachment style serves to increase self-esteem through improved intimacy. The anxious attachment style is connected to low self-esteem (Mikulincer & Goodman, 2006), and the connection between damaged attachments and self-esteem has also been explored through studies of marital infidelity (Eaves & Robertson-Smith, 2007; Ward, 2001). The low self-esteem of anxiously attached individuals (those overly concerned with rejection and abandonment) leads them to use sex to please or appease their partners, reassure their self-worth, or cope with a partner's negative affect. The avoidant attachment style (those exhibiting low anxiety with varying degrees of avoidance) is more complex, often associated with high self-esteem selectively based on self-assessed personal competence rather than successful or supportive personal relationships (Davis, Shaver, & Vernon, 2004).

Recent adult attachment studies have suggested that the availability, responsiveness, and supportiveness of romantic partners in time of need help avoidant or anxiously attached partners feel more secure (Mikulincer & Goodman, 2006). However, these characteristics must exist in the context of a specific relationship; they are necessary but not in themselves sufficient. For example, when one or both partners in an intimate relationship have attachment anxiety, the anxious persons may become preoccupied with the possibility of abandonment. This preoccupation can lead to behaviors that further undermine intimacy. This seems especially true of those with low self-esteem. Individuals with avoidance attachment disorder may seek to avoid intimate sexual encounters, but pursue sex with casual partners. Partner responsiveness, rather than just simple self-disclosure, is critical; supportive listening, emotional openness, identification, and responsiveness to needs are necessary to overcome attachment difficulties.

INTERVENTION STRATEGIES

From the previous discussion it is clear that activities must encourage intimate and safe discussion of sexual concerns, encourage the differentiation of the self, and promote secure attachment, leading to improved self-esteem and increased sexual satisfaction.

Development of the Sexual Self

Many sexuality therapists use sexual history taking and the sexual genogram to help assess and evaluate couples' current sexual functioning and relationship dynamics. The "three-fights-in-one" concept (Sells, Giordano, & King, 2002) interprets couples conflicts based on the historical injury in each member of the couple, the history of conflict in the couple, and the nature of the current fight. Using this model, couples able to differentiate historical injury from past and current conflict are better able to resolve conflict and maintain intimate relationships. As a result, in this activity, each partner in the couple is asked to help the other review the history of his or her sexual self and to understand how a historical sense of his or her sexual self is connected to the current conflict. The emphasis here is on using the sexual genogram and teaching the couple to ask each other open-ended questions exploring how the sexual self developed, with an emphasis on adolescent experiences. This activity is structured to reinforce positive feedback as a way of building the couple's sexual self-esteem. The couple is asked to stay focused on four areas: (1) *when* they made decisions to engage or not engage in various types of intimate behaviors, at what age, and what they can remember influenced their decision-making process; (2) *how* their body image affected their sexual and intimate (dating) behaviors in adolescence; (3) *what* experiences they had with intimate sexual communication, and where, when, and with whom they learned about sexual boundaries; and (4) any *negative experiences* they may have had with sexual coercion and violence. Sharpe (2003), in her review of adult sexuality from a developmental perspective, suggests that partnered young adults become more sensitive to differences in sexual experience between them, and that the negotiation and reconciliation of those differences can be an attempt to achieve true intimacy. An emphasis on the cultural messages conveyed by parents or other family members and the community is also encouraged.

Sexual Intimacy Circles

This part of the sexual history taking can be enhanced through creating sexual intimacy circles. Each member of the couple is asked to remember himself of herself as an adolescent. Each draws a diagram of concentric circles; the center is labeled "My Self." Each circle out from the self is labeled as a less intimate group of people. For example, the next-level circle could be labeled "intimates," the next circle "family," the next circle "friends," the next circle "acquaintances," and so on. Then, each member of the couple adds to each circle the type of intimate information and sexual behaviors they—as adolescents—felt were appropriate to the group associated with that circle. For example, the intimate circle might be associated with sexual intercourse, but limited personal information, while the family circle could be associated with very intimate personal information but not sexual intercourse. This activity can also explore experiences with sexual coercion and violence; such experiences are often identified by high levels of (forced) sexual behaviors and low or no levels of intimate communication, though they may occur in any circle. It may be that forced sexual behaviors are associated with intimate communication, and in these cases, feelings of guilt and shame may also need to be addressed.

A special note about processing shame-based experiences is warranted here. The linked between shame-evoking experiences and low self-esteem is well documented, suggesting that feelings of shame about past experiences (especially experiences in which the individual had no control) may be damaging to global self-esteem. Couples should be encouraged to utilize positive feedback with each other in confronting feelings of shame and in reinforcing positive coping, current worthiness, and acceptance.

In this activity, special emphasis is placed on separating the ideal self from the real self, that is, distinguishing what family or other significant adults told them was right (ideal) from what they actually did (real). In cases where there is significant conflict between the two, participants may benefit by drawing and filling in a second diagram, distinguishing between the ideal and real. This activity also helps to explore the connection between culture and intimate communication. This can be especially important either when each member of the couple identifies with different cultural backgrounds, or when the effects of multiple cultural identities make communication between the couple more complex. For couples in which culture, multiple identities, or cultural conflict is especially important, an additional intimacy circle just focused on culture may be critical.

Emphasis is placed on helping the couple ask each other nonjudgmental, nonevaluative, open-ended questions. The goal is to develop a picture of how the adult sexual self developed, through the influence of adolescent experience. Couples should be encouraged to use supportive and responsive listening strategies to create an environment of emotional openness, feelings of closeness, and connection— all essential elements of positive feedback.

Who Is in the Bed With Us?

This activity is a humorous attempt to encourage couples to examine the positive and negative messages from others that run through their minds during intimate and sexual behaviors. Difficulties in sexual performance have been linked to "interfering thoughts that precede and/or occur during sexual relations" (Wincze & Carey, 2001, p. 144), especially in men. Negatively evaluative messages have a particularly negative effect on sexual self-esteem. In exploring the relationship between investment in gender conformity and sexual satisfaction, Sanchez, Crocker, and Boike (2005) have found that both men and women who based their self-esteem on others' approval tended to invest in messages that promote gender conformity, and that this undermines their autonomy in sexual relationships and lowers sexual satisfaction.

Couples explore with each other the messages—real or implied—from each other, other people, and entities (such as specific television shows or magazines) that they feel negatively evaluate their sexual behaviors. Special emphasis is placed on media and cultural messages. For example, a woman who is recently a mother might say, "My mother is in bed with us telling me that mothers are not sexual," or "That Victoria's Secret catalog is in bed with us, and it's telling me I'm too fat to be sexually attractive." Couples work together, listing as many types of messages as they can that they feel might be influencing their sexuality. This activity often leads to important insights about the influence of negative messages on self-esteem and intimacy.

CASE STUDY

Mary is a 23-year-old woman. She has been married to Mark for six months. Both are second-generation Puerto Rican Americans with very close ties to their families of origin. Mary is originally from a small borough in southern New Jersey and attended a private liberal arts college in the East. She and Mark are currently living in Philadelphia, and she works as a second grade teacher in a bilingual class-room for children. Mark has lived in Philadelphia all his life. He did not attend college, but went directly to work in his father's business from high school. Mark is 25 years old and has a young son from a brief previous marriage. Mark's son and ex-wife were living in Puerto Rico, but Mark encouraged her to allow his son to live with him, believing that this son would be provided with better educational opportunities. His son ended up as a student in Mary's class, and this is how Mark and Mary first met.

Mary was raised in a middle-class Puerto Rican family with two older sisters and a younger brother. She was raised by both her parents, who have been happily married for over 30 years. Her family is very close and supportive of her education, even when she left home for college. Mary's family is very traditionally Roman Catholic, and she has a strong personal sense of spirituality. Some aspects of her faith include beliefs that sacrifice on earth aids in later salvation, that misfortune in life is inevitable, and especially that she should not have sex before marriage. Mary has had several relationships with men, including a two-year relationship during her senior year of high school and her first year of college. Throughout her life she has held to her beliefs about sex, despite pressure from boyfriends and college friends to change them.

Mark is the eldest child of a working-class Puerto Rican Roman Catholic fam-ily, with seven brothers and two sisters. Mark was also raised with both his parents, but their relationship has been full of stress and conflict. Mark's dad has occasion-ally been abusive to his mom, and Mark is strongly determined never to turn into his dad, no matter what. Further, as is often the case in Puerto Rican families, Mark is especially close to his mother (McGoldrick et al., 2005). Though Mark works closely with his dad every day, his mother's abuse has never been openly discussed, at least in part because of the traditional family structure and religion. Mark has dated many women and had sexual relationships with all of them. He reports that his brief marriage was a "mistake," and that he had never really been in love until he met Mary. He wonders sometimes if he is good enough for her, but has kept these thoughts to himself.

Mary has sought out counseling because she fears her sexual relationship with Mark is unsatisfying to him. While he has not complained, Mary senses that they do not have sex often enough for Mark. Even after six months of marriage, Mary still feels inhibited and shy, especially around sexual issues. She often feels over-whelmed by thoughts that she is not attractive enough for him and that he will cheat on her with a more "sexually appealing" woman. She thus exhibits signs of low body image esteem and lacks feelings of worthiness. Mary knows that many of her insecurities stem from a secret she has never shared with Mark: She was raped.

At the beginning of her senior year in high school, she accepted a ride home from an event with a Puerto Rican boy that she had known throughout high school. On several occasions they kissed and had done some light petting in the car on the way home from events they sometimes attended together. One night, they stopped on the way home, parked, and began to kiss. He made advances toward having sex with her and she protested, but he did not listen and eventually raped her. They both had been drinking, and Mary felt tremendous guilt about many aspects of her behavior that night. Mary never told anyone what happen.

She denied to herself that the rape occurred, though she reported feeling depressed and worthless most of the time. She eventually confided in a college friend but was still depressed, angry, and distrustful of men. She immersed herself in her schoolwork and extracurricular activities and became the coordinator of the sexual assault awareness committee at her college, even while separating herself psychologically from women who also had been sexually assaulted. During her senior year, she decided that she had to start dealing with her own rape experience. Instead of seeking therapy, Mary shared the experience with some friends who also had been raped. She never told Mark about the assault.

Mary reported that she is not ready to do a sexual genogram with Mark, but would participate in the sexual intimacy circles. As they both worked together to explore their circles, they discussed how their backgrounds had helped shape their beliefs about to whom to tell intimate information. Ironically, they both came to see that they tend to share intimately more with women than men. Mary began to see that it was not easy for her to share intimately with Mark. On the other hand, Mark had always talked easily to women, but had never been able to talk about important issues with his dad. Mark began to see how he expects Mary to take the responsibility of "opening up" to him. He discovered that he had assumed that not being abusive to Mary was "not being like his dad," and that he must take some responsibility himself to talk about his emotions. Mark and Mary recognized that their somewhat covert, traditional Puerto Rican communication style was having a negative and stressful effect on their ability to be intimate. They started to discuss how they wished that their inner circle consisted of sharing their most intimate information with each other, and decided that they must create a communication relationship between them that is open, trusting, and safe. Having a positive experience sharing their intimacy circles built their confidence to share more deeply. Both reported that the positive feedback from each other was helping to build their confidence, their sexual self-esteem, and their global self-esteem. They helped each other feel better about themselves. Based on this feedback, they learned how they share common values and associated their love for each other with these common values. Eventually, Mary was able to tell Mark about the rape without fear or shame.

CONCLUSION

This chapter has reviewed the ways in which self-esteem impacts the sexual problems of adults and couples. From this discussion, it is clear that sexual experiences from one's adolescence have a profound effect on self-esteem, especially regarding intimacy and sexual issues. Young adults leave their adolescence with a variety of experiences that serve to enhance or damage sexual self-esteem. Adults must possess positive self-esteem in order to develop healthy differentiation and attachment necessary to healthy adult sexual relationships. The activities included in this chapter are designed to encourage mutual exploration of adolescent experiences, promote healthy differentiation and attachment, and create a positive self-esteem-building experience.

REFERENCES

Asher, N. (2007). Made in the (multicultural) U.S.A.: Unpacking tensions of race, culture, gender, and sexuality in education. *Educational Researcher, 36,* 65–73.

Bowen, M. (1978). *Family theory in clinical practice.* New York: Jason Aronson.

Butler, J. (1991). *Gender trouble: Feminism and the subversion of identity.* New York: Routledge.

Conklin, S. C. (2007). Sex education. In *Encyclopedia of educational psychology.* Thousand Oaks, CA: Sage.

Davis, D., Shaver, P. R., & Vernon, M. L. (2004). Attachment style and subjective motivations for sex. *Personality and Social Psychology Bulletin, 30,* 1076–1090.

Eaves, S. H., & Robertson-Smith, M. (2007). The relationship between self-worth and marital infidelity: A pilot study. *The Family Journal, 15,* 382–386.

Frable, D. (1997). Gender, racial, ethnic, sexual, and class identities. *Annual Review of Psychology, 48,* 139–163.

Franklin, A. (1999). Invisibility syndrome and racial identity development in psychotherapy and counseling African American men. *The Counseling Psychologist, 27,* 761–793.

Liebowitz, S., Castellano, C., & Cuellar, I. (1999). Factors that predict sexual behaviors among young Mexican American adolescents: An exploratory study. *Hispanic Journal of Behavioral Sciences, 21,* 470–479.

Lieser, M. L., Tambling, R. B., Bischof, G. H., & Murry, N. (2007). Inclusion of sexuality in relationship education programs. *The Family Journal, 15,* 374–380.

Mandara, J., Murray, C., & Bangi, A. (2003). Predictors of African American adolescent sexual activity: An ecological framework. *Journal of Black Psychology, 29,* 337–356.

McGoldrick, M., Giordano, J., & Garcia-Preto, N. (2005). *Ethnicity & family therapy* (3rd ed.). New York: Guilford Press.

Meier, A. M. (2007). Adolescent first sex and subsequent mental health. *America Journal of Sociology, 112,* 1–28.

Mikulincer, M., & Goodman, G. S. (2006). *Dynamics of romantic love.* New York: Guilford Press.

Noll, J., Trickett, P., & Putnam, F. (2000). Social network constellation and sexuality of sexually abused and comparison girls in childhood and adolescence. *Child Maltreatment, 5,* 323–228.

Parmer, T., & Gordon, J. (2007). Cultural influences on African American sexuality: The role of multiple identities on kinship, power, and idealogy. In M. Tepper & A. Owens (Eds.), *Sexual health—Moral and cultural foundations* (Vol. 3, pp. 173–201). Westport, CT: Praeger.

Sanchez, D. T., Crocker, J., & Boike, K. R. (2005). Doing gender in the bedroom: Investing in gender norms and the sexual experience. *Personality and Social Psychology Bulletin, 31,* 1445–1455.

Sanchez, D. T., & Kwang, T. (2007). When the relationship becomes her: Revisiting women's body concerns from a relationship contingency perspective. *Psychology of Women Quarterly, 31,* 401–414.

Schnarch, D. (1997). *Passionate marriage: Love, sex, and intimacy in emotionally committed relationships.* New York: Henry Holt and Company.

Seidler, V. J. (2007). Masculinities, bodies, and emotional life. *Men and Masculinities, 10,* 9–21.

Sells, J. N., Giordano, F. G., & King, L. (2002). A pilot study in marital group therapy: Process and outcome. *The Family Journal: Counseling and Therapy for Couples Families, 10,* 156–166.

Selverstone, R. (1989). Where are we now in the sexual revolution? *SIECUS Report, 17,* 7–12.

Sexuality Information and Education Council of the United States. (2008). *Sexuality Information and Education Council of the United States.* Retrieved September 29, 2008, from http://www.siecus.org/

Sharpe, T. H. (2003). Adult sexuality. *The Family Journal, 11,* 420–426.

Smith, C. V. (2007). In pursuit of 'good' sex: Self-determination and the sexual experience. *Journal of Social and Personal Relationship, 24,* 69–85.

Snell, W. E., & Papini, D. R. (1989). The sexuality scale: An instrument to measure sexual-esteem, sexual-depression, and sexual-preoccupation. *Journal of Sex Research, 26,* 256–263.

Spencer, J., Zimet, G., Aalsma, M., & Orr, D. (2002). Self-esteem as a prediction of initiation of coitus in early adolescents. *Pediatrics, 109,* 581–585.

Sue, D., & Sue, D. (2003). *Counseling the culturally diverse: Theory and practice* (4th ed.). New York: John Wiley & Sons.

Turner, S., Kaplan, C., & Badger, L. (2006). Adolescent Latinas' adaptive functioning and sense of well-being. *Affilia, 21,* 272–281.

Wade, J. (2003). Evolutionary theory and African American self-perception: Sex differences in body-esteem predictors of self-perceived physical and sexual attractiveness, and self-esteem. *Journal of Black Psychology, 29,* 123–141.

Ward, D. (2001). Self-esteem and dishonest behavior revisited. *Journal of Social Psychology, 126,* 709–713.

Wincze, J. P., & Carey, M. P. (2001). *Sexual dysfunction: A guide for assessment and treatment* (2nd ed.). New York: Guilford.

Wyatt, G. (1999). Beyond invisibility of African American males: The effects on women and families. *The Counseling Psychologist, 27,* 802–809.

14

Alcohol and Other Drug Use and Self-Esteem in Young Adults

BRANDON HUNT AND MARY H. GUINDON

*T*he transition into young adulthood from adolescence requires completing a variety of developmental tasks that include becoming more independent, developing new relationships, including intimate relationships, and beginning a career. Depending on people's level of self-esteem, as well as their coping skills and support system, this transition can include alcohol and other drug (AOD) overuse and abuse. The focus of this chapter is on counseling young adults struggling with AOD-related concerns to move into recovery by helping them improve their self-concept and develop more positive self-esteem.

Young adults begin to individuate from their parents in adolescence and continue to be influenced by their peer group more than by older adults. Peer relationships continue to be important in young adulthood because they provide opportunities for young adults to compare their values, beliefs, and mental and physical abilities with people who are similar to them. This social comparison helps them feel validated and gives them a sense of belonging, but it can add pressure to engage in behaviors such as AOD use that they may not be comfortable with to gain acceptance from their friends and acquaintances (Feldman, 2006; Gorbett & Kruczek, 2008).

USE OF ALCOHOL AND OTHER DRUGS IN YOUNG ADULTHOOD

Use of alcohol and other drugs is a behavior common among young adults. The prevalence of AOD use and abuse is highest during late adolescence and young adulthood, particularly among college students, and the rate of drug abuse is highest in young adulthood. By the 12th grade, 72% of students have had an entire drink, 26% report engaging in binge drinking, and 55% report having been drunk (National Institute on Alcoholism Abuse and Alcoholism [NIAAA], 2009a). The rate of diagnosis of AOD dependence/abuse is also highest among young adults between the ages of 18 and 25 (Arnett, 2005; Lewis, Phillippi, & Neighbors, 2007), whether they are in college, the military, or the workforce (NIAAA, 2009a).

Research has also shown that higher use of AOD during adolescence predicted higher use of AOD in young adulthood as well as alcohol-related problems, and that chronic use of alcohol in adolescence was related to aggressive behavior, relationship problems, and mental health concerns, including suicidal ideation, regardless of gender (Duncan, Alpert, Duncan, & Hops, 1997). NIAAA (2009b) reports that approximately four in five college students drink, including almost 60% of 18- to 20-year-olds. About 41% of all college students reported drinking five or more drinks in the previous two weeks, and more than 40% of college students, regardless of age, reported binge drinking at least once during the previous two weeks, although rates vary across campuses. Furthermore, excessive college drinking leads to injuries, assaults, sexual abuse, unsafe sex, academic problems, vandalism, and even death. Clearly, alcohol and the use of other drugs in young adults and the reasons for it are of grave concern to clinicians, colleges, the workplace, and society.

As Cooper (1994) noted, there are four motivations for young people to use alcohol, and presumably other drugs. First, alcohol can help people obtain or maintain a positive mood and outlook. Second, drinking can make social activities more fun. Third, people drink to conform to the desires of others (e.g., peer pressure), and fourth, people drink as a way to cope with or reduce negative feelings, such as anxiety or sadness. Arnett (2005) identifies four features specific to young adults that increase the risk of AOD overuse, abuse, and dependence. First, young adulthood involves significant identity exploration. During this stage, young people are discovering who they are and what they want from friendships, romantic relationships, and careers. Part of this self-exploration involves the use of AOD to expand their awareness and experiences (i.e., sensation seeking), but some young adults may use substances to relieve the tension related to this time of uncertainty. The transition into young adulthood is ripe with change and instability, which is the second feature. As young people engage in identity exploration, they go through a variety of changes in terms of where they live, who they spend time with, where they work, and who they date, often without a clear guide or road map of where they are headed. While many of these changes may be exciting, they can also create anxiety and discomfort, and young people may turn to AOD as a form of self-medication.

The third feature specific to this transition is that young adults are very self-focused. This may be the first time they have been truly independent and can make their own decisions without getting consent or permission from parents or other authority figures. There is a shift in the level of social control they experience. Often their relationships are in transition as they individuate from parents and family and begin to develop new relationships, both social and romantic. For some, AOD can act as the major social lubricant, yet this is not always the case. Lewis et al. (2007) found that young people who have higher morally based self-esteem drink less alcohol and are more likely to engage in activities that do not revolve around AOD. Young adults who have been using AOD, particularly those who have been overusing or abusing, are often drawn to new friends who engage in similar behaviors, particularly if their old friends do not support or encourage their AOD use. In other words, they seek out new significant others who will validate their newly emerging different sense of worth.

All of these changes and transitions leave young people in a state of "feeling in-between," which Arnett (2005) defines as the fourth feature of young adulthood (p. 245). They are no longer adolescents, but they do not see themselves as adults yet. The age at which young people marry, if they choose to marry, and have children—events used to serve as markers for adulthood—continues to increase, which extends this phase between adolescence and adulthood. Society typically accepts the use of AOD by young people in this "in between" phase, particularly college students, which encourages overuse and makes it difficult to separate users from potential abusers.

SELF-ESTEEM ISSUES FOR YOUNG ADULTS WITH AOD CONCERNS

Studies with late-stage adolescents and young adults show that having positive self-esteem is important to maintaining physical and mental health, and for preventing problems like AOD overuse, aggression, and engaging in delinquent or criminal behavior. High self-esteem is related to achievement, positive work experiences, the ability to set and reach goals, and developing positive coping skills. High self-esteem also helps young adults persevere when faced with the possibility of failure. Low self-esteem can lead to negative consequences, including engaging in abusive relationships; AOD overuse and abuse; engaging in unprotected sex, which can lead to sexually transmitted diseases and unintended pregnancies; self-injurious behavior; disordered eating; and increased involvement in aggressive and criminal activities (see, for example, Trzesniewski et al., 2006). Low self-esteem can also lead to an increased vulnerability to criticism and rejection, causing young people to inflate their feelings of inadequacy and perceived incompetence, which can lead to depression and anxiety. Orth, Robins, and Roberts (2008) report evidence that low self-esteem predicts subsequent levels of depression, although depression does not predict low self-esteem.

Involvement in social relationships provides young adults with a sense of community and support. However, young adults with low self-esteem tend to seek out negative feedback as a way to reinforce their negative sense of self, and their low self-esteem may result in avoidance of social interactions. This reinforces their negative self-worth and self-esteem because they do not receive the validation and social support they want and need from others (Orth et al., 2008). Some young adults may use AOD to help them cope with their insecurity and tenuousness around their relationships, and behaviors that result from using AOD can lead to further alienation from the people who matter most to them.

As noted earlier, self-esteem begins to increase during the transition into adulthood, but this may not be the case for young adults who are potential problem drinkers. People with alcohol dependence have lower self-esteem than nonproblem drinkers, regardless of gender, although a few studies have found that alcoholic men have relatively high levels of self-esteem. One explanation for this discrepancy is that self-deception and social acceptability may influence the men to justify their heavy alcohol use, as opposed to women, who are viewed negatively if they engage in heavy drinking (Corbin, McNair, & Carter, 1996). This may be particularly true among college students, where the expectation is that young adults will actively engage in AOD use and exploration.

Given the high incidence of heavy drinking among college students, Corbin et al. (1996) investigated the relationship between self-esteem and three levels of alcohol use: abstinence, moderate drinking, and heavy drinking. They found that for male college students, as their alcohol consumption level increased, so did their self-esteem, although they found no differences in self-esteem between the moderate and heavy drinkers. For females, women who did not drink had higher levels of self-esteem than either group of women who drank, with women in the heavy drinking group having the lowest levels of self-esteem. They also noted that women appeared to be "at greater risk for low self-esteem associated with heavy alcohol consumption" (Corbin et al., 1996, p. 10). While it is unclear whether the problem drinking led to decreased self-esteem or the reverse, the authors made a valid point that helping young women increase their self-esteem may help them control their problem drinking. Glindemann, Geller, and Fortney (1999) also investigated the relationship between self-esteem and alcohol consumption by assessing blood alcohol levels, and found that students with lower self-esteem were significantly more intoxicated than students with higher self-esteem upon leaving a fraternity party. Lillie (2002) reported that women who drink alcohol, particularly women who abuse alcohol, have lower self-esteem than both women who do not drink and men who do drink. Women who have low self-esteem are also more likely to overuse or abuse alcohol, which leads to even lower self-esteem, creating a cycle that can be challenging to break. Women who are able to develop stronger self-esteem, however, became more mentally healthy and are less likely to relapse.

While there appears to be link between low self-esteem and overuse and abuse of AOD, there is a lack of consistent evidence that focusing on increasing self-esteem has an effect on AOD recovery. Despite the number of studies investigating the relationship between self-esteem and AOD use, the findings are mixed, and it is unclear whether low self-esteem leads to increased AOD use or vice versa. Regardless, counselors need to assess self-esteem in young adults who are in AOD treatment.

ASSESSING SELF-ESTEEM IN YOUNG ADULTS WITH AOD CONCERNS

AOD treatment for young adults requires assessment of both their AOD use and their self-esteem. There are a number of good AOD paper-and-pencil inventories, but conducting an interview is also an effective way to assess for AOD overuse, abuse, and dependence, and creates an opportunity to begin building a counseling relationship. A good AOD assessment includes the following (Myers & Salt, 2007):

1. History of AOD use and abuse that includes the substances used, when, and how (e.g., intravenous, oral); patterns and changes in use; and consequences of use (e.g., ending relationships, arrests, being fired from a job)
2. Family history of AOD use and abuse
3. Physical and mental health status and medical concerns
4. Family and social functioning
5. Education and employment history
6. Sexual history
7. Legal concerns

Clinicians can use an interview format to gather information about their clients' level of self-esteem, including discussing the consequences their AOD overuse or abuse has had on their lives, sense of worth, and self-esteem. Counselors can help clients explore the consequences of their behavior physically, psychologically, socially, vocationally, spiritually, and sexually to assess the effects of their AOD overuse and abuse on the various domains of self-esteem that matter most to them.

If the assessment is completed during or soon after the person has gone through detoxification, the client and counselor should revisit the responses several weeks later to see what new information the client has to add. As people move into sobriety, they gain more clarity about their use and its consequences, and they may also feel more comfortable with the counselor and be more willing to share information about their AOD use history and experiences. It is best not to complete the assessment as the person is detoxing since this process can skew people's responses.

INTERVENTION STRATEGIES

There are several challenges inherent in counseling people with AOD issues. First, they lack internal motivation for treatment as a result of the addiction itself. Second, their interpersonal styles are not conducive to building a counseling relationship. They may have issues with trust, which makes it difficult to establish a counseling alliance, as a result of the secrecy of their AOD use and abuse history. Third, clients are ambivalent about changing their AOD using behavior as a result of the reinforcing quality of AOD use, as well as the reason they began to overuse and abuse AOD in the first place (Glidden-Tracey, 2005).

When beginning to address concerns about self-esteem with people in recovery, it is essential not only that clients no longer use AOD, but that they have some period of sobriety beyond detoxification. In AOD treatment the initial focus is on educating clients about their addiction, helping them come up with short-term plans for not using (e.g., minimizing time with or avoiding friends and family who still use AOD, attending 12-step meetings to create a new support network), as well as developing a relapse prevention plan. By its very nature, addiction works to keep clients in a situation where they continue to use, even when they want to stop, even when they place themselves in harm's way to continue to use, and even when they stop engaging in activities and relationships that once had great meaning for them so that they can keep using.

As clients move into longer periods of sobriety, they are ready to explore the consequences of their AOD addiction, as well as the underlying issues and concerns that may have led to their using AOD in the first place. This exploration should include discussion about the role of their self-esteem in their AOD use. For example, a woman may talk about how she had a good job and good friends and felt confident about herself. It was important to her to be in a romantic relationship, although her selective self-esteem in this area was low. She began dating a heroin user even though she had concerns about his AOD use. She said she started to snort heroin with him on weekends so that he would not end the relationship. Her addiction developed rapidly and she began to take money from work to support their habit. She was arrested for embezzlement and was sentenced to a work release program. In counseling, she explored why she made the choice to date her former partner and how she feels about that choice now. In this case, she initially showed good domain-specific self-esteem and generally strong global self-esteem, but her low selective self-esteem in romantic relationships was weighted far more heavily (i.e., it mattered more to her) than other domains, leading her to her making choices that had a negative effect on her life.

Many clients use AOD to avoid recollection of negative life experiences, including destructive feedback from significant others, and associated feelings. Moving into recovery and beginning to explore these experiences can increase the likelihood clients will relapse, so counselors need to help clients develop effective relapse prevention plans as well as help clients come to terms with and work through their guilt and shame related to behaviors they may have engaged in when they were using AOD. Kaskutas (1996) found that women involved in the Women for Sobriety program showed a significant improvement in their self-esteem in the first year of recovery. On the other hand, Trucco, Connery, Griffin, and Greenfield (2007) found that while self-esteem scores improved following AOD treatment, there appeared to be no relationship between improved self-esteem and treatment. Although the findings are mixed about the role of self-esteem in preventing relapse, counselors should use every opportunity to educate clients about relapse prevention and developing a relapse prevention plan, what they can do if relapse occurs, and how competence and worthiness might play a role.

Several interventions can be effective. Counselors can help clients create a lifeline of their AOD history. On one line that runs from birth to present age, clients list their AOD use history. On a second line, they list significant life events and the effects they had on both global and various domains of their self-esteem. Together, clients and clinicians explore the patterns that emerge from comparing the two lifelines. Another option is to have clients complete a genogram of AOD use in their family of origin. As part of the discussion, counselors can ask clients to talk about their perceptions of how AOD use affected self-esteem in significant family members.

Among the many suitable alternatives, one simple approach to help young adult clients in recovery rebuild their self-esteem is to provide individual counseling developed around Branden's (2006) pillars of self-esteem: living consciously, self-acceptance, self-responsibility, self-assertiveness, living purposefully, and practicing personal integrity. Compatible with 12-step programs, these pillars create a framework for clients to follow and mirror the core elements of self-esteem, as supported by research. The focus is on competence, achievement, feedback from significant others, worthiness, and feelings of acceptance, all of which are based on clients' personal values and beliefs. The intention is to rebuild the clients' sense of self and self-esteem by educating them about how to make positive and life-affirming decisions, how to trust their own decisions and wishes, and how to repair and rebuild their relationships with other people so they can begin to see their own worth and value again. An essential part of this approach is to treat clients holistically, ensuring they are taking care of their physical and social needs, while using counseling to help them address their psychological and emotional needs. Some clients also benefit from attending group and individual counseling, in addition to attending 12-step programs like Alcoholics Anonymous and working with a 12-step sponsor.

There are a variety of techniques that can be implemented in counseling sessions to help clients start rebuilding their self-esteem as they continue to work on their recovery. One activity involves helping clients identify *bridge people* in their lives. Bridge people are the individuals who provide support, encouragement, validation, and motivation as people transition from one phase of life experience to another, providing a bridge from the known to the unknown (see Carlock, 1999). In this case, the unknown is a life without alcohol and other drugs. Using an adaptation of Carlock's circle of support, clients draw a circle on a piece of paper with their name in the middle of the circle. Then they draw lines radiating out from the circle and write the names of people who have served as supports throughout their lifetime, including people who have showed a special interest in them or nurtured them, even in some small way. The goal of this activity is to help clients become aware of messages they received as children and adolescents about their worth, capabilities, abilities, strengths, and weaknesses, so they can more accurately assess, with the help of the counselor, which messages are accurate and which messages should finally be expunged. Clients can highlight the people they believe are supportive of their continued recovery so they can begin to visualize the support system and bridge people who can help them in this new phase of their lives. This activity addresses cognitive and affective elements of global and situational self-esteem, as well as Branden's (2006) pillars of living consciously and self-acceptance.

Another technique, also adapted from Carlock (1999), is to have clients list two or three new experiences or activities they will engage in between sessions or over the next several weeks. The activities can include trying a new recreational activity like fishing, reading a book on a new topic, or volunteering their time to help a local charity. The purpose is twofold. First, it provides an opportunity for clients to expand their horizons by trying something interesting to them that they may have never made time for or had the courage to do in the past. Second, it provides clients with new activities that can be an opportunity to experience successful accomplishments and increase competence, as well as ways to meet new people to affiliate with, substituting for the time they previously spent on their AOD use. This activity addresses cognitive and behavioral elements of global and situational self-esteem, as well as Branden's (2006) pillars of living consciously, self-assertiveness, and living purposefully.

An activity that can be helpful for clients in recovery is one recommended by 12-step programs. Step 4 states that people will take a "searching and fearless moral inventory" of themselves (Alcoholics Anonymous, 2008, p. 59). Counselors can help clients begin taking an honest and complete inventory of their actions and intentions before and during their addiction. This inventory-taking process provides an opportunity for clients to accept responsibility for their actions and begin to make amends to themselves for what they did and why, not excusing their behaviors but allowing them to accept responsibility for their choices and move past the guilt and shame. During this process counselors and clients can explore how their decisions and behaviors affected specific domains of their self-esteem, and how self-esteem domains influenced their decisions and behaviors. Step 9 involves making amends to people who have been harmed because of the clients' AOD addiction (Alcoholics Anonymous, 2008, p. 59). Counselors can help clients make decisions about when and how they want to make amends, and they can also help clients figure out how to make amends when they cannot locate the person or when the person is not willing to speak with them. The activities of taking an inventory and making amends addresses cognitive, affective, and behavioral elements of global and situational self-esteem, as well as Branden's (2006) pillars of living consciously, self-acceptance, living purposefully, and practicing personal integrity.

ROLE OF THE COUNSELOR

The counselor's role, when working with people in recovery as well as when working with people with self-esteem issues, is to provide a supportive environment for clients to start developing trust in both the counselor and the counseling process as they explore the reasons for their AOD addiction. At the same time, counselors need to be honest and direct, using gentle confrontation to help clients become honest about the consequences of their AOD use. Lillie (2002) found that women who were engaged in counseling that was supportive, genuine, accepting, and nonjudgmental were more likely to be successful in treatment, which led to increased feelings of confidence and hope about their recovery. If the praise and support are not grounded in the reality of the clients' thoughts, feelings, and behaviors, they will not be able to hear or accept the counselors' comments.

Counselors serve as allies, providing a safe place for clients to begin making amends to themselves and others, while learning to assert themselves and change the dynamics of their relationships. Counselors can help clients navigate necessary changes in a positive and proactive manner. Given the level of denial and challenges with trust that arise with some AOD clients, it is essential that counselors are authentically engaged with clients, serving as teachers and role models about how to engage in honest and support relationships. This not only helps clients with their AOD recovery, but also provides support and validation as clients work on increasing their self-esteem. By helping young adults seek out and become involved in healthy relationships that do not encourage the overuse or abuse of AOD, counselors can help them increase and maintain good levels of self-esteem through positive feedback and authentic support.

CASE STUDY

Mario is a 26-year-old White male with a strong sense of his Italian-American identity and his Roman Catholic faith. As a child he had a very close relationship with his maternal grandmother, who died five years ago. She was his primary caregiver since both of his parents worked outside of the home. Mario stated his parents were "social drinkers," although his description of their drinking behaviors seems more consistent with binge drinking, which is similar to his own alcohol abuse history. Although he reports doing some drinking in high school, he did not "drink a lot" until college. By the time he was 19, he was consuming "a couple of beers" a day and binge drinking on weekends.

Mario had been referred for eight weeks of intensive outpatient alcohol counseling as a result of a charge of driving under the influence. He was sober for six months after this treatment but started drinking again when his girlfriend of four years broke up with him. He believes their breakup was the result of his refusal to drink "socially" with her. Mario had relapsed for three months, stopped drinking again by attending daily AA meetings, and has now been sober for nine months, attending AA meetings once a week. He is becoming frustrated because his sponsor will not allow him to talk about anything other than his alcoholism.

Although actively engaged in his recovery program, Mario recently began to experience problems with motivation and productivity at work, where he previously felt competent and confident. He has worked as an accountant since he graduated from college. Because he engaged in his addiction only on the weekends, he was able to stay relatively productive. After two sessions with the Employee Assistance Program counselor at work, he was referred to a counselor who specialized in addictions.

During the first session, Mario discussed his concern about wanting to start drinking again. He said he did not think he deserved to be happy. He worried that he did not give back enough to people who were supportive of him and his recovery, but believed they helped him only because they "feel sorry" for him. Mario was grieving over the end of his four-year relationship, had not considered dating since, and thought he was not "good enough" for any woman even though he wanted to be married and have children. Although Mario had a strong, supportive group of male friends who valued him, and felt confident in his abilities as an accountant, especially during sobriety, he had low social self-esteem and put more weight on his romantic relationships, although his selective self-esteem was lowest in this domain. The counselor determined that this lack of self-worth could put his recovery in jeopardy. At the end of the first session, Mario and his counselor agreed to meet for eight sessions to focus on maintaining his sobriety and increasing his sense of self-worth in romantic relationships.

The counselor started the second session by educating Mario about the role of self-esteem in his sobriety and how different activities completed inside and outside of counseling could help him increase his sense of self-worth and maintain his recovery. She summarized Branden's pillars of self-esteem to provide a straightforward framework for Mario to understand and begin to work on his self-esteem. The counselor and Mario agreed to focus on self-acceptance and self-responsibility as a way for him to begin to see the role he played in romantic relationships, focusing on the messages he learned as a child from his family and society about what a man is supposed to be. During this session they discussed the connection between his alcohol abuse and his sense of worthiness and how that affected his relationships with romantic partners.

During the third session, Mario drew two lifelines—one focused on his alcohol abuse history and the other focused on romantic relationships—that allowed him to begin to see patterns that existed between the two. He and his counselor talked about ways that his various selective self-esteem domains affected the events on both lifelines, and he talked about how he used alcohol when dating to feel more confident and desirable. This awareness was the focus of the remaining sessions as Mario moved to a deeper level of understanding of what he wanted in a romantic partner and a relationship, as well as what he had to bring to a relationship. Since he had never dated a woman when he was not drinking, he explored steps he could take to begin dating again while maintaining his recovery. As a way to meet new people and help others, Mario started volunteering with a local organization that consisted of single people who wanted to give back to their community.

During this time Mario and his AA sponsor began work on Step 4, where he focused on his behaviors and attitudes in his previous romantic relationships. This helped him understand what he had done that may have been hurtful or harmful to women he dated, how he felt about himself in those situations, and also some of the positive qualities he brought to his relationships. Rebuilding his social self-esteem helped Mario learn to trust his judgment and decision-making abilities, and provided him with skills to develop stronger and more supportive relationships with other people, and potentially with a life partner.

CONCLUSION

There is a strong relationship between AOD use and abuse and self-esteem and self-worth. While there are mixed results about the role self-esteem plays in treatment, there is evidence that improving self-esteem helps people maintain their recovery and helps prevent relapse. When counseling people about their AOD history, it is important that counselors focus on the role self-esteem played in the clients' use of AOD since lower self-esteem can lead to overuse and abuse, particularly if people start using during adolescence. By helping clients learn ways to increase their sense of competence, worthiness, and self-acceptance, counselors can help clients not only achieve recovery but maintain their recovery.

REFERENCES

Alcoholics Anonymous. (2008). *The big book* (4th ed.). Retrieved November 8, 2008, from http://www.aa.org/bbonline/

Arnett, J. J. (2005). The developing context of substance use in emerging adulthood. *Journal of Drug Issues, 35,* 235–253.

Branden, N. (2006). Nurturing self-esteem in young people. In M. H. Kernis (Ed.), *Self-esteem issues and answers: A sourcebook of current perspectives* (pp. 238–243). New York: Psychology Press.

Carlock, C. J. (1999). *Enhancing self-esteem.* Philadelphia: Accelerated Development.

Cooper, M. L. (1994). Motivations for alcohol use among adolescents: Development and validation of a four-factor model. *Psychological Assessment, 6,* 117–128.

Corbin, W. R., McNair, L. D., & Carter, J. (1996). Self-esteem and problem drinking among male and female college students. *Journal of Alcohol and Drug Education, 42,* 1–14.

Duncan, S. C., Alpert, A., Duncan, T. E., & Hops, H. (1997). Adolescent alcohol use development and young adult outcomes. *Drug and Alcohol Dependence, 49*(1), pp. 39–48.

Feldman, R. S. (2006). *Development across the life span* (4th ed.). Upper Saddle River, NJ: Pearson Prentice Hall.

Glidden-Tracey, C. E. (2005). *Counseling and therapy with clients who abuse alcohol or other drugs: An integrative approach.* Mahwah, NJ: Lawrence Erlbaum Associates.

Glindemann, K. E., Geller, E. S., & Fortney, J. N. (1999). Self-esteem and alcohol consumption: A study of college drinking behavior in a naturalistic setting. *Journal of Alcohol and Drug Education, 55,* 60–71

Gorbett, K., & Kruczek, T. (2008). Family factors predicting social self-esteem in young adults. *The Family Journal: Counseling and Therapy for Couples and Families, 16,* 58–65.

Kaskutas, L. A. (1996). Predictors of self-esteem among members of Women for Sobriety. *Addiction Research, 4,* 273–281.

Lewis, M. A., Phillippi, J., & Neighbors, C. (2007). Morally based self-esteem, drinking motives, and alcohol use among college students. *Psychology of Addictive Behaviors, 21,* 398–403.

Lillie, N. (2002). Women, alcohol, self-concept and self-esteem: A qualitative study of the experience of person-centred counselling. *Counselling and Psychotherapy Research, 2,* 99–107.

Myers, P. L., & Salt, N. R. (2007). *Becoming an addictions counselor: A comprehensive text.* Boston: Jones and Bartlett.

National Institute on Alcoholism Abuse and Alcoholism. (2009a). *Research findings on college drinking and the minimum legal drinking age.* Retrieved February 27, 2009, from http://www.niaaa.nih.gov/Publications/

National Institute on Alcoholism Abuse and Alcoholism. (2009b). *Statistical snapshot of college drinking.* Retrieved February 27, 2009, from http://www.niaaa.nih.gov/Publications/

Orth, U., Robins, R. W., & Roberts, B. W. (2008). Low self-esteem prospectively predicts depression in adolescence and young adulthood. *Journal of Personality and Social Psychology, 95,* 695–708.

Trucco, E. M., Connery, H. S., Griffin, M. L., & Greenfield, S. F. (2007). The relationship of self-esteem and self-efficacy to treatment outcomes of alcohol-dependent men and women. *American Journal on Addictions, 16,* 85–92.

Trzesniewski, K. H., Donnellan, M. B., Moffitt, T. E., Robins, R. W., Poulton, R., & Caspi, A. (2006). Low self-esteem during adolescence predicts poor health, criminal behavior, and limited economic prospects during adulthood. *Developmental Psychology, 42,* 381–390.

Section V

Midlife

*I*n the 40 to 60 age range, wide variations in development exist. Midlife adult development is "more an account of differences than a description of universals" (Bee & Boyd, 2003). In fact, the upper and lower limits for defining midlife can vary by at least 10 years. Many people who are well into their 70s can still be considered in midlife when their physical and mental health, well-being, and outlook on life are not compromised. It seems to be that the beginning of midlife is triggered not by chronological age or noticeable physical changes, but by an internal, emotional realization. When people make a shift from counting the years they have been alive to the years they have left to live, middle age has begun. They reassess their life structure—the basic pattern of their lives—and their place in the world (Levinson, 1978, 1996).

Throughout life, human development consists of alternating periods of stability and upheaval (Levinson, 1978). Midlife is second only to adolescence in this regard. People seem to have a sense of urgency to "finally get things right": They want to reach for goals previously deferred or foreclosed upon, or find new goals more compatible with their temperaments or interests. They want to live authentically by their own values, based on life experiences rather than on strict adherence to the internalized values of childhood. The feminine aspects of the self begin to emerge for men; the masculine aspects begin to emerge for women (Jung, 1933/1971).

For some, a new sense of awareness of discrepancies between one's lifelong assumed conventions and one's own behavior results in greater ego integration and differentiation; but for others, ego development plateaus and further development stops (Loevinger, 1976).

Differences in physical/biological, cognitive, social, and emotional areas of life are likely related to cohort and idiosyncratic effects of personal, social, cultural, and family histories. Nevertheless, commonalities appear in inevitable declines and compensatory gains, all of which have the potential to impact self-esteem levels and stability. Physical competence decreases, career goals may go unrealized, intimate relationships may disappoint or disappear, and families may not materialize or may drastically change. Yet midlife can be the most productive time of life, when many people make significant achievements that can bring them great life satisfaction. Thus, midlife can be a time of great accomplishment and also of great turmoil.

Physical change is a gradual process throughout adulthood, yet by midlife cannot be denied. Changes in vision, hearing, muscle/fat ratio, and bone mass; skin loosening and wrinkling; and loss of reproductive capacity, and sexual response or performance contribute to "a revised physical self-image, which often emphasizes fewer hoped-for gains and more feared declines" (Berk, 2006, p. 508). Although the majority of midlife adults enjoy good health, illness and chronic disease as well as death rates increase. Heart disease and cancer are the two most common causes of death. With a decrease in immune system protection, chronic diseases manifest in greater frequency at midlife. Many are a result of heredity or poor lifelong health and fitness choices or both. Chronic diseases have higher incidence rates among those of lower economic status, especially African Americans, Latinos, and Native Americans (Centers for Disease Control, n.d.). Most "ailments, although largely treatable with medications or diet, can trigger distress because they signal aging, which is neither desirable nor valued in our culture" (Lachman, 2004, p. 307).

Cognitive functioning also begins to change at midlife, showing both losses and gains. Fluid intelligence—information processing ability—began declining in early adulthood and intensifies at midlife. Perceptual and memory speed decrease, although the drop is generally small until late in this stage. There is a lessening of the ability to retain information in working memory. For some, intellectual functioning dramatically declines as a result of environmental factors or illness. However, verbal abilities increase from early adulthood into midlife, as does crystallized intelligence—accumulated knowledge, proficiency, and expertise—and for some, creativity is at its peak. Most midlife adults become adept at solving problems; they have an increased ability to synthesize disparate information as relativistic, dialectical reasoning becomes more refined. Midlife adults are more able to successfully resolve for themselves the dialectical issues of achievement versus relationships, being an individual versus fulfilling a prescribed role, immediate gratification versus deferred pleasure, and freedom versus security (Wrightsman, 1994).

Social and emotional changes at midlife can be significant as multiple life roles are modified or vanish all together. For many, career is the most important role, yet for others upward mobility is less important, achievement and mastery become more central, and leisure pursuits occupy more time (Boylan & Hawkes, 1988). Parenting roles are either relinquished as children mature and leave home, or they are greatly diminished and transformed. Many people add a new role as caregivers to aging parents. Primary relationships can come to an end, or they can be renewed and reenergized, depending upon how each partner negotiates his or her own midlife transition. Gender differences mean that men and women accept midlife challenges differently. Women now in the later years of midlife, for example, had fewer opportunities for finding fulfilling work outside of the home when they were younger. Some have met the challenge of midlife by seeking training and entering professional careers for the first time. They will likely work well into the third phase of life or face economic hardship or poverty, especially in the wake of divorce. On the other hand, women today soon to enter midlife—born in the 1965–1970 cohort—"have the greatest access to resources that enhance self-esteem, such as higher education, higher-status occupations, and fewer family obstacles to work, which resulted in higher levels of self-acceptance compared to the older cohorts" (Carr, 2004, as cited in Lachman, 2004, p. 309). Most men now at midlife have had fewer experiences with nontraditional roles that exemplify younger cohorts and will follow a more typical developmental trajectory of career role maintenance and decline and increased desire for the centrality of other life roles (Super, 1990).

"Midlife adults are at the height of assuming responsibility for others and midlife is typically the time of greatest influence and most frequent intergenerational contact" (Lachman, 2004, p. 326). Midlife adults are now fully in Erikson's (1959/1980) generativity versus stagnation stage that for many began in the latter part of young adulthood. They must successfully resolve the need to support and give back to the next generation. Some resolve this stage through the parenting role; others through creativity, volunteering, concern for the future of the environment, equality, and myriad other ways to take care of, guide, or influence others. Midlife adults who are unable to successfully negotiate the generativity stage stagnate and are in danger of leading lives of self-absorption, oftentimes quite unhappily.

In general, self-esteem in midlife remains stable. In normal development, self-esteem has been shown to peak in midlife before it begins a decline in old age (Robins & Trzesniewski, 2005). However, when people experience maturational changes or great changes in their environment, lower self-esteem stability can be expected to occur. Transitions in midlife can spawn such changes, although not all people experience a crisis at midlife (Livson, 1981; Valliant, 1977). It may be that the social clock associated with major life events accounts for the difference. Major life events are expected occurrences across life, such as educational accomplishments, marriage, or birth of children. Neugarten and Hagestad (1976) found that off-time events—those that occur at unexpected times, such as a pregnancy during menopause or forced early retirement—are more difficult and stressful than on-time events, such as the death of a parent in old age. Nonevents (those expected events that never happen—the child never born, the job never attained, etc.) become painfully evident by midlife and are particularly stressful. They have the potential to impact self-esteem through the mechanism of perceived social comparison. Trzesniewski, Donnellan, and Robins (2003) have indicated that self-esteem levels have been shown to react to social evaluation and can change in response to external feedback. Inevitable changes at midlife and "shifting social circumstances ... may lead to changes in social roles and corresponding shifts in identity.... These events may challenge some individuals' view of themselves and thus produce idiosyncratic changes that reduce the stability of self-esteem" (p. 216). During the natural process of reassessing one's life to date, some individuals can perceive themselves wanting in areas of significance to them, thus affecting their trait self-esteem. Lack of expected achievement, whether at home or work, can lead some people to be more unforgiving and critical of themselves, causing them to reevaluate selective self-esteem domains. The impact of nonevents or the onset of illness can shake an individual's sense of worth as well. Endless possibilities in reevaluations exist at midlife, many of which can impact self-esteem, either positively or adversely. This chapter discusses three important issues: identity of lesbians and gay men, career development, and chronic illness.

REFERENCES

Bee, H., & Boyd, D. (2003). *Lifespan development* (3rd ed.). Boston: Allyn & Bacon.

Berk, L. E. (2006). *Development through the lifespan* (4th ed.). Boston: Allyn & Bacon.

Boylan, R. J., & Hawkes, G. R. (1988). Perceptions of life changes in middle adulthood: A survey of managers' work and personal adaptations. *Journal of Social Behavior Personality, 3*, 177–190.

Centers for Disease Control and Prevention. (n.d.). *Mortality/deaths*. Retrieved February 20, 2009, from http://www.cdc.gov/nchs/fastats/deaths.htm

Erikson, E. H. (1980). *Identity and the life cycle*. New York: Norton. (Original work published 1959)

Jung, C. G. (1971). The stages of life (R. F. C. Hull, Trans.). In. J. Campbell (Ed.), *The portable Jung* (pp. 33–22) New York: Viking. (Original work published 1933)

Lachman, M. E. (2004). Development in midlife. *Annual Review of Psychology, 55*, 305–331.

Levinson, D. J. (1978). *The seasons of a man's life*. New York: Knopf.

Levinson, D. J. (1996). *The seasons of a woman's life*. New York: Knopf.

Livson, F. B. (1981). Patterns of personality development in middle-aged women: A longitudinal study. *International Journal of Aging and Human Development, 7*, 107–115.

Loevinger, J. (1976). *Ego development*. San Francisco: Jossey-Bass.

Neugarten, B. L., & Hagestad, G. O. (1976). Age and the life course. In R. H. Binstock & E. Shanas (Eds.), *Handbook of aging and the social sciences* (pp. 35–55). New York: Von Nostrand Rhinehold.

Robins, R. W., & Trzesniewski, K. H. (2005). Self-esteem development across the lifespan. *Current Directions in Psychological Science, 14*, 158–162.

Super, D. E. (1990). A life-span life-space approach to career development. In D. Brown, L. Brooks, & Associates (Eds.), *Career choice and development* (2nd ed., pp. 197–261). Hillsdale, NJ: Lawrence Erlbaum Associates.

Trzesniewski, K. H., Donnellan, M. B., & Robins, R. W. (2003). Stability of self-esteem across the life span. *Journal of Personality and Social Psychology, 84*, 205–220.

Valliant, G. E. (1977). *Adaptation to life*. Boston: Little, Brown.

Wrightsman, L. S. (1994). *Adult personality development: Theories and concepts* (Vol. 1). Thousand Oaks, CA: Sage.

15

Lesbians and Gay Men at Midlife

JOY S. WHITMAN

A t midlife, individuals begin to ask themselves who they are, how they want to spend the second half of their lives, whether they are content with what they have accomplished, and if they want to make changes in the time they have left. For those who do not have a history of being oppressed because of sexual identity, these questions are often answered without the burden of shame or discrimination. For them, looking back is not a look at the struggle oftentimes accompanying coming out as lesbian or gay and the challenges it may have presented; looking forward is not encumbered with the possibility of coming out now in midlife with the losses that may follow or with the concern of furthering a career without fear of being outed in the workplace as a result of greater visibility. Being lesbian and gay at midlife, therefore, engenders a variety of concerns and joys that therapeutically need to be understood in order to facilitate the establishment of healthy identity.

For lesbians and gay men, the establishment of identity and intimacy stages does not follow the same path as that of heterosexuals, and for those lesbian and gay men now in midlife, the path has been influenced by past social and political events. To better understand lesbians and gay men in midlife, these differences must be explored. This chapter, therefore, will offer an overview of those midlife issues for gay men and lesbians and their connection to self-esteem. Therapeutic intervention for lesbians and gay men coming out at midlife will be discussed along with their intersection to development of positive self-esteem.

THEMES OF MIDLIFE FOR LESBIANS AND GAY MEN

Many themes associated with midlife for lesbians and gay men need to be understood historically and contextually. Midlife for lesbian and gay men from a life course perspective "assumes an open system shaped by social and historical process as well as by expectable and eruptive life changes within individual lives" (Cohler, Hostetler, & Boxer, 1998, p. 267). These historic events are not limited to

1. The Stonewall riot of 1969 (a pivotal moment in gay history and a symbol of gay resistance during which lesbians and gay men defended themselves against harassment and arrest from police during a morals raid at a gay bar in New York) and the various social and political events post-Stonewall in the 1970s
2. Changes in the declassification of homosexuality as a mental illness from the *Diagnostic and Statistical Manual (DSM)* in 1973, and its complete removal from the *DSM* in 1986
3. The Defense of Marriage Act of 1996 that federally permits states to choose not to recognize same-sex marriages and forbids this recognition at a federal level
4. The 2003 U.S. Supreme Court decision to invalidate sodomy laws
5. The passage (or rescinding) of same-sex marriage laws in Massachusetts, Iowa, Connecticut, and Vermont, the rescinding of it in California, and the availability of same-sex marriage in countries such as Spain, Belgium, Canada, The Netherlands, Sweden, Norway, and South Africa.

These events legally, socially, and psychologically impact lesbians and gay men, and the life course perspectives of these individuals at midlife must be contextualized within this history of discrimination.

As a result of shifting political and social climates, historical cohorts are created, and these cohorts develop their sexual identities differently (Baron & Cramer, 2000; Kertzner, 2001). Older midlife lesbians and gay men internalized the stigma of same-sex attraction, which impacted their self-esteem and compromised their coming out processes, in different ways than those in their younger years of midlife. For example, Schope's (2002) study of gay men pre-, during, and post-Stonewall and the influences on self-disclosure found that gay men 50 and older (pre-Stonewall) were less likely to disclose their sexual identities than those men who came out during and post-Stonewall. Gay men and lesbians who are in their 40s now are able to more freely come out because of the Stonewall riots, while their older midlife cohorts still hold on to the stigma that instigated the riots. This must also be understood in the context of ethnic and cultural identities as well. Not all gay and lesbian individuals with racial and ethnic minority identities value coming out. This may be due to the fear of losing the support from their ethnic or racial communities (Icard, 1985; Loiacano, 1989), perceiving coming out as a "White phenomenon" (Adams & Kimmel, 1997, p. 133), or adhering to cultural prohibitions against doing so (Chan, 1997; Greene, 1997). Little is known, though, about how historical cohorts of various ethnic and racial minority identities differ in terms of coming out.

Furthermore, the stigma of identifying as lesbian or gay can interfere with the development of a personal and sexual identity and the formation of intimate relationships (Cohler et al., 1998). This disruption can cause foreclosure or delay of these developmental tasks as perceived within the traditionally understood developmental life cycle and can result in lesbians and gay men at midlife begin-ning to consider long-term relationships and responsibilities of parenting at a time when their heterosexual cohorts have settled into marriage and are sending their children to high school and college. Cohler et al. (1998) speak to the idea that lesbians and gay men are "off-time with respect to certain normative life events and developmental tasks" (p. 278). Moreover, the stigma of a lesbian or gay identity plays a part in the absence of developmental markers often well understood for heterosexual women and men (Isensee, 2005; Kertzner, 2001). Dating, marriage, anniversaries, and childbirth are socially sanctioned milestones of development, and without those markers, it is more complicated for lesbians and gay men to situate themselves along their own developmental trajectory. How does a lesbian or gay man know if she or he is engaging in developmentally appropriate behavior when the markers set for that behavior are created within a heterosexist frame and social context? This lack of markers can cause disequilibrium, and as one partici-pant in Kertzner's (1999) study of gay men at midlife stated, "I think it's when you have a family and all of a sudden your kids are in high school or your kids are in college, that can make you middle-aged" (p. 51).

However, lack of developmental markers can also offer freedom from tradi-tional gender role scripts and make available the creation of different developmen-tal norms for lesbians and gay men (Weinstock, 2000). Having already confronted rigid gender roles through the process of coming out (Friend, 1991), lesbians and gay men are unshackled from the prescribed markers guiding heterosexual indi-viduals, and without those limited gender prescriptions, can embrace midlife with adaptability. Without the expectation of marriage and parenting, lesbians and gay men at midlife can experience greater role flexibility within relationships and along their life course. This can result in meeting the crises of midlife with resilience. Brown, Allen, Sarosy, Quarto, and Cook (2001) emphasize this point, noting how, for example, gay men learned earlier in life to transgress traditional gender roles and are therefore able to care for themselves and engage in self-care activities such as cooking and cleaning. Linked to these experiences, Friend (1991) proposed that the crisis of coming out and the losses managed during that process help with the potential crises of aging. Self-esteem can be enhanced as a result of the compe-tence gained through the challenges of coming out. Crisis competence has been met (Kimmel, 1978), to some degree, and "older gay and lesbian people who have had experience in reconstructing the arbitrary definitions of what homosexuality and gender mean are also more likely to be able to transfer these affirmative pro-cesses to their identities as older people" (Friend, 1991, p. 111).

The convergence of the absence of developmental markers and strict adher-ence to traditional gender roles with the changing social and political landscape, granting more rights and options to gay men and lesbians for marriage, adoption, surrogacy, and insemination, is resulting in the growing phenomenon of lesbians and gay men at midlife choosing to parent (Donaldson, 2000; Weinstock, 2000). As noted, due to the stigma and psychological sequel surrounding coming out, especially before and during the gay liberation movement, lesbians and gay men at midlife often solidified their identities at a later developmental period than did heterosexual individuals. Parenting, for these lesbians and gay men, was not a consideration in their 20s or 30s, as they focused more on exploring and strengthening their lesbian and gay identities and experiencing intimacy with same-gender partners. Now, in their 40s and 50s, many midlife lesbians and gay men have obtained a secure identity, sustained intimate relationships, and are ready to have children. The route they take to do so, the social stigma surrounding them and their children, and the meaning it has for lesbians and gay men at midlife are considerations that must be explored.

The central theme of generativity in midlife is accomplished in a variety of ways, and for lesbians and gay men, this manifests in nontraditional as well as traditional forms. While some do so through choosing childbearing and adoption, others do so through volunteer work or creative expression. Additionally, de Vries and Blando (2004) and Hostetler (2000) offer a range of examples illustrating how lesbians and gay men are generative. These consist of involvement in community and political activism around lesbian, gay, bisexual, and transgender (LGBT) issues in order to give back to their communities and to enhance the lives of future LGBT people; participation in preservation and restoration efforts of gay structures and urban centers through oral history projects and gay archives; and selection of careers that include teaching and mentoring.

Generativity can also be expressed through the creation of intergenerational relationships (Hostetler, 2000; Kimmel, 2004) that constitute one's family of choice. The concept of family of choice is well known in the lesbian and gay communities and is understood as those relationships that take the place of kin relationships and can include current and ex-partners, members of one's family of origin, and close friends (Weston, 1997). Whereas many lesbians and gay men experience rejection by their family of origin and the negative effect on their self-appraisal, families of choice affirm and validate lesbians and gay men, and therefore enhance their self-esteem. This underscores the importance of friends and community in the transition for lesbian and gay men into midlife. Tully's (1989) study of midlife lesbians recognizes the high involvement with friendship networks that were looked to for emotional and physical caregiving. These community connections help to decrease depression and fear of aging (Hunter, 2005), increase self-acceptance and self-esteem, and buffer against homophobia (Weinstock, 2000).

The relationships established not only buffer against homophobia and heterosexism but also help with the health crisis gay men have faced as a result of the impact of AIDS on the community. For gay men at midlife, the AIDS pandemic has had a significant effect on their psychological development, physical health, and progression into midlife. Gorman and Nelson (2004) remind us of the disproportionate number of gay men in midlife and born before 1955 affected by HIV/AIDS and the loss of their cohort due to this disease. The various issues presented to them and to men who are HIV+ include enhanced awareness of mortality and the expectation of a shortened life; possible disability due to the various antiretroviral treatment effects on the body; depression accompanying the loss of friends, partners, and cohorts and control over one's body; and stigma associated with both aging and being HIV+ (Gorman & Nelson, 2004; Isensee, 2005; Kertzner, 2001). HIV– men may also experience survivor guilt (Gorman & Nelson, 2004). However, for some gay men who are HIV+, meaning can be found in the diagnosis, fostering a "spiritual awakening" causing greater self-reflection at this time in his life (Gorman & Nelson, 2004, p. 84). A more intimate and conscious relationship with their bodies is evoked as well (Kooden & Flowers, 2000).

What's more, the body, for gay men, has a qualitatively different meaning than it does for lesbians, as "gay men are deeply invested in their bodies, and many feel that their body is their best asset—not only for sex, but for feelings of attractiveness, power, and success" (Kooden & Flowers, 2000, p. 28). Therefore, aging for gay men brings to the forefront the issues of body image and beauty and the potential loss of visibility within the gay male community. As gay men enter into midlife and move toward their older years, and as their bodies naturally change, they begin to lose the currency their bodies afforded them (Jones, 2001). With an emphasis in gay culture on youth and beauty, gay men in midlife can feel marginalized and less attractive (Kertzner, Myer, & Dolezal, 2004), resulting in lower self-esteem. Yet in terms of sexual functioning, the limited research available indicates that even though sexual activity decreased, sexual satisfaction did not (Pope & Schultz, 1991). It is their perception of their value as attractive and sexually vibrant men, however, that is in jeopardy.

In contrast, for lesbians at midlife, the changes they experience in their bodies are less traumatic, as "lesbians tend to recognize and value a woman in her entirety" (Kooden & Flowers, 2000, p. 28), and focus on psychological and emotional elements of their personhood in addition to their bodies. Additionally, the midlife physical change of menopause can prompt many positive changes, as it is perceived differently sexually for lesbians than it is for heterosexual women. In a study of women age 43 to 68, Cole and Rothblum (1991) found that these women did not have concerns about their waning sexuality or sexual performance, with 46% of the women reporting no change in frequency and 29% indicating an increase in quality since onset. Moreover, they experienced enhanced freedom and acceptance of self. It is easy to imagine that experiencing greater acceptance of self leads to higher self-esteem.

Additional concerns for midlife lesbians and gay men that warrant mentioning include

1. Homophobia and heterosexism in the healthcare system and the hesitance to seek medical care at a time when health-related issues begin to emerge
2. The ability to receive domestic partner benefits for healthcare coverage (Baron & Cramer, 2000)
3. Financial disadvantages for lesbians due to sexism in the workplace and its resulting effect on planning for retirement (Barker, 2004)
4. Career choices in light of existing homophobia in the workplace
5. The fear of discrimination or being outed as one moves up the career ladder (Embrick, Walther, & Wickens, 2007)

Finally, a significant theme for lesbians and gay men is that of coming out at midlife. Narratives of lesbians and gay men reveal how this transitional period of midlife is pivotal to their coming out and living authentically (Jensen, 1999;

Johnston & Jenkins, 2004; Rickards & West, 2006). The reasons for coming out at midlife vary among lesbians and gay men, although most commonly reported are the inability to continue to live disingenuously, the confrontation of myths and stereotype of what it means to be a lesbian and a woman, the connection with other lesbians and gay men and undeniable attraction to someone of the same gender, and the feeling of being stagnant in one's life (Jensen, 1999; Johnston & Jenkins, 2004; Rickards & West, 2006).

Although the reasons to come out are compelling, the losses accompanying coming out in midlife are many, and lesbians and gay men must confront these losses to successfully manage the transition, including the potential loss of privilege, status, power, identity, career, family, friends, and children (Hunter, 2005; Johnston & Jenkins, 2004; Rickards & Wuest, 2006; Woolf, 1998). Managing these losses can take a toll on positive self-esteem; however, doing so well can result in a sense of competence and enhance feelings of worth as well. To face these possible losses, lesbians and gay men must prepare themselves psychologically and financially, and they will need to learn how to navigate the new communities to which they now belong. Woolf (1998) notes that to facilitate a smooth transition, the women in her study had to acknowledge a lesbian identity as acceptable and engage in behavioral, cognitive, and sociocultural shifts. These paradigm shifts of self-identification are essential to the healthy integration of a lesbian or gay identity, and the connection to self-esteem is irrefutable.

SELF-ESTEEM AND COMING OUT AT MIDLIFE

Self-esteem is to be understood in regard to the traits that are responsive to change and the contribution of these more mutable traits to an overall appreciation of the self. The process of developing self-esteem must be acknowledged as occurring in relationship with others since self-appraisal is in response to others' feedback and approval. The importance of relationships and their contribution to self-esteem is highlighted by Baldwin (2006), who rightfully recognizes that "self-esteem dynamics are virtually always, at some deep level, tied with relationship dynamics—even when the connection may not be conscious or apparent" (p. 359). Coming out at midlife, or at any time in one's life, is intimately connected to relationship dynamics as lesbians and gay men navigate the questions of to whom, when, and how to come out in order to minimize loss of relationships and damage to their self-esteem as others approve or disapprove of their sexual identities.

In a related manner, self-esteem is an appraisal of self that develops over time as a consequence of both engaging in behaviors that one values and creating skills to encounter the challenges of life (Mruk, 2006). This process results in the development of traits that one integrates into a definition of self. Self-esteem, therefore, is the product of one's ability to meet challenges in life and find self-worth in the process as one self-appraises both situational and relatively stable traits. This frame provides a better way to understand how the self-esteem of lesbians and gay men coming out at midlife may be affected by living in a homophobic and heterosexist world. Given that development of self-esteem occurs in relationship with others and in response to others' feedback and approval, the cultural messages, both explicit and implicit, that denigrate the worthiness of a lesbian or gay male identity and challenge the competence of lesbians and gay men must be appreciated for their damaging effects. These messages are ones that indicate lesbians and gay men do not deserve the same civil rights, healthcare, societal and financial benefits, social status and privilege, and psychological safety granted to heterosexual individuals because of their sexual identities. Lesbians and gay men are denied over 1,100 federal rights (see Human Rights Campaign, 2008). When coming out as lesbian or gay at any age, these messages and the resulting realities of being lesbian or gay need to be managed in ways so that lesbians and gay men do not incorporate these messages into their identities. Otherwise, the result is internalized homophobia or internalized homonegativity, a "process in which negative family and community attitudes are internalized …, creating a lack of self worth that has ramifications for differentiation of self" (Spencer & Brown, 2007, p. 258). High internalized homophobia has been correlated with low self-esteem (Szymanski & Chung, 2001), isolation, (Shidlo, 1994; Szymanski, Chung, & Balsam, 2001), and psychiatric symptoms (Hershberger & D'Augelli, 1995). It is therefore essential that women and men coming out as lesbian and gay in midlife neutralize the harmful information and then appraise it positively prior to integrating it into their selective and global self-esteem.

The task for women and men coming out at midlife is further complicated because an identity as heterosexual has been created and well established by midlife. Having presented to their families, communities, and workplaces as heterosexual, women and men who come out at this juncture will be faced with many of the issues discussed earlier in the chapter. Loss of status in the workplace and community, rejection by family and friends, and temporary loss of identity as they attempt to reestablish themselves are real fears and, for some, realities. Relationships with spouses and partners are changed, and ruptures in other close relationships, such as those with children, may occur. In light of the connection of self-esteem to relationships and the feedback we obtain about ourselves in relationship with others, women and men coming out at midlife and facing rejection from those with whom they have established deep and enduring connection must be appreciated for the difficult task that it can be. For lesbians and gay men of color, families who have buffered them from and taught them how to manage racism may not want to know about their sexual identity. Rejection from those who have protected them can be notably damaging to self-esteem, and coming out to those communities might be avoided.

INTERVENTION STRATEGIES

The question that must be asked is, what aids in self-acceptance and self-esteem for women and men coming out at midlife? There are a variety of ways to approach this issue, and in this section, I explore the importance of addressing internalized homonegativity, integrating the impact of sociopolitical contexts, facilitating relationships with lesbians and gay men, fostering resilience, and reframing positive aspects of lesbians and gay men.

Addressing Internalized Homonegativity

In general, coming out at any age requires an LGBT affirmative approach that normalizes same-sex attractions and contextualizes internalized homonegativity as a product of societal and cultural homophobia and heterosexism. Given the internalization of damaging societal messages, moving into a lesbian or gay identity requires therapists to unearth this information and sift through what it means to be lesbian or gay. For those women and men born before Stonewall, that may require a discussion about a period in their histories when same-sex attractions were illegal and deemed psychologically disordered. Younger midlife women and men may be more concerned with parenting and how to do so as a lesbian or gay man while managing the stigma of their identities. In either case, an in-depth examination of the internalized stigma and how this internalization process has impacted the client's self-esteem is necessary. Additionally, the individual's cultural community's attitudes and beliefs about same-sex attractions necessitate attention. This includes religious and gender role prescriptions about relationships and sexuality and involves helping the individual incorporate multiple identities.

Integrating the Impact of Sociopolitical Contexts

In addition to taking an approach that uproots intrapsychic trauma, Russell and Bohan (2006) suggest "bringing the political into psychotherapy, encouraging the client to see her/himself not as a free-standing individual who contains the germ implanted by external homophobia but as a participant in socio-linguistic exchanges that suffuse the collective experiences of us all" (p. 13). In doing so, political events are weaved into the therapeutic process. This approach can work well with lesbians and gay men coming out at midlife, as it addresses the importance of historical events that have informed the individual's beliefs about same-sex attractions. It also invites clients to actively engage in experiences that challenge oppression. Given the theme of generativity at this life stage, lesbians or gay men coming out at midlife can find opportunities to address internalized homonegativity by "engaging in political activism targeting that bias" and involving themselves in "community-based anti-homophobia education as an antidote" (p. 6). Through community activism, they can heal their own wounds of homophobia and contribute to the safety and political freedoms of future generations of LGBT individuals.

Facilitating Relationships With Lesbians and Gay Men

Furthermore, relationships with other lesbians and gay men are paramount to the development of healthy self-esteem when coming out at midlife (Jensen, 1999; Rickards & Wuest, 2006; Woolf, 1998). Seeing positive images of lesbians and gay men with whom they can identify is important. It combats internalized homophobia and makes possible the transition to a healthy identity. Particularly for women and men of color, relationships with other lesbians and gay men of color are significant, given the existing racism in the White lesbian and gay communities (Adams & Kimmel, 1997). For gay men, facilitating connection with men that are both HIV+ and HIV– will help them demystify any misconceptions they have about the disease and educate them about safer sex practices. Finding communities of lesbians and gay men who have successfully navigated their own coming out and who are of the same cohort can provide self-esteem modeling for midlife lesbians and gay men who do not yet know the language of these new communities and who can do so in ways that resonate with their stage of life.

Fostering Resilience

A strength-based approach that focuses on resilience is essential to exploring the many ways clients have previously handled issues of adversity. Individuals in midlife have faced prior challenges, and meeting hardships well enough is essential to creating positive self-esteem. By situating the process of coming out within the client's life history of challenges, it is possible for the clinician to build on previous experiences and to use those cognitive, affective, and behavioral skills already in place. Reminding clients of their abilities and resources, internal and external, and reflecting on their resilience in a realistic manner can assuage fears and allow for exploration of this emerging identity. The benefit to enhanced self-esteem is clear as lesbians and gay men at midlife review their competence in managing the challenges of living out and proud.

Positive Aspects of Being Lesbian and Gay

Additionally, reference to the literature on positive psychology and the experiences of lesbians and gay men indicates that being lesbian or gay can have many positive aspects, such as "insight and awareness, key tools for making meaning out of one's life and circumstances … [and] increased empathy and compassion for themselves and others" (Riggle, Whitman, Olsoh, Rostosky, & Strong, p. 214). Lesbians and gay men coming out at midlife and striving for authenticity may need to hear this as they attempt to make meaning of their lives and their experiences. This study also revealed how integrating an identity that challenges normative gender roles can free individuals to adopt a greater range of behavior and become creative in expression as they live their lives more authentically. Rather than solely focusing on the challenges of coming out at midlife, the clinician can help clients focus on the joys of doing so.

CASE STUDY

Elena is a 50-year-old first-generation Mexican American woman who is coming out as lesbian. She has been married to a man, Bob, for 27 years, and together they have two daughters who are now in their early 20s. She describes herself as middle class, educated with a master's degree in business, and successful professionally as a manager in a small company. Although raised a Catholic, she presently does not practice her religion in a formalized manner. She is the eldest of four children, and all but one live close to Elena. Her parents are still alive and live within close proximity. In their 70s, they are in good health and are encountering only minor health concerns. Elena too is in good health and is experiencing the onset of menopause.

Elena acknowledged attractions to women throughout her life but never acted on any of them. She first noticed her interest in women when she had a strong connection to her best friend in high school, and then again in college, with various crushes on roommates and friends. Close relationships with women were acceptable in her family and the Mexican community in which she was raised, yet Elena knew her interest in her friends was more than what is usually acceptable, even within the Latino culture. In addition, because of strong messages received and integrated from the Catholic Church, her family, and her Mexican community, she denied her feelings and felt ashamed for having them. She dated men exclusively and met her husband while in college. As she followed the expected, heterosexually and culturally defined traditional path of marriage and childbearing, Elena continued to notice her emotional and physical attractions to women. Most recently, and pivotal to her coming out, was a growing attraction to Meredith, a newly hired manager in her company who is out as lesbian. Elena formed a quick and close relationship with Meredith and is no longer willing to deny her interest in exploring her powerful connection to women.

Elena is aware of the internal psychological conflict and relational challenges she faces in coming out. Much of her identity is connected to her Mexican heritage, and she is concerned about rejection from her family and community. Although she knows she can keep private her sexual identity, and may even be encouraged to do so through covert messages within her family and Mexican community (Greene, 1997), her fear of continuing to live an inauthentic life is causing much anxiety for her. She is faced as well with the decision of whether to self-disclose to her husband, of European descent with an Irish and English cultural history. He has consistently been somewhat distant emotionally with Elena. She fears his reaction and the reactions of her daughters, with whom she has very close relationships.

Therapeutically, there are many ways to intervene to enhance Elena's self-esteem as she considers the complexity of her experience. Coming out to herself as lesbian needs to be explored within the context of her culture, gender, and historical cohort. How does she understand herself as a Mexican woman who is 50 years old and coming out as lesbian? It is important to help her situate herself sociopolitically in regard to the historic events of her life and those for lesbians and gay men. During her adolescence, same-sex attractions were pathologized and criminalized, and she has witnessed many changes in the law and psychological communities, as well as societal perceptions of lesbians. How did her family and community absorb these changes, and what has been their influence on her perspective and her belief in her self-worth? As an adult, how did she internalize the messages she heard, and how did she manage the stigma? Given that self-esteem is a product of feedback from others, this part of the therapeutic process will require careful attention. The evaluation of others she places on the identity of lesbian will impact her self-esteem.

As a woman in a Latino family, Elena learned to quiet her sexuality. Coming out now in midlife requires her to confront this long-standing prohibition, which can be unsettling. In Jensen's study (1999), one of the major themes for these women coming out at midlife was the mystery of sex, as they had little education about their bodies and sex, and did not have permission to be sexual. Elena will need to explore her understanding of herself as sexual and romantic with another woman and her worthiness as a lesbian, and to integrate this part of herself into her sexual and global self-esteem. Unpacking and then connecting this aspect of herself as a Latina lesbian can pose a threat to her identity as a Latina, and helping her find ways to be true to both identities will be critical, as both identities constitute important domains that impact on her global self-esteem.

Relationally, Elena may encounter multiple rejections. Helping her manage any potential loss to her self-esteem as a product of these rejections is critical. It may be best to explore to whom she can come out first, who may be the least likely to reject her, and who can help her manage any potential losses. Role playing with her how she will come out to this individual in a manner that helps her communicate the joy and love she is experiencing will allow her to approach coming out from a strength-based perspective. She also needs to explore to whom she will not come out and how she will manage her identity around those individuals without pathologizing her decision to keep private this information. Attention to any division she may feel in regard to authenticity and the impact on her self-esteem at this juncture will be critical, as will a discussion of the resilience she has developed in the past when faced with racism, as a way to face possible rejection of those who are unable to support her lesbian and Latina identities. Finally, she should be connected to resources and organizations, such as Parents, Families, and Friends of Lesbians and Gays, which can support her and her family through the coming out process by normalizing doubts and fears, creating new compassionate relationships, and embracing her identities. The feedback she can receive from these new relationships can aide in establishing a sense of worthiness and competence that will strengthen her self-esteem.

CONCLUSION

This chapter addresses significant themes for lesbians and gay men at midlife and their connection to self-esteem. These themes offer insight into how lesbians and gay men at midlife encounter the challenges of coming out and living in a homophobic and heterosexist society, and how, at this juncture in their lives, they can use their resilience to enhance their self-esteem as they strive to live the second part of their lives authentically and with dignity, creating their own paths and life trajectories that normalize their sexual identities.

REFERENCES

Adams, C. L., & Kimmel, D. C. (1997). Exploring the lives of older African American gay men. In B. Greene (Ed.), *Ethnic and cultural diversity among lesbians and gay men* (pp. 132–151). Thousand Oaks, CA: Sage.

Baldwin, M. (2006). Self-esteem and close relationship dynamics. In M. H. Kernis (Ed.), *Self-esteem: Issues and answers; A sourcebook of current perspectives* (pp. 359–366). New York: Psychology Press.

Barker, J. C. (2004). Lesbian aging: An agenda for social research. In G. Herdt & B. de Vries (Eds.), *Gay and lesbian aging: Research and future directions* (pp. 29–72). New York: Springer.

Baron, A., & Cramer, D. W. (2000). Potential counseling concerns of aging lesbian, gay, and bisexual clients. In R. M. Perez, K. A. DeBord, & K. J. Bieschke (Eds.), *Handbook of counseling and psychotherapy with lesbian, gay, and bisexual clients* (pp. 207–223). Washington, DC: American Psychological Association.

Brown, L. B., Alley, G. R., Sarosy, S., Quarto, G., & Cook, T. (2001). Gay men: Aging well! In D. C. Kimmel & D. L. Martin (Eds.), *Midlife and aging in gay America* (pp. 41–54). Binghamton, NY: Harrington Park Press.

Chan, C. S. (1997). Don't ask, don't tell, don't know: The formation of a homosexual identity and sexual expression among Asian American lesbians. In B. Greene (Ed.), *Ethnic and cultural diversity among lesbians and gay men* (pp. 240–248). Thousand Oaks, CA: Sage.

Cohler, B. J., Hostetler, A. J., & Boxer, A. M. (1998). Generativity, social context, and live experience: Narratives of gay men in middle adulthood. In D. P. McAdams & E. de St. Aubin (Eds.), *Generativity and adult development* (pp. 265–309). Washington, DC: American Psychological Association.

Cole, E., & Rothblum, E. D. (1991). Lesbian sex at menopause: As good as or better than ever. In B. Sang, J. Warshow, & A. J. Smith (Eds.), *Lesbians at midlife: The creative transition* (pp. 184–193). San Francisco: Spinster Books.

de Vries, B., & Blando, J. A. (2004). The study of gay and lesbian aging: Lessons for social gerontology. In G. Herdt & B. de Vries (Ed.), *Gay and lesbian aging: Research and future directions* (pp. 3–28). New York: Springer.

Donaldson, C. (2000). Midlife lesbian parenting. In M. R. Adelman (Ed.), *Midlife lesbian relationships: Friends, lovers, children, and parents* (pp. 119–138). Binghamton, NY: Harrington Park Press.

Embrick, D. G., Walther, C. S., & Wickens, C. M. (2007). Working class masculinity: Keeping gay men and lesbians out of the workplace. *Sex Roles, 56,* 757–766.

Friend, R. A. (1991). Older lesbian and gay people: A theory of successful aging. In J. A. Lee (Ed.), *Gay midlife and maturity* (pp. 99–118). Binghamton, NY: Haworth Press.

Gorman, E. M., & Nelson, K. (2004). From a far place: Social and cultural considerations about HIV among midlife and older gay men. In G. Herdt & B. de Vries (Ed.), *Gay and lesbian aging: Research and future directions* (pp. 73–93). New York: Springer.

Greene, B. (1997). Ethnic minority lesbians and gay men: Mental health and treatment issues. In B. Greene (Ed.), *Ethnic and cultural diversity among lesbians and gay men* (pp. 216–239). Thousand Oaks, CA: Sage.

Hershberger, S. L., & D'Augelli, A. R. (1995). The impact of victimization on the mental health and suicidality of lesbian, gay, and bisexual youths. *Developmental Psychology, 31,* 65–74.

Hostetler, A. J. (2000). Lesbian and gay lives across the adult years. In B. J. Cohler & R. M. Galatzar (Eds.), *The course of gay and lesbian lives: Social and psychoanalytic perspectives* (pp. 193–251). Chicago: University of Chicago Press.

Human Rights Campaign. (n.d.). *Rights and protections denied same-sex partners.* Retrieved September 27, 2008, from http://www.hrc.org/issues/5478.htm

Hunter, S. (2005). *Midlife and older LGBT adults: Knowledge and affirmative practice for the social services.* Binghamton, NY: Haworth Press.

Icard, L. D. (1985). Assessing the psychological well-being of African American gays: A multidimensional perspective. *Journal of Gay & Lesbian Social Services, 5,* 25–49.

Isensee, R. (2005). *Are you ready? The gay man's guide to thriving at midlife*. Lincoln, NE: iUniverse, Inc.

Jensen, K. L. (1999). *Lesbian epiphanies: Women coming out in later life*. Binghamton, NY: Harrington Park Press.

Johnston, L. B., & Jenkins, D. (2004). Coming out in mid-adulthood: Building a new identity. *Journal of Gay & Lesbian Social Services, 16*, 19–42.

Jones, B. E. (2001). Is having the luck of growing old in the gay, lesbian, bisexual, transgender community good or bad luck? In D. C. Kimmel & D. L. Martin (Eds.), *Midlife and aging in gay America* (pp. 13–14). Binghamton, NY: Harrington Park Press.

Kertzner, R. M. (1999). Self-appraisal of life experience and psychological adjustment in midlife gay men. *Journal of Psychology & Human Sexuality, 11*, 43–64

Kertzner, R. M. (2001). The adult life course and homosexual identity in midlife gay men. *Annual Review of Sex Research, 12*, 75–92.

Kertzner, R., Myer, I., & Dolezal, C. (2004). Psychological well-being in midlife and older gay men. In D. C. Kimmel & D. L. Martin (Eds.), *Midlife and aging in gay America* (pp. 97–115). Binghamton, NY: Harrington Park Press.

Kimmel, D. C. (1978). Adult development and aging: A gay perspective. *Journal of Social Issues, 34*, 113–130.

Kimmel, D. C. (2004). Issues to consider in studies of midlife and older sexual minorities. In G. Herdt & B. de Vries (Ed.), *Gay and lesbian aging: Research and future directions* (pp. 265–283). New York: Springer.

Kooden, H., & Flowers, C. (2000). *Golden men: The power of gay midlife*. New York: Harper.

Loiacano, D. K. (1989). Gay identity issues among Black Americans: Racism, homophobia, and the need for validation. *Journal of Counseling and Development, 68*, 21–25.

Mruk, C. J. (2006). *Self-esteem research, theory, and practice* (3rd ed.). New York: Springer.

Pope, M., & Schultz, R. (1991). Sexual attitudes and behavior in midlife and aging homosexual males. In J. A. Lee (Ed.), *Gay midlife and maturity* (pp. 169–177). Binghamton, NY: Harrington Park Press.

Rickards, T., & Wuest, J. (2006). The process of losing and regaining credibility when coming-out at midlife. *Health Care for Women International, 27*, 530–547.

Riggle, E. D. B., Whitman, J. S., Olson, A., Rostosky, S. S., & Strong, S. (2008). The positive aspects of being a lesbian or gay man. *Professional Psychology: Research and Practice, 39*, 210–217.

Russell, G. M., & Bohan, J. S. (2006). The case of internalized homophobia: Theory and/as practice. *Theory & Psychology, 16*, 343–366.

Schope, R. D. (2002). The decision to tell: Factors influencing the disclosure of sexual orientation by gay men. *Journal of Gay & Lesbian Social Services, 14*, 1–21.

Shidlo, A. (1994). Internalized homophobia: Conceptual and empirical issues in measurement. In B. Greene & G. M. Herek (Eds.), *Lesbian and gay psychology: Theory, research, and clinical applications* (pp. 176–205). Thousand Oaks, CA: Sage.

Spencer, B., & Brown, J. (2007). Fusion or internalized homophobia? A pilot study of Bowen's differentiation of self hypothesis with lesbian couples. *Family Process, 46*, 257–268.

Szymanski, D. M., & Chung, Y. B. (2001). The lesbian internalized homophobia scale: A rational/theoretical approach. *Journal of Homosexuality, 41*, 37–52.

Szymanski, D. M., Chung, Y. B., & Balsam, K. F. (2001). Psychosocial correlates of internalized homophobia in lesbians. *Measurement and Evaluation in Counseling and Development, 34*, 27–38.

Tully, C. (1989). Caregiving: What do midlife lesbians view as important? *Journal of Gay & Lesbian Psychotherapy, 1*, 87–103.

Weinstock, J. S. (2000). Lesbians friendships at midlife: Patterns and possibilities for the 21st century. In M. R. Adelman (Ed.), *Midlife lesbian relationships: Friends, lovers, children, and parents* (pp. 1–32). Binghamton, NY: Harrington Park Press.

Weston, K. (1997). *Families we choose: Lesbians, gays, kinship.* New York: Columbia University Press.

Woolf, P. F. (1998). Mid-life transition to lesbian: Expanding consciousness of women. *Anthropology of Consciousness, 9,* 49–72.

16

Career Development
and Self-Esteem

SPENCER G. NILES, CHARLES JASON JACOB,
AND LINDSEY MARIE NICHOLS

F ew things are more personal than a career choice. Perhaps the substantial surge in downsizing has helped most people realize that when career situations go awry, the ripple effects are quite personal and, often, devastating. Herr (1989) notes that high levels of career uncertainty and occupational dissatisfaction are positively correlated with high levels of psychological and physical distress. High levels of unemployment have been associated with increased rates of chemical dependency, interpersonal violence, suicide, criminal activity, and admissions to psychiatric facilities (Herr, Cramer, & Niles, 2004). Clearly, individuals with an authentic sense of positive self-esteem rarely commit such acts. Thus, difficult career situations often translate to difficult life situations, and such situations will negatively impact a person's self-esteem.

It is also reasonable to suggest that when people experience low self-esteem, they often struggle considering career options, implementing their career choices, or managing their careers once their choices have been implemented. If, as Super (1957) contended, the choice of an occupation is the implementation of one's self-concept in an occupational role, then low self-esteem will undoubtedly cloud one's self-perceptions and negatively influence one's career decision-making process. Thus, today, most people acknowledge that positive career development experiences can foster positive global and contingent self-esteem, and low self-esteem can limit the person's opportunities for experiencing positive career situations by restricting the person's perceived opportunities. The relationship between career development and self-esteem is strong and bidirectional.

WORK AND SELF-ESTEEM

The close relationship between career development and self-esteem is evident throughout U.S. history. This relationship was evident in a speech made nearly 30 years ago by then-U.S. Secretary of Education Terrence Bell:

> Work in America is the means by which a person is tested as well as identified. It is the way in which a youngster becomes an adult. Work shapes the thoughts and life of the worker. A change in atmosphere and lifestyle can be effected by changing the way one earns a living. For most of us in adult life, being without work is not living. (Riegle, 1982, p. 114)

Such orientations to work reflect largely a majority culture American view toward work, which emphasizes individual control in career development (e.g., motivation, discipline, perseverance, goal directedness) and deemphasizes the role that sociological/contextual variables (e.g., the opportunity structure, the economy, socioeconomic status) play in shaping one's career. Thus, if a person has a "successful career," people tend to make a number of very positive attributions to the person who is a success. The corresponding assumption is that the "unsuccessful" person is inferior. The denial of the sociological factors influencing the pattern of one's career development, and the centrality of work in culture, become problematic for many people because such assumptions underscore the ways in which people link work with self-esteem (Subich, 1993). Obviously, if a positive sense of self-esteem is substantially dependent upon how one feels about his or her work contributions, then one's self-esteem can unravel fairly quickly if one's work situation goes awry (Herr et al., 2004).

Linking work with self-esteem also becomes problematic when we develop unrealistic expectations for work. For example, O'Toole (1981) suggests that "when it is said that work should be meaningful, what is meant is that it should contribute to the self-esteem, to the sense of self-fulfillment, through the mastering of one's self and one's environment, and to the sense that one is valued by society" (p. 15). Although these are clearly desirable experiences, issues such as dehumanizing work conditions, unemployment, prejudicial hiring practices, downsizing, and mismatches between people and their jobs lead to the conclusion that for many people, work is anything but meaningful. Denying contextual factors influencing career situations can lead people to engage in excessive self-blame when work experiences are negative for reasons beyond the worker's control.

Not only do many workers experience negative work situations and job dissatisfaction today, but many also do not know how to improve their situations. A poll conducted by the National Career Development Association (NCDA, 1989) revealed that a significant percentage of Americans (39%) did not have a career plan, and an even larger percentage of Americans (69%) did not know how to make informed career choices. It is reasonable to suggest that the current work situation is even more complex and more challenging today. Many workers experience record unemployment and substantial underemployment, with most economists and government officials predicting that the economy "will get worse before it gets better."

Many adults have information and skill deficits related to career planning and career self-management. Many people have also had limited opportunities to engage in systematic self-exploration for career development, and they are unclear about their training and educational needs. Results from the same NCDA (1989) poll indicate that almost half of all U.S. workers experience job-related stress and think that their skills are being underutilized in their jobs. If these are the experiences of many, and if we link work with self-worth, then it seems reasonable to suggest that the need for understanding the relationship between self-esteem and career development is substantial and urgent.

The challenges inherent in the new economy (fewer work opportunities, greater job insecurity, greater costs for durable and nondurable goods with stagnant or dwindling pay levels, pressure for engaging in lifelong learning, etc.) predict negative career outcomes for adults with insufficient career self-management knowledge, skills, and awareness. Due to the often concomitant experience of negative career outcomes and negative self-esteem, the press for increasing understanding related to these two issues becomes obvious.

SELF-ESTEEM AND CAREER DEVELOPMENT RESEARCH

Although some researchers have investigated the link between self-esteem and career development, it is somewhat surprising that a more substantial amount of research in this area does not exist. Researchers have tended to focus more on the relationship variables, such as personality type and occupational satisfaction; career development and career self-efficacy (a related but distinct construct); and career adaptability and occupational satisfaction.

Much of the research that includes self-esteem as a variable of interest is based upon developmental or cognitive career development theories. For example, Betz (2001) postulated that self-esteem has a relationship with career development, particularly as a moderator in the development of career goals. Betz references Super's (1990) emphasis on the influence of self-esteem in relation to vocational self-concept, but integrates this with the self-efficacy construct. She cites Korman's (1967) claim that "self-esteem operates as a moderator of the vocational choice process in that individuals with high self-esteem would seek those vocational roles that would be congruent with one's self-perceived characteristics, whereas this would be less likely the case for those individuals with low self-esteem" (p. 56). Betz (2001) also makes reference to Holland and his view that "individuals with low self-esteem may not act on their interests and suggests that interventions designed to increase an individual's range of experiences would be useful in increasing self-efficacy" (p. 56). Betz (2001) identifies these constructs as having different implications related to career development, citing self-esteem as "the overall affective evaluation of one's own worth, value, or importance" (Blascovich & Tomaka, 1991, p. 115) as opposed to self-efficacy, which concentrates on specific performance ability-related beliefs. Judge and Higgins (1998) have suggested that combining the implications of self-efficacy and self-esteem could result in increased job satisfaction and performance predictions. As a whole, this body of literature suggests that the differences and similarities between the two forms of self-evaluation have implications related to career development that can be used to better understand the needs of individuals struggling with career-related issues.

Changing Landscape of Self-Esteem

Important to an understanding of the relationship between self-esteem and career development is the changing definition of self-esteem as a construct, particularly the notion that increasing self-affirmation leads to globally positive outcomes. Baumeister has been at the forefront of research related to self-esteem within the last two decades, with some of this earlier scholarship focusing on how individuals reconcile self-esteem with performance and self-regulation. In one study, Baumeister, Heatherton, and Tice (1993) had participants complete a measure of self-esteem, after which they were instructed to play a video game that involved a basic test of manual dexterity. After playing the game for several minutes, participants were offered a chance to earn a small cash prize for subsequent performance on the video game—the catch was that they would be required to set their own benchmark for success, based on how confident they were in their ability to perform. Half of the subjects were randomly assigned to an "ego threat" condition, during which the explanation of potential benefits by the researcher included a suggestion that setting low benchmarks for success might be a good idea "if you don't think you have what it takes" (p. 145). The hypotheses were that people with high self-esteem set unrealistic goals for themselves, and those individuals struggle with completing goals when faced with a potential ego threat. Support for the latter hypothesis was confirmed, as those subjects with high self-esteem had a much higher rate of failure when confronted with the ego threat condition than their lower self-esteemed counterparts. The implication for career development, in this case, is that self-esteem where performance of tasks is concerned (such as tasks related to job performance) can be detrimental, as overconfidence in our abilities may be challenged by either poor performance or potential ego threats.

In more recent research, Baumeister and colleagues have found limited support for the idea that increasing self-esteem is useful in improving either task performance or psychological well-being. In one study, students performing poorly in an undergraduate psychology course were provided with a series of positive affirmations regarding self-esteem via e-mail, with the expectation that increasing self-esteem would help to improve self-worth and in turn foster improvements in academic performance. The opposite was found to be true: While students who received positive affirmations via e-mail did note slight improvements in self-esteem, overall test scores worsened from the beginning of the experiment to its conclusion (Forsyth, Lawrence, Burnette, & Baumeister, 2007). Similar findings have been noted in investigating the idea of discrepant high self-esteem, when an individual's expressed self-perceptions are higher than his or her internal self-perceptions (Zeigler-Hill, 2006, p. 123). In a review of data obtained from undergraduate students completing measures of implicit self-esteem, explicit self-esteem, and narcissism, it was found that individuals with high explicit self-esteem and low-implicit self-esteem reported higher levels of narcissism (Zeigler-Hill, 2006). Collectively, this research suggests that attempts to alter our self-esteem through outward affirmations are questionable, and that the notion of increasing self-esteem as a great social panacea has been largely misinformed (Krueger, Vohs, & Baumeister, 2008).

Organization-Based Self-Esteem

Perhaps most relevant to the arena of career development is a newer domain of selective self-esteem that has been suggested: organization-based self-esteem (OBSE). Organization-based self-esteem has been described by its progenitors as the amount of confidence individuals place in themselves to be productive and worthy members of a particular organization (Pierce & Gardner, 2004). Using data collected from 2,444 individuals completing questionnaires, a 10-item instrument was developed to measure OBSE, with evidence to suggest reliability and validity of the measure (Pierce, Gardner, Cummings, & Dunham, 1989).

Gardner, Van Dyne, and Pierce (2004) have conducted research that lends support to the hypothesis that levels of OBSE can be altered by external factors, which in turn can promote more effective job performance. In examining the rates of pay for employees of a construction company, OBSE, and employee performance as measured by the employer, it was found that pay level was related to organization-based self-esteem, which had a subsequent effect on job performance; specifically, higher pay led to a more favorable perception of value by the employer, which in turn led to better job performance (Gardner et al., 2004, p. 316).

Payne (2007) has found evidence to suggest that an employee's organization-based self-esteem may have an impact on the manner in which they express dissatisfaction with their employment. In a sample of 179 employees that completed both Pierce's measure of OBSE and a measure of organizational dissent, employees with high levels of organization-based self-esteem were more likely to communicate dissent to their supervisors; employees with low OBSE were more likely to vent their concerns to co-workers, though they were not significantly different from employees with moderate OBSE (Payne, 2007). In this case, the degree to which an employee felt confident in his or her abilities had a significant impact on the likelihood that complaints would be heard (and potentially resolved) by management, as opposed to fellow co-workers.

Implications

Self-esteem and career development research results highlight the link between these two constructs. This link has important implications for career development theory and practice. For instance, if positive career development and positive self-esteem are related, then career development programs become critical at essentially every level of career development. Although career development theorists tend not to address self-esteem directly, cognitively oriented career development theories address various ways in which self-referential thinking can influence career development goals and actions. Thus, in the following section we discuss the three primary cognitively oriented career theories. Specifically, we discuss these theories in light of self-esteem.

CAREER DEVELOPMENT THEORY

Cognitive theories of career development address an important dimension of the career decision-making process (i.e., factors that influence how we think about ourselves and our world). Often, it is the person's cognitions, especially one's sense of self-esteem, that determine whether one is willing and motivated to select an educational or career path. The major cognitive theories of career development are social cognitive career theory, cognitive information processing, and the social learning theory of career decision making.

Social Cognitive Career Theory

Social cognitive career theory (SCCT; Lent & Brown, 1996) incorporates the triadic reciprocal model, developed as part of social cognitive theory by Bandura (1986), to describe the complex relationship between self-efficacy beliefs, outcome expectations, and personal goals in the career decision-making process. Self-efficacy beliefs are "people's judgments of their capabilities to organize and execute courses of action required to attain designated types of performances" (Bandura, 1986, p. 391). These beliefs, or self-judgments, are shaped both positively and negatively within four domains: (1) personal performance accomplishments, (2) vicarious learning, (3) social persuasion, and (4) physiological states and reactions (Bandura, 1986). In the case of personal performance accomplishments, successful accomplishment in any of these domains results in a more positive self-efficacy belief in that particular domain, while failures lead to more negative domain-specific self-efficacy beliefs.

Self-efficacy beliefs play an essential role in the career decision-making process. For example, self-efficacy beliefs tend to move either toward or away from tasks and occupations, depending upon the person's belief in his or her capacity to develop the capabilities required for successful performance. Self-efficacy beliefs provide answers to "Can I do it?" questions.

Outcome expectations are behavior-specific belief expectations that are developed in the context of extrinsic reinforcement (i.e., tangible rewards), self-directed consequences (i.e., pride of accomplishment), or outcomes resulting from the activity itself (being "in the zone"; Lent, Brown, & Hackett, 1996, p. 381). In other words, these describe what a person expects to happen if he or she takes action. Although outcome expectations have less influence on behavior than self-efficacy beliefs, they still play an important role in the career decision-making process. These expectations may manifest themselves through questions such as: "Do I have a chance of getting the scholarship if I apply?" "Will I get a job after completing the training program?" "What job opportunities will be available to me if I pursue college study?"

Personal goals relate to a person's determination to obtain a particular outcome by engaging in activities designed to achieve that outcome over time (Bandura, 1986). Goals help organize and determine one's career-oriented behaviors over extended periods of time. Personal goals may be found in statements such as: "I will get a second part-time job to stay in school." "I will stay in this physics course because it is required to get into an engineering major."

The interaction of these three factors informs beliefs about one's perceived competence and ability to play a central role in the career decision-making process. This interaction is seen as interlocking and bidirectional in that all three factors impact the other two.

SCCT is a useful career theory for addressing career concerns that incorporate self-esteem issues because low self-esteem tends to accompany low self-efficacy and negative outcome expectations. According to Lent and Brown (1996), "Higher self-efficacy and anticipated positive outcomes promote higher goals, which help to mobilize and sustain performance behavior" (p. 318). One can easily add to this statement the qualifier "as long as one possesses high self-esteem." Career interventions include challenging inaccurate self-efficacy beliefs, outcome expectations, or low self-esteem, concerning components of worthiness or competence, or both, because these can cause one to prematurely foreclose on occupational options due to barriers that are perceived as insurmountable.

A card sort exercise is one suggested approach to interest exploration (Lent & Brown, 1996). Occupations are sorted into three categories: (1) those one would choose, (2) those one would not choose, and (3) those one would question. The focus of the intervention is then on the last two categories. The client is asked which occupations he or she might choose if he or she had the skills (perceived competence and self-efficacy beliefs), and which he or she might choose because he or she thinks the occupation offers them something he or she values (outcome expectations). A similar question can be posed relative to the worthiness component of self-esteem (i.e., Which occupations might they choose if they had a more positive sense of self-esteem?). The client is also asked which occupations he or she definitely would not choose. The list of occupations determined from the first two card sort categories is then examined for accuracy in terms of self-esteem salience, self-efficacy, and outcome expectations, and in terms of the degree to which self-esteem might be influential.

Several interventions are available to career practitioners to help clients modify their self-efficacy beliefs and strengthen their self-esteem. When clients have sufficient ability, but low self-efficacy beliefs or low self-esteem due to factors such as sex role stereotyping and racism, career counselors can encourage relevant vicarious learning experiences such as observing successful occupational and self-esteem role models. These clients can also be encouraged to gather ability-related data to counteract these inaccurate beliefs from friends, family, and teachers. The goal is to help clients experience and examine success experiences to strengthen their weak self-efficacy beliefs and low self-esteem.

Cognitive Information Processing

The cognitive information processing (CIP) approach to career counseling (Peterson, Lumsden, Sampson, Reardon, & Lenz, 2002) addresses the role that cognitions play in career and educational planning. This approach stems from the three-factor Parsonian model of career decision making (i.e., develop self-understanding and occupational knowledge to arrive at a career choice), but also includes current knowledge about cognitive information processing. The CIP model is useful for counselors in that it provides an additional layer to understanding the process of career decision making (metacognitions).

Four assumptions provide the theoretical foundation of the CIP model. First, there is an interaction between cognitive and affective processes that occurs during any career decision. Second, available cognitive operations and knowledge determine an individual's capacity for solving career problems. Third, knowledge structures and, therefore, career development are always evolving. Finally, the aim of career counseling is to enhance the client's information processing skill set (Peterson et al., 2002). The cognitive processes described by this model occur in four career decision-making domains: (1) self-knowledge, (2) occupational knowledge, (3) decision-making skills, and (4) metacognitions. The fourth domain, metacognitions, adds to the traditional foundation of most career theories by incorporating self-talk, self-awareness, and the monitoring and control of cognitions. This fourth dimension of the CIP model also represents the stage in which the dynamic interactions between self-esteem and career decision making play out. These four domains are often presented as a pyramid, with self-knowledge and occupational knowledge acting as the base, decision-making skills as the middle, and metacognitions as the apex (Sampson, Peterson, Lenz, & Reardon, 1992).

The pyramid model is an excellent framework for guiding career interventions. Each of the four domains may represent an element of a person's development to be addressed with an intervention designed specifically for that domain. For example, self-knowledge deficits may require formal or informal values assessments, occupational knowledge deficits may be addressed with informational interviews or internships, and negative self-talk, especially as may related to negative self-esteem, may best be addressed through counseling (Peterson et al., 2002).

Social Learning Theory of Career Decision Making

Krumboltz and his colleagues developed the social learning theory of career decision making (SLTCDM; Mitchell & Krumboltz, 1996). This theory is based on the application of Bandura's (1977) social learning theory to career decision making. Bandura's theory emphasizes the influence of reinforcement theory, cognitive information processing, and classical behaviorism on human behavior. Social learning theory "assumes that people's personalities and behavioral repertoires can be explained most usefully on the basis of their unique learning experiences while still acknowledging the role played by innate and developmental processes" (Mitchell & Krumboltz, 1996, p. 234). Social learning theory also assumes that "humans are intelligent, problem-solving individuals who strive at all times to understand the reinforcement that surrounds them and who in turn control their environments to suit their own purposes and needs" (Mitchell & Krumboltz, 1996, p. 236).

Krumboltz and his colleagues drew upon these theoretical assumptions in developing SLTCDM. Specifically, in SLTCDM, four factors that influence career decision making are identified:

1. Genetic endowments and special abilities. Genetic endowments are inherited qualities, such as sex, race, and physical appearance. Special abilities, such as intelligence, athletic ability, and musical and artistic talents, result from the interaction of genetic factors and exposure to selected environmental events.
2. Environmental conditions and events. Factors in this category are generally outside our control and can involve a wide variety of cultural, social, political, historical, and economic forces.
3. Instrumental and associative learning experiences. Instrumental learning experiences involve antecedents, behaviors, and consequences. Associative learning experiences occur when a neutral stimulus is paired with a positive or negative stimulus or consequences.
4. Task approach skills. These include the individual's work habits, mental set, emotional responses, cognitive processes, and problem-solving skills.

Although these four factors (i.e., genetic endowment and special abilities, environmental conditions and events, instrumental and associative learning experiences, and task approach skills) influence people differently, there are generally four ways in which they can influence career decision making. First, they lead to the formation of self-observation generalizations. Self-observation generalizations are overt or covert statements evaluating one's actual or vicarious performance or self-assessments of one's interests and values (Mitchell & Krumboltz, 1996), or conclusions regarding one's self-esteem. Learning experiences lead people to draw conclusions about themselves. People compare their performance with the performance of others and to their own performance expectations. Individuals then use these comparisons to draw conclusions about their performance capabilities. Conclusions about interests and values also result from learning experiences. In SLTCDM, interests link learning experiences with specific actions. Self-observations about values are, in essence, statements about the desirability of specific outcomes, behaviors, or events (Mitchell & Krumboltz, 1996). For example, the statement that "it is important that my job provides ample time for me to be with my family" is a values-related self-observation generalization about desirable outcomes resulting from previous learning experiences. Self-esteem self-observations emanating from negative learning experiences (e.g., "My boss continually berates my effort and my performance; thus, I must be both lazy and incompetent") offer fertile ground for counseling-based interventions. A second outcome of the four factors influencing career decision making can be labeled as worldview generalizations. These are generalizations about the nature and functioning of the world (e.g., "It's not what you know, it's who you know," "Once you choose a job, you cannot change your mind") formed from learning experiences. The accuracy of worldview generalizations is dependent on the learning experiences shaping such generalizations. Clearly, inaccurate worldview generalizations (e.g., "It's not what you know, it's who you know") can lead to negative self-esteem (e.g., "If it doesn't matter what I know or how hard I work, then my effort does not matter and I do not matter"). A third outcome of the four factors influencing career decision making is the development of additional task approach skills. Mitchell and Krumboltz

(1996) define these outcomes as "cognitive and performance abilities and emotional predispositions for coping with the environment, interpreting it in relation to self-observation generalizations, and making covert and overt predictions about future events" (p. 246). As noted earlier, task approach skills both influence career decision making and are outcomes of learning experiences that shape individuals' career development. Task approach skills critical to career development are those involved in decision making, problem solving, goal setting, information gathering, and values clarifying. Finally, the four factors influencing career decision making lead individuals to take actions related to their career planning. These actions can include implementing an occupational choice, entering a training program, applying to graduate school, changing jobs, or taking other overt steps to make progress in one's career planning.

Cognitive theories of career development address an important dimension of the career decision-making process (i.e., factors that influence how people think about themselves and the world). Often, it is the person's cognitions, especially one's sense of self-esteem, that determine whether one is willing and motivated to select a career path.

CASE STUDY

Thomas is a 45-year-old African American male who has presented for career counseling at an urban career center. At his initial appointment he states that he heard that career counselors do testing on interests and that he would like to take this type of test "to find out what he should do for the rest of his life." He notes that he decided to pursue career counseling now because his wife had been "nagging" him to get some help.

Thomas reported that he had been in the Navy for the past 27 years. He joined the Navy after graduating from high school because there were no jobs in the rural community where he grew up in the midwestern United States. He spent the majority of his naval career on ships and submarines where his expertise was in radar and sonar maintenance, and where he managed crews of 15–50 personnel. He enjoyed his maintenance work but stated that, at times, being a supervisor was "very frustrating." Often, he thought it was just easier to do the work himself rather than relying on others to get the job done. When he was not chosen for a higher rank, he decided to retire from naval service.

After leaving the Navy, Thomas began looking for employment as a manager, but after eight months of job searching, he had received no offers of employment. Although income from his retirement and his wife's part-time employment has been sufficient to meet the mortgage and basic utility bills, Thomas has borrowed heavily to meet other expenses, and he and his wife are rapidly depleting the savings intended for the education of their children. They have two sons, ages 16 and 18, and one daughter, age 12.

Thomas reported that lately he had been feeling tired most of the time. Even his hobbies—gardening and horticulture, which have fascinated him since his boyhood days in 4-H—are not satisfying now. He confesses that he has been drinking rather heavily for the past month and that there are some days when he just stays at home in his bathrobe watching television. He hopes that the results of an interest test will help him "get back on track."

Thomas clearly is struggling with the interplay between self-esteem and career development. Being denied promotion in the military and engaging in an unsuccessful job search seem to have damaged his self-esteem and self-efficacy to the point that he now demonstrates obvious signs of depression. Interventions with Thomas would need to demonstrate sensitivity to both self-esteem and career development issues.

Career developmentally, he seems to be reengaging in Super's exploration stage tasks, as he has reentered civilian life at age 45—something he has not experienced since he was a teenager. On a positive note, he brings substantial information to his exploring. He has a wealth of data from his time in the military that he can draw upon to help crystallize a current sense of self relative to his values, interests, and skills. His exploration must also factor in his life structure, which obviously includes multiple life roles (Super, 1980). In addition to being a worker, he is also a spouse and a father, roles with strong self-esteem salience for him. He questions his capacity to parent competently, especially as that relates to what he may view as his responsibility to be the provider of financial resources within the family. Given his employment situation, he would not be surprised if he were engaged in excessive negative self-talk, thereby perpetuating the downward spiral of his self-esteem. His career counselor would need to listen for negative self-referential statements and view them as opportunities to encourage Thomas to engage in cognitive restructuring. For example, the vast amount of evidence indicates that he has been a very supportive father and spouse. He clearly cares about his family and takes his family responsibilities seriously. He has provided for his spouse and children through his military service. He is now engaged in finding new work opportunities in a challenging economy. The fact that he has not yet found a job may be leading him to internalize this lack of success in ways that diminish his self-esteem. Rather than simply give up the search, however, he is meeting with a counselor to explore other possibilities. All signs of someone who cares about his career and his family, facts that the counselor should reinforce to Thomas. By reinforcing these facts, the counselor would be engaged in positively influencing Thomas's self-observation generalizations (Mitchell & Krumboltz, 1996) and metacognitions (CIP). Related to this, Thomas would seem to be a prime candidate for a job search support group in which he could share with other job seekers his thoughts and feelings regarding the search.

To further bolster his self-esteem and also assist him in his career self-management process, Thomas's career counselor could engage him in a functional skills or accomplishments interview. Specifically, Thomas can be asked to list three things he has accomplished in his life about which he feels particularly proud (e.g., an accomplishment during his time in the military). The career counselor's role in this process is to encourage Thomas to describe in detail what he did to make the accomplishment happen. As Thomas describes his actions, the career counselor listens closely for all functional skills that Thomas identifies (e.g., organizing, managing, implementing orders effectively). The career counselor writes down all skills he hears as Thomas tells his story. Once this has been completed for the first accomplishment, Thomas and the career counselor engage in the same process with the second activity and then the third. At the conclusion of this interview, Thomas and the career counselor review the entire list of functional skills that Thomas used in the three activities. At this point, it will be important for the career counselor to encourage Thomas in how he felt as the counselor read the list of skills. The intent here is to reinforce the many functional skills Thomas has demonstrated in his life, something that a person struggling with self-esteem needs to hear. Once Thomas and the career counselor have reviewed the skill list, they can then review it with the goal of identifying those skills that Thomas enjoys using the most, and in which his selective self-esteem is most heavily weighted. By focusing on the skills Thomas possesses and enjoys using, the career counselor and Thomas can then begin to brainstorm career options that connect with his skills and interests. At this point, the career counselor can focus on providing Thomas with positive reinforcement (Mitchell & Krumboltz, 1996) for his accomplishments. The goal here is both helping him to move forward with specific career goals while also helping him to increase his self-esteem, thereby influencing his self-observation generalizations (Mitchell & Krumboltz, 1996). At this point, Thomas may be ready to engage in career decisionmaking and move forward strategically with a job search directed toward occupational options that match important self-characteristics he possesses. In Super's terms, he will turn from crystallizing and specifying an occupational choice to implementing one.

CONCLUSION

Although there has been some research investigating the relationship between self-esteem and career development, more understanding of this relationship is needed on both the theory and practice levels. It seems clear that when both issues are present, the need for a holistic intervention approach increases (i.e., one that addresses the more traditional career development tasks related to educational and career planning while also addressing the client's self-esteem concerns). The challenges in the new economy make the need for increased understanding of these issues even more urgent. As the increased realization of the personal dimensions of career development grows, we urge researchers and practitioners to more aggressively address the relationship between self-esteem and career development in their work.

REFERENCES

Bandura, A. (1977). *Social learning theory*. Upper Saddle River, NJ: Prentice Hall.

Bandura, A. (1986). *Social foundations of thought and action: A social-cognitive theory*. Upper Saddle River, NJ: Prentice Hall.

Baumeister, R. F., Heatherton, T. F., & Tice, D. M. (1993). When ego threats lead to self-regulation failure: Negative consequences of high self-esteem. *Journal of Personality and Social Psychology, 64*, 141–156.

Betz, N. (2001). Career self-efficacy. In S. H. Osipow, F. T. L. Leong, & A. Barak, *Contemporary models in vocational psychology: A volume in honor of Samuel H. Osipow* (pp. 55–77). Mahwah, NJ: Lawrence Erlbaum Associates.

Blascovich, J., & Tomaka, J. (1991). Measures of self-esteem. In J. P. Robinson, P. R. Shaver, & L. S. Wrightsman (Eds.), *Measures of personality and social psychological attitudes* (pp. 115–160). San Diego, CA: Academic Press.

Forsyth, D. R., Lawrence, N. K., Burnette, J. L., & Baumeister, R. F. (2007). Attempting to improve the academic performance of struggling college students by bolstering their self-esteem: An intervention that backfired. *Journal of Social and Clinical Psychology, 26,* 447–459.

Gardner, D. G., Van Dyne, L., & Pierce, J. L. (2004). The effects of pay level on organization-based self-esteem and performance: A field study. *Journal of Occupational and Organizational Psychology, 77,* 307–322.

Herr, E. L. (1989). Career development and mental health. *Journal of Career Development, 16,* 5–18.

Herr, E. L., Cramer, S. H., & Niles, S. G. (2004). *Career guidance and counseling through the lifespan* (6th ed.). New York: Pearson.

Judge, T. A., & Higgins, C. (1998). Affective disposition and the letter of reference. *Organizational Behavior and Human Decision Processes, 75,* 207–221.

Korman, A. K. (1967). Self-esteem as a moderator of the relationship between self-perceived abilities and vocational choice. *Journal of Applied Psychology, 51,* 65–67.

Krueger, J. I., Vohs, K. D., & Baumeister, R. F. (2008). Is the allure of self-esteem a mirage after all? *American Psychologist, 63,* 64–65.

Lent, R. W., & Brown, S. D. (1996). Social cognitive approach to career development: An overview. *Career Development Quarterly, 44,* 310–321.

Lent, R. W., Brown, S. D., & Hackett, G. (1996). Career development from a social cognitive perspective. In D. Brown, L. Brooks, & Associates (Eds.), *Career choice and development* (3rd ed., pp. 373–416). San Francisco: Jossey-Bass.

Mitchell, L. K., & Krumboltz, J. D. (1996). Krumboltz's theory of career choice and counseling. In D. Brown, L. Brooks, & Associates (Eds.), *Career choice development* (3rd ed., pp. 233–280). San Francisco: Jossey-Bass.

National Career Development Association. (1989). *Gallup poll on work in America.* Columbus, OH: Author.

O'Toole, J. (1981). Work in America. In J. O'Toole, J. L. Schiber, & L. C. Wood (Eds.), *Working: Changes and choices* (pp. 12–17). New York: Human Sciences Press.

Payne, H. J. (2007). The role of organization-based self-esteem in employee dissent expression. *Communication Research Reports, 24,* 235–240.

Peterson, G. W., Lumsden, J. A., Sampson, J. P., Reardon, R. C., & Lenz, J. G. (2002). Using a cognitive information processing approach in career counseling with adults. In S. Niles (Ed.), *Adult career development: Concepts, models, and practices* (3rd ed., pp. 99–120). Tulsa, OK: National Career Development Association.

Pierce, J. L., & Gardner, D. G. (2004). Self-esteem within the work and organizational context: A review of the organization-based self-esteem literature. *Journal of Management, 30,* 591–622.

Pierce, J. L., Gardner, D. G., Cummings, L. L., & Dunham, R. B. (1989). Organization-based self-esteem: Construct definition, measurement, and validation. *Academy of Management Journal, 32,* 622–648.

Riegle, D. W., Jr. (1982). Psychological and social effects of unemployment. *American Psychologist, 21,* 113–115.

Sampson, J. P., Jr., Peterson, G. W., Lenz, J. G., & Reardon, R. C. (1992). A cognitive approach to career services: Translating concepts into practice. *Career Development Quarterly, 41,* 67–74.

Subich, L. M. (1993). How personal is career counseling? *Career Development Quarterly, 42,* 129–131.

Super, D. E. (1957). *The psychology of careers.* New York: Harper & Brothers.

Super, D. E. (1980). A life span, life-space approach to career development. *Journal of Vocational Behavior, 16,* 282–298.

Super, D. E. (1990). A life-span life-space approach to career development. In D. Brown, L. Brooks, & Associates (Eds.), *Career choice and development* (2nd ed., pp. 197–261). Hillsdale, NJ: Lawrence Erlbaum Associates.

Zeigler-Hill, V. (2006). Discrepancies between implicit and explicit self-esteem: Implications for narcissism and self-esteem instability. *Journal of Personality, 74,* 119–143.

17

Chronic Health Issues

REBECCA L. BRICKWEDDE

Angela was in perfect health and felt fully in control of her life. There were many projects she planned to undertake, many professional as well as personal goals. She was energetic, optimistic, and enjoyed her life with her family and friends. Then one day her health began to waver and she was diagnosed with a chronic illness. From one day to the next, everything changed. Now her life revolves around fear and doctor appointments. The carefree life she once experienced is gone, replaced by the need to submit to a world of uncertainty and concerns. She feels she is no longer in control of her own life, as she must submit to doctors' orders and rely on the help of others. Her self-identity, her perceived role in her family, and her self-worth are suffering.

S ome say it is like falling into an abyss, where all is unknown. "Walking out of the physician's office, the patient's head swirls with questions ... the feeling is one of being adrift in a sea of uncertainty, with all anchors gone and previous points of reference rendered meaningless" (Pollin, 1995, p. 49). Bolen (1996) described it as a soul experience: "Illness is both soul-shaking and soul-evoking for the patient.... We lose an innocence, we know vulnerability, we are no longer who we were before this event, and we will never be the same" (p. 14).

Chronic health problems include, but are not limited to, asthma, epilepsy, nervous system injuries, diabetes, arthritis, Alzheimer's disease, heart disease, stroke, cancer, HIV/AIDS, and multiple sclerosis. Losses of a limb, whether through illness, accident, or war, as well as surgical removal of a body part, are chronic health issues that also merit attention. Chronic disorders can interfere with self-esteem, especially when they affect a person's appearance or ability to function successfully.

SELF-ESTEEM ISSUES OF PERSONS
EXPERIENCING CHRONIC HEALTH ISSUES

Self-esteem is one of the identifiable factors known to affect both adaptation and adjustment to chronic illness; chronic health issues affect both global and selective self-esteem. How one sees and evaluates oneself, regarding competence and identity, can be radically altered by a medical crisis, or the onset of a chronic illness. Patients must learn to cope with and adapt to their illness, deal with its symptoms, and manage the stress of treatment procedures. "Coping with a chronic illness requires substantial effort and a great capacity to adjust to new and changing circumstances" (Kuijer & DeRidder, 2003, p. 313). Factors affecting adaptation include baseline levels of symptom severity, time since diagnosis, social comparison, self-esteem, optimism, and perceived approach to goals (Yardley & Dibb, 2007).

Pollin (1995) identified eight predictable adjustment issues that persons diagnosed with chronic illness tend to have in common. These include control, self-image, dependency, stigma, abandonment, anger, isolation, and death. Self-image is second only to control issues as the most pressing concern. Upon diagnosis, the patient faces a fear of losing control, followed by grief over the loss of their prior sense of self and personal independence, as well as a fear of becoming a burden to the family. Depending on the illness, impairment, or disfigurement, the patient will experience different levels of stigma. Profound fears of abandonment arise and patients come face to face with their anger. Social, physical, and emotional isolation become a challenge, and finally, varied death-related issues begin to dominate.

Self-esteem is part of self-identity and "may be discordant for many individuals with visible disabilities" (Livneh & Antonak, 2005, p. 13). "Patients who undergo critical physical changes often suffer a loss of self-esteem. It is essential to deal with the change in body image and to help the patient institute a compensatory means of accommodation" (Landgarten, 1981, p. 335). The self-esteem element of worthiness comes into question for many coping with a threatening diagnosis. Because they often withdraw from normal activity, patients may experience erosion in their sense of identity, as they often feel they no longer can fill essential roles at home and must increase time off from work (Sherman & Simonton, 2001).

Research by Robins, Trzesniewski, Tracy, Gosling, and Potter (2002) indicates that "the profound physical and emotional changes associated with aging may have a more negative impact on self-esteem than on other aspects of psychological adjustment" (p. 431). For the person who must experience chronic illness in midlife, self-esteem is challenged early, and the need to maintain good self-esteem is crucial. Favorable self-appraisal and a feeling of competence and mastery in the midst of the uncertain challenge of a chronic illness are heightened when there is hope, optimism, and a sense of control. Substantial evidence indicates that hope and optimism play vital roles in adaptation to chronic illness. To be able to envision and expect the best possible outcome involves hope; choosing to see the best side of a given situation involves optimism. Yet remaining optimistic and hopeful in the face of a chronic illness is challenging.

Facing a medical crisis, being diagnosed with a chronic illness, and learning to live with a chronic illness, confront and test the stability of one's self-esteem, both globally and selectively. How one is able to deal with and adapt to the illness plays an important role in determining one's overall level of self-acceptance and the possibility of a successful outcome. Patients with chronic illnesses report the loss of personal control, threats to self-esteem, restricted feelings of competence, and increased vulnerability (Fife, 1994, as cited in Brannon & Feist, 1997). Regaining a sense of control, maintaining hope, as well as learning to identify and assert one's needs are essential components to the preservation of one's self-esteem while learning to live with a chronic medical condition. The fear of losing control of one's life and the changes in self-image and self-esteem that chronic illness brings can be addressed in the counseling process through a variety of intervention strategies.

INTERVENTION STRATEGIES

Psychoeducational interventions are particularly useful at early phases of diagnosis and treatment. Casado-Kehoe and Ballard (2006) stressed the importance of client education in order to feel more in charge of their progress and to be an effective part of the decision-making process. Being apprised of common emotional changes and challenges brought about by chronic illness, and learning coping skills such as relaxation and assertiveness training, can help patients come to terms with their conditions. Learning to communicate assertively with medical providers and being directed toward useful patient education programs and resources for additional information on the specific illness can clear up misconceptions about treatment and side effects.

People with chronic illness are often viewed negatively with stigmatizing perceptions. They may be treated with discriminatory practices that result in reduced self-esteem, increased life stress, and withdrawal from social encounters (Livneh & Antonak, 2005). Because feedback from significant others is an important element in one's self-esteem, it is important to explore close relationships and process stigma's potential negative effect on the patient. Pollin (1995) listed avoidance, discrimination, hostility, fear, disgust, condescension, and simple curiosity as possibilities patients may have to endure, depending on their condition. Counselors should encourage patients to join social support peer groups of others with their condition, in addition to strengthening self-acceptance and promoting the understanding and teaching skills necessary to constructively confront stigma.

Changes in thoughts and feelings can directly affect body responses, and emotions can trigger changes in the immune system (Myers & Sweeney, 1995). "People's emotions—both positive and negative—play a critical role in the balance of immune functions" (Sarafino, 1998, p. 120). Many researchers have pointed out that high levels of stress can increase susceptibility to illness and the progression of disease; numerous studies report the relationship between stress and ill health. Stressors can disrupt immune function, whereas well-being can bolster it and buffer the effects of stressors. Because self-esteem has been shown to buffer stress, boosting self-esteem and managing perceived stress are important objectives in the treatment of those with chronic illness.

A number of mind–body health approaches can be used in the counseling setting. Roberts (1999) stressed the importance of nurturing the client's soul, defining soul as "that depth of our being where a personal reflective knowledge resides, and becomes accessible to us through non-rational means…. The world of reverence, feeling, imagination, poetry, art, music, ritual, symbol, and existential longing all provide gateways to that place where our unique self connects with something greater than ourselves, and provides opportunities for understanding and meaning" (p. 84). These creative approaches to healing and enhancing self-esteem are particularly useful to clients who are in the midst of a medical crisis, or adapting to long-term illness.

Approaches often used to complement traditional medical treatment discussed here are (1) art therapy, (2) guided imagery, (3) active imagination, and (4) assertiveness training. Believing in the process of these interventions and having options among them can be empowering, giving clients a feeling of control over their illness and their overall stressful circumstance. "Perceived control is associated with emotional well-being, successful coping with stress, [and] better physical health…. Having an internal locus of control has been associated with lower levels of anxiety and depression and higher levels of self-esteem and life satisfaction" (Myers & Sweeney, 2005a, p. 22).

Art Therapy

The creative process of art, especially drawing images, can be effective for those confronting serious illness. Self-esteem is enhanced and perception of pain is often reduced during the creative process of art making. It can provide "an experience of normalcy, if only for the time one is engaged in creative activity" (Malchiodi, 1998, p. 174). Clients can be asked to draw their illness metaphorically and symbolically, allowing the image to emerge as it will. The emotions behind the images can then be processed. Because achievement is an integral element of self-esteem, it is important to provide experiences in which patients can experience success. Art materials serve as an opportunity for clients to be in charge of their own decision-making while gaining "awareness about their ability to still be productive and to problem-solve. It is this small measure of accomplishment which serves as the foundation for patients to build future trust in themselves and hope" (Landgartern, 1981, p. 336). Gladding (2005) suggested that introducing clients to classic paintings can also arouse feeling responses that may open the door to insight on repressed issues or issues they desire to discuss.

The mandala, first introduced by Jung, is a symbol of wholeness and satisfies a need for order. It is useful in reconciling and understanding particular polarities, or opposites, in one's life, and can be used as an expression of the self-healing process. Useful for perception and exploration of self-identity and self-worth, Klagsbrun et al. (2005) described a mandala activity with cancer patients in which "each participant created an individual mandala using symbols and/or words to remind them of their personal self-care and support tools" (p. 120).

Restorying can be an effective technique for increasing the sense of control that is so essential to maintaining self-esteem. In one example, patients drew two timelines depicting positive and negative events covering the same period of time (see Eeltink & Duffy, 2004). Positive events are added to openings in stories of reduction and deterioration in order that "the negative experiences intermingle with the positive ones and a new enriched story of life and what life means in the presence of illness and fear can then emerge" (p. 285). Sherman and Simonton (2001) have emphasized the importance of creating new flexible and adaptive narratives, after reevaluating rigid, self-defeating ones. They suggest making conjoint family drawings to facilitate communication about illness-related changes in the family, as well as writing and posting affirming messages derived from the positive constructions of meaning that patients attach to their illnesses. Many patients find it an empowering coping strategy to decorate these affirming messages with bright colors and meaningful symbols. These messages may consist of family mottos, positive attitudes, or hopeful thoughts (e.g., "1 in 10 people survive for longer than five years with this type of cancer, and I could be one of those survivors"; Ornstein & Sobel, 1988, p. 243). Patients can be helped to "become more aware of self-defeating beliefs" (Curtis & Juhnke, 2003, p. 165).

Hiltebrand (as cited in Klagsbrun et al., 2005) "noted that art therapy offers cancer patients the 'opportunity to express emotion, enhance relaxation, increase communication, reduce pain and empower themselves through vital participation in a life affirming activity'" (p. 112). "The process of art making is recognized as important to physical healing, whether it be in the form of recovery or rehabilitation, learning to cope with illness or symptoms, or finding meaning for the experience of serious or life-threatening illness" (Malchiodi, 1998, p. 169).

Guided Imagery

Gladding (2005) stated that "the use of imagery is one of the most powerful of our human faculties ... imagery is a tool for working with and working through one's environment and circumstances" (p. 66). Benson (1996) has reminded us that "when people are jolted by symptoms they associate with serious illness, their images of themselves as strong, vigorous, and healthy are often instantly dampened or destroyed.... Panic and fear, with their accompanying arousal of the fight or flight response, take colossal bites out of self-esteem" (p. 207). Guided imagery, as directed meditation or hypnosis, can be tailored to help chronic illness patients remember instances of competence to regain their positive image of themselves. More than 30 years ago, Lazarus (1977) suggested encouraging clients to recall something that they did quite well and to dwell on that incident, recapturing feelings of achievement and accomplishment. Patients can be asked to imagine themselves as they once were, strong, vigorous, and healthy. Imagery can be used as a way to awaken reference memories and experiences in which the joy and success of being themselves, while living and expressing their truth, were present (Miller, 1997). When one focuses on an image, the brain reconstructs the image that was stored in the memory "by recreating the pattern of nerve cell activity" (Benson, 1996, p. 76) that occurred when the image was originally viewed. The brain interprets imagined and real scenes the same way. Guided imagery capitalizes on the capacity of imagination to create images that have a potent impact on the mind and body (Owen, 2006). The mind and nervous system cannot distinguish between fantasy and actual external stimuli.

In fact, guided imagery is used to augment the treatment of a variety of diseases and health conditions in hospitals around the world. For example, Halpin, Spier, CapoBianco, and Barnett (2002) found that guided imagery can be used to reduce preoperative anxiety and postoperative pain in surgery patients. Limonick (2001) reported the use of guided imagery in reversing weight loss in cancer patients, as well as easing pain and fatigue. Simonton's use of guided imagery with cancer patients, as measured by a seven-year outcome study, led to longer terms of survival (Simonton & Henson, 1992/2002). Ornish (1991) has promoted and successfully utilized imagery in his program for reversing (and preventing) heart disease.

Achterberg (1996) stated that imagery is "the communication system between body and mind. It is how the mind learns of things of the body and how the mind translates information to the body." To aid in the image formation, and enhance the belief system, Achterberg (1985) suggested beginning by "developing a solid understanding of the way the body functions, and by gathering information on the health condition…. Hope and belief in becoming one of the positive health statistics stir the imagination into action" (pp. 102–103). Achterberg (1985) listed three major components of the imagery, which include the disease, the treatment, and the defenses. She stated:

> The therapist's goal at this point is to create a canvas upon which the intimate knowledge of disease can then be drawn, but not to program or suggest images. It is upon the initial hunches, the emotions, the strength given to the disease and the defenses rallied against it that therapy is based…. The more symbolic images, as opposed to those that are realistic or anatomically correct, are better predictors of good health outcome. (p. 105)

Imagery is the language that serves the body, the mind, and the soul. It is often paired with relaxation skills, in an effort to calm the individual and create an atmosphere more conducive to concentration on imagery goals. Relaxation techniques, as well as guided imagery, can help to foster a sense of personal control regarding illness and its effects, as well as reinforce hope. Relaxation, however, has its own rewards for those with chronic conditions, including a sense of calm and reduced heart and metabolic rates. Strong evidence suggests that self-regulatory relaxation techniques can reduce chronic pain in a variety of medical conditions (National Institutes of Health, 1995).

Sarafino (1998) cited a number of examples in which relaxation training is helpful with various forms of chronic illness, including its use with arthritis patients to control stress, with diabetic patients to manage blood glucose levels, with epileptics to manage seizures, with asthma patients to manage asthma attacks, and with cancer patients to reduce chemotherapy-induced nausea. Guided imagery can decrease pain perception and reduce anxiety (Ackerman & Turkoski, 2000), and has been used successfully in a variety of treatment issues with cancer patients (Casado-Kehoe & Ballard, 2006).

Active Imagination

The method of active imagination, first developed by Jung, can be used with chronic illness patients to enhance self-esteem by increasing feelings of competence and strengthening self-image.

It lends "a voice to sides of the personality … that are normally not heard" (Sharp, 1991, p. 13). Jaffé (1977/1979) described the process as "a conscious submerging in the unconscious, whose contents are then observed, pictured, and meditated upon" (p. 115). It can be differentiated from guided imagery as a process in which an individual consciously observes and meditates on the contents of the unconscious. Hollis (2001) stressed that psychic energy is carried by images, and these images "may rise spontaneously from one's own unconscious" (p. 49). "In active imagination consciousness respectfully approaches the image, activates it through engagement, and then pays attention to what the image wishes to do" (Hollis, 2004, p. 142). Images that arise include symbolic expressions of psychological or physical difficulties; overcoming these difficulties in the imagination leads to overcoming them in the psyche. These images aid in "the conversion of a lived experience into a feeling, an idea, a behavior and a value system whose source lies beneath consciousness altogether…. Only when the invisible becomes manifest as image can we discern and track it" (Hollis, 2003, p. 27).

Active imagination, as a means of self-expression for the unconscious, can also be accomplished through musical improvisation, painting, sculpting, or dancing. Singer (1994) explained that "the common feature of all varieties of active imagination is its dependence upon a view of the unconscious that recognizes its contents as containing innate structures (archetypes) which inevitably define the potentialities and the limitations of the personality" (p. 288). Thus, active imagination is a powerful resource in healing and maintaining whatever specific elements of self-esteem have been compromised as a result of illness.

Assertiveness Training

A feeling of competence in expressing oneself assertively leads to a greater sense of efficacy, and the ability to be assertive can increase a sense of self-worth. Becoming aware of and expressing one's own ego identity is an important developmental task in midlife (Hollis, 2003). Passivity can be extremely detrimental in those with life-threatening illness. Sperry (2005) noted that the chronic illness of one of his patients, who had a personal style of submissiveness, seemed to magnify the influence of this style on relational dynamics. Assertiveness training can be implemented to teach new ways of communicating and negotiating and can also aid in overcoming fear. Becoming more assertive, expressing emotions freely, refusing to participate in defeat, and taking charge of one's life, *even if one was never able to before*, are key elements to developing a survivor mentality. Siegel (1986/1998) called these survivors "exceptional patients" and asserted his belief that making these changes while suffering from a life-threatening disease could save or prolong their lives well beyond medical predictions. "Exceptional patients refuse to be victims. They educate themselves and become specialists in their own care. They question the doctor because they want to understand their treatment and participate in it. They demand dignity, personhood, and control, no matter what the course of the disease" (p. 24).

Cognitive restructuring can help replace patients' passive methods of coping with more active and assertive problem-solving coping strategies (Eeltink & Duffy, 2004). Expressing emotions is an important aspect of assertiveness. Pert (1997) stated that "when emotions are repressed, denied, not allowed to be whatever they may be, our network pathways get blocked, stopping the flow of the vital feel-good, unifying chemicals that run both our biology and our behavior" (p. 273).

Siegel (1986/1998) maintained that "the most important kind of assertiveness a patient can demonstrate is in the formation of a participatory relationship with the doctor" (p. 172). In fact, he found that those who play an active and more assertive role in their treatment had a better chance of becoming long-term survivors. "Families [and patients] can be assisted to communicate more actively and assertively with medical providers so they have a clearer understanding of the road ahead" (Sherman & Simonton, 1999, p. 46). This assists them in their need and effort to maintain competence and mastery.

ROLE OF THE COUNSELOR

The counselor can play a vital role in fostering the qualities of a sense of hope, control, and assertiveness, all of which can have a positive impact on self-esteem while learning to live with a chronic medical condition. Siegel (1986/1998) maintained his belief that there is no such thing as false hope in the patient's mind, and strongly suggested that the concept be discarded from the medical vocabulary.

Control issues are among the most powerful concerns for people adjusting to chronic illness. To assist patients in regaining their sense of control, the counselor can help them identify the areas where they feel powerless and give expression to feelings of loss of control. The goal is to "reinforce the patient's confidence in his or her own ability to cope with the demands of the medical condition" (Pollin, 1995, p. 51). Having a number of options helps to increase a sense of control and a feeling of competency, leading to healthier outcomes. Recalling positive coping with difficult past experiences can increase self-esteem and suggest that clients have the necessary control and coping skills to deal with the general, as well as the current, uncertainty of life (Eeltink & Duffy, 2004; Pollin, 1995). For many, a life-threatening illness "mobilizes an inner warrior, and taps into a wish to live…. [It] then serves as a wake-up call to the importance of life, and in the process of coping …, the patient discovers strengths" he or she never knew he or she had (Bolen, 1996, pp. 50–51). Those who develop this inner warrior, this *fighting spirit*, may actually have improved clinical outcome. Cancer patients with a fighting spirit were shown to have "significantly higher survival [rates] than those with stoic acceptance or helplessness/hopelessness at 5, 10 and 15 years after diagnosis" (Greer et al., as cited in Stolbach, 2003, p. 17).

Counselors can help clients reassess their options and choose new goals that fit their current capabilities. For example, Fischer, Salewski, and Küch (2007) found that the well-being of patients was increased when intervention options took into account the impact of interruptions in their goal striving due to chronic disease or an accident. The counselor's goal is to help the patient allow a "different self-image to emerge that integrates all of the new realities in the patient's life" (Pollin, 1995, p. 56). To do this, the counselor must determine the patient's pre-illness sense of self so the focus can be placed on strengthening remaining attributes and identifying losses and grieving them. The patient can learn that "he or she has not lost everything; not all of one's positive attributes are undermined by a medical condition" (p. 60). A mourning process triggered by the crisis experience at the onset of the chronic illness or disability must include the identification of the remaining attributes as well as personality strengths (Livneh & Antonak, 2005). Previous healthy levels of self-esteem can now be rallied to fight the illness. The strongest elements of the patient's personality "become the bedrock on which an adaptive process can be built. Patients are helped ... to become aware of the ways in which they are already coping and to strengthen those that are most positive" (Pollin, 1995, p. 60).

Self-efficacy involves competency, and a feeling of competence in the form of mastery is one of the integral elements of self-esteem. Younger, Finan, Zautra, Davis, and Reich (2008) likened a high sense of personal mastery to self-efficacy and found that "a sense of personal mastery likely lessens the psychological impact of the disease" (p. 530). They also identified control as an aspect of mastery, recognizing the unique clinical implications of control for those with chronic illness.

The chronic illness diagnosis can dramatically change the way in which one lives life. One must effectively ask, "Do I have the illness or does the illness have me?" Continuing on with the other aspects of one's life that are not directly affected by the illness can aid in restoring and maintaining a sense of control and improved self-esteem. It is important for both patients and families to be able to take time out from focusing on the illness. A "break from the cycle of worry" (Casado-Kehoe & Ballard, 2006) can be accomplished by structuring time when illness is not the focus and maintaining as normal a life as possible.

Spirituality can be included in counseling goals. Roberts (1999) stressed that "therapists must be aware that nurturance of the soul is unique to each client" (p. 84). To some, it is important to find meaning in the illness. Sherman and Simonton (1999) maintained that these meanings are "powerful determinants of adjustment" (p. 47), and therefore should be included in the therapy. "The subjective meaning ascribed to the illness has a powerful impact.... Cultural models of illness also shape the meaning ascribed" (p. 45).

ASSESSMENT AND EVALUATION

The *Wheel of Wellness* (Myers & Sweeney, 2005a) can be used as a basis for assessment and interventions for those with chronic illnesses. Health psychology, behavioral medicine, and psychoneuroimmunology were all utilized in the foundation of this model. It includes primary areas of focus on sense of worth, sense of control, emotional awareness, and coping, as well as problem solving and creativity. Two formal assessment methods based on the *Wheel of Wellness* are the Wellness

Evaluation of Lifestyle (WEL; and its successor, the Five-Factor Wellness Inventory 5F-WEL; Myers & Sweeney, 2005b).

The Silver Lining Questionnaire (SLQ; Sodergren & Hyland, 2000) can be used to measure aspects of adversarial growth, or *positive consequences of illness*, in the case of chronic illness. Bride, Dunwoody, Lowe-Strong, and Kennedy (2008) introduced the revised version (SLQ-24), after factoring 24 of the SLQ-38 items into five subscales: improved personal relationships, greater appreciation for life, positive influence on others, personal inner strength, and changes in life philosophy, noting that "each subscale reflects a theme of adversarial growth previously reported in the literature" (p. 672).

Owen (2007) developed a short, informal self-rating scale that could prove to be helpful with this population. The Self-Esteem Evaluation Scale (SEES) is a useful tool to help counselors introduce clients to "the idea of self-esteem and its central position in nearly all aspects of our behavior and personality" (p. 28). The Tennessee Self-Concept Scale (TSCS; Roid & Fitts, 1988) lends itself especially well to this population, in that it has a subscale, which pertains particularly to the physical self.

CASE STUDY

Lynn, 45, a professional with a husband and two teenage children, was diagnosed with a prolactinoma after an MRI of her brain revealed a tumor. It was in close proximity to her optic nerve, potentially jeopardizing her eyesight should it enlarge. She was hospitalized for further testing, the tumor was found to be benign, and surgery to remove it was recommended. She declined. Upon discharge, she sought another medical opinion. The doctor found no indication for surgery and started her on medication that was known to shrink prolactinomas just enough to contain their growth. Already dealing with the normal physical and emotional changes that come with midlife, Lynn was overwhelmed with fear and felt her self-esteem plummeting. She sought out counseling for the first time in her life. MRIs over the course of the next 2½ years revealed that the adenoma had actually slowly and completely dissolved, leaving only scar tissue. In the following five years, there was no recurrence.

Throughout the course of her illness, several counseling interventions were implemented that seemed to aid in her self-esteem adjustment and health recovery. After processing her fear and her grief over her lost sense of a healthy self, reasons for optimism and hope were explored. She was encouraged to ask the doctors questions and to read about her medical condition and her medication. Research on her medication found that in rare cases, the prolactinoma did, in fact, disappear. The counselor capitalized on this fact to instill hope and help Lynn restore a sense of control.

The concepts of the mind–body connection were reviewed as well as the clinical uses of imagery. After preparing a script, a guided imagery tape was recorded, using her own voice, reminding her of all of the positive strengths and goals in her life. She described an image of the tumor melting away like a snowball on a hot stove. She was asked to listen to this tape twice a day, which gave her a sense of mastery and accomplishment.

She was encouraged to draw her pituitary gland, depicting it as healthy, fully functioning, and tumor-free. She chose to make it bright yellow, as if it were bathed with bright, healing light. A small example was laminated and she was instructed to keep it with her and concentrate on this healing image often throughout the day. Using active imagination, symbols and metaphors emerged that reflected positive meaning in her illness. These themes were then explored. She was asked to make small posters of sayings that had always given her strength. She chose to illustrate some of them with her meaningful symbols. She was instructed to place the posters in her home where she would see them often. She was asked to bring photos depicting a time in which she felt vibrantly healthy and happy. She gathered photo images of herself with those whom she loved dearly. She was instructed to look through the photos often and imagine herself experiencing health and happiness in the present and in the future. All these techniques helped Lynn feel competent in the management of her own illness and increased her global self-esteem to its pre-illness level.

Life satisfaction and well-being were explored. She chose to embark on some changes that gave her life more meaning and increased her sense of competence and control. Assertiveness strategies were reviewed, which led her to begin to more assertively set limits with others, so that she would no longer overextend herself. She came to her own conclusion that all of these positive changes had actually been brought about by her illness.

CONCLUSION

Chronic illness negatively impacts self-esteem. One's self-image, self-identity, and sense of control deteriorate and self-worth is questioned. This leads to an overall deterioration in both global and selective self-esteem. Counseling and the use of the aforementioned intervention strategies can effectively restore and maintain high self-esteem.

REFERENCES

Achterberg, J. (1985). *Imagery in healing: Shamanism and modern medicine*. Boston: Shambhala.

Achterberg, J. (Speaker) (1996). *The power of the imagination in healing* [Heilen mit inneren Bildem] (Cassette Recording No. ISBN3-8302-0155-9). Muensterschwarzach, Germany: Vier-Tuerme-Verlag.

Ackerman, C. J., & Turkoski, B. (2000). Using guided imagery to reduce pain and anxiety. *Home Healthcare Nurse, 18*, 524–530.

Benson, H. (with Stark, M.). (1996). *Timeless healing: The power and biology of belief*. New York: Scribner.

Bolen, J. S. (1996). *Close to the bone: Life threatening illness and the search for meaning*. New York: Simon & Schuster.

Brannon, L., & Feist, J. (1997). *Health psychology: An introduction to behavior and health* (3rd ed.). Pacific Grove, CA: Brooks/Cole.

Bride, O. M., Dunwoody, L., Lowe-Strong, A., & Kennedy, S. M. (2008). Examining adversarial growth in illness: The factor structure of the silver lining questionnaire (SLQ-38). *Psychology and Health, 23*, 661–678.

Casado-Kehoe, M., & Ballard, M. (2006, April). *For better or for worse: Empowering families to survive cancer*. Education session presented at the Annual Convention of the American Counseling Association/Canadian Counselling Association, Montreal, Canada.

Curtis, R. C., & Juhnke, G. A. (2003). Counseling the client with prostate cancer. *Journal of Counseling & Development, 81*, 160–167.

Eeltink, C., & Duffy, M. (2004). Restorying the illness experience in multiple sclerosis. *The Family Journal: Counseling and Therapy for Couples and Families, 12*, 282–286.

Fischer, D., Salewski, C., & Küch, D. (2007). Personal goals and subjective well-being in chronically ill patients. *Health Psychology Review, 1*, 112–113.

Gladding, S. T. (2005). *Counseling as an art: The creative arts in counseling* (3rd ed.). Alexandria, VA: American Counseling Association.

Halpin, L. S., Spier, A. M., CapoBianco, P., & Barnett, S. D. (2002). Guided imagery in cardiac surgery. *Outcomes Management, 6*, 132–137.

Hollis, J. (2001). *Creating a life: Finding your individual path*. Toronto: Inner City Books.

Hollis, J. (2003). On *this journey we call our life: Living the questions*. Toronto: Inner City Books.

Hollis, J. (2004). *Mythologems: Incarnations of the invisible world*. Toronto: Inner City Books.

Jaffé, A. (Ed.). (1979). *C.G. Jung: Word and image* (K. Winston, Trans.). Princeton, NJ: Princeton University Press. (Original work published 1977)

Klagsbrun, J., Rappaport, L., Speiser, V. M., Post, P., Byers, J., Stepakoff, S., et al. (2005). Focusing and expressive arts therapy as a complementary treatment for women with breast cancer. *Journal of Creativity in Mental Health, 1*, 107–137.

Kuijer, R. G., & DeRidder, D. T. D. (2003). Discrepancy in illness-related goals and quality of life in chronically ill patients: The role of self-efficacy. *Psychology and Health, 18*, 313–330.

Landgarten, H. B. (1981). *Clinical art therapy: A comprehensive guide*. New York: Brunner/Mazel.

Lazarus, A. A. (1977). *In the mind's eye: The power of imagery therapy to give you control over your life*. New York: Rawson Associates.

Limonick, M. D. (2001, April 16). Guided imagery: Mind over malignancies. *Time, 157*, 60.

Livneh, H., & Antonak, R. F. (2005). Psychosocial adaptation to chronic illness and disability: A primer for counselors. *Journal of Counseling & Development, 83*, 12–20.

Malchiodi, C. A. (1998). *The art therapy sourcebook*. Los Angeles: Lowell House.

Miller, E. E. (1997). *Deep healing: The essence of mind/body medicine*. Carlsbad, CA: Hay House.

Myers, J. E., & Sweeney, T. J. (1995, March). *The characteristics of healthy individuals and families: Strategies for optimizing development during drawdown*. Seminar presented at the European Branch–American Counseling Association Professional Development Learning Institute, Wiesbaden, Germany.

Myers, J. E., & Sweeney, T. J. (2005a). The wheel of wellness. In J. E. Myers & T. J. Sweeney (Eds.), *Counseling for wellness: Theory, research, and practice* (pp. 15–28). Alexandria, VA: American Counseling Association.

Myers, J. E., & Sweeney, T. J. (2005b). Assessing wellness: Formal and informal approaches. In J. E. Myers & T. J. Sweeney (Eds.), *Counseling for wellness: Theory, research, and practice* (pp. 39–57). Alexandria, VA: American Counseling Association.

National Institutes of Health. (1995). *Integration of behavioral and relaxation approaches into the treatment of chronic pain and insomnia.* (NIH Technology Assessment Statement, October 16–18, 1995, pp. 1–34). Retrieved August 23, 2004, from http://odp.od.nih.gov/consensus/ta/017/017_statement.htm

Ornish, D. (1991). *Dr. Dean Ornish's program for reversing heart disease.* New York: Ballantine Books.

Ornstein, R., & Sobel, D. (1988). *The healing brain: Breakthrough discoveries about how the brain keeps us healthy.* New York: Simon & Schuster.

Owen, D. W., Jr. (2006, May). *Spontaneous and structured fantasy in counseling: Putting inner experience to work.* Seminar presented at the European Branch–American Counseling Association Professional Development Learning Institute, Speyer, Germany.

Owen, D. W., Jr. (2007, August). Tools for the counselor: Self-Esteem Evaluation Scale. *Neues Perspectives for the European Counselor, 19,* 28–29.

Pert, C. B. (1997). *Molecules of emotion: The science behind mind-body medicine.* New York: Scribner.

Pollin, I. (1995). *Medical crisis counseling: Short-term therapy for long-term illness.* New York and London: W.W. Norton.

Roberts, S. (1999). The spiritual dimension of the wellness model and its implications for counseling. *New Jersey Journal of Professional Counseling, 55,* 79–86.

Robins, R. W., Trzesniewski, K. H., Tracy, J. L., Gosling, S. D., & Potter, J. (2002). Global self-esteem across the life span. *Psychology and Aging, 17,* 423–434.

Roid, G. H., & Fitts, W. H. (1988). *Tennessee Self-Concept Scale* (rev. manual). Los Angeles: Western Psychological Services.

Sarafino, E. P. (1998). *Health psychology: Biopsychosocial interactions* (3rd ed.). New York: John Wiley & Sons.

Sharp, D. (1991). *C.G. Jung lexicon: A primer of terms & concepts.* Toronto: Inner City Books.

Sherman, A. C., & Simonton, S. (1999). Family therapy for cancer patients: Clinical issues and interventions. *The Family Journal: Counseling and Therapy for Couples and Families, 7,* 39–50.

Sherman, A. C., & Simonton, S. (2001). Coping with cancer in the family. *The Family Journal: Counseling and Therapy for Couples and Families, 9,* 193–200.

Siegel, B. S. (1998). *Love, medicine & miracles: Lessons learned about self-healing from a surgeon's experience with exceptional patients.* New York: HarperPerennial. (Original work published 1986)

Simonton, O. C., & Henson, R. (2002). *The healing journey.* Lincoln, NE: Authors Choice Press. (Original work published 1992)

Singer, J. (1994). *Boundaries of the soul: The practice of Jung's psychology* (rev. ed.). New York: Doubleday.

Sodergren, S. C., & Hyland, M. E. (2000). What are the positive consequences of illness? *Psychology and Health, 15,* 85–97.

Sperry, L. (2005). A therapeutic interviewing strategy for effective counseling practice: Application to health and medical issues in individual and couples therapy. *The Family Journal: Counseling and Therapy for Couples and Families, 13,* 477–481.

Stolbach, L. L. (2003). Does "fighting spirit" improve medical outcomes of cancer patients? *Advances in Mind-Body Medicine, 19,* 17–18.

Yardley, L., & Dibb, B. (2007). Assessing subjective change in chronic illness: An examination of response shift in health-related and goal-oriented subjective status. *Psychology and Health, 22,* 813–828.

Younger, J., Finan, P., Zautra, A., Davis, M., & Reich, J. (2008). Personal mastery predicts pain, stress, fatigue, and blood pressure in adults with rheumatoid arthritis. *Psychology and Health, 23,* 515–535.

Section VI

Late Life

In late life, aging is more noticeable than at midlife and there are even greater differences in the rates of aging. The combination of genetics, environment, and earlier health and lifestyle choices determine longevity and quality of life. Rates of change are related not only to age, but also to whether one is still physically adept and functionally healthy (the young-old) or in physical decline (the old-old). Normal aging consists of changes that are universal, progressive, and irreversible. Throughout life, age can be measured not only by the passage of time, or chronological age, but by biological age—progression of biological development and physical health, psychological age—the measure of psychological and mental functioning, social age—the passage through socially defined markers of development, and perceived age—one's view of oneself in the other measures of age, or how old one feels. It is perhaps perceived age that best determines self-esteem and life satisfaction. As in every other phase of life, social class and economic status affect the downward trajectory in aging.

Physical changes of aging are apparent in outward signs—wrinkling and sagging skin, gray to white and thinning hair, ages spots, and decreasing height and possibly weight—and in declining sensory functioning; the breakdown of cardiovascular, respiratory, nervous system, digestive, and immune systems; and deterioration of mental and motor functioning. Sleep disturbances are the norm. Illness and chronic disease increase substantially. Yet there is considerable support for the positive influence of exercise in staving off effects of aging. Exercise has also been shown to be effective with older sedentary adults in reducing depressive symptoms; change in physical self-esteem predicts change in depressive symptoms (Motl et al., 2005).

Cognitively, older people process new information more slowly and have more difficulty retrieving long-term memories. Although language comprehension does not decline in normal elderly people, word retrieval and verbal planning decrease. Differences in individual cognitive functioning are greater in old age than in any other time of life (Berk, 2006). Many of these differences are accounted for by how active late-life people are in pursuing mentally challenging experiences, such as taking classes, working on puzzles of all kinds, and pursuing new opportunities, whether friendships, travel, volunteerism, or work. Lifelong learning in any form leads to new friends, a broader understanding of the world, and the perception of competence (Berk, 2006). Pursuit of creativity in many forms can keep people of all ages, but most especially late-life adults, productively engaged, and thus impact life satisfaction.

Social and emotional changes are most tied to the many inevitable losses people experience as they progress through the last stage of life. Loss of physical vitality, decreases in all five senses, loss of family and loved ones through changing roles or death, and loss of meaningful work, whether paid or unpaid, mean significant adjustments. Depression is prevalent among those older people who have debilitating illness and disease. Bereavement is a common risk factor for depression as well. When faced with loss, some older people experience depression or even commit suicide, while others show resilience and adapt to new circumstances.

Although not part of normal aging, almost 20% of people over the age of 55 experience mental disorders. Most prevalent are anxiety disorders (11.7%) and depressive disorders (4.4%); suicide frequency is highest after age 65 (U.S. Public Health Service, n.d.). Memory complaints are more likely related to depression than to decline in memory performance (U.S. Public Health Service, n.d.). With decreasing physical stamina, illness, and relinquishing many life roles, many elderly people feel a lack of control and agency. Some elders give up control by having to acquiesce to the desires and demands of well-meaning children or grandchildren; others lead lives with little attention from these significant others. Intergenerational conflicts and misunderstanding can affect late-life adults in profound ways. Older people may learn to be helpless in the face of their changing situations, and thus are more vulnerable to emotional and physical crises (Myers, 1989). Subgroups based on ethnicity and socioeconomic needs and circumstances have special concerns, particularly when their issues fall outside the mainstream, dominant culture view of aging.

Many late-life adults continue to resolve Erikson's (1959/1980) generativity versus stagnation stage throughout life. Late-life adults now enter the last Eriksonian stage, ego integrity versus despair, in which individuals reflect on and analyze their lives. This appears to be a natural process in aging during which older people attempt to reach closure for the life experience. Resolution of this stage means fully accepting oneself and responsibility for one's life, coming to terms with the past, and feeling satisfaction with and fulfillment of the self. Ego integrity leads to wisdom, renunciation of the accumulations of life, and reconciliation with death, accepting it as an inevitable part of life. Those who are not able to successfully negotiate this stage may face despair and fear death.

With regard to self-esteem, evidence suggests that it declines in old age, substantially for some but less so or not at all for others (Robins & Trzesniewski, 2005; Trzesniewski, Donnellan, & Robins, 2003). Resilience in many forms, including perception of control and being socially engaged and physically active, has been shown to contribute to healthy levels of self-esteem in this age group. Resilience in psychological well-being shows little change in those with high levels of self-esteem (Collins & Smyer, 2005). High collective self-esteem, in which late-life adults see themselves positively as part of a broad network of similar others, seems to delay absence of perceived control, decline of activity, and onset of chronic health problems (Bailis, Chipperfield, & Helgason, 2008). Siegrist, Von Dem Knesebeck, and Pollack (2004) found that productivity in the form of paid or unpaid work and other socially valued activities seem to be related to the need for self-efficacy and self-esteem. On the whole, although losses can take a toll on selective self-esteem, global self-esteem appears to continue to remain relatively the same for many people. Those with low self-esteem in earlier life may have greater difficulty in later life, and those with appropriately high levels of self-esteem may have an easier time resolving their losses. This section presents information in these areas of late adulthood: the effects of loss on self-esteem, intergenerational relationships in Asian Americans, and the positive effects of creativity in late life.

REFERENCES

Bailis, D. S., Chipperfield, J. G., & Helgason, T. R. (2008). Collective self-esteem and the onset of chronic conditions and reduced activity in a longitudinal study of aging. *Social Science & Medicine, 66*, 1817–1827.

Berk, L. E. (2006). *Development through the lifespan* (3rd ed.). Boston: Allyn & Bacon.

Collins, A. L., & Smyer, M. A. (2005). The resilience of self-esteem in late adulthood. *Journal of Aging and Health, 17*, 471–489.

Erikson, E. H. (1980). *Identity and the life cycle.* New York: Norton. (Original work published 1959)

Motl, R. W., Konopack, J. F., McAuley, E., Elavsky, S., Jerome, G. J., & Marquez, D. X. (2005). Depressive symptoms among older adults: Long-term reduction after a physical activity intervention. *Journal of Behavioral Medicine, 28*, 385–394.

Myers, J. E. (1989). *Adult children & aging parents.* Alexandria, VA: American Association of Counseling and Development.

Robins, R. W., & Trzesniewski, K. H. (2005). Self-esteem development across the lifespan. *Current Directions in Psychological Science, 14*, 158–162.

Siegrist, J., Von Dem Knesebeck, O., & Pollack, C. E. (2004). Social productivity and well-being of older people: A sociological exploration. *Social Theory & Health, 2*, 1–17.

Trzesniewski, K. H., Donnellan, M. B., & Robins, R. W. (2003). Stability of self-esteem across the life span. *Journal of Personality and Social Psychology, 84*, 205–220.

U.S. Public Health Service. (n.d.). Older adults and mental health. In *Mental health: A report of the surgeon general.* Retrieved February 15, 2009, from http://www.surgeongeneral.gov/library/mentalhealth/chapter5/sec1.html

18

Self-Esteem and the Third Phase of Life

LEE J. RICHMOND AND MARY H. GUINDON

O
lder Americans—once divided into categories of young-old, old, and old-old—now form one group differentiated not by age but by physical ability and mental agility. Consequently, the three groups are collapsed into one group called *the third phase of life*. Older Americans comprise the fastest growing segment of the population, unprecedented in the nation's history. According to a recent report from the Centers for Disease Control (2007a), in the year 2030 there will be 71 million older Americans. The first wave of the baby boomers will be 85 years old and the youngest boomers will be 65 (Wacker & Wacker, 2007). Aging baby boomers will double today's population of those 65 years of age and older, accounting for 20% of the total U.S. population, and exerting tremendous influence on our collective future.

The expected growth of the aging population poses many social challenges shaping the manner in which all future Americans will live. The new demographics will affect how people are housed and the manner in which they live in their houses; how office buildings are constructed and the physical and social needs of workers; the structure of recreation facilities and the structure of recreation itself. The fact that increasing numbers of people will live longer raises huge challenges to social security and healthcare, critical concerns of older adults. Their perception of financial well-being and a sense of physical wellness both lead to a sense of being in control, a major component of self-esteem in the elderly. Concern about health could be greatly eased if a high quality of life and attention to active engagement could be ensured for older adults. The findings of many studies of the elderly document that self-esteem is correlated positively with good health, and that both self-esteem and good health are negatively correlated with depression. The surgeon general's report the *State of Aging and Health in America* (Centers for Disease Control, 2007b) clearly states that style of life, which includes healthy

eating, regular physical activity, and avoidance of tobacco, is predictive of longevity. Furthermore, chronic illness and the absence of depression and economic
burden are correlated with well-being and a sense of contentment in later years
(Guralnik & Kaplan, 1989).

SELF-ESTEEM IN AGING AND RELATED RESEARCH

Self-esteem is a primary factor in quality of life. In the persons of all ages, positive self-esteem comes from a sense that one is adequate enough and competent
enough to manage the tasks that one either selects or inherits in life. Crocker and
Park (2004) examined why people pursue self-esteem and hypothesized that people search for high levels of self-worth in order to manage their fears and anxieties. In the elderly, due to a succession of losses, a multitude of factors are likely
to cause anxiety and fear, and almost all of them are related to loss. These losses
range in severity from the loss of youth and beauty, to the loss of physical agility,
to the loss of close friends and relatives, to the loss of a partner or spouse (Hayslip,
1995). Therefore, in older people, self-esteem is a very complex matter that cannot be viewed solely as a lack of gain; esteem cannot be seen independently of the
other losses that the elderly endure. Acceptance and ability to cope with losses and
energy and the will to maximize gains influence how third-phase adults cope, and
there is no one size fits all.

The ability to cope with what comes in life is perhaps the single most important
factor influencing how older people view the self. For most people, self-esteem
either stays the same or diminishes during the third phase of life. In a comprehensive study of global self-esteem across the life span, Robbins, Tresniewski,
Tracy, Gosling, and Potter (2002) reviewed cross-sectional data collected from
326,641 individuals and found that self-esteem declines sharply around age 70.
The researchers attribute their findings to negative assaults on well-being, such as
declining health, lack of sufficient social support, bereavement, and a decline in
socioeconomic status. Nevertheless, some people are able to adjust to age-related
inevitabilities and do not lose their sense of self-worth. In a hardy few, self-esteem
actually increases.

Presumably, Nola Ochs is such a person. She exudes resilience and positive
self-regard. As featured in the October 7, 2008, issue of *AARP Magazine*, Ochs,
a 95-year-old great-grandmother of 16, is also a recent graduate of Kansas State
University, the oldest person ever to receive a degree. In her full-page picture, she
is seen smiling, perhaps because of her newly earned BA in history. Ochs intends
to continue her studies. "I am considering a Master's Degree" (p. 64), she is quoted
as saying, possibly personally experiencing what research demonstrates, that lifelong learning is one of the best ways of enhancing self-esteem by addressing both
achievement and worthiness.

Ochs is not alone. A remarkable number of aging adults maintain healthy and
fulfilling lives well into old age. The idea of old age is changing, and research continues to demonstrate that one's evaluation of self affects mental and emotional
wellness. Positive esteem can assist people through life transitions into very old age
(Pachana, 2008). When self-esteem is positive, cognitive function is maintained,

and many older adults find it possible to live independently (Luszcz & Lane 2008). For the most part, people with good health, which includes absence of hypertension, arthritis, and back pain (Guralnik & Kaplan, 1989), and high income (Wagnild, 2003) are the most likely to maintain esteem as they age.

Ranzijn, Keeves, Luszcz, and Feather (1998) studied perceived usefulness and competence in the self-esteem of older adults and found that older adults do not necessarily relate these variables to economics or to jobs. For senior adults, usefulness and competence are most frequently associated with knowledge, the ability to deal with life events wisely, and the capacity to help others do the same, possibly indicating a shift in the salience of personal values.

Krause (1996) pointed out that older persons participating in public welfare programs experience diminished feelings of self worth: men more than women. Krause and Borawski-Clark (1995) studied social class difference in the self-esteem of older adults and found that contact with friends, support provided to others, and satisfaction with the support that one gives are related to social class in older people. Findings indicated that social class standing relates to the kind and amount of support that one is able to give later in life. Older adults in upper-income brackets or with a high degree of education differ from those in lower-income brackets or little education in the amount of support that they can give to friends and others in their social network. Thus, higher and lower income and greater and less education affect the amount and kind of activities in which one can engage when giving support to others, and the satisfaction one can gain from social network members. This is not surprising, and it can easily be concluded that people who are poor and uneducated have far less access to the resources associated with self-esteem than their wealthy and educated cohort. Krause and Shaw (2000) also examined whether providing emotional support to others bolsters self-esteem in older adults over time, and whether the salubrious effects of helping others are more likely to be enjoyed by persons of high social status. The data suggest that all older people benefit from giving social support to others, but that persons in lower socioeconomic strata are more vulnerable to the amount of support they provide to others because the effect of their support dissipates quickly and is less effective because providers lack the resources and social skills necessary to deliver assurance effectively. Furthermore, low-income receivers of support can experience the huge number of problems that come with poverty. This can contribute to the likely diminishing of self-esteem over time in people with little income and meager education, whether they are the givers or receivers of social support.

The feeling of being in control is related to self-esteem. Shaw and Krause (2001) examined racial difference with regard to control and found that African Americans have less sense of personal control than do White Americans, though older Blacks and older Whites both experience loss of control to varying degrees. Some people compensate for this loss through involvement in religious activity. Elderly Black people are more involved in religion and in a church community than are elderly White people, and those Blacks who do participate in religious activity gain more spiritual support and general optimism from it than do Whites (Krause, 2002). Taken as a whole, however, racial studies on self-esteem are inconclusive since the issue of race seems to be confounded by the fact that socioeconomic status is not always independent of race. General studies of religion and self-esteem in the older population indicate that religion is a mediating factor for depression and stress. However, it can serve to enhance self-esteem only when the individual perceives God as beneficent rather than punitive.

Older adults, for good or ill, are often exempt from the burdens of social living but may also be eliminated from some of its joys. Retirement incomes can free elders who have been previously involved in gainful occupations from employment. For many older adults, it is a joy to be free to decide what new roles and activities in which they would like to engage and to what extent. For other elders, even thinking about new roles and new activities is a chore, and they may choose not to become involved at all.

Three basic theories of aging, each of which captures some truth and has some merit, may account for this difference in attitude and behavior. One of these theories, and perhaps the most familiar, is called disengagement. The *disengagement theory* holds that older people become preoccupied with their inner lives, perhaps in an anticipation of death. They therefore choose to abandon former activities and take on few, if any, new ones. The opposite of disengagement theory is *activity theory*. Some older women and men disengage from old roles, not in anticipation of death, but in order to find new meaning and enjoyment in life. New roles may include marriage or remarriage, different employment, volunteer or club activity, and further education (as in the case of Ochs). When one takes on new roles in order to find new meaning or excitement in life, activity can be a surrogate for one's prior definition of self, or it can be the assumption of an emerging new and satisfying identity. Pop psychology pushes activity theory, proclaiming it a potential producer of self-esteem. However, endless activity has the potential for self-exhaustion. Furthermore, if the new role or new activity is acquired with the expectation of finding a new and perhaps more perfect idea of self than that in which one has chosen to engage, the result may be disappointment. The third theory, *socioemotional selectivity theory*, asserts that people become more selective with age—a process that does not begin or end with age, but is lifelong. Contact with family and friends diminishes gradually, and new activities and relationships, when sought, are sought less for basic information or general interaction than as a result of specific experiences perceived to afford pleasant emotional consequences. A majority of healthy aging adults prefer to remain independent, residing either in homes that they manage, located in familiar communities, or in residential communities designed for adult living. According to the socioemotional activity theory, older adults engage in social activity of their own choosing.

Professionals who design or who participate in interventions for older adults should be aware not only of the three disparate theories, but also of the fact that there are people who seem to have attitudes and behaviors congruent with each. Interventions on behalf of persons in the third phase of life should be planned accordingly.

LOSSES IN THE THIRD PHASE OF LIFE

The self-esteem issue in older people, as previously stated, is related to problems of loss. Whether primary or secondary, each loss can be regarded as an assault on self-esteem. In the poor and less educated, and in the less healthy, the assault is often more severe than in others. Sometimes due to lack of resources, the result is devastating. In those people who are more physically healthy or more affluent, the result of the loss can vary, but in whomever self-esteem is lost, it is always related to other losses.

Some of the most serious losses in later life, those losses called primary losses, are (1) loss of health, (2) loss of significant relationships, and (3) loss of work. All of these losses have subsets that are sometimes called secondary losses in that they derive from the primary three. Nevertheless, they are serious and should be understood as such. Underscore the fact that each loss, primary or secondary, brings with it the potential loss of self-esteem.

Loss of Health

Illness-related losses include onset diseases such as cancer, diabetes, or Alzheimer's, or chronic, expected, common illnesses such as hypertension, arthritis, and back pain. Long-term or permanent loss can also result from injury-related occurrences, such as a fall. Loss of health may be defined also as loss of balance, loss of vision, loss of bladder control, loss of immediate memory, and loss of hearing. The latter two are perhaps the most common losses experienced in some degree by almost all of those in the third phase of life.

Aging affects memory by changing the way the brain stores information, making recall more difficult. This affects recent memory rather than memories that are stored. Forgetting the names of people that one just met is a common experience for adults over 65. It is not only embarrassing and inconvenient, but it can affect one's awareness of competence and, in some cases, interfere with accomplishments and achievements.

One-third of all persons between the ages of 65 and 74 have hearing problems. About half the people who are 85 and older have a hearing loss that can seriously affect their lives (MedicineNet, 2008). Much that is said to people with hearing problems is lost, resulting in embarrassment and loss of self-regard. The inability to contribute to a conversation or the awkwardness that could occur when one is unable to answer a question may prove to be upsetting, and may lead to negative feedback from others at a time when their support is most needed.

Loss of Significant Relationships

Those in the third phase of life experience repeated loss of relationships. The loss can result from a move or relocation, but it more often is associated with the death of a loved one, generally a spouse but sometimes a child or grandchild, or close friend. In the instance of the death of someone dear, grief is certainly normal. Death can cause people to question their very existence and worth. Generally at the end of the grief period self-esteem returns, but when the grief turns to depression, it does not. Older adults have few people with whom they can express their fears. Death and fear of death are difficult to discuss.

So is fear of loss of attractiveness and loss of sexual potency. Either can lead to fear of forming or maintaining loving relationships or to a significant decrease in the sexuality component of selective self-esteem. Aging men have few peers with whom they could or would discuss the less firm erections that occur with age, and few older women talk about their fears of pain due to lessening vaginal elasticity. In both older men and older women, sexual arousal is slower and less intense. Nevertheless, neither gender loses interest, nor does either lose total sexual capability. At every age human beings seek intimacy, and the ability to engage in sexual activity is an esteem issue (Bloom, 2000; Pochapin, 2008).

Loss of Work

Most individuals must relinquish the worker identity through the loss of work after retirement or involuntary termination in later life. Loss of work means diminished income. It also may mean loss of identity. For the person who has an immediate need for money, the former may be the most important, but for the person with adequate financial resources, the loss of identity can prove the most devastating. Many individuals who work outside the home are heavily invested in the role-defining characteristics of work that can affect the level and stability of their self-esteem. Organization-based self-esteem may be a heavily weight-selective self-esteem domain for most workers. The loss of this major life identity can be devastating for those who have foreclosed on other identities, leaving them floundering and without purpose.

INTERVENTION STRATEGIES

Asoka Selvarajah, PhD, formerly a practicing nuclear physicist at CERN, now writes about growth and spirituality. According to Selvarajah (2000), self-esteem it is at the core of people's problems and *"THE* major challenge of our era."* Rather than addressing their problems, people frequently externalize them. Lack of esteem can be remedied only when individuals turn inward and address what their underlying issues and problems really are. Clinicians, therefore, must take into consideration the wide range of losses that can affect persons in the third phase of life and what can be done to prevent or be a remedy for them.

Strategies Targeting Specific Losses

In addition to individual counseling, workshops involving large or small group activities related to the losses that occur with normal aging are good interventions in that they do several things at one time. Workshops where several people participate normalize whatever the issue, and when the underlying problem is either compensated for or remedied, the result is an increase in self-esteem. Counselors who want to help older Americans increase their esteem first need to deal with the problem that led to its loss.

Prevention is key to addressing health losses that can be associated with aging. Health management through proper diet, exercise, dental care, and an informed use of prescribed medications is within one's control, and counselors can help people follow a health regimen. Though it is embarrassing and difficult to talk about, loss of bladder control is a manageable situation when counselor and client are able to openly discuss it (Merkelj & Quillen, 2001).

Hearing losses can frequently be corrected with a hearing device. However, before a hearing device is used, the person in need of it must be encouraged to acknowledge that a problem exists and own the problem. Many older people deny that they have hearing problems because admitting to them calls attention to another loss, that of any semblance of youth and control. There are others who are simply too vain to wear a hearing aid. Supporting the use of wearing hearing aids or amplifying devices that sometimes vanity or denial prevents, while at the same time normalizing the need for them, can be very helpful.

Loss of memory, according to the American Academy of Family Physicians (2008), can also be easily dealt with when acknowledged. A simple intervention might be a brief workshop designed to normalize the situation. Keeping a list or putting keys in the same place every time are just two ideas that could be "taught" in such a workshop. Repeating names when meeting new people and making associations between things are exercises that can be modeled and rehearsed. On the other hand, there are cognitive losses that are not a part of normal aging, and those cannot be normalized. Not being able to keep track of daily happenings, not being able to make simple choices, not being able to handle money, and not being able to learn new concepts are not a part of normal aging, and for cognitive problems of this sort, medical interventions are necessary.

Strategies for *loss of significant relationships* vary significantly, depending upon the kind of loss. For some, following through on goals to reach out to new friends may be all that is necessary. Intervention strategies for loss of a loved one, however, usually involve much support and skill. Grief groups may be the treatment option of choice and can be either self-help groups or groups led by a professional. If grief turns to depression, psychotherapy is the intervention of choice. All counselors should familiarize themselves with the *Handbook of Counseling and Psychotherapy With Older Adults* (Duffy, 1999)

When dealing with the issue of sexuality losses, sex counseling is becoming a subspecialty for counselors whose primary area is gerontology. Many older individuals may need to be taught to reevaluate the early messages they received about sexuality. They can learn to see themselves as desirable, sexual human beings.

In the case of *loss of work*, people who are economically disadvantaged, especially those members of minority groups, have the greatest and most immediate need for placement or public assistance, and many community agencies and churches are set up to handle their needs. They are in the need of multiple services.

For those who are not economically disadvantaged and anticipate retirement, the best intervention strategy occurs before full-time work ends. Preretirement workshops are the intervention of choice in that they deal with identity issues as well as issues related to how to finance retirement. Focused on self and next steps, preretirement workshop participants can examine their lives in the light of their knowledge, skills, and interests as filtered through their values. Standardized assessment inventories such as the Myers-Briggs Type Indicator (CPP, 2008) and the Five-Factor Wellness Inventory (Myers, 2005; Myers & Sweeney, 2005), along with nonstandardized self-discovery activities in workshops, are commonly used. For example, workshop participants can be asked to draw a split picture about roles that they currently are playing in their work, learning, leisure, and family, and the roles that they would like to play in the future. They identify factors that restrain them from engaging in activities of choice and factors that could help them overcome the restraints. They then develop an individual life plan (ILP).

Although this kind of workshop is suggested as a preretirement exercise, retirees could benefit from it as well. The goal of the workshop is the enhancement of self-esteem in the participants. The holistic emphasis is based on the life role–life space theory of Donald Super (1980). The objectives of finding a new identity part of the workshop might help senior adults explore where they are in life and design a desired personal future. They are encouraged to

1. Recognize the challenges that come from their various life roles
2. Value where they are in life now
3. Appreciate their current strengths
4. Understand the tension between traditional expectations and contemporary realities
5. Adjust current roles to satisfy future goals
6. Identify interests, knowledge, and skills
7. Filter interests' knowledge and skills through their values
8. Achieve a creative balance that will lead to wholeness
9. Develop an individual life plan

Cognitive Therapy

By using cognitive restructuring techniques, counselors can help older adults change the way they address their losses and themselves and help them rediscover their coping skills. Through the use of cognitive therapy, counselors can help older clients gain control of their self-talk. Negative self-talk increases the loss of self-esteem in many older people. On the other hand, positive affirmations can help them gain positive esteem. Older persons should be introduced to objective thinking about aging (Luszcz & Lane, 2008) and to realize that the ability to cope with problems and interact socially remains within their grasp.

Cognitive therapy techniques can be used to assist people who need to take control of how they spend their time or how they live their social life. Supportive counseling techniques are helpful when encouraging elders to make choices about whom one chooses to see and what one chooses to do. Enabling older people to control that which they wish to control fits with the socioemotional theory of aging. It also fits well with theories of self-esteem. By using the techniques of cognitive therapy, counselors can help older clients turn their symptoms into strengths and their strengths into social contributions (Adler, 1956; Savickas, 1997).

DIVERSITY ISSUES

As previously stated, the greatest diversity in aging is health and wealth. The healthy, wealthy, and well educated are distinct from people less fortunate when it comes to self-regard and personal esteem. Different kinds of services are needed between the people who have and those who have not. Many elderly distrust and reject any kind of counseling or therapy and tend to solicit help, if seriously needed, first from family and then from clergy. But the resistance to seeking professional help is greater in ethnic and racial minorities (McGoldrick, Giordano, & Garcia Preto, 2005). Furthermore, when elderly adults do seek help from counselors, psychologists, and social workers, there is a problem of trust, and the professional may have a great deal of difficulty earning it. Immigrants may have difficulty understanding the English language, making both trust and hope elusive.

Many older people may have had negative relations with professionals over the years. Krause and Rook (1993) have demonstrated that negative relationships, however specific at first, tend to generalize and frequently lead to a decrement in health. People with a lifetime of negative relationships have no reason to trust a counselor or a health agency. Krause and Rook found that interpersonal difficulties are chronic stressors. Therefore, when working with elderly, disadvantaged people of any race or ethnicity, counselors take the time to get to know their clients. They should also become familiar with the communities in which their clients live, including the community agencies and churches that may be able to offer some support to clients. Below are some tips for working with older clients from diverse racial and ethnic groups (McAuliffe, 2008):

1. Take time to introduce the concept of counseling and psychotherapy. It is unfamiliar to many.
2. Face the person and speak reasonably loud and clearly, especially with immigrants who may have difficulty understanding English.
3. Make an effort to understand the culture from which your client comes.
4. Be aware that an immigrant may feel diminished for not understanding, and sometimes not liking, American ways.
5. Realize that intergenerational conflicts may be larger in ethnic and racial minority groups.
6. Understand that among some cultures, particularly Asian cultures, older people may demonstrate deep respect; while, inwardly, they may not agree with, nor intend to do anything about what is being suggested to them by the counselor.

ROLE OF THE COUNSELOR

Counselors can work with groups and individuals in both proactive and reactive ways. They can help people solve problems that lead to a sense of loss and help them combat a sense of loss after it occurs. One may not be able to regain one's youthful eyesight, but one can control the manner in which one views things. With effective counseling, to paraphrase John Milton (1667/1940), one's torments can become one's elements. Translated into less poetic language, the role of the counselor when working with senior adults, whether in individual counseling or in groups, is to aid in the maintenance and enhancement of their self-esteem by therapeutic methods in either programs or direct service. Recognizing and empathizing with the fears of elders offers consolation that is sometimes hard for older people to come by. When counselors help older clients accept the aging process rationally and not let emotions get the better of them, self-esteem grows stronger. Most importantly, counselors can help older clients stop comparing their present self with their self of former days or to others. It serves no purpose. It can lead to unrealistically low evaluations of many self-esteem domains.

In brief, counselors should help clients accept and, if possible, celebrate whatever age they are. Steven Slon, editor of *AARP Magazine*, wrote a brief article about his love of biking (October 2008). He called the piece "Taking My Lumps." He described a day in late spring when past age 50 he engaged in a sport that he loves and went bicycling. He hit a bump and went flying over the handlebars. Landing on his head, he broke two ribs. As he tells it: "The bad news was the aches and pains of healing; the good news was the bike was left intact" (p. 6). However, the real point of the editorial is that being older holds both wonderful opportunities and some difficulties. The important thing is to be alive. In a side panel, the *AARP Magazine* placed a small feature depicting Harriett McBride Johnson, a civil rights attorney born with a degenerative neuromuscular disease and not expected to live past her teens. At the age of 52, Johnson is quoted as saying: "When I die I might as well die alive."

Perhaps the major task of counselors who work with people in the third phase of life is to help them remain truly alive and open to their future. In order for counselors to help older people love and respect the age that they are, counselors must overturn their own misconceptions about aging. If counselors believe that depression and anxiety are a natural part of growing old, they are wrong, because neither anxiety nor depression is the natural state for people of any age. When counselors believe that, after a certain age, people can no longer change, they do older people and themselves a disservice. People who wish to change can do so at any age. And, despite this chapter's recitation of the many losses that elders face, there are also gains. According to a recent survey conducted by the Australian Psychological Society (2008), one of the gains that people report, strange as it may sound, is time: to take part in community activities, to spend with family, and to engage in leisure activities. Another gain, according to Cohen (2005), occurs in the brain. It seems that brain function becomes more, not less, efficient as people age because in old age people are able to use the right and left hemisphere at the same time. This creates a synergy that allows healthy older adults to think creatively. Erikson (1963) regarded age as a time when the people who have mastered identity diffusion develop integrity, or oneness with self and humankind. Thus, the positive advantages of aging are time, life experience, knowledge, greater wisdom, and a mature perspective on life.

The role of the counselor with people already engaged in positive aging is to learn from them and engage them by offering creative aging opportunities, such as workshops, growth groups, and individual counseling, in which clients can exercise their self-knowledge and wisdom in order to decide how they best want to spend their time and resources, be it for education, paid or nonpaid work, or travel and other leisure.

On the whole, elderly people need more time than younger people, so give them the time they need. Take extra time when teaching skills. Make adaptations as needed. Use furniture that does not require deep bending when clients sit down, and use furniture that has arm rests to assist one when getting up. Work with good lighting. Be patient and relaxed. Repeat instructions. Above all else, show deep and sincere respect. These simple things will do much to avoid diminishing the sense of worthiness in older clients, and enhance their esteem for self.

CASE STUDY

Anne, mother of two grown daughters and grandmother of seven young children, was 76 years old when her husband of 55 years died 6 years ago. The third of seven children, Anne was a quiet woman who throughout her life suffered bouts of depression and low self-esteem. She had only a high school education and went to work in her father's grocery store. Although Anne was a pretty girl and a pretty woman who remained quite attractive all of her life, she was never satisfied with how she looked. Married at age 21, Anne never worked outside of her home other than in the office in her husband's construction business, a business that she helped to build though she never took any credit for it. She had made only three friends throughout her life, and two of them had passed away. At the time of her husband's death, Anne had enough money to go anywhere she wanted to go and do anything she wanted to do, but she had never been "on her own," had no idea of what "she wanted," and didn't think she had the ability "to do much." Most of the time, Anne stayed at home. She spent her time watching TV and speaking on the telephone to her one living sister and to her one living friend, who had moved away. She enjoyed seeing her daughters, who worried about her and came to visit her as often as they could. Once a week Anne went to the hairdresser and to the supermarket to buy a week's supply of food. Familiar with depression from her former bouts of it, Anne was surprised that she was not as deeply saddened by her husband's death as she expected; she was numb.

One of Anne's daughters took charge by insisting that Anne join a women's 10-week grief group held at a local hospital and driving her there. By the fourth session, Anne surprised herself by speaking up. By the seventh session Anne started to drive herself to group. She also started going out to lunch with two other women in the group. After the group ended, and with the help of the group leader, Anne found a counselor with whom she would work individually. More and more, Anne began to leave her house. She would not drive far, but her daughters were in range and she began visiting them instead of waiting for them to come to her. She enjoyed seeing her grandchildren. She kept contact with some of the women from her grief group, and when one of them invited her to a church luncheon, Anne went. For the first time in her life, she started to take agency and concurrently her self-esteem improved.

CONCLUSION

The story of Anne is not an atypical story for women of her generation, but as the youngest boomers age, the story will change somewhat. Both women and men will be less sheltered in youth, and almost all will have worked outside of the home. The boomers for the most part will be more worldly than Anne, and many, though not all, will be further educated. But for people, the loss issues discussed in this chapter are timeless, and the self-esteem issues that they bring will remain. An increasing number of counselors and other wellness professionals, sensitive to the issues, will be needed to help a growing population in the third phase of life both cope and thrive.

REFERENCES

Adler, A. (1956). *The individual psychology of Alfred Adler* (H. I. Ansbacher & R. R. Ansbacher, Eds.). New York: Basic Books.

American Academy of Family Physicians. (2008). *Memory loss with aging: What's normal, what's not.* Retrieved September 22, 2008, from http://www.familydoctor.org

Australian Psychological Society. (2008). *Positive ageing.* Retrieved November 8, 2008, from http://www.psychology.org.au.publications/tip_sheets/ageing

Bloom, P. (2000). *Sex in the elderly.* Retrieved November 8, 2008, from http://www.global-aging.org/health/us/sexelderly.htm

Centers for Disease Control and Prevention. (2007a). *Health information for older adults.* Retrieved October 8, 2008, from http://www.cdc.gov/aging/info.htm

Centers for Disease Control and Prevention. (2007b). *State of aging and health in America.* Retrieved February, 25, 2009, from http://www.cdc.gov/aging/saha.htm

Cohen, G. D. (2005). *The mature mind: The positive power of the aging brain.* New York: Basic Books.

Crocker, J., & Park, L. (2004). The costly pursuit of self-esteem. *Psychological Bulletin, 130,* 392–414.

CPP. (2008). *CPP, Inc., unveils new Myers-Briggs Type Indicator(R) (MBTI(R)) qualifications program.* Retrieved October 8, 2007, from http://www.reuters.com.article.pressrelease/idUS5100390+12-Mar-2008+PRN20080312

Duffy, M. (Ed.). (1999). *Handbook of counseling and psychotherapy with older adults.* New York: John Wiley & Sons.

Erikson, E. H. (1963). *Childhood and society* (2nd ed.). New York: W. W. Norton & Company.

Guralnik, J. M., & Kaplan, G. A. (1989). Predictors of healthy aging: Prospective evidence from the Alameda County study. *American Journal of Public Health, 79,* 703–708.

Hayslip, B. (1995). *Helping older adults cope with loss.* Dallas: TLC Group.

Krause, N. (1996). Welfare participation and self-esteem in later life. *The Gerontologist, 36,* 665–673.

Krause, N. (2002). Church-based social support and health in old age: Exploring variations by race. *Journal of Gerontology, 57B,* S332–S347.

Krause, N., & Borawski-Clark, E. (1995). Social class differences in social support among older adults. *The Gerontologist, 35,* 498.

Krause, N., & Rook, K. S. (2003). Negative interaction in late life: Issues in the stability and generalizability of conflict across relationships. *Journal of Gerontology: Social Sciences, 58B,* 88–99.

Krause, N., & Shaw, B. A. (2000). Giving social support to others, socioeconomic status, and changes in self-esteem in late life. *Journal of Gerontology: Social Sciences, 55B*, S323–S333.

Luszcz, M. A., & Lane, A. (2008). Executive function in cognitive aging. In S. M. Hofer & D. F. Alvin (Eds.), *The handbook on cognitive ageing: Interdisciplinary perspectives* (pp. 193–206). Thousand Oaks, CA: Sage.

McAuliffe, G. (2008). What is culturally alert counseling? In G. McAuliffe & Associates, *Culturally alert counseling: A comprehensive introduction* (pp. 2–44). Thousand Oaks, CA: Sage.

McGoldrick, M., Giordano, J., & Garcia Preto, N. (2005). Overview: Ethnicity and family therapy. In M. McGoldrick, J. Giordano, & N. Garcia Preto (Eds.), *Ethnicity and family therapy* (3rd ed., pp. 1–40). New York: Guilford Press.

MedicineNet. (2008). *Hearing loss and aging: Senior health, aging, elder care, and health conditions.* Retrieved October 8, 2008, from http://www.medicinenet.com/script/main/art.asp?articlekey

Merkelj, I., & Quillen, J. H. (2001). Urinary incontinence in the elderly. *Southern Medical Journal, 94,* 952–957.

Milton, J. (1940). *Paradise lost.* New York: Heritage Press. (Original work published 1667)

Myers, J. E. (1999). Adjusting to role loss and leisure in later life. In M. Duffy (Ed.), *Handbook of counseling and psychotherapy with older adults* (pp. 41–56). New York: John Wiley & Sons.

Myers, J. E., & Sweeney, T. (2005).*WEL inventory.* Palo Alto, CA: Mindgarden, Inc.

Pachana, N. (2008). Resilience in older age. *Australian Psychological Society.* Retrieved October 29, 2008, from http://www.psychology.org.au./publications/inpsych/resilience

Pochapin, M. (2008). *Sex and the elderly woman.* Retrieved November 8, 2008, from http://www.globalaging.org/health/us/sexwomen.htm

Ranzijn, R., Keeves, J., Luszcz, M., & Feather, N. T. (1998). The role of self-perceived usefulness and competence in the self-esteem of elderly adults: Confirmatory factor analyses of the Bachman Revision of Rosenberg's Self-Esteem Scale. *Journal of Gerontology, 53B,* P96–P104.

Robins, R. W., Trzesniewski, K. H., Tracy, J. L., Gosling, S. D., & Potter, J. (2002). Global self-esteem across the life span. *Psychology and Aging, 17,* 423–434.

Savickas, M. L. (1997). The spirit in career counseling: Fostering self-completion through work. In D. P. Bloch & L. J. Richmond (Eds.), *Connections between spirit and work* (pp. 3–26) Palo Alto, CA: Davies-Black.

Selvarajah, A. (2000). *Self-esteem: The problem behind all problems.* Retrieved September 18, 2008, from http://www.selfgrowth.com/articles/Selvarajah13.html

Shaw, B. A., & Krause, N. (2001). Exploring race variations in aging and personal control. *Journal of Gerontology: Social Sciences, 56B,* S119–S124.

Slon, S. (2008, October). E Street: Taking my lumps. *AARP Magazine.*

Super, D. E. (1980). A life-span, life-space approach to career development. *Journal of Vocational Behavior, 16,* 282–298.

Wacker, R. R., & Wacker, K. A. (2007). Community resources for older adults. *On the threshold of a new era* (pp. 3–12). Thousand Oaks, CA: Sage.

Wagnild, G. (2003). Resilience and successful aging: Comparison among low and high income older adults. *Journal of Gerontological Nursing, 29,* 42–49.

19

Asian American Elders in U.S. Culture*

BRYAN S. K. KIM AND YONG S. PARK

Mr. Huang is a 66-year-old Taiwanese American who immigrated to the United States last year to join his daughter and her family after his wife passed away in Taiwan. Although he was initially hesitant about moving to the United States, he felt that it was the only option because he was retired from his calligraphy business and has no other children living in Taiwan; he has another daughter, but she lives in Canada. Mr. Huang also felt that by moving in with his daughter, he could see his two grandchildren, whom he has not been able to see regularly.

Although the time immediately after joining his daughter and her family was filled with happiness, Mr. Huang soon began to feel sad and lonely. He missed his life in Taiwan, his wife, and his network of close friends. In addition, he does not speak English, does not know how to drive a car, and spends most days staying home and waiting for his grandchildren to return from school and his daughter and her husband to return from work. But even when the grandchildren are home, he is unable to communicate with them fluently because the children do not speak Taiwanese very well. When Mr. Huang does venture outside his home, he finds himself feeling very nervous and scared of the strange neighborhood, where only a few people are walking on the sidewalks and there are so many cars. All of this has caused him to feel useless, without a purpose in the remainder of his life, and to experience a lack of self-esteem.

Furthermore, he has noticed that his daughter's views about the world seemed to have changed dramatically since she left Taiwan 15 years ago to attend college in the United States. For example, his daughter has asked him to help around the house by cleaning and doing the laundry, which he never had to do in Taiwan.

---

* This research was supported in part by the Asian American Center on Disparities Research (National Institute of Mental Health grant: 1P50MH073511-01A2).

He has noticed that his daughter's behavior toward her husband seems "bossy" and very disrespectful. Given all of these experiences, he has begun to feel very frustrated about living in the United States, in addition to thinking that he might be a burden to his daughter. However, he also knows that returning to Taiwan is not an option.

As you read this vignette, what thoughts come to your mind about Mr. Huang's self-esteem? Given the difficulties he is experiencing, what do you think are his selective and global levels of self-esteem?

The purpose of this chapter is to describe the various psychological challenges that are faced by Asian American elders, which in turn affect their self-esteem. We will begin with a description of the demographic, historical, and cultural characteristics of elderly Asian Americans. Then, we will provide a discussion of how self-esteem might be conceptualized differently in Asian cultures than in the dominant U.S. culture, highlight several risk factors that might negatively impact Asian American elders' self-esteem, and describe specific intervention strategies that may be utilized by mental health professionals when working with Asian American elders to address their low self-esteem.

DEMOGRAPHIC, HISTORICAL, AND CULTURAL CHARACTERISTICS

According to the U.S. Bureau of the Census (2004), Asian Americans comprise 12.9 million individuals, or 4.5% of the U.S. population. Among this group, 2.13 million Asian Americans, or 16.5% of the total Asian American population, are 55 years and older. Also within this group are 1.07 million Asian Americans who are 65 years and older, representing 8.3% of the total Asian American population. While these numbers indicate a large number of people who can be categorized under the Asian American elderly population, the high degree of within-group variability makes it difficult to characterize them as a homogeneous group. One of the most important indicators of this variability is ethnicity. Although Asian Americans have been classified as a single group because of their common origins in the Asian continent, they include over two dozen ethnic groups representing a wide range of geographical origins, including East Asian countries such as China and Japan; Southeast Asian countries such as Vietnam, Philippines, and Indonesia; and South Asian countries such as India and Pakistan. These groups vary significantly in language, traditions, customs, societal norms, and immigration history.

Another important within-group variable is immigration histories. Many Asian American elderly are three, four, or five generations removed from ancestors who entered the United States between the mid-1800s and early 1900s during the Gold Rush and Transcontinental Railroad eras in California and the sugar plantation period in Hawaii. Others are second-generation Americans whose parents entered the United States during World War II and the Korean War. There are also first-generation Asian Americans who entered the United States after the passing of the Immigration Act of 1965 or after the U.S. military forces pulled out of Southeast Asia in 1975 (Takaki, 1989). Furthermore, like Mr. Huang, Asian Americans consist of individuals who arrived from various Asian countries as recently as last year or even yesterday. This diversity of the length of residence in the United States suggests that the Asian American elderly population represents a dramatic range in the degree to which they have adapted to the norms of the dominant U.S. culture or have retained the norms of the traditional Asian culture. Two constructs that represent these processes are acculturation (the process of adapting to the norms of the dominant group) and enculturation (the process of retaining the norms of one's indigenous group; Kim & Abreu, 2001). Current theories of acculturation and enculturation suggest that first-generation individuals (i.e., immigrants) experience low levels of acculturation and high levels of enculturation, whereas individuals who are several generations removed from immigration would be expected to experience high levels of acculturation and low levels of enculturation. However, there are also individuals (e.g., second generation) who could be experiencing high levels of both acculturation and enculturation, thereby representing biculturalism.

To better understand the worldview of Asian American elders, it is useful to be aware of traditional Asian values that help to shape it. In the process of developing a measure of Asian cultural values (Asian Values Scale), Kim, Atkinson, and Yang (1999) conducted a comprehensive review of the literature, a nationwide survey of Asian American psychologists, and focus groups to identify value dimensions that are commonly observed among Asians. The results yielded the following value dimensions:

1. Ability to resolve psychological problems (e.g., one should use one's inner resources and willpower to resolve psychological problems)
2. Avoidance of family shame (e.g., the worst thing an individual can do is to disgrace his or her family reputation)
3. Collectivism (e.g., group interests and goals should be promoted over individual interests and goals)
4. Conformity to family and social norms and expectations (e.g., individuals should not make waves and should avoid disrupting the status quo)
5. Deference to authority figures (e.g., authority figures are deserving of respect)
6. Educational and occupational achievement (e.g., success in life is defined in terms of one's academic and career accomplishments)
7. Filial piety (e.g., children are expected to manifest unquestioning obedience to their parents)
8. Importance of family (e.g., honor and duty to one's family are very important, more important than one's own fame and power)
9. Maintenance of interpersonal harmony (e.g., one should always try to be accommodating and conciliatory and never directly confrontational)
10. Placing other's needs ahead of one's own (e.g., an individual should consider the needs of others before considering one's own)
11. Reciprocity (e.g., an individual should repay another person's favor, that is, repay those people who have helped or provided assistance to the individual)

12. Respect for elders and ancestors (e.g., young people should never confront their elders, talk back to them, or go directly against their wishes)
13. Self-control and restraint (e.g., ability to control emotions is a sign of strength)
14. Self-effacement (e.g., it is important to minimize or depreciate one's own achievements)

These value dimensions offer insight as to how Asian American elders might formulate and interpret their sense of self-esteem.

SELF-ESTEEM ISSUES OF ASIAN AMERICAN ELDERS

This section describes how self-esteem might be conceptualized by the Asian American elderly population and is based on traditional Asian cultural norms. Hence, it is specific to the experiences of highly enculturated and low acculturated Asian Americans (i.e., traditional Asian Americans). To the extent that individuals are low enculturated and highly acculturated, the description may not apply.

Asian Americans tend to exhibit a relatively lower rate of personal self-esteem than their European American counterparts. Interdependent self-construal (e.g., collectivistic thinking)—a trait commonly associated with Asian Americans—was found by Singelis, Bond, Sharkey, and Lai (1999) to be related to lower rates of personal self-esteem. In a more recent study, Heine and Hamamura (2007) conducted a meta-analysis of Asian Americans and European Americans in regard to various operational definitions of self-esteem, finding that among 91 cross-cultural comparisons, Asian Americans reported a lower tendency to self-enhance while European Americans exhibited a clear self-serving bias. While these research findings suggest that Asian Americans may struggle with lower rates of personal self-esteem, it is unclear whether these disparities are an outcome of unique psychosocial risk factors faced by Asian Americans, or whether the findings are an artifact of varying values and norms that Asian culture has toward self-esteem. To clarify the latter point, it could be that personal self-esteem is not as strongly encouraged or valued in traditional Asian cultures, thereby resulting in studies that suggest self-esteem disparities.

Asian Cultural Values and Norms Surrounding Self-Esteem

Contrary to popular belief, cross-cultural psychologists suggest that the need to enhance self-esteem is largely a culture-bound phenomenon rather than a universal one. Heine, Lehman, Markus, and Kitayama (1999) point out that the "universal assumption" that people need to evaluate themselves positively is an artifact of Western philosophical thought and a product of research that was conducted primarily with White, North American samples. From the cross-cultural perspective, the needs and desires of the group may take priority to the needs for personal self-esteem. Asians are likely to exhibit a group-serving bias (i.e., a tendency to overevaluate one's group in positive terms; Heine & Lehman, 1997). Furthermore, in a study that examined Japanese nationals, Kitayama, Takagi, and Matsumoto

(1995) found that the Japanese participants failed to exhibit a self-serving attribution bias (i.e., perceiving self in overly competent and optimistic terms). In respect to Japanese language, Heine et al. (1999) observed that the terms *self-confident* and *self-respect*, qualities that are viewed as desirable in Western cultures, may have connotations for conceit and arrogance.

As opposed to self-enhancement, traditional Asian culture may be encouraging of a critical view of self and, in turn, value individuals who practice humility and self-effacement. The purpose of being self-critical may be consistent with the Asian cultural value placed on collectivism (Kim et al., 1999), which emphasizes the importance of fitting in and fulfilling roles and responsibilities that are ascribed to the individual by the group. From this perspective, differentiating oneself from other group members or "standing out" would not be an adaptable trait. To reinforce this value, there is a well-engrained adage in the Japanese culture that "a nail that sticks out gets hammered in."

Because belongingness and fitting in is a value and a norm in traditional Asian culture, internal attitudes, such as people's assessments of their individual characteristics and strengths (e.g., interests, skills, values, and personalities), may not have as strong an influence in defining the sense of self. Instead, self-esteem may be largely determined by external and relational factors. Several scholars (see Uba, 1994, for review) have corroborated traditional Asian Americans' propensity for having an "external locus of control"—a belief that external factors control the outcome of a person's life. Given the focus on external factors, self-esteem may be strongly influenced by how well one fulfills externally defined roles and responsibilities, and is affected by the approval one receives from others in terms of one's contribution to the group. The way success is defined in Japanese culture is largely based on how a person "fulfills consensually defined standards of excellence within a given context" (Heine & Lehman, 1997, p. 1279).

The manner in which one organizes one's sense of self and behaviors in respect to external contingencies is reflected in the concept of face. Ho (1976) provides a comprehensive definition of face: "respectability and/or deference which a person can claim for himself from others, by virtue of the relative position he occupies in his social network and the degree to which he is judged to have functioned adequately in that position" (p. 883). A key determinant of a person's esteem (or respect in this instance) is contingent on how well one functions in one's social position. In other words, self-esteem from the purview of face management may be performance driven, and thus more aligned with the competence component of self-esteem.

Along with the need to fulfill group responsibilities may be the ulterior concern for the loss of face (i.e., saving face). Based on an extensive literature review, Zane (2000) concisely defined loss of face as the "threat or loss of one's social integrity" and identified four common face-threatening situations for Asian Americans: threats to social status, acting in an unethical manner, failing to uphold social propriety, and lacking self-discipline. In the unfortunate circumstance that the person is not able to save face, shame may be the predominant emotion experienced (Ha, 1995; You, 1997). For Asian American elders, a shame response is a powerful sanction, one that may ultimately result in the person, and perhaps the whole family, being pressured to relinquish membership from a particular social group or community of co-ethnics. Furthermore, research has shown that a shame response has strong and negative implications for a person's self-esteem (Yelsma, Brown, & Elison, 2002).

The gravity of a shame response may compel Asian American elders to do what is in their power to avoid bringing shame to themselves and to their family. One way Asian American elders can protect themselves from losing face and the concomitant shame response is by conforming to social propriety—socially acceptable conduct and speech (*Merriam-Webster's Collegiate Dictionary*, 2003). Heine et al. (1999) provide a more descriptive definition specific to traditional Asian culture: "The individual is protected by layers of insulating rituals—such as codes of formal communication; highly conventionalized forms of greetings; rules for posture, gesture, and so forth—all of which serve to prevent the exposure of the individual self to others" (p. 773). In other words, by adhering to social propriety, the person is able to maintain harmony with other group members and, as a result, not bring negative attention or shame to self. Although social propriety may protect the individual from loss of face or shame, the person sacrifices the freedom to be a unique self in the group. One no longer has the autonomy to assert individual needs and desires, and in this group context, the individuals' need for positive self-esteem may often be pushed aside for the greater goals of the collective.

Self-Esteem: Shifting From the Individual to the Collective

In traditional Asian culture, personal self-esteem may play a subsidiary role to collectivism, saving face, and avoiding shame. Therefore, when working with Asian American elderly clients who adhere to traditional Asian values, self-esteem needs to be reconceptualized not as an individualist construct but as one that takes into consideration social and collective factors. This is important because for traditional Asian American elders, a "truly meaningful existence is conceivable only in relation to others" (Suh, 2002, p. 1378).

The concept of selective self-esteem (that stresses the situational and transitory nature of self-esteem) may be culturally relevant to Asian American elderly because traditional Asian culture tends to emphasize external and contextual factors of self-esteem, as opposed to intrinsic factors. More specifically, Asian Americans' evaluation of self may be largely dependent on fulfilling specific roles, positions, and tasks within varying social and situational contexts.

In addition to selective self-esteem, another culturally appropriate conceptualization with Asian American elderly clients may be the construct of collective self-esteem (CSE). Luhtanen and Crocker (1992) have argued that evaluation of self-worth is largely based on a person's knowledge of, emotional significance attached to, and role in being a member of a particular social group. They identified four domains of collective self-esteem: private CSE—how individuals privately evaluate their social group or groups; public CSE—how individuals believe others evaluate their social groups; importance to identity—the role of group membership in self concept; and membership CSE—how well a person functions as a member of his or her social group. Similar to selective self-esteem, these CSE domains depart from the individualistic and global assumptions embedded in personal self-esteem, and give consideration to social-contextual factors that influence self-esteem. These domains may be particularly relevant for first-generation Asian American elderly who in their Asian countries of origin were held in high regard and positioned on top of the social order based on filial piety and value of respecting elders. In the United States, however, Asian American elderly are faced with challenges of navigating an ethnically heterogeneous society that may place them in a subordinate position, due to their ethnic minority and elderly status, which in turn may diminish their CSE.

Finally, borrowing from evolutionary psychology, the sociometer theory may be useful for understanding the role of self-esteem for Asian Americans. From this perspective, self-esteem is considered a sociometer or gauge of how well a person functions in various interpersonal contexts (Kirkpatrick & Ellis, 2001). Underlying the self-esteem sociometer is the psychological mechanism to which the self is socially constructed based on reflected appraisals of how others view the self (Leary & Baumeister, 2000).

RISK FACTORS RELATED TO SELF-ESTEEM

While there may be cultural normative reasons for the lower rates of personal self-esteem that are observed among Asian Americans, research shows that lower self-enhancement may be associated with various measures of distress among Asian Americans, including depression, social avoidance, and fear of negative evaluation (Norasakkunkit & Kalick, 2002). Thus, it is important for clinicians to address unique psychosocial risk factors that may place Asian American elders at risk for low self-esteem.

Erosion of Family Structure and the Care for Elders

According to traditional Asian family structure, elders are expected to control and hold authority over the younger family members. In turn, younger members are expected to respect and obey their elders. When Asian families immigrate to the United States, the family structure can be compromised when the roles of the parents and children are reversed. A prominent example of role reversal involves the issue of language. Many Asian immigrant parents, like Mr. Huang, may not be proficient in English; therefore, they may need to depend on their English-speaking children to help them navigate and function in their new cultural surroundings. Furthermore, because self-esteem may be strongly influenced by external validation and approval from significant others, Asian American elders may experience lowered self-esteem when younger, more acculturated generations are less reliant on their elders for guidance and decision making.

Additionally, the erosion of the traditional Asian family structure may result in care-taking conflicts that may further distress Asian American elderly. According to McLaughlin and Braun (1998), adult-aged Asian children are largely responsible for their elderly parents' care, which often includes living with and providing their basic care. However, when the authority and influence of Asian elders are undermined, the parents may not be able to enforce co-residence with their children. Instead, Asian American elderly may be placed in nursing homes, further diminishing their place of authority in the family.

Parent–Child Family Conflict

The 2002–2003 University of California at Davis National Latino and Asian American Study surveyed over 2,000 Asian Americans and found that Asian Americans who endure family conflict are at a threefold greater risk of attempting suicide (Sue, 2008). Family conflict may arise when traditional Asian parents implement parenting behaviors (i.e., authoritarian style) that expect their children to unconditionally obey their wishes and fulfill family obligations (Chao, 2001). These expectations may be incongruent with their acculturated children's need for autonomy. Recent studies examining Asian American college students have found that parents' Asian cultural orientation and the parent–child difference of Asian cultural values is associated with higher family conflict (Ahn, Kim, & Park, 2008; Lee, Choe, Kim, & Ngo, 2000) and conflict in the areas of academic and career, dating and marriage, and family expectations (Ahn et al., 2008). The case of Mr. Huang illustrates the psychological stressors that can arise when there is a gap between parents and children on their cultural values orientation.

Acculturative Stress

On an average day, Asian Americans traverse through a multitude of social contexts, all of which have associated social norms. Although some Asian Americans are able to achieve bicultural effectiveness and successfully adapt to varying cultural situations, others may be overwhelmed by the constant negotiating of their cultural identities and values. The *Diagnostic and Statistical Manual of Mental Disorders* (American Psychiatric Association, 2000) has recognized cultural differences as a legitimate source of mental disorder, and has aptly labeled it acculturation problem. Recently, Kim and Park (2007) suggested that East Asian Americans are particularly vulnerable to acculturative stress since traditional Asian values and behaviors tend to be construed as ineffective or irrelevant in mainstream Western culture. For example, Asian Americans' tendency toward indirect communication may be viewed as passive and ineffective, in contrast to the trait of assertiveness, which includes direct and open communication (Park & Kim, 2008). With respect to self-esteem, Asian Americans may have difficulty in reconciling Asian cultural expectations to minimize self-enhancement with Western expectations of openly expressing a positive sense of self.

Racism and Discrimination

Asian Americans have been subject to racism and discrimination, on both personal and systemic levels, since their first arrival to the United States. Early on, Asian American immigrants were stereotyped with derogatory characterizations such as "filthy," "immoral," "treacherous," and "inassimilable aliens" (Takaki, 1989; Wong, 1995). Even Asian Americans born and raised in the United States were viewed as perpetual foreigners, as harshly noted by General De Witt's reference to Japanese Americans during the time of World War II: "Jap is Jap regardless of birthplace" (c.f. Takaki, 1989). These negative stereotypes underscore issues of larger, systemic racism against Asian Americans that included immigration acts that excluded Asians, the discriminatory internment of Japanese citizens without due process of law, and findings that Asian Americans are less likely to be promoted and earn as much as their White counterparts when education and work experience are equal (see Leong, 1998, for review). Taken together, mental health providers need to be attentive to the effects of racism and discrimination on their Asian American elderly clients. Racism can result in lower self-esteem, learned helplessness, and depression.

Micro-Aggressions

In addition to overt and systemic forms of racism, Sue, Bucceri, Lin, Nadal, and Torino (2007) have argued that racism against Asian Americans has become more subtle and ambiguous. Referred to as racial micro-aggressions, Sue et al. (2007) defined this new form of racism as "brief and commonplace daily verbal, behavioral indignities, whether intentional or unintentional, that communicate hostile, derogatory or negative racial slights and insults that potentially have harmful or unpleasant psychological impact on the target person or group" (p. 72). Micro-aggression can be more harmful than overt racism. Predominant themes of micro-aggressions are: (1) alien in own land (e.g., perpetual foreigners), (2) ascription of intelligence (e.g., "all Asians are smart in math and science"), (3) denial of racial reality (e.g., invalidation of discriminatory experiences, "Asians are new Whites"), (4) exoticization of Asian American women, (5) invalidation of interethnic differences, (6) pathologizing cultural values/communication styles, (7) second-class citizenship, and (8) invisibility (e.g., being overlooked or left out).

For Asian American elderly, the micro-aggression of invisibility may be particularly salient. In their countries of origin, the elderly tend to be at the forefront of society; they are sociopolitical leaders, heads of households, and revered by the community at large. In their new social environment, however, Asian American elders may face the reality that their status is less respected or desirable. This social reality aggravates an already dire situation because their minority status and cultural differences may already alienate them from mainstream American society. Asian American elderly may be given the feedback from the broader U.S. society that they are unimportant, which in turn negatively influences their self-esteem.

Underemployment Upon Immigration

Another common challenge for Asian American elders may be underemployment upon immigration in comparison to their preimmigration educational and occupational abilities. Hurh and Kim (1989) provided an analysis of immigrant educational and occupational transition, and found that the average Asian immigrant makes the transition during his or her most economically productive years. Before immigration, a large majority had a college education, but upon immigration, they were not able to obtain many professional or prestigious occupations. Considering the traditional Asian value placed on academic and occupational achievement (Kim et al., 1999), Asian American elders' experiences with underemployment may have a negative impact on their self-esteem when their preimmigration statuses do not carry over to their new environment, especially if they previously occupied prestigious educational and occupational positions. Self-esteem can be adversely affected for Asian immigrants because it is largely performance and achievement driven. They are frustrated when they are unable to engage in careers that are commensurate with their training and abilities.

INTERVENTION STRATEGIES

Given the risk factors described earlier, many Asian American elders are in need of psychological services. Mental health professionals should be aware of their attitudes toward seeking professional psychological help, ways to conduct culturally appropriate psychological assessment, possible usefulness of indigenous healing methods, and possible modification of conventional counseling methods.

Attitudes Toward Seeking Professional Psychological Help

Research in the past three decades has found that Asian Americans tend not to seek psychological services, and even if they enter treatment, they tend to terminate prematurely (e.g., Snowden & Cheung, 1990; Kim, Brenner, Liang, & Asay, 2003). There are no particular reasons why Asian Americans, in comparison to other cultural groups, should have a lower rate of psychological problems. In fact, given the risk factors Asian American elders face, it seems reasonable to expect that the need for mental services among this group will be high. It could be that underutilization of psychological services among Asian Americans is related to Asian cultural norms. Less acculturated Asian Americans tend to have less favorable attitudes toward seeking services than their more acculturated counterparts. In terms of enculturation, studies have shown that high adherence to Asian cultural values was associated with both less favorable attitudes toward seeking psychological help and less willingness to see a mental health professional (Kim, 2007; Kim & Omizo, 2003). Consequently, mental health professionals should consider conducting more outreach services in the form of educational materials describing the potential benefits of psychological services. Mental health agencies should attempt to hire more Asian American mental health professionals to attract Asian American clientele and serve as strong self-esteem models for them. When working with Asian American elderly clients who are strongly enculturated, mental health professionals should be sensitive to collective self-esteem needs and discuss issues of shame and embarrassment about seeking help (i.e., loss of face).

Indigenous Healing Methods

If traditional, highly enculturated Asian American elderly clients might not do well with conventional forms of counseling, even with the augmentation of culturally sensitive interventions, mental health professionals could consider referring the clients to practitioners of indigenous healing practices. An example of an indigenous healing method is *ta'i chi ch'uan*. Ta'i chi ch'uan involves an exercise that has the purpose of inducing relaxation and meditation (Sandlund & Norlander, 2000) and underscores competence-based self-esteem.

Modification of Conventional Counseling

If it appears that Asian American elderly clients can benefit from conventional forms of counseling, care must be taken to modify the treatment with culturally relevant and sensitive strategies. There have been a number of research studies on therapist variables and counseling interventions that may be effective with Asian American clients. Kim, Ng, and Ahn (2009) found, based on analogue studies, that Asian American clients favor ethnically similar counselors over ethnically dissimilar counselors and counselors with similar attitudes, more education, older in age, and similar personality. Asian American clients also favor a logical, rational, and directive counseling style over a reflective, affective, and nondirective one, especially if the counselor is an Asian American. The findings also suggest that Asian American clients view culturally sensitive counselors as being more credible and culturally competent than less sensitive counselors, and judge culturally responsive counselors as more credible than culturally neutral counselors.

Studies that have employed actual counseling settings with real clients (Kim, Li, & Liang, 2002; Kim, Ng, & Ahn, 2005, 2009) are consistent with Sue and Zane's (1987) notion of gift giving. For practitioners to be perceived as culturally responsive and to reduce clients' premature termination, they should focus on the strategy of gift giving—helping clients experience immediate and concrete benefits in the initial sessions. Examples of gifts are a resolution of a presenting problem, in particular, anxiety reduction, depression relief, cognitive clarity, normalization, and skills acquisition, which have the potential to enhance self-esteem. Ethnic minorities in general and Asian Americans in particular need to attain meaningful gains early in counseling, and "gift giving demonstrates to clients the direct relationship between working in therapy and alleviation of problems" (Sue & Zane, 1987, p. 42).

Another model that can be helpful when using the modified counseling approach is the three-dimensional model of multicultural counseling (Atkinson, Thompson, & Grant, 1993). The model includes three factors—acculturation (high or low), locus of problem of etiology (internal or external), and goal of counseling (prevention or remediation)—a combination of which suggests the use of one of eight helper roles: adviser, advocate, change agent, consultant, facilitator of indigenous support systems, facilitator of indigenous healing methods, counselor, and conventional psychotherapist.

In addition to culture-based modification of conventional counseling, mental health professionals should consider referring Asian American elderly clients to organizations serving Asian Americans. For example, Korean Americans tend to seek support from church priests and other parishioners, and thus, it may be beneficial to help establish a connection between Korean elderly clients with local Korean churches in the community. Similarly, it may be helpful to refer traditional Vietnamese American Buddhist clients to temples in which priests can provide supportive services.

ASSESSMENT

Despite the general reluctance among many Asian American elders in seeking mental health services, many of them do enter counseling. However, they may enter with a great deal of skepticism and culture-related concerns, which, if left unattended, could lead to premature termination from counseling. Hence, it is important for mental health professionals to conduct a thorough assessment of the clients at the beginning of the counseling relationship. As with any clients, mental health professionals should assess the nature, severity, and duration of the problem, and the ways in which the problem had been addressed in the past. In addition, it is very important for mental health professionals to obtain information about the factors related to clients' cultural background, which could lead to more relevant and helpful counseling relationships and interventions. Such cultural factors for assessment include (1) acculturation and enculturation levels, (2) attitudes about counseling, (3) experiences with oppression, (4) possible presence of culture-specific psychological disorders, and (5) availability of other sources of support.

ROLE OF THE MENTAL HEALTH PRACTITIONER

The self-esteem, both personal and collective, of Asian American elderly may be improved by implementing interventions, counselor roles, and assessment strategies that are tailored to be sensitive to the cultural experiences of this population. For example, by modifying interventions to fit with indigenous ways of healing, therapists communicate that they value and view clients' cultural practices as legitimate and provide positive feedback. Furthermore, by considering alternative counseling roles, the therapist may be indirectly saving or protecting face of the elderly client. The counseling process may be demeaning to Asian American elders because counseling usually expects clients to openly share about their personal problems to a stranger. Furthermore, the counseling experience tends to be individualistic in nature, as the focus of therapy usually puts emphasis on the client's personal cognitions, emotions, and behaviors. Therefore, whenever appropriate, it can be helpful to refer Asian American elderly to indigenous or community resources that are culturally congruent with their collective sense of self.

CASE STUDY

As Mr. Huang continued to suffer from sadness, loneliness, and low personal and collective self-esteem, his daughter decided that something needed to be done. Fortunately, she had a good friend who is a mental health professional and referred the daughter and Mr. Huang to a local mental health agency specializing in multicultural counseling and therapy with counselors that speak Taiwanese. At their first appointment, the counselor obtained information to determine whether conventional counseling could be helpful or if Mr. Huang should be referred to an indigenous healer. After a thorough assessment, the counselor decided on modified conventional counseling, indigenous healing, and additional support services in the community.

In terms of modified conventional counseling, the counselor decided to work with Mr. Huang, in the Taiwanese language, to explore his sense of grief for leaving Taiwan and particularly about being so far away from where his wife is buried. The counselor soon learned that Mr. Huang was suffering from low self-esteem partly because he felt that he was not fulfilling his role as a husband and the head of the family, and felt very guilty about leaving his wife's remains in Taiwan. The counselor encouraged Mr. Huang to visit the local Taiwanese Buddhist temple to pray for his wife's well-being in the next world. During this process, the counselor provided Mr. Huang with additional "gifts" in the form of information about the nature of the grieving process and cognitive techniques to cope with feelings of guilt and sadness. Also, the counselor helped Mr. Huang understand the processes of acculturation and enculturation that he was undergoing and how he might cope with the high level of acculturative stress he was experiencing. Furthermore, the counselor helped Mr. Huang to achieve some level of biculturalism by exploring the cultural differences between Taiwan and the United States and how he might be able to bridge the two cultures for himself. This helped Mr. Huang to feel more hopeful about overcoming the cultural barriers, which led to an improvement in his sense of competence.

In addition to this counseling work, the counselor referred Mr. Huang to a local practitioner of ta'i chi ch'uan who could help Mr. Huang to engage in physical exercise to raise his mood and experience a sense of accomplishment. This also allowed Mr. Huang to meet other Taiwanese Americans in the community, giving him opportunities to reinforce collective self-esteem. The counselor also introduced Mr. Huang to a local Taiwanese community center where he could go every day to meet other Taiwanese Americans. Given Mr. Huang's training as a calligrapher and its salience to him, the center helped Mr. Huang set up a calligraphy class where he could teach other people in this art. Having this opportunity allowed Mr. Huang to feel a sense of worth and usefulness in the community. In addition, this "work" led Mr. Huang to meet other calligraphers in the community with whom he met regularly in social settings.

After about six weeks of these interventions, Mr. Huang shared with the counselor that he felt much better and that he has a renewed sense of purpose and usefulness. He reported that he no longer felt guilty and had a more positive view of himself and his abilities to live in the United States. These statements were strong indications that his self-esteem had increased significantly.

CONCLUSION

In this chapter, we described how self-esteem might be experienced by Asian American elders. First, in the hope of avoiding stereotyping, we discussed important within-group variability such as ethnicity, immigration history, and acculturation and enculturation levels. Then, we described traditional Asian cultural values that might be salient for many Asian American elders and how these values might shape their worldviews and influence their self-esteem. In particular, we highlighted how self-esteem might be conceived differently by Asian American elders based on their more collective and interdependent worldviews. We then described potential risk factors, such as family conflict, acculturative stress, racism and discrimination, and underemployment, that might lead to a decrease in self-esteem. Finally, we offered various strategies that might be helpful when mental health professionals work with Asian American elders.

REFERENCES

Ahn, A. J., Kim, B. S. K., & Park, Y. S. (2008). Asian cultural values gap, cognitive flexibility, coping strategies, and parent-child conflicts among Korean Americans. *Cultural Diversity and Ethnic Minority Psychology, 14*, 353–363.

American Psychiatric Association. (2000). *Diagnostic and statistical manual of mental disorders* (4th ed., text rev.). Arlington, VA: Author.

Atkinson, D. R., Thompson, C. E., & Grant, S. K. (1993). A three-dimensional model for counseling racial ethnic minorities. *The Counseling Psychologist, 21*, 257–277.

Chao, R. K. (2001). Extending research on the consequences of parenting style for Chinese Americans and European Americans. *Child Development, 72*, 1832–1843.

Ha, F. I. (1995). Shame in Asian and Western cultures. *American Behaviorist Scientist, 38*, 1114–1131.

Heine, S. J., & Hamamura, T. (2007). In search of East Asian self-enhancement. *Personality and Social Psychology Review, 11*, 4–27.

Heine, S. J., & Lehman, D. R. (1997). The cultural construction of self-enhancement: An examination of group-serving biases. *Journal of Personality and Social Psychology, 72*, 1268–1283.

Heine, S. J., Lehman, D. R., Markus, H. R., & Kitayama, S. (1999). Is there a universal need for positive self-regard? *Psychological Review, 106*, 766–794.

Ho, D. Y. (1976). On the concept of face. *American Journal of Sociology, 81*, 867–884.

Hurh, W. M., & Kim, K. C. (1989). The "success" image of Asian Americans: Its validity, and its practical and theoretical implications. *Ethnic and Racial Studies, 12*, 512–538.

Kim, B. S. K. (2007). Adherence to Asian and European American cultural values and attitudes towards seeking professional psychological help among Asian American college students. *Journal of Counseling Psychology, 54*, 474–480.

Kim, B. S. K., & Abreu, J. M. (2001). Acculturation measurement: Theory, current instruments, and future directions. In J. G. Ponterotto, J. M. Casas, L. A. Suzuki, & C. M. Alexander (Eds.), *Handbook of multicultural counseling* (2nd ed., pp. 394–424). Thousand Oaks, CA: Sage.

Kim, B. S. K., Atkinson, D. R., & Yang, P. H. (1999). The Asian values scale: Development, factor analysis, validation, and reliability. *Journal of Counseling Psychology, 46,* 342–352.

Kim, B. S. K., Brenner, B. R., Liang, C. T. H., & Asay, P. A. (2003). A qualitative study of adaptation experiences of 1.5-generation Asian Americans. *Cultural Diversity and Ethnic Minority Psychology, 9,* 156–170.

Kim, B. S. K., Li, L. C., & Liang, C. T. H. (2002). Effects of Asian American client adherence to Asian cultural values, session goal, and counselor emphasis of client expression on career counseling process. *Journal of Counseling Psychology, 49,* 342–354.

Kim, B. S. K., Ng, G. F., & Ahn, A. J. (2005). Effects of client expectation for counseling success, client–counselor worldview match, and client adherence to Asian and European American cultural values on counseling process with Asian Americans. *Journal of Counseling Psychology, 52,* 67–76.

Kim, B. S. K., Ng, G. F., & Ahn, A. J. (2009). Client adherence to Asian cultural values, common factors in counseling, and session outcome with Asian American clients at a university counseling center. *Journal of Counseling and Development 87,* 131–142.

Kim, B. S. K., & Omizo, M. M. (2003). Asian cultural values, attitudes toward seeking professional psychological help, and willingness to see a counselor. *The Counseling Psychologist, 31,* 343–361.

Kim, B. S. K., & Park, Y. S. (2007). East and Southeast Asian Americans. In G. McAuliffe (Ed.), *Culturally alert counseling: A comprehensive introduction.* Thousand Oaks, CA: Sage.

Kirkpatrick, L. A., & Ellis, B. J. (2001). An evolutionary-psychological approach to self-esteem: Multiple domains and multiple functions. In G. J. O. Fletcher & M. S. Clark (Eds.), *Blackwell handbook of social psychology: Interpersonal processes* (pp. 411–436). Oxford: Blackwell.

Kitayama, S., Takagi, H., & Matsumoto, H. (1995). Causal attribution of success and failure: Cultural psychology of the Japanese self. *Japanese Psychological Review, 38,* 247–280.

Leary, M. R., & Baumeister, R. F. (2000). The nature and function of self-esteem: Sociometer theory. In M. P. Zanna (Ed.), *Advances in experimental social psychology* (Vol. 32, pp. 1–62). San Diego: Academic Press.

Lee, R. M., Choe, J., Kim, G., & Ngo, V. (2000). Construction of the Asian American Family Conflicts Scale. *Journal of Counseling Psychology, 47,* 211–222.

Leong, F. (1998). Career development and vocational behaviors. In L. C. Lee & N. W. S. Zane (Eds.), *Handbook of Asian American psychology* (pp. 359–400). Thousand Oaks, CA: Sage.

Luhtanen, R., & Crocker, J. (1992). A collective self-esteem scale: Self-evaluation of one's social identity. *Personality and Social Psychology Bulletin, 18,* 302–318.

McLaughlin, L. A., & Braun, K. L. (1998). Asian and Pacific Islander cultural values: Considerations for health care decision making. *Health & Social Work, 23,* 116–126.

Merriam-Webster's collegiate dictionary. (11th ed.). (2003). Springfield, MA: Merriam-Webster.

Norasakkunkit, V., & Kalick, S. M. (2002). Culture, ethnicity, and emotional distress measures: The role of self-construal and self-enhancement. *Journal of Cross-Cultural Psychology, 33,* 56–70.

Park, Y. S., & Kim, B. S. K. (2008). Asian and European American cultural values and communication styles among Asian American and European American college students. *Cultural Diversity and Ethnic Minority Psychology, 14,* 47–56.

Sandlund, E. S., & Norlander, T. (2000). The effects of tai chi chuan relaxation and exercise on stress responses and well-being: An overview of research. *International Journal of Stress Management, 17,* 139–149.

Singelis, T. M., Bond, M. H., Sharkey, W. F., & Lai, C. S. Y. (1999). Unpackaging culture's influence on self-esteem and embarassability: The role of self-construals. *Journal of Cross-Cultural Psychology, 30*, 315–341.

Snowden, L. R., & Cheung, F. H. (1990). Use of inpatient mental health services by members of ethnic minority groups. *American Psychologist, 45*, 347–355.

Sue, D. W., Bucceri, J., Lin, A. I., Nadal, K. L., & Torino, G. C. (2007). Racial microaggressions and the Asian American experience. *Cultural Diversity and Ethnic Minority Psychology, 13*, 72–81.

Sue, S. (2008, August 18). *Suicide among Asian Americans* [press release]. UC Davis News and Information. Retrieved September 19, 2008, from http://www.news.ucdavis.edu/search/news_detail.lasso?id=8738

Sue, S., & Zane, N. (1987). The role of culture and cultural techniques in psychotherapy: A critique and reformulation. *American Psychologist, 42*, 37–45.

Suh, E. M. (2002). Culture, identity consistency, and subjective well-being. *Journal of Personality and Social Psychology, 83*, 1378–1391.

Takaki, R. (1989). *Strangers from a different shore: A history of Asian Americans.* New York: Penguin Books.

Uba, L. (1994). *Asian Americans: Personality patterns, identity and mental health.* New York: Guilford Press.

U.S. Bureau of the Census. (2004). *U.S. interim projections by age, sex, race, and Hispanic origin.* Retrieved October 28, 2004, from http://www.census.gov/ipc/www/usinterimproj

Wong, K. S. (1995). Chinatown: Conflicting images, contested terrain. *MENUS, 20*, 3–15.

Yelsma, P., Brown, N. M., & Elison, J. (2002). Shame-focused coping styles and their associations with self-esteem. *Psychological Reports, 90*, 1179–1189.

You, Y. G. (1997). Shame and guilt mechanisms in East Asian culture. *Journal of Pastoral Care, 51*, 57–64.

Zane, N. W. S. (2000). *Loss of Face Scale.* Retrieved September 19, 2008, from http://psychology.ucdavis.edu/aacdr/measures/zanelof.pdf

20

Creativity and Self-Esteem in Later Life

SAMUEL T. GLADDING AND BETH MARTIN

C ontrary to prevalent beliefs, much creativity occurs in later life. Johann Wolfgang von Goethe completed *Faust* at 80, Titian painted masterpieces at 98, Arturo Toscanini conducted at 85, Oliver Wendell Holmes wrote Supreme Court decisions at 90, Thomas Edison worked in his laboratory until he was 84, and Benjamin Franklin helped to frame the U.S. Constitution at 80.

Yet the power of dominant myths that older adults are not creative is still pervasive. Many individuals, regardless of age, view older adults as lower in status, less exciting, and primarily passive instead of seeing them as continuing to or even beginning to utilize their talents. In this chapter, seven creative art forms—music, movement, imagery, visual art, literature, drama, and humor—will be examined in regard to how they can be used to creatively help older adults increase their self-esteem and assist them in living more productively.

SELF-ESTEEM ISSUES IN OLDER ADULTS

Several difficult changes can accompany aging: Older adults often experience increasing financial constraints and severity of health issues, while social status and basic functioning are decreasing. Hunter, Linn, and Harris (1982) connect older adults' reports of poor health, depression, anxiety, and external locus of control orientation to low self-esteem. Robins, Trzesniewski, Tracy, Gosling, and Potter (2002) highlight several developmental issues that can contribute to a drop in self-esteem as people continue to age. Losing a spouse, losing social support, dealing with declining physical health, cognitive impairments, and declining socioeconomic status all have the potential to be detrimental, though the degree to which self-esteem is affected may depend on other variables, such as gender, ethnic group, and socioeconomic status. These differences may contribute to the somewhat inconsistent literature regarding how self-esteem may change in the later years (Robins et al., 2002). Yet several studies have shown little to no self-esteem losses as people enter old age despite challenges.

Feelings of competence and achievement, of course, can dwindle with the aging process if one begins to lose mental or physical capacities. They may also decrease if what is considered creative is restricted to what may be accomplished primarily at one age span in life and not the entire life span. Given that one's perceptions of competence and achievement are so closely linked to the perception of self-worth, it would make sense that older persons might be susceptible to decreases in self-esteem if they were mentally or physically limited or if the definition of creativity was too narrow for individuals to meet its standards. However, such circumstances are the exception, not the rule, in the aging process, as Cohen (2000) has shown. Most individuals live fully until a few months or a few years up to the time of their death, and definitions of creativity continue to be broad. Therefore, in working with older adults regarding their creativity and self-esteem, it is crucial to put an open rather than narrow definition on what these two entities entail.

Robins et al. (2002) interpret Erikson's (1968) writings on the final stages of life: "The decline in self-esteem might not be part of a larger pattern of deteriorating emotional health in old age but rather a specific shift in self-conceptions that contributes to a more modest and balanced view of the self" (p. 431). Self-esteem and general well-being will be affected more by how an aging individual views these events and changes than by their intrinsic nature (Torres & Hammarstroem, 2006). The conceptualization of self-esteem in old age varies from individual to individual. Clients may maintain healthy self-esteem levels as they age; it should not be assumed that self-esteem plummets with each year after retirement. The job of helpers is to support clients' resiliency as they grow and develop through the end of their lives.

BUILDING SELF-ESTEEM IN LATER LIFE THROUGH THE CREATIVE ARTS

As a group, older adults do not lose their ability to be creative, although creativity may be expressed in different ways. The ability to think in an integrative and original way based on subjective experiences may be the hallmark of such mature creativity as crystallized intelligence comes more into play (Sasser-Coen, 1993). Researchers are posing new ideas about what creativity can look like for older adults. "If one considers creativity from a developmental perspective, interventions that stimulate individuals' reflection, restructuring, and synthesis of ideas and wisdom also could be characterized as creative activities" (Flood & Phillips, 2007, p. 392).

Divergent thinking, associated with creativity in younger adults, is usually not as prevalent in older adults. Yet recent literature (Cohen, 2000, 2006; Reed, 2005) has broadened the conceptualization of creativity to encompass activities throughout the life stages. This broadening is in line with Erikson's (1968) conceptualization of healthy older adults as developmentally being involved in generativity of two kinds. Communal generativity is connecting with and caring for others. Agentic generativity is producing a contribution to a particular community or to society at large (McAdams & St. Aubin, 1992, as cited in Adams-Price & Steinman, 2007). Although later acts of creativity may be quite different from those found in early adulthood, produced works may also be a continuation of their earlier creativeness. Either way, self-esteem is enhanced when older adults actively engage in creativity. Only those older adults who fall into Erikson's category of despair, have been despondent most of their lives, or are now depressed or demented suffer low self-esteem and other maladies due to age.

In addition, increased longevity, improved health, and a decline in ageism have changed opportunities for the development of creativity and improved self-esteem in older adults. Shifting the way both helping professionals and the surrounding society look at and value older adults' creative acts can open doors for a developmental, strengths-based approach to helping seniors explore creativity and their own potentials. New definitions of what creativity is and at what life stages creativity is manifested are two other means for improving self-esteem in older adults. At the same time, keeping an open mind and realizing the factual nature of aging is also crucial in working with older adults on issues of creativity and self-esteem.

Big C creativity—producing something new and useful in society—is rarely found in the general population, let alone the subpopulation of those over age 60. Rather, little c creativity—the solving of daily problems—tends to be the domain of most people regardless of age (Cohen, 2000; Csikszentmihalyi, 1996). Many times this little c creativity is expressed through artistic endeavors. The creative arts range from those that are primarily auditory or written (e.g., music, drama, and literature) to those that are predominantly visual (e.g., painting, mime, dance, and movement). Many overlaps exist between these two categories, and in a number of cases two or more art forms may be combined creatively, such as literature and drama in the form of enactment or dance and music, as in the form of ballet. We will address these creative arts in conjunction with self-esteem enhancement since involvement with them is most likely to make a difference in the lives of older adults.

MUSIC, CREATIVITY, AND OLDER ADULTS

Older adults generally report increased positive feelings when listening to music in their everyday lives (Laukka, 2007). Playing or making music with older persons has several goals, including the promotion of social interaction, the enhancement of self-worth, the encouragement of self-expression, and the recall of past events (Rio, 2002; Sherman, 2006). Reported benefits of producing or listening to music on a regular basis in older age include sharing and connecting with others, linking and remembering life events, stress relief, a sense of temporary escape, and spiritual connection (Hays & Minichiello, 2005).

Ways of conducting musical sessions vary. They may be carried out in a formal or improvised manner, as well as individually and collectively. When sessions are formal, individuals or groups follow a schedule, and music is played in order to promote personal and interpersonal gains. If the sessions are less formally conducted, on the other hand, more spontaneity and interaction may occur with less music.

In maximum-participation groups, members select their own music and theme. In less democratic groups, most of the selections are made by the leaders, with particular foci in mind. Contemporary or early American songs set a tone and a mood that encourage talk and interaction.

In reminiscence or in present-oriented self-focused social groups, music can be the key to encouraging the discussion of past or present feelings and thoughts about events, such as learning, romance, loss, and family life. Typically, music is initially played that revolves around a particular theme, such as the importance of home or family. Such an activity usually takes place after the group as a whole has warmed up by participating in a brief sing-along of familiar songs that include their own accompaniment of clapping and foot tapping. This approach helps participants incorporate the past into the present in a creative way through the telling of stories or story anecdotes, and even has been found to be effective in helping reduce depressive symptoms in 73- to 94-year-olds with dementia (Ashida, 2000).

MOVEMENT, CREATIVITY, AND OLDER ADULTS

A reasonable amount of physical movement is beneficial to older adults and has been shown to increase self-esteem. Particularly when combined with music, creative movement may be used with older adults to help them achieve better body awareness and functioning in their everyday movements. Rhythmic music, for example, acts as a stimulus for helping those with gait disorders improve the flow of their walk (Berrol, Ooi, & Katz, 1997; Staum, 1983). In this process, the beat of the music serves as a cue for individuals in anticipating a desired rate of movement. As older adults continue to use music as inspiration for practicing movement functions, they can maintain or rebuild a sense of achievement and confidence in this domain. Hackney, Kantorovich, and Earhart (2007) found that older adults with Parkinson's disease improved their balance and gait after taking Argentine tango dance lessons designed for their physical capabilities. Study participants reported feeling more confident in their ability to balance themselves. Such gains in selective self-esteem can be reinforced by the positive social interactions participants tend to have in dance courses. Haboush, Floyd, Caron, LaSota, and Alvarez (2006) suggest that dance courses seem approachable to adults who may be hesitant to seek professional help for their mental health. After participants learn or refamiliarize themselves with creative movements, they can practice what they have learned at home (with or without a partner) and continue to reap self-esteem benefits of creative movement.

Authentic movement is another type of creative movement that has been shown to help perceptions of self-esteem in women with physical ailments (Dibbell-Hope, 2000). "The mover moves in her own time, at her own pace, and from her own impulse, and can therefore move comfortably and safely within any physical limitations" (p. 53). Participants are encouraged to see themselves as experts on their bodies, and the group facilitator uses free association and clinical observation techniques to encourage the process.

In another therapeutic group activity known as *passive-active* (Fisher, 1989), designated active members make statues out of the passive members (within reason), but the passive members may "come alive" at any time, and likewise, the active members may become passive at any time. The enjoyment of this type of play is found in creating the statues and in the element of surprise.

IMAGERY, CREATIVITY, AND OLDER ADULTS

Both free and guided imagery may be especially powerful tools in working with older persons in bringing out their creativity and bolstering their self-esteem, showing them that they can change their thoughts in any situation. Guided imagery exercises allow those who are growing older to take relaxed trips in time either to a place they long to visit or back to a place they have enjoyed before (Fisher, 1989). These imaginary trips are followed with a process session in which individuals share with the counselor and group members their experiences in verbal or nonverbal forms, such as talking or drawing. They may recall or create times and settings that are valuable to them and to which they may retreat during times of stress or distress.

Pain from chronic conditions, illness, or injury is a fact of life for many older adults. Guided imagery techniques have been used successfully to help with pain management (Fors, Sexton, & Goetestam, 2002) and anxiety (Antall & Kresevic, 2004).

Free imagery is a largely unstructured strategy in which music is played in the background and participants are asked to "dance in their minds." After the experience ends, those who are mobile may actually act out what they envisioned, and the less physically agile may move their limbs to the beat of the music while remaining seated. Movement may bring out previously unknown innovations and become a source of pride and pleasure.

Focused visual imagery can also improve the functioning of older clients who have mild cognitive impairments. For instance, Abraham, Neundorfer, and Terris (1993) found that 46 nursing home residents (aged 71–97 years) made a significant improvement in their cognitive abilities over a 24-week period when imagery experiences were used to help them. These researchers structured their focused visual imagery group around six themes—relaxation, protection (from anxiety and stresses that come with change), self-esteem, control (i.e., working out conflicts in symbolic form), energy (including strategies for increasing energy), and transition (e.g., dealing with aging, loss, and relocation).

VISUAL ART, CREATIVITY, AND OLDER ADULTS

Later life is filled with almost as many changes as adolescence, such as becoming grandparents, being liberated from work responsibilities, and being free to enjoy leisure time; other changes involve major life losses, such as "physical decline, sexual changes, changes in dependency status, and role of receiver" (Wald, 2003, p. 295). In both the areas of gain and loss, the visual arts can be helpful. Indeed, history is filled with examples of aging adults who combined experience with creativity, such as "Michelangelo, Titian, Tintoretto, Hals, Picasso, and Grandma Moses" (p. 296).

Using the visual arts as a creative medium is an excellent approach for many older persons looking to feel better about themselves and their environments (Weiss, 1999). As a preventative and remedial force against low self-esteem, visual art endeavors can take many forms—pictures or models of events in memory from childhood, school, work, trips, holidays, and special events are all examples. Photography, applied arts and crafts, and the spontaneous use of art are also accessible and helpful to older adults. A study based on interviews with older art show participants (Fisher & Specht, 1999) yielded reports of increased self-esteem. These senior artists were able to "transcend the negative aspects of life by focusing on the positive and fostering the optimization versus the minimization of potential" (p. 465). Participants felt a renewed sense of purpose when they engaged in creative activities and also were pleased with the social support they found through creating and sharing their art together.

The use of photography, especially the use of old pictures, is an excellent way to help older adults participate in the life review process that is so important to fostering a sense of ego integrity. The procedure used in introducing this activity can vary depending on the setting. For example, practitioners employed in an older adult day care center can ask members of the center to bring in photographs of their lives. On the other hand, if they are employed in an inpatient facility where clients do not have ready access to their personal possessions, they may have to be more active and find some "representative photographs." The idea is to help older adults identify positive early recollections while reframing negatives to promote a sense of progress or achievement toward the goal of improving or maintaining self-esteem.

Applied art, like visual art, can also help foster aspects of self-esteem. A recent qualitative study (Adams-Price & Steinman, 2007) asked middle-aged women who make jewelry to describe their experiences and beliefs with their creative endeavor. Every participant reported some sort of psychological benefit associated with their jewelry making, and about a quarter of the interviewed women connected their creative endeavors to increased feelings of well-being, happiness, and self-worth. The women were proud of their specific talent, jewelry making, and also benefited on a more global level from their creative work.

"Art on occasions" is the indirect suggestion of an older adult art therapist, Maxine Toch Frankenfelder (1988), who began an art therapy program at age 73 and upon graduation worked in a psychogeriatric day treatment center. In introducing art to her participants, she began by drawing a mandala and then drew circles within circles that she colored. The group she worked with followed her lead and improvised, too. On the occasions of members becoming ill, she had members of the group make cards. At the termination of the experience she had members draw the "saddest pictures they could imagine, but add a ray of hope. The images ranged from a weeping willow with a bit of sunshine to a Madonna and child" (p. 253). Thus, using the visual arts with older adults was a way to help them show care for others and at the same time care for themselves, both of which speak to sense of worth.

LITERATURE, CREATIVITY, AND OLDER ADULTS

Reading or writing is often quite therapeutic for older populations. Haber (2006) notes that while older adults have traditionally been held in high regard in many societies for the wisdom passed along through their stories, their role as storytellers in the United States has been deemphasized and devalued over time. In recent years, the life review process has become a popular tool in helping older clients reclaim this storyteller role and find new meaning in how they have lived. A life review involves having individuals write an autobiography using family albums, old letters, personal memories, and interviews with others to gather and integrate life experiences into a significant whole. Ideally, this effort produces wisdom and satisfaction while alleviating pain and regrets as individuals strive to find meaning in the sum of their experiences or in specific memories. A marked and somewhat sustained increase in self-esteem occurs among older persons who participated in the process of writing a life review (Botella & Feizas, 1993; Chiang, Lu, Chu, Chang, & Chou, 2008). Chiang et al. (2008) found that their North Taiwanese participants generally were able to redefine their beliefs about what constitutes a successful life journey and, in doing so, "alter their individual negative understanding" (p. 10) about past events. On the other hand, another study (Wang, Hsu, & Cheng, 2005) did not yield a statistically significant change in self-esteem for elderly Taiwanese participating in life review programs. More research is necessary to explore culturally sensitive and consistently effective ways to facilitate life reviews.

Another literary way of working with older persons involves reading works by those within their age range. Books by Koch (1977), such as *I Never Told Anybody: Teaching Poetry Writing in a Nursing Home*, and Kaminsky (1974), such as *What's Inside You It Shines Out of You*, are classics in illustrating the creative potential of older adults and their insightful wisdom. Furthermore, reading these works helps to sensitize older adults and those who work with them to facts and feelings about aging. It assists them in creating understanding and empathy through an enjoyable experience and can have the benefit of an increased sense of worthiness.

In an experience that involves group work with older people, residents in nursing homes and other long-term care facilities can do reaction readings of poetry, during which they read poems aloud together as a group (i.e., a choral reading). They "then react to the content of the poems with their own knowledge, opinion, emotion, and imagination" (Asmuth, 1995, p. 415). In such an activity, residents are performers as well as the audience. They are stimulated emotionally and intellectually. Furthermore, their self-concepts and cohesiveness as a group can improve as these poetry readers gain confidence in their reading and responses. Given the connection between perceived social support and self-esteem (e.g., Bailey & McLaren, 2005), this work can be helpful to self-esteem development among older populations. Some examples of poems that have been found helpful in reaction reading include "Tree" by Joyce Kilmer, "They Have Yarns" by Carl Sandburg, and "Mother to Son" by Langston Hughes. As adults create, grapple with, and discuss their readings and writings, their self-esteem benefits from social interaction, increased mastery and understanding of the experiences and self, and a sense of achievement upon the life review's completion.

DRAMA, CREATIVITY, AND OLDER ADULTS

Older adults (aged 60–86) who participated in one month of theater training showed improvements in self-esteem and overall well-being (Noice, Noice, & Staines, 2004). This training consisted of short drama exercises rather than line memorization and role development for a play, and the group leader emphasized participants' unique abilities to explore creative and dramatic interactions: "As the instructor put it, 'nobody can be as good a *you* as *you*'" (p. 570). As older adults participate in noncompetitive dramatic exercise, they may feel better about specific acting or expressive abilities as well as more comfortable with themselves in a more global sense.

A somewhat recent trend in working with older persons is the use of developmental drama. In this approach, counselors work to help disoriented or depressed older adults connect with their past and their present, and with each other in a positive way. Employing a group format, members are actively engaged in a sustained manner (Johnson, 1986). The developmental nature of drama progresses from greeting, to unison activities, to expression of group themes, to personification of images, to playing, to closing rituals. Members are encouraged to interact with their fellow group members and to recognize and own their emotions. For example, in *phoning home*, group members call a significant person in their lives and either resolve difficulties or express gratitude. Overall, drama, especially that developed by older adults, is helpful in resolving past issues and moving into the present purposefully.

HUMOR, CREATIVITY, AND OLDER ADULTS

Humor is also much appreciated by many older people and is used by them at times in creative ways to feel better about themselves and their environments. Kruse and Prazak (2006) surveyed older adults to learn what is most humorous, and found interactions with children and joke telling to be most popular. The wit of persons at advanced ages is often quite keen (Nahemow, 1986). Although humor comprehension may decline somewhat with age, affective appreciation of humor and the ability to emotionally react to humor tend to remain consistent (Shammi & Stuss, 2003). One general advantage older persons have over other age groups is their appreciation of more diverse forms of humor, since they have more experiences from which to draw. Certain themes, such as sexuality, wisdom, and death, are more common than others.

Laughter and humor also help older adults develop their ability to cope with life's stressors and losses (Marziali, McDonald, & Donahue, 2008), which in turn benefit adults' global self-esteem. Berk (2001) summarizes the many psychological and physiological benefits of laughter for older adults, and recommends that health educators present information regarding these benefits to elderly groups when possible. However, poorly timed or otherwise inappropriate humor can be harmful to clients in a delicate emotional state (Tennant, 1990) and damage their sense of worth.

In addition to verbally encouraging and using humor, nonverbal actions on the part of counselors who work with older populations can bring out the best and the lightest within members when warranted. For instance, if an older person takes the role of a doormat in a relationship with others, a therapist might literally have the client lie down and act out this helpless part (Raber, 1987). Such humorous enactments create an impression in the midst of fun and laughter, and put individuals in the position of change as well (Watzlawick, 1983).

ROLE OF THE COUNSELOR

Newman and Newman (2009) encourage helping professionals to acknowledge the limitations faced by older adults with whom they work, especially the oldest of the old. They suggest supporting these individuals by helping them strive for a reasonable level of independence, autonomy, and self-esteem. Counselors and clients can work together to define *reasonable*. Giordano (2000) presents a summary of client-centered communication skills that can facilitate this ongoing process with older clients. Guindon (2002) cautions that counselors should not assume that a particular area of self-evaluation is or is not important to clients regardless of age. Rather, as in other areas of helping, counselors should listen first, make broad assumptions second, and assess the reality of what needs to be or can be done third.

Practitioners should cultivate their own creativity and work on improving their own self-esteem. They can engage and participate in the creative arts, such as singing in a choir, painting with watercolors, or writing short stories. The beauty of such a strategy is that it is not only enriching in itself, but may well spill over to the work they do with older adults. By cultivating creative efforts, practitioners and the older adults with whom they work may well be sensitized to the creative processes and move toward greater self-awareness.

EFFECTS OF CULTURAL BACKGROUNDS AND DIVERSITY ON OLDER ADULT CREATIVITY AND SELF-ESTEEM

By its very nature, creativity is multicultural and diverse. By participating in it and being productive, older adults court a healthy sense of accomplishment. In addition, creativity is universal, and displaying creativity enhances feelings of achievement that are not limited by age or background. Basically, there is not a country or ethnic group in the world devoid of creative thoughts and actions and the benefits that they bring (Gladding, 2005).

Besides being culturally encompassing and diverse, creativity and the creative arts help individuals, especially in later life, understand the meaning of life and aging more fully. The creative arts contribute to well-being and life satisfaction because they extend beyond those who give them life. Overall, the promotion and encouragement of creativity in older adults helps them integrate and concentrate on life in a more holistic way and feel they are more alive.

CASE STUDY

When Cassie turned 70, she decided to quit her work as a cleaning specialist. She had begun the work initially by default when a neighbor, Sally, invited Cassie to accompany her to houses she had contracted to clean, to earn some extra cash, while Cassie's kids were in school. Cassie enjoyed the work at first. She thought it was good exercise and it helped her balance her life. However, as the years went on, Cassie knew she had more abilities than the now full-time job allowed her to show. Nevertheless, she never looked for any other kind of employment.

Feeling unfulfilled and lacking a sense of competence, Cassie decided that in retirement she would spend her time and her life more productively. She thought initially of going back to school but decided she could never keep up. She also thought of other trades but realized she had paid her dues in regard to work. Therefore, when a local senior center announced a six-week dance and movement series, Cassie signed up. Her physical self-esteem had always been both high and salient, so it sounded like fun, and she liked staying active.

As she expected, more women than men showed up for the sessions. Yet, the facilitator emphasized that the dancing and movement the group of 10 older adults would do was not designed for partners. Each session was focused on the individual within the group. Session 1, and the remaining sessions, started with warm-up movements and ended with cool-down movements. Thus, at the beginning and ending of the sessions, Cassie found herself moving in slow motion, which she particularly liked because it helped her be more aware of what her body was doing, and she felt a sense of accomplishment.

During the six weeks, Cassie learned European and Caribbean folk dances, elementary tap dancing, a peace movement, and how to time her body in some free movement ways to coincide with the music she heard in the background. It was great exercise, and participating in a nonjudgmental experience increased her global self-esteem. In addition, Cassie met other people and made new friends, which enhanced the sense of belongingness essential to healthy self-esteem. At the end of the class, she felt refreshed, empowered, and invigorated. She even saw a new dimension to herself—Cassie the dancer, as opposed to Cassie the cleaner.

CONCLUSION

Creativity and self-esteem are not confined to the young. Rather, the creative spirit and the high self-regard that often accompanies it are qualities found throughout the life cycle in different ways and at distinct times. Older adults may be quite creative and psychologically healthy. The creative process can help them find, maintain, or keep their innovation and integrity. Through the use of the creative arts, older adults may gain insight, develop an understanding of life's deeper meanings, and understand the aging process, themselves, and others even better. Different aspects of life begin at different times, but the essentials of being integrated and healthy in later life can be fostered through utilizing creativity and the creative arts and have the benefit of bolstering selective domains of self-esteem as well as general self-esteem.

REFERENCES

Abraham, I. L., Neundorfer, M. M., & Terris, E. A. (1993). Effects of focused visual imagery on cognition and depression among nursing home residents. *Journal of Mental Imagery, 17*, 61–76.

Adams-Price, C. E., & Steinman, B. A. (2007). Crafts and generative expression: A qualitative study of the meaning of creativity in women who make jewelry in midlife. *International Journal of Aging and Human Development, 65*, 315–323.

Antall, G. F., & Kresevic, D. (2004). The use of guided imagery to manage pain in an elderly orthopaedic population. *Orthopaedic Nursing, 23*, 335–340.

Ashida, M. (2000). The effect of reminiscence music therapy sessions on changes in depressive symptoms in elderly persons with dementia. *Journal of Music Therapy, 37*, 170–182.

Asmuth, M. V. (1995). Reaction reading: A tool for providing fantasy imagery for long-term care facility residents. *Gerontologist, 35*, 415–419.

Bailey, M., & McLaren, S. (2005). Physical activity alone and with others as predictors of sense of belonging and mental health in retirees. *Aging & Mental Health, 9*, 82–90.

Berk, R. A. (2001). The active ingredients in humor: Psychophysiological benefits and risks for older adults. *Educational Gerontology, 27*, 323–339.

Berrol, C. F., Ooi, W. L., & Katz, S. S. (1997). Dance/movement therapy with older adults who have sustained neurological insult: A demonstration project. *American Journal of Dance Therapy, 19*, 135–160.

Botella, L., & Feizas, G. (1993). The autobiographical group: A tool for the reconstruction of past life experience with the aged. *International Journal of Aging and Human Development, 36*, 303–319.

Chiang, K., Lu, R., Chu, H., Chang, Y., & Chou, K. (2008). Evaluation of the effect of a life review group program on self-esteem and life satisfaction in the elderly. *International Journal of Geriatric Psychiatry, 23*, 7–10.

Cohen, G. (2000). *The creative age: Awakening human potential in the second half of life.* New York: Avon Books.

Cohen, G. D. (2006). Research on creativity and aging: The positive impact of the arts on health and illness. *Generations, 30*, 7–15.

Csikszentmihalyi, M. (1996). *Creativity: Flow and the psychology of discovery and invention.* New York: Harper Perennial.

Dibbell-Hope, S. (2000). The use of dance/movement therapy in psychological adaptation to breast cancer. *The Arts in Psychotherapy, 27*, 51–68.

Erikson, E. H. (1968). *Identity: Youth and crisis.* New York: W. W. Norton and Company.

Fisher, B., & Specht, D. (1999). Successful aging and creativity later in life. *Journal of Aging Studies, 13*, 457–472.

Fisher, P. P. (1989). *Creative movement for older adults.* New York: Human Sciences.

Flood, M., & Phillips, K. D. (2007). Creativity in older adults: A plethora of possibilities. *Issues in Mental Health Nursing, 28*, 389–411.

Fors, E. A., Sexton, H., & Goetestam, K. G. (2002). The effect of guided imagery and amitriptyline on daily fibromyalgia pain: A prospective, randomized, controlled trial. *Journal of Psychiatric Research, 36*, 179–187.

Frankenfelder, M. T. (1988). For later days—a fulfillment. *Arts in Psychotherapy, 15*, 251–254.

Gladding, S. T. (2005). *Counseling as an art: The creative arts in counseling* (3rd ed.). Alexandria, VA: American Counseling Association.

Giordano, J. A. (2000). Effective communication and counseling with older adults. *International Journal of Aging and Human Development, 51*, 315–324.

Guindon, M. H. (2002). Toward accountability in the use of the self-esteem construct. *Journal of Counseling and Development, 80,* 204–214.

Haber, D. (2006). Life review: Implementation, theory, research, and therapy. *International Journal of Aging and Human Development, 63,* 153–171.

Haboush, A., Floyd, M., Caron, J., LaSota, M., & Alvarez, K. (2006). Ballroom dance lessons for geriatric depression: An exploratory study. *The Arts in Psychotherapy, 33,* 89–97.

Hackney, M. E., Kantorovich, S., & Earhart, G. M. (2007). A study on the effects of Argentine tango as a form of partnered dance for those with Parkinson disease and the healthy elderly. *American Journal of Dance Therapy, 29,* 109–127.

Hays, T., & Minichiello, V. (2005). The contribution of music to quality of life in older people: An Australian qualitative study. *Ageing and Society, 25,* 261–278.

Hunter, K. I., Linn, M. W., & Harris, R. (1982). Characteristics of high and low self-esteem in the elderly. *International Journal of Aging and Human Development, 14,* 117–126.

Johnson, D. R. (1986). The developmental method in drama therapy: Group treatment with the elderly. *Arts in Psychotherapy, 13,* 17–33.

Kaminsky, M. (1974). *What's inside you it shines out of you.* New York: Horizon.

Koch, K. (1977). *I never told anybody: Teaching poetry writing in a nursing home.* New York: Random House.

Kruse, B. G., & Prazak, M. P. (2006). Humor and older adults: What makes them laugh? *Journal of Holistic Nursing, 24,* 188–193.

Laukka, P. (2007). Uses of music and psychological well-being among the elderly. *Journal of Happiness Studies, 8,* 215–241.

Marziali, E., McDonald, L., & Donahue, P. (2008). The role of coping humor in the physical and mental health of older adults. *Aging & Mental Health, 12,* 713–718.

Nahemow, L. (1986). Humor as a data base for the study of aging. In L. Nahemow, K. A. McCluskey-Fawcett, & P. E. McGhee (Eds.), *Humor and aging* (pp. 3–26). New York: Academic.

Newman, B. M., & Newman, P. R. (2009). *Development through life: A psychosocial approach* (10th ed.). Belmont, CA: Cengage Learning/Wadsworth.

Noice, H., Noice, T., & Staines, G. (2004). A short-term intervention to enhance cognitive and affective functioning in older adults. *Journal of Aging and Health, 16,* 562–585.

Raber, W. C. (1987). The caring role of the nurse in the application of humor therapy to the patient experiencing helplessness. *Clinical Gerontologist, 7,* 3–11.

Reed, I. C. (2005). Creativity: Self-perceptions over time. *International Journal of Aging and Human Development, 60,* 1–18.

Rio, R. (2002). Improvisation with the elderly: Moving from creative activities to process-oriented therapy. *The Arts in Psychotherapy, 29,* 191–201.

Robins, R. W., Trzesniewski, K. H., Tracy, J. L., Gosling, S. D., & Potter, J. (2002). Global self-esteem across the life span. *Psychology and Aging, 17,* 423–434.

Sasser-Coen, J. R. (1993). Qualitative changes in creativity in the second half of life: A lifespan developmental perspective. *Journal of Creative Behavior, 27,* 18–27.

Shammi, P., & Stuss, D. T. (2003). The effects of normal aging on humor appreciation. *Journal of the International Neuropsychological Society, 9,* 855–863.

Sherman, A. (2006). Toward a creative culture: Lifelong learning through the arts. *Generations, 30,* 42–45.

Staum, M. (1983). Music and rhythmic stimuli in the rehabilitation of gait disorders. *Journal of Music Therapy, 20,* 69–87.

Tennant, K. F. (1990). Laugh it off: The effect of humor on the well-being of the older adult. *Journal of Gerontological Nursing, 16,* 11–16.

Torres, S., & Hammarstroem, G. (2006). Speaking of 'limitations' while trying to disregard them: A qualitative study of how diminished everyday competence and aging can be regarded. *Journal of Aging Studies, 20*, 291–302.

Wald, J. (2003). Clinical art therapy with older adults. In C. A. Malchiodi (Ed.), *Handbook of art therapy* (pp. 294–307). New York: Guilford.

Wang, J. J., Hsu, Y. C., & Cheng, S. F. (2005). The effects of reminiscence in promoting mental health of Taiwanese elderly. *International Journal of Nursing Studies, 42*, 31–36.

Watzlawick, P. (1983). *The situation is hopeless, but not serious.* New York: Norton.

Weiss, J. C. (1999). The role of art therapy in aiding older adults with life transitions. In M. Duffy (Ed.), *Handbook of counseling and psychotherapy with older adults* (pp. 182–196). New York: John Wiley & Sons.

Conclusion

MARY H. GUINDON

To be yourself in a world that is constantly trying to make you something else is the greatest accomplishment.

—Ralph Waldo Emerson

You have come to the end of this book. My hope is that you now have a good idea of what self-esteem is and feel better prepared to address self-esteem issues whomever your client of interest and wherever your work setting may be. It seems no matter what concerns our clients may bring to us, sooner or later we—or they—may very well realize that self-esteem is part of the issue. You have seen that sometimes self-esteem is an area for possible intervention in and of itself through targeted strategies and other times it can be attended to as a part of a broader issue. This book provides only a small sampling of the many types of people and problems that may present with self-esteem issues. I realize that many more specific populations could have been addressed. Nevertheless, you have the tools necessary to adapt self-esteem strategies to the people and problems you are most likely to encounter. As you consider what you have found useful in this book, I also hope that you will reflect on what you need to do to responsibly and successfully apply self-esteem strategies that will make a difference in the lives of your clients. Last, I hope that you will continue to add effective self-esteem intervention tools to your practitioner's toolbox. To that end, I have some recommendations.

First, we must all be accountable for what we mean by self-esteem. Credible and viable results take no less. Any theory of self-esteem and, ultimately, any intervention, rests on how it is defined. Additionally, those professionals with whom we work should be made aware of the lack of clarity in the meaning of the construct and held accountable for their usage of this term, if we are to raise the word "self-esteem" to its level of importance as a core part of personality. Many intervention strategies can be effective when practitioners know and apply the self-esteem system knowledge base and match treatment goals to the particular self-esteem need. Without this knowledge, it may be that practitioners will inadvertently enhance self-esteem through the interventions they routinely use, but they may also miss opportunities to recognize and address self-esteem problems or, worse still, add to the instability of their clients with low self-esteem or with dangerous, narcissistic high self-esteem. We are in a long-overdue era of social responsibility and advocacy. We must ensure that we are socially responsible in how we look at the role of self-esteem in the helping professions and advocate for its accurate application.

Second, all helping professionals should receive adequate training in the meaning of self-esteem through courses, workshops, and educational materials that have an empirical, rigorous research base behind them. Bednar and Peterson (1995) reminded us more than a decade ago that "Any mode of treatment, like science itself—indeed, like therapy itself—is an evolving, growth-oriented process (p. 409). The resurgence of interest in self-esteem as an area of academic inquiry in this century should yield more support for some existing strategies, offer new ways of understanding the construct, and provide outcomes research that give us more options in how self-esteem can be successfully operationalized in the field. Practitioners should adjust the focus of treatment planning accordingly.

Third, at the same time, there continues to be a need for outcomes-based research upon which mental health practitioners and educators can draw. The professional literature on self-esteem, while offering substantial research on strategies, is far and away conceptual in nature. Although important in advancing the self-esteem discourse, its relevance to practice tends to be indirect. Interventions should be a critical element of research interest, as one of its main purposes in the helping professions is to inform practice. Much more work needs to be done to investigate the puzzling inconsistencies and weak effects that so many research studies show. Is it that self-esteem is not really a meaningful construct, despite the overwhelming amount of interest in it over more than a century? Or is it that we need to better refine our methods of conceptualizing its many aspects and assessing its artifacts? Sociologists and personality, developmental, and social psychologists continue to lead the way in the self-esteem discourse. Despite an impressive array of studies, researchers in the applied fields of professional counseling, social work, marriage and family therapy, and the other related helping professions, as those most concerned with treatment, need to add their voices in greater numbers to refine the construct and its applications, and present viable outcomes results.

Fourth, assumptions cannot not be made that existing programs represented as addressing self-esteem needs do, in actuality, address those needs. It is true that any resource that provides interventions strategies might be appropriate if the clinician takes the time to analyze it for alignment with the self-esteem body of knowledge and extract materials that fit the self-esteem issue of their client. The contributors to this book have shown how this can be done. They conceptualized self-esteem within the context of a specific problem or disorder. They showed us that clinicians can use existing interventions to successfully affect self-esteem by being informed about how the self-esteem system and its many elements are impacted by those interventions.

However, if consultants and vendors and other self-esteem "experts" who claim to offer solutions for self-esteem issues are unable to provide a practical definition of self-esteem grounded in the professional literature, they may not be offering programs that address self-esteem requirements. Educational materials (books, workbooks, videos, and, especially, Web sites) must be viewed with a skeptical eye. We must ascertain what, in fact, these materials are addressing. While some are useful and helpful in self-concept building and may use developmentally sound principles, they may not attend to self-esteem regardless of the word "self-esteem" interjected into the material. Few, if any, programs that generically purport to raise self-esteem are effective. They just don't ring true to clients, most especially students, who en masse are told they are worthy, competent, inherently loveable, or whatever just by existing, as lofty an ideal as that seems to be. Such programs certainly are not likely to have the intended effect on those who have low levels of selective and global self-esteem. Worse yet, such wholesale unearned positive feedback may very well account for legions of entitled individuals who expect to be rewarded for little expenditure of effort, and who feel neither accountable for their actions nor compelled to act on behalf of the greater good.

People at each developmental stage have unique self-esteem needs. There are no simplistic solutions or immediate results for an area of personality as complex and recalcitrant to change as self-esteem. Still, people can change their self-esteem. As Virginia Satir was known to say, "It's just a question of when and in what context" (as cited in Carlock, 1999, p. xiv). Vulnerable clients need our respect and our expertise, not a quick fix with little chance of helping and a possible potential for harm.

Fifth, practitioners should be trained and well versed in the use of self-esteem appraisal methods and, if qualified, in the use of appropriate assessment instruments. This book covers a few of them. You have enough knowledge of the construct to choose among these or use others that can be adapted. Making no assumptions about the presented characteristics of self-esteem is important. As we have seen, low—or high—self-esteem attributes can be in the eye of the beholder, particularly in those untrained in its definitions. Because self-evaluation is the basis of self-esteem, the observer's own personal and societal values can cloud judgment. Remaining objective and using multiple measures will help us better approximate level, stability, domains, and salience—those areas that our clients are most invested in—that matter the most to them both positively and negatively.

Fifth, as a self-esteem model to your clients, you should pay special attention to your own self-esteem needs. You might benefit from training that emphasizes exercises to bring into awareness how your own self-esteem developed and continues to play out today. Peer support groups can offer opportunities for self-esteem enhancement in the company of informed colleagues. Peer group supervision, of course, is a way to process clients' self-esteem needs and collaborate on possible effective self-esteem interventions for vulnerable clients. Peer supervision also offers a forum to engage in the personal self-work necessary to recognize and resolve selective (both trait and situational) self-esteem issues about your own competence and worthiness that might get in the way of your clients' progress.

This book was planned with the intent of providing you a comprehensive overview of the field of self-esteem. Low or high, self-esteem has motivational significance that lasts a lifetime. Without awareness of its meaning and significance, the term itself will continue to sink into the domain of talk shows and "pop" psych, which may encourage abdication of responsibility for actions in the name of "low self-esteem," without offering any real assistance to those who need it most. As professionals, it is incumbent upon all of us to understand the meaning of self-esteem, to use consistent terminology, to ensure that curricula and interventions are appropriate and grounded in the existing body of knowledge, to develop programs that fit throughout the mental health community, and to advocate for its accurate usage.

REFERENCES

Bednar, R. L., & Peterson, S. R. (1995). Self-esteem: Paradoxes and innovations in clinical theory and practice (2nd ed.). Washington, DC: American Psychological Association.

Carlock, C. J. (1999). *Enhancing self-esteem.* (3rd ed.). New York: Taylor & Francis.

Appendix A: Resources

BOOKS

Although there are thousands of books available on self-esteem, not many are directly related to the needs of practitioners and also clearly grounded in the self-esteem body of knowledge. Many of the following books are classics in the field. Although several of them are not recent, they have stood the test of time and are still available.

Baumeister, R. (Ed.). (1993). *Self-esteem: The puzzle of low self-regard*. New York: Plenum.

> Written by a social psychologist, this book presents a review of the self-esteem construct with a focus on the meaning and consequence of low self-esteem. Although more than 15 years old, it is still in print and widely quoted in other sources. It has some utility for the practitioner because it presents information that is central to the understanding of personality, mental health, and social adjustment.

Bednar, L. L., & Peterson, S. R. (1995). *Self-esteem: Paradoxes and innovations in clinical theory and practice* (2nd ed.). Washington, DC: American Psychological Association.

> Although information is not up to date, this book is still in use and targeted to practitioners. It offers a model for diagnosing and treating self-esteem issues in psychological disorders. The book includes information about self-esteem and discusses its many paradoxes. It offers clinical applications, including chapters on developmental considerations, the therapeutic relationship, and considerations of marital and family therapy, and children's development.

Branden, N. (2001). *The psychology of self-esteem: A revolutionary approach to self-understanding that launched a new era in modern psychology* (anniversary ed.). San Francisco: Jossey-Bass. (Original work published 1969)

> This edition of the original and now classic book includes an updated epilogue with a 31-week self-esteem sentence completion exercises. The author explores the need for self-esteem and how self-esteem "affects our values, responses, and goals." Although mainly for the popular market, it has utility for practitioners.

Carlock, C. J. (Ed.). (1999). *Enhancing self-esteem* (3rd ed.). New York: Taylor & Francis.

> Although this book has not been updated in 10 years, it is a very good techniques book that includes lots of activities. It defines self-esteem and explains how it forms, is maintained, and can be changed. The authors offer interventions that incorporate cognitive, emotional, and behavioral aspects of individuals and include anticipated outcomes. It addresses several key problematic self-esteem issues, such as parenting, body image, gender, children, and life transitions.

Harter, S. (2001). *The construction of the self: A developmental perspective*. New York: Guildford Press. (Original work published 1999)

> Also not recent, this landmark book presents extensive research-based information on the formation of a sense of self, along with normative developmental and individual variables. It includes discussions on the causes and consequences of low self-esteem. It is an outstanding theoretical and empirical work that includes Harter's discussions of clinical cases. It also includes some useful information on designing intervention programs practitioners may find useful.

Kernis, M. (Ed.). (2006). *Self esteem: Issues and answers*. New York: Psychology Press (Taylor & Francis Group).

> This edited text is perhaps the most comprehensive on the topic and includes short chapters from leading contributors from clinical, developmental, personality, and social psychology. It is most suitable as a resource for researchers and academics, although it has utility for the practitioner by including several chapters on therapeutic interventions.

McKay, M., & Fanning, P. (2000). *Self-esteem: A proven program of cognitive techniques for assessing, improving, and maintaining your self-esteem* (3rd ed.). Oakland, CA: New Harbinger Publications.

> This now classic and widely used self-help self-esteem book, although not primarily intended for practitioners, presents such thorough information that practitioners can use it to guide them in developing cognitive/behavioral strategies and programs. It includes a section for therapists. Other companion books include:
>
> McKay, M., Fanning, P., Honeychurch, C., & Sutker, C. (2005). *The self-esteem companion*. Oakland, CA: New Harbinger Publications.
>
> Schiraldi, G. R. (2001). *The self-esteem workbook*. Oakland, CA: New Harbinger Publications.

Mruk, C. J. (2006). *Self-esteem research, theory, and practice: Toward a positive psychology of self-esteem* (3rd ed.). New York: Springer.
> Written for practitioners and researchers, it does a creditable job on the use of terms, major self-esteem theories, and reviewing current research. It includes a five-week self-enhancement program.

Owens, T. J., Stryker, S., & Goodman, N. (Eds.). (2001). *Extending self-esteem theory and research: Sociological and psychological currents.* New York: Cambridge University Press.
> Primarily sociological in focus, this edited book concentrates on extending the work of Morris Rosenberg. It presents information about self-esteem, beginning with self-esteem's conceptualization and measurement, and examines the role of self-esteem in society and within and across various domains and contexts of the human experience. Primarily for academicians, it is not targeted toward practitioners but does include some useful information.

WEB SITES

As Debbie M., one of my students, put it, "Searching the word *self-esteem* on the Internet is like trying to count stars in a night sky." Despite the overwhelming number of Web sites that search engines produce, relatively few show evidence that they actually are aware of the self-esteem body of knowledge or its research base. That does not mean you cannot find many useful resources. When looking through self-esteem Web sites online, ask yourself these questions:

1. Is self-esteem defined?
2. If so, is the definition grounded in the current body of knowledge?
3. How useful is this Web site in my current or future work?
4. Would I recommend this site to a colleague? A client? A student? A parent? Why or why not?

If you are not able to answer these questions to your satisfaction, move on. The following Web sites are those that I have found to be most responsible.

The Rosenberg Self-Esteem Scale: http://www.bsos.umd.edu/socy/Research/rosenberg.htm
> This is the site at the University of Maryland Sociology Department where information on the Rosenberg Self-Esteem Scale can be found. It includes Rosenberg's definition of self-esteem.

International Council for Self-Esteem: www.self-esteem-international.org
> From the Web site: "The Council serves as a resource for anyone interested in research, training, materials, and resources related to self-esteem." It is a membership site, with members from countries all over the world.

National Association for Self-Esteem: www.self-esteem-nase.org
> In 1986, the National Council on Self-Esteem (now National Association of Self-Esteem [NASE]) defined self-esteem as "the experience of being capable of meeting life's challenges and being worthy of happiness," and emphasizes personal responsibility and accountability. NASE states that its purpose "is to fully integrate self-esteem into the fabric of American society so that every individual, no matter what their age or background, experiences personal worth and happiness." It is a large organization with many local chapters.

Center for Children's Health Media/Kids Health: www.kidshealth.org
> The Nemours Foundation's Center for Children's Health Media, through this Web site, offers families advice and "comfort about a wide range of physical, emotional, and behavioral issues that affect children and teens." A search on the word *self-esteem* brings up information useful for parents, teachers, and children themselves.

Nathaniel Brandon: http://www.nathanielbranden.com
> Known as the father of self-esteem, Nathaniel Brandon's Web site offers articles, essays, and links on self-esteem and considerably more. Although this is a commercial site, it is worth a look.

The Self Esteem Shop: http://www.selfesteemshop.com
> The Web site provides books and a multitude of other resources. It states: "Self Esteem Shop's mission is to provide outstanding resources that promote healing, inspiration, and personal growth." However, only 11 books came up under the search *self-esteem*, and they would need to be scrutinized closely using the aforementioned questions.

Appendix B: Example of a Group Self-Esteem Intervention Program[*]

Number of sessions: 8

Length of each session: 90 minutes

Number of participants: 8–12 (screen for appropriateness)

Target populations: Same-sex group; cognitively high functioning; older adolescents/young, midlife, and third-phase adults

The following example is a women-only group and can be run by one or two facilitators. It can easily be adapted to other high-functioning groups.

SESSION 1: MANAGING CHANGE

Purpose: To begin instilling a desire for action and an awareness of choice. To set up a future self-affirmation.
Supplies: Small sticky note paper (Post-its®).

HANDOUT 1

What is your favorite color? _____

Write down three descriptive adjectives that best describe this color for you:

1. _____

2. _____

3. _____

Source: Adapted from Sher, B. (1983). *Wishcraft: How to get what you really want.* New York: Ballentine Books.

Facilitation: The participants write down a favorite color and as many positive adjectives as possible to describe it. Each woman reads her list to the group. When she has finished, each woman states the three adjectives most descriptive of her, preceded by "I am ____." For example, "I am happy. I am sunny. I am calm." The facilitator distributes Post-it notes and

[*] Parts of this program are adapted from McKay, M., & Fanning, P. (2000). *Self-esteem: A proven program of cognitive techniques for assessing, improving, and maintaining your self-esteem* (3rd ed.). Oakland, CA: New Harbinger Publications.

suggests that each woman write the sentences on it and attach the note to the mirror she most often looks in.

The facilitator turns to the topic of change, describing change as resulting from a combination of several factors: recognizing dissatisfaction, a clear idea of what is needed to change the dissatisfaction, knowledge of the initial steps to take to effect change, and belief in one's ability to change. Particular attention is paid to the latter, and clients process their thoughts and feelings about change. The facilitator ends by defining self-esteem and explaining the concepts of worthiness and competence.

SESSION 2: BECOMING AWARE OF NEGATIVE THINKING

Purpose: To bring into awareness negative self-talk and to begin feeling a sense of choice and personal control.

Supplies: Plain paper lunch bags.

HANDOUT 2

Fill in the blanks.

I can't _____ .

I must _____ .

I should have _____ .

I need _____ .

I should _____ .

Facilitation: The session begins by completing the sentences on Handout 2. After reading their lists, the members are asked to change *can't* to *won't*, *must* to *can*, *should* to *will*, *need* to *want*, and *should have* to *chose not to* or to *could have _____ but didn't*. The members read aloud and explore the original and restructured sentences. The facilitator suggests that these and other negative ways of thinking belong to the category of garbage and distributes plain paper lunch bags. Each participant is asked to symbolically get rid of her garbage by throwing into the bag a piece of paper, tissue, trash, and so forth, whenever she catches herself engaging in negative thinking exemplified by the word in this exercise. The women are asked to keep this bag with them wherever they go and continue the exercise until the next session.

SESSIONS 3: EXPLORING THE MEANING OF WORTHINESS

Purpose: To explore and accept one's self-worth.

Supplies: Paper and markers/crayons; plastic garbage bag.

Facilitation: The third session begins by processing feelings about the bag homework. At some point members will begin expressing negative feelings about carrying the bags (how cumbersome they are, how ridiculous she feels, etc.). Participants gain insight that carrying around negative, destructive thoughts is similar. The analogy is graphic, simple, and easily understandable. The participants commit to carrying the bags until the next session.

The problem of human worth is explored. Using guided imagery, each woman is asked to recall one specific time or event in her life when she felt accepted just for being herself. The facilitator asks each member to describe the time or event to the group. When all members have described their special moments, the facilitator points out that each has already acknowledged her personal worth as evidenced by her own experience (McKay & Fanning, 2000). Each woman draws a symbolic picture of what she visualized and how she feels when she is unconditionally accepted. The facilitator suggests that she put it on the mirror next to the Post-it note to remind her that her personal worth always exists.

The women are asked if they are ready to dispose of their negative, destructive thinking, that is, their old garbage. Individually, each woman throws her bag in the plastic garbage bag provided as the group members support her action and commits to using more positive self-talk.

SESSION 4: EXPLORING THE MEANING OF FEEDBACK FROM SIGNIFICANT OTHERS

Purpose: To provide a basic understanding of the formation of the self-concept.

To introduce the concept of selective domains as components of self-esteem.

Supplies: A small notebook or journal.

HANDOUT 3

PART I. Answer these questions from the time you were 8–12 years old. Include feedback that was nonverbal as well as verbal.

1. What were you told about your intelligence? By whom?

2. Who did you think was smarter, boys/men or girls/women? Who told you so?

3. What were you told you should do/be when you grow up? By whom?

4. What did you know about making friends? How did your friends treat you?

5. What were you told about appearance and the importance of your looks? What were you told about your weight? By whom?

6. What were you told when you did household chores? Indoors? Outdoors? By whom?

7. Where did you fit into your family? What was your role? Who told you so?

8. Who took care of you? How did they feel about it?

9. What were you told about your ability to solve problems? By whom?

10. What were you told about your ability to work with numbers? By whom?

11. What were you told about your ability to do well in sports? By whom?

12. What were you told about your ability to draw, dance, and sing? By whom?

PART II. Considering the feedback you received as a child, answer the following questions:

1. Which of these messages do you believe today?

2. For those beliefs that you still hold, what experiences have shown you that they are accurate?

3. For those beliefs that you no longer hold, what do you now believe? What experiences caused you to change your mind?

4. How do these beliefs impact on your work/home/relationships/life today?

Facilitation: The concept of feedback from significant others and parental injunctions as critical elements in the formation of self-esteem is introduced. Through the use of Handout 3, participants are encouraged to contemplate the processes through which their views of self-developed; to explore the societal demands placed on them; and how these concepts and the expectations may contribute to their self-esteem. The importance of feedback from significant others in both their past and present life is processed.

The women are asked to make a contract to give and receive appropriate positive feedback to and from each other. They are asked to give and receive without alibi at least one sincere and truthful compliment to one other group participant before the next session. (This is especially effective with inpatient groups.) They are also asked to try to listen for positive feedback from the significant others now in their life. The facilitator gives each woman a journal in which to record any feedback that she receives until the next session.

SESSION 5: RECOGNIZING COGNITIVE DISTORTIONS

Purpose: To bring cognitive distortions into awareness; to introduce the concept that reality is filtered through one's perceptions according to individual needs, beliefs, habit patterns, and so forth.

Facilitation: The women process the preceding session's homework assignment. Many will not recall receiving a compliment from another group member until they are confronted with accurate information from those who offered the compliments. This realization sets the scene for a discussion of cognitive distortions. Having experienced graphic examples of discounting and filtering, the women give greater credibility to the probability of other distortions operating in their lives. The members are encouraged to share their journal entries.

The facilitator instructs the women in the process of disputing the distortion and substituting positive self-talk for negative self-talk. The women are asked to become more aware of their negative self-talk and its sources through journaling.

They are given an affirmation statement to be practiced daily: Each member is to stand in front of her mirror and look at herself as if she has never seen this person before. She is to say aloud, "I accept you just the way you are right now." The facilitator states that it is not necessary that she believe the statement in order to say it.

SESSION 6: EXPLORING THE MEANING OF COMPETENCE

Purpose: To develop recognition of one's uniqueness and to begin building a positive identity based on one's authentic achievement.

Facilitation: The women begin by processing the *affirmation of self* exercise from the last session. The facilitator's encouragement is crucial to the success of this exercise. At no time should the women be made to feel they have failed if they were unable to accomplish the entire assignment. Each step, even just an attempt to stand in front of the mirror, should be treated as a success. The processing of feelings and the completion of small, successive steps toward accomplishment for those that find it difficult can be an exciting, rewarding, often cathartic experience for all participants.

The group now turns to discussing their experiences with recognizing and disputing their negative self-talk. The facilitator then explains the competence element of self-esteem. The participants are encouraged to remember one accomplishment of which they were proud at any time in the past. They go back over their lives and describe the actions they took to bring the accomplishment to completion. They are encouraged to talk about their assets and special skills, to own their areas of competence based on realistic appraisals, and describe them without apology to the group members. At the end of this session, the facilitator asks the women to answer the question "Who are you?" with just one authentic "I am _____" statement. Some will find this difficult, because they have little sense of identity as unique human beings; others will use one of the statements from their Post-it note. Once again, the facilitator suggests they continue writing in their journals, making entries on all the preceding homework assignments. They are also asked to write out by the next session the statement "I am _____" 15 times.

SESSION 7: BEGINNING ACCEPTANCE OF SELF

Purpose: To build self-acceptance despite one's perceived shortcomings; to reinforce authentic behavior through acceptance of appropriate feedback from group members.

Supplies: An adjective checklist.

Facilitation: The group again processes the *affirmation of self* homework and their journal entries. They then read their "I am _____" identity statements. They process feelings surrounding their statements. Inevitably, these statements include those first written on the Post-it note in the first session. The facilitator assists participants in accepting these positive statements as legitimate aspects of themselves.

Each participant is given an adjective checklist and asked to check as many words that apply to her, then to narrow the list to the five that are most descriptive of her positive self. In turn, the facilitator asks each participant to provide one adjective that best describes one of the women. She is asked not to comment but rather to listen openly and to write down each word on the back of the adjective checklist sheet. The process continues for each participant. As each woman's feedback list is completed, she is encouraged to read it aloud to the group along with her own checklist choices. Often there are startling similarities between the two lists. They realize that other participants have seen and accepted them as they really are, even when they were not aware of it. They can now begin to take steps toward generalizing such acceptance into their everyday lives.

SESSION 8: MAINTAINING SELF-ESTEEM; CLOSURE

Purpose: To reinforce positive changes. To develop plans for applying the insights learned.

Facilitation: After processing the previous weeks' assignments, the facilitator presents a self-acceptance graduation ritual useful in establishing a sense of closure. The women are invited to stand in a circle. Each in turns stands in front of every other woman and accepts this statement: "[Name], I accept you just the way you are right now." The participant is encouraged to respond with "I accept myself, too." She proceeds around the circle until every member has had a chance to affirm her acceptance. The session ends as members express their feelings, fears, and hopes for themselves, each other, and the future. The facilitator reinforces the positive changes made and offers suggestions on reading lists, videos, and self-help and support groups.

Author Index

Subject Index